D1094443

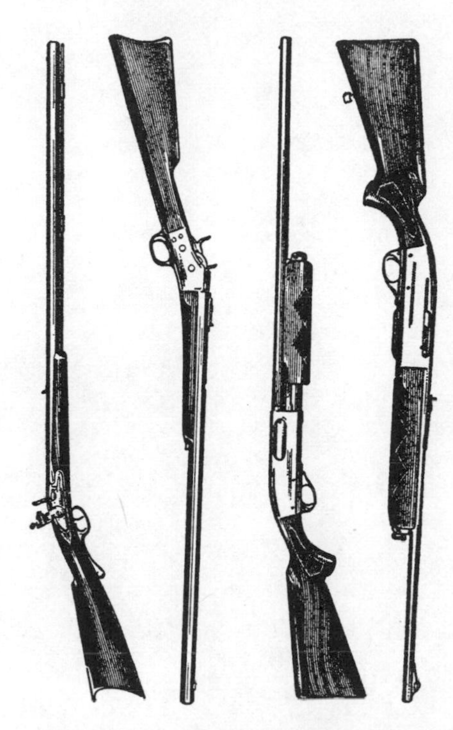

# REMINGTON ARMS

*In American History*

BY ALDEN HATCH

LIBRARY OF CONGRESS CATALOG CARD NUMBER: 72-96373

PRINTED IN THE UNITED STATES OF AMERICA

# CONTENTS

PART I—*Enterprise on the Mohawk*



PART II—*Enterprise at Bridgeport*

# Enterprise on the Mohawk

## Chapter 1

# The First of Ten Million Guns

The tenuous line of civilization was the width of the flatlands and lesser slopes of the Mohawk Valley. Nowhere was it more than ten miles across, and at Little Falls, sixty-five miles above Schenectady, abrupt, constricting walls of pre-glacial rock compressed it to a scant three hundred yards. From Albany to Oneida Lake, the pale green plaques of cultivated fields clung to the silver wire of the river. Pressing down upon their outer edges was the vast, immobile power of millions of square miles of primeval wilderness. It seemed as though the forest but stood aside for a brief space before the mighty trees should close their ranks and march again to the water's edge, obliterating that slight scar on its perfection.

Appearances were deceptive. For the life of the wilderness was static, having stood changeless for a hundred thousand years, while the force that flowed up river was enormously dynamic, being the irresistible tide of human migration.

By the early years of the nineteenth century, other tiny imperfections began to obtrude on the solid, dark green surface of the forest, small clearings on the plateaus behind the mountain rampart of the river. The light patches of the open fields appearing, spreading, joining, were the bridgeheads of the pioneers.

In one such clearing, in the area called Litchfield, some four miles back from the German Flatts and the river, the square stone house of Eliphalet Remington stood in three hundred acres of land he had mostly cleared himself. Being a Yankee, lately from Connecticut, Remington pronounced his name E-life-alet, though the York Staters persisted in calling him "Eliffalit."

Remington's land was ringed by the hundred-foot-high palisade of trees except on the south where it joined the clearing of his neighbor, Samuel Merry. Its only connection with civilization was the rutted wagon track that followed Staley's Creek through a deep cleft in the rocky hills, known as the Gulph, from the hamlet of Crane's Corners to the River Road which ran along the south bank of the Mohawk.

Remington was a man of substance—his house and the fine furniture that filled it proved that. He was a man of piety—with his own hands he had built the little wooden church at Crane's Corners. He had imagination and the will to seize opportunity at the right moment, otherwise he would have stayed in the comfortable town of Suffield, Connecticut, instead of adventuring to the fringes of civilization. He was a solid man who built always for the future. He had three daughters and a son.

Eliphalet Remington, II, "Lite" to his family and friends, lay asleep in a soft feather bed in the northeast bedroom of his father's house. Abigail, his young wife, lay beside him. The sun rose at four fifty-four A.M. on that morning early in August, 1816, and a first shaft of light, piercing the fringe of trees that rimmed the Remington fields, touched Lite's long, chiseled nose. He awoke, and remembering his plans for the day, heaved himself out of his feathered nest.

Abigail stirred and muttered, "Is the night over already?"

"Yes," said Lite. "But don't you move. The women say you must be extra careful of the first child."

"You're so good, Lite," she answered. "I'll keep him safe for you. Are you going to start the Gun today?"

"Sure as shootin'," her husband said. "The hay is in and things are slow at the forge. Father says I can use it."

He put on a rough homespun shirt and pantaloons—broadcloth was for Sundays—pulled on his leather half boots, and went down to the hearty New England breakfast his mother had ready for him. He ate quickly, scarcely speaking to his parents, for in his mind he was already working the iron to form the barrel of his gun.

Legend says that young Remington asked his father for a gun; that he was refused on the grounds it was too costly, and that he went straight off and made one for himself. Legend indubitably lies. For in an era when game supplied most of the meat for every larder and the forest was still full of "noxious animals"—the bear, the black wolf and the gray, and the sleek, dangerous panther—a gun was not a luxury but a necessity. The Remingtons never lacked necessities. Nor was Lite Remington the man to go off at half-cock and make a gun by inspiration. Not without careful study and planning would he undertake it.

So throw the legend out; it's not in key with the characters of the men involved. The truth is that Remington, having carefully studied methods of gun-making, and minutely examined all the rifles he could reach, decided that he could make a better gun than he could buy. He was, of course, quite right.

Lite finished his breakfast quickly, kissed his mother, and said to his father, "Stop by the forge when you can and give me the benefit of your advice."

"If you don't know more than I do about gun-making after all that studying, you'd better give it up right now," his father answered. "But I'll have a look at it all the same."

Young Remington went out of the kitchen door, being careful not to bang it for Abigail's sake. He cut straight across the hayfield in which the cows were now in pasture, toward the tall trees that rimmed the edge of the Gulph. Ignoring the wagon track that quartered down its steep slopes to the ford near the sulphur springs, he slipped and slid down an almost vertical foot path between the great tree trunks that rose branchless for fully sixty feet before spreading out their thick canopy of leaves. The August heat was already on the fields, but in the wooded gorge the air was almost chilly, and the steady rushing sound of the creek, tearing over its bed of boulders, made it seem cooler still.

The new stone building that housed the forge and smithy, which Mr. Remington had built the year before, stood right on the water's edge. When it was operating, a wooden flume several hundred feet long carried water from a dam at the bend of the creek above the ford to the big waterwheel with its twelve-foot wooden paddles. The water gate was shut, the flume was empty and the wheel stood still. Lite would not need it today.

Remington threw open the big door of the forge and left it so—it would be hot in there later. The interior of the shop was a scene of cluttered order. Nearest the doors was the wooden ox sling, a sort of stout, four-poster gallows on which oxen were hoisted to be shod since they could not give their feet to the smith like horses. On racks along the walls hung dozens of horseshoes and even more of the little half shoes for the oxen's cloven hooves. Wagon wheels with shiny new iron tires leaned against the stone walls. In one corner were piled a heterogeneous assortment of parts for agricultural implements: harrow teeth and cultivator prongs, ox yokes, hoes, crowbars and the metal parts of other farmers' tools, including iron facings for wooden plows (it would be three years yet before Jethro Wood of Cayuga County invented the first all-metal plow).

In another heap were iron parts that the Remingtons made for the grist mills which were springing up on virtually every creek that had sufficient head of water to turn a wheel. Mixed up with them were heavy sleigh shoes, curved to fit over the wooden runners of the only vehicle that could be used in that country from December to March.

In one corner of the shop stood the brick forge, its interior chimney already blackened with soot. Close beside it were the big circular tub bellows, a good six feet in diameter, mounted horizontally on a wooden frame. Within easy reach was the heavy triangular anvil, its iron column secured to a wooden block. The tools of the trade were racked handily by: sledge hammers, grooving hammers, wedge-shaped pritchel hammers for punching nail holes in the horseshoes, mandrels, rasps, paring knives, long-handled iron ladles for dishing out molten metal, chisels, gouges, files and powerful scissor tongs for handling the white-hot iron. At the south end of the building nearest to the waterwheel were the big grindstones, laboriously cut from a red sandstone cliff in the Gulph.

Lite Remington hung a leather apron from his neck and went straight to the forge, where he started a fire of charcoal bought from the charcoal burners, who worked their pits back in the hills where the great trees provided an apparently inexhaustible supply of raw material. While the fire was getting started, Remington selected a rod of iron that he himself had smelted down from ore from the mine in Frank's Fort Gulph and scrap iron traded in by the farmers who bought the finished product of the forge.

It took better than half an hour to get the fire exactly right. Then Lite shoved his bar of iron into the furnace and, swinging on the pole of the bellows, pumped it up and down, forcing jets of air into the coals which sparked and sizzled. The iron rod was dark against the fire, then glowing faintly, and finally a cherry red that seemed brighter than the coals. Judging the right instant exactly from long experience, Lite seized the bar with the tongs and expertly swung it across the anvil. Holding it thus with his left hand, he raised a heavy hammer with his right.

Stop here and take a look at him, for as the first blow rings upon the glowing metal, history will be made, and that small bar of iron will become the first of ten million guns bearing the name of Remington. Lite had a long, loose-jointed body, which in Sunday broadcloth seemed deceptively slender. Now, poised in tension for the blow, thighs and buttocks strained the rough cloth of his trousers, his bare arms were bunched with muscle and the rigid cords of his neck made a perfect pattern of human power.

So far he might have stood as the prototype of the young workman, the essence of physical strength and skill, single of purpose and beautifully adapted to that end. But the head poised on his straining neck seemed strangely out of key. It was a delicate head, long and well-shaped, with curly, dark hair growing to a widow's peak on the high forehead. Lips and nose were finely chiseled, eyebrows delicately sketched above large, dreamy eyes. Even in the flush of furnace heat and hard labor, sweat beading and dripping from the point of his classic nose, Lite Remington looked like a poet, which he was.

The hammer described a perfect arc and smashed down on the white-hot iron, sending up a spray of sparks. With the deceptive ease of practiced skill, Remington struck again and again in ringing rhythm. The end of the rod was beaten flat to a thickness of about one half of an inch. When cooling turned it from red to pale pink, Remington swung it back to the bed of the furnace, and pumped the bellows once more. Thus he worked it until the rod was changed to a long metal bar, one-half inch wide and one-half inch thick. Then he worked backward over it until thickness and width were as nearly uniform as human skill could make them. This was the first step.

The legend built around that gun has it completed in a single day. Of course, that's nonsense. It took a practiced gunsmith a week to make a gun, and must have taken Remington at least as long. After he had forged his length of iron, he took an arbor—that is, another rod of iron .40 of an inch in diameter—and fixed it in his vise. This was the core around which he must build up his barrel, for there were as yet no tools in the world that would drill a straight hole through three feet or more of metal. Since the diameter of the arbor must be a little smaller than the bore of the finished gun after reaming, it would be .45 caliber. That seems rather large, now, when few rifles are bigger than .30 caliber, but it was average then.

Remington brought the strip of iron to red heat again, placed an end of it over the arbor and slowly bent the softened metal around the core so that it fitted in a tight spiral. Every few inches he would have to reheat it. It was close, arduous work, done with painstaking exactitude, for on the tightness and evenness of the coil and the quality of the weld depended the whole success of the undertaking.

While Lite worked, his father came in to offer approval and advice, and farmer customers dropped by to purchase goods and offer their opinions, since in those times almost every man was forced to have a smattering of the blacksmith's craft.

The job was done at last. Lite had a tightly wound spiral of metal some forty-two inches long with a .40 of an inch hole running through it. Once more he laid it in the bed of coals and this time brought it to white heat. Then he sprinkled borax and sand on it to make it weld, and seizing it in his tongs pounded it vigorously on the stone floor. This was called "jumping." It jarred the malleable edges of the spiral strip against each other so the heat-activated molecules, running together, were welded into a solid tube of iron. Because only eight inches could be heated at once, Remington repeated this process six times. There was the rough barrel of the gun.

Remington plunged it, with a hiss and flash of steam, into a tub of water to cool. When he could touch it without burning his fingers, he drew out the arbor and eagerly raised the barrel, warm and dripping; he sighted along it to answer the vital question: Was it straight? As far as his eye could tell, it was. Then he looked through it, aiming at the open doors, and it seemed to him there was a slight divergence. To check this, he made a plumb line with a piece of string and a small weight, and dropped it down the tube. About a foot below the muzzle, the string almost touched the side of the barrel.

Marking the spot carefully, Remington rested the tube on two pieces of metal and taking a soft lead hammer tapped it smartly, several times. When he tried his plumb line again it was almost right. Two more slight taps, and now the line ran dead center down the length of the barrel, which was actually as straight as a string.

For the last day's work on the barrel, Lite needed power. That morning he went first to the dam and hoisted the sluice gate. A fine head of water roared down the flume. Cascading over the end, it smashed down in flying spray on the twelve-foot wheel, which shuddered and groaned and began to turn. Inside the forge the grindstones were revolving. Remington drove tapering wooden spindles into both ends of his barrel to act as handles, then pressed it vertically against the grindstone. The abrasive surface bit into the iron, sending forth a bright river of sparks. Lite gradually moved it down against the wheel, cutting a flat, smooth surface the length of the barrel. Eight such surfaces were cut to give the gun the octagon-shaped barrel that was then the fashion.

It took the better part of a day to grind the barrel. When it was done, Lite lifted it and caressed the polished metal. But the inside of the barrel was still rough, and he had no tools for reaming and rifling it.

The following day, Remington put on his best black broadcloth suit so that he would be properly attired for a visit to the metropolis of Utica. He slung a knapsack, packed with plenty of meat and bread, over his shoulder, clapped a tall beaver hat on his head and, carrying his barrel in one hand and his father's rifle in the other for protection against possible panthers, set out for town.

Because it was much shorter and easier going than the River Road, he followed the old Oneida Trail along the crests of the hills. As soon as he left his father's fields, he plunged into the great woods; it was a little like diving into clear, cool water. The hot August sun was strained by the almost impenetrable ceiling of leaves to a dim green gloom, through which Lite saw an endless vista of dark, columned tree trunks rising to the high Gothic groining of branches and leaves. The white pole of an occasional birch was like a marker placed to show the way. Except for a thin spread of low ferns, there was no underbrush in that forest—the dense shade killed all vegetation that could not reach up to the light. The great trees stood a good twenty feet apart, so the only obstacles that Remington encountered were an occasional huge log fallen across the trail. Under his feet the forest floor, laid down through centuries by fallen trees and leaves and rotting vegetation, was delightfully springy to walk on.

Though the forest was so vast and dim, Lite did not feel lonely, for it was anything but silent. Indeed, it was as noisily conversational as a county-wide quilting bee. Away above him in the upper stories of the trees there was a tremendous traffic of birds. Crows, blackbirds and jays wrangled and disputed with hoarse croaks and shrill jabbering. Woodcock, plover and partridge talked to each other, and wild pigeons flocked in thousands, cooing low. Squirrels raced up and down the broad, bare tree trunks like flashes of gray light, and, on the ground, sudden scurryings indicated that minks, raccoons and other such valuable vermin were getting out of the way, while occasionally a deer flashed across a corridor at the limit of vision.

Remington noted the lively life around him with pleasant anticipation of the day when the gun should be finished; but today he was traveling, not hunting, and he never broke his easy ground-covering stride, even while his imagination delighted in picturing the creatures who made all that commotion. But fanciful though he was, he probably never produced a mental image of the absurdity of his own angular person, top-hatted and in formal black, pacing through the aboriginal forest.

Except for a charcoal burner's aromatic pit and a thin trickle of humanity that he saw in the deep crack of Frank's Fort Gulph, he encountered no other signs of civilization until, after better than three hours walking, he struck the down slope to Utica. There the forest ended abruptly and he came out in the dazzling sunlight of open fields. Below him were the houses of the fast-growing town, straggling from the hills to cluster thickly at the water's edge. He saw the brand-new mills and factories, fine church spires and the turmoil of commerce along the wharves. The Mohawk's thin blue band, curving away between the hills, was speckled with activity. It was the one break in the great Appalachian mountain barrier from the St. Lawrence to the Cumberland Gap, and through it funneled the mass migration of settlers, pouring out of the East to fill the vast vacuum of the fertile Western plains.

The river was crowded with long, high-sided bateaux and the big eight-oared Durham boats, with square sails set before the favoring wind. Oxen drew the new Pennsylvania wagons up the roads that ran along both banks, while other families moved westward on foot or on horseback, and occasionally in fine four-horse coaches.

Nor was all the traffic upriver. The fertile farms of the Mohawk

Valley, the Genesee and the Finger Lakes were the breadbasket of the Eastern seaboard. Their produce and cargoes of salt from the famous salt springs of Syracuse were floated down the Mohawk in strange lozenger-shaped vessels, half raft, half scow, that were called "arks."

Utica, with its population of twelve hundred, was the biggest city Remington knew. As he walked down the steep hill of Genesee Street, it seemed very metropolitan to him and, in fact, it made up in bustle what it lacked in size. He inquired for the shop of Morgan James, a young man about his own age, who was making himself a reputation as a gunsmith.

Remington approached young Mr. James with his barrel, and stated his need. James took it in his hands and hefted expertly. He peered along it and through it, and turned it over and over, inspecting the forging with particular care. Lite looked on with the agonized concentration of an artist exhibiting his latest work. This was the first authoritative critique of his labors.

James soon put him out of his misery. "That's a fine barrel," he said. "Straight as a string. It'll only take me a couple of hours to ream it for you, but the rifling is a long job."

He secured it firmly in the narrow, wooden bed of his rifling machine, and introduced a nut auger mounted on the end of a slender five-foot rod. He turned the rod by a hand crank with infinite care, moving inch by inch into the barrel, cutting a smooth shining surface.

While the gunsmith worked, Remington never moved from the shop. He had no desire to explore the familiar sights of Utica. The grog shops and taverns by the wharves, crowded even at noon with teamsters and river men, were genuinely sickening to his fastidiously puritanical mind. However, the new mills and the glass and cotton factories interested him intensely, for woven in with the poetic streak in his nature was a hard strand of practical ambition. The two elements of his character were twisted together like the steel and iron of an imported Damascus gun barrel to form the pattern of the man.

On previous visits to town, he had invariably visited its factories to examine new additions to their machinery and discuss economic problems with their owners. The rattle and bang of machinery, the crash of wooden spindles or the grating roar of slow-turning grindstones were a discordant symphony that drew him as strongly in one direction as the music of the forest did in another. It seemed to him a striking evidence of the fantastic prosperity of the times that experienced mill hands now made as much as two hundred dollars a year. Where young workmen could do that, the sky was clearly the limit for an ambitious man with a little capital. Remington had every intention of jumping on the band wagon of industrial expansion, and he regarded the forge in the Gulph as a good base from which to leap.

However, he had no time for factories this day; he wanted to study every move the master gunsmith made. So he ate his lunch in the shop, sharing a slab of ham and cheese and bread with James, while he cross-questioned the gunsmith about his craft.

When the reaming was done, they peered through the barrel in turn to admire its smooth sheen. Then James fastened it in the rifling machine again, and, substituting a special cutting tool for the auger, began the infinitely delicate task of cutting spiral grooves inside the barrel. The bit cut a tiny fraction of an inch at a time, and James worked with an intensity that was matched only by his patience.

As soon as the light began to fade, the gunsmith knocked off. Remington spent the night with him and induced James, who loved his trade, and was to become famous at it, to talk about the history and technique of his craft. James took him way back to the beginning of America, and described the clumsy guns with which the Pilgrims had miraculously managed to stand off the Indians and supply themselves with game. Their matchlocks were so heavy that they usually required a forked stand to steady the barrel, and the charge was fired by a slow-burning match like a piece of punk for lighting firecrackers. Then had come the wheelock, in which a clockwork mechanism turned a steel wheel against a piece of flint throwing a stream of sparks into the priming pan. Finally, the familiar flintlock was invented by Dutch chicken thieves, who called it the *snaphance* or hen snatcher.

All of these guns had been smooth bore and you were lucky to hit the broad end of a potato patch with one. It was the German and Swiss immigrants, whose descendants are the Pennsylvania Dutch, who brought the rifle to America. Their first rifles were German Jaegers weighing twenty pounds or more. They were unwieldy compared to the smooth-bore flintlocks then in general use, but with one you could actually hit a squirrel in the top of a tree. The trouble was that nobody could carry a Jaeger through the woods, and, besides that, it took special tools and about ten minutes to reload, by which time the pioneer would likely be lacking one scalp.

The immigrant German gunsmiths went to work on this problem. In many small, individual shops they developed a long, slender graceful rifle that weighed less than ten pounds and could be fired two or three times a minute. This was the "Kentucky rifle"—it should have been called the "Pennsylvania rifle." It was perfected about 1730, and became the most famous gun in the world.

"The rifle made the conquest of the Western wilderness possible," James told Lite, "but we Easterners were awfully slow about taking it up. We stuck to smooth bores until after the Revolution, and only now are rifles really becoming common hereabouts. It's still hard to get a good barrel. You've made a dandy."

James finished the rifling job the next morning. When Remington paid him his fee, which was four of the double reales (two-bit pieces worth twenty-five cents each) which were still the small currency of the country districts, he felt that he had received more than his money's worth.

To complete his barrel, Remington had to bore a small touch hole near its base for the powder train, and forge a plug which he screwed into the rear end for the breech block. The firing mechanism was to be the universal flintlock. Remington forged the parts and finished them with a hammer, a cold chisel and a file. The lock consisted of a lock-plate, to which he brazed a priming pan; a vertical strip of steel, which was held against the priming pan by a powerful spring, and a hammer, actuated by another spring, holding a piece of flint. When the trigger was pulled the hammer slammed the flint down the face of the steel uncovering the priming pan and throwing a stream of sparks into the priming powder from whence a flash of fire passed through the touch hole to the main charge.

In the evenings, Lite worked on the stock of the gun, shaping it from a straight-grained block of walnut with a draw knife, and whittling it out so that it fitted flush against the breech plug, and exactly accepted the curves of the lock. He smoothed it down with a small block of sandstone—sandpaper had not been invented—and polished it with wild beeswax. The barrel was coated with hazel-brown, an excellent preservative made of uric acid and iron oxide.

On a Saturday evening he assembled the gun, securing the stock and metal parts with hand-wrought screws and pins.

Not all the game in the world would have induced so strict a Methodist as Lite Remington to fire his gun off on Sunday. Besides, the sound of a shot breaking the Sabbath calm would have brought down on his head the ire of the godly neighbors. But he would have been less than human had he not swung the new rifle to his shoulder fifty times that day.

He did not need the sun to wake him Monday morning. He took his gun, powder horn, newly molded bullets and greased patches to the field in back of the house. There he loaded with a heaping measure of black powder—might as well know if she'd take it—rammed it home and drove in the patch and bullet. He shook a pinch of powder into the priming pan and cocked the gun. Then he laid it on the ground with its butt against a tree, and tied a piece of string to the trigger. If she was going to blow up, he was too prudent to put his face in the way. He backed off, and knew a moment of irresolution while he thought of all the work that gun had cost him. Then he pulled the string.

There was a terrific explosion and the gun gave a convulsive leap vomiting clouds of smoke. Lite ran, through the choking fumes, and picked up his gun. She wasn't hurt a bit.

Then came the real test. Lite reloaded with a normal charge; and, aiming carefully at the bole of an ancient oak, pulled the trigger. The crash made his ears ring, and smoke blanked out everything in front of him. When it cleared, he saw the oak absolutely unscathed.

He fired again with the same lack of result, but on the third try, he got the hang of the thing. The bullet, centered beautifully in the irregular circle of bark, was the first of uncounted Remington bull's-eyes. It gave Lite a high sense of accomplishment, which seemed to him almost absurdly exaggerated. After all, what had he done beyond building a gun that could send a bullet on a fine, straight path? The answer to that rhetorical question was beyond his wildest imaginings.

## Chapter 2

# Remingtons from Way Back

Just what difference it makes who sired whom in the multiple ancestry of any human being is a nice question. The individual is—himself; a unique personality created by such a puzzling complex of genes and cells and environmental influences that even the most microscopic study of inherited strains cannot explain him. There he stands on his two feet, and in the end you must take him as he comes. However, origins have a genuine interest, so the biographer must explore the branches of the family tree.

The first Remingtons of record appear to have lived in the Village of Remington in the Parish of Gisbarne in Robblesdale, Yorkshire. There is mention of an improbable line of clergymen, each named Richard Remington, and born exactly thirty-five years apart, in 1500, 1535 and 1570. The last Richard seems pretty authentic since he was an archdeacon and Rector of Lockington in Yorkshire. His will was proved in 1615. It was his youngest son, John, who first displayed the Remington gumption by taking his wife and two small sons and sailing for America in 1637.

Another school of genealogists, headed by the gunmaker's last living grandson, Franklin Remington, maintains that John was the son of Sir Thomas Remington of Lockridge Abbey. Franklin has a seventeenth-century picture to prove it—a family group of Sir Thomas, his lady and their twenty children in the drawing room of the Abbey. The artist was a whimsical fellow who depicted four of the Remington children, who died in infancy, as wraithlike mummies in tiny coffins arranged symmetrically on the parlor rug.

Whomever John descended from, the American Remingtons soon made themselves known. With other Yorkshiremen, they founded the new settlement of Rowley near Salem, Massachusetts. Two years later John Remington appeared before the General Court in Boston to take the oath of freeman, and is shown among the persons made free on March 22, 1639. That seems to indicate that he may have indentured himself as somebody's servant to get the price of his passage. Indentured or not, he was a leader for, in 1640, he "is desired to drill the militia company at Rowley." In 1645, he was a sergeant of militia and: "1647, May 26, the Rowley Company chose John Remington their Lieft."

John appears to have been one of the few military-minded Remingtons; though there is a rather foggy suggestion that a later John Remington served on General Washington's staff in the Revolution. Be that as it may, the progenitors of the gun makers seem to have been singularly peaceable folk. The most distinguished of them was Uncle Jonathan, born in 1677, who climbed the legal ladder from Professor of Law at Harvard, to Judge of the Probate Court of Boston and finally to Judge of the high and mighty Appellate Court of Massachusetts.

In general, the Remingtons just minded their own business and prospered mildly. They married nice girls, also of pure English descent to judge by such names as Mehitable Walker, Margaret Scott, Sarah Winchel and Patience Mason; and they had many children, mostly sons.

Thomas Remington, a grandson of the gallant "Lieft" of the Rowley Militia, moved to Suffield, in Litchfield County, Conneticut, about 1677; and there the family stayed for more than a century. Skipping several generations who did nothing notable, we come to the twins, John and Josiah, born in Suffield in 1745, and history begins to hover closer. John married Patience Mason in 1767. She promptly produced a son, who was christened Eliphalet, born October 13, 1768. Thirteen months later John Remington died. His twin, Josiah, lived to play a minor role as an agent of destiny.

There is very little reliable information about the childhood of

Eliphalet Remington, Senior. However, the man was well known, so it is possible to work backward and reconstruct the youth. By the time the spotlight of history focused on Eliphalet, he was an extremely substantial citizen; so it can be assumed that he had an excellent upbringing. Just how his widowed mother managed to support him and give him a firm grounding of character is unknown, but she certainly did. She also instilled in him a strong faith in God and the Methodist Church; and saw to it that he got a reasonable amount of education and learned a trade—that of carpenter—to which he later added an extensive knowledge of blacksmithing and the metal working crafts.

Young Remington must have been a competent, self-reliant youth with a good deal of hustle. By the time he was twenty-three he was prosperous enough to support a wife. In 1791, he married Elizabeth Kilbourn. As was the custom then, they lost no time in starting a family. Their first child, Elizabeth, was born in 1792, and Eliphalet Remington, II, was born on October 28, 1793.

The Remingtons were exceedingly comfortable in Suffield. They were one of its oldest families; they were known and liked by all, and Eliphalet was reasonably prosperous. But he was also very ambitious; just waiting for the right opportunity. It came in the form of letters from Litchfield, New York.

That was a time when civilization was moving westward with the inevitability of a glacial drift. The Revolution had halted it briefly; but when the war ended in the glorious morning of a new nation, the tide rolled on faster than ever. Soldiers of the Connecticut Line, who had marched with Arnold up the Mohawk Valley, came back with tall tales of an enormously fertile land where the wheat grew thicker and the corn taller than any New Englander had ever seen. And there were no boulders in the fields!

After a century and a half of abuse, the thin Connecticut soil was wearing out. There were a lot of men who were tired of wrestling with it. A whole group of them left Litchfield County to take up forest land on the plateau south of the Mohawk at Fort Herkimer.

Because the ties of home are strong even in the most dauntless pioneers, they named their new township Litchfield; and wrote enthusiastic letters home. Eliphalet got several from them, and from his Uncle Josiah, who had bought 680 acres of forest in Glen's Purchase north of Little Falls, extolling the advantages of the new land. Once the trees were cut down and burned, the most tremendous crops would grow with hardly any attention, for the deep "muck" that had been the forest floor was incredibly fertile. If you were careful not to cut out the stumps, but plowed around them, it not only saved a lot of trouble, but they held the precious soil from slipping away, and the rotting wood kept it fertilized for years. It was, in fact, a farmer's paradise. However, there were too many farmers and not enough craftsmen. Most of the agricultural implements had to be imported at great cost, and were not much good. Horses and oxen had to be driven miles to be shod; and lines formed in front of the smithies. There was a rare opportunity for young men with a trade.

That was the sort of thing Eliphalet wanted to hear. He knew that he could be comfortable all his life in Suffield—already he had accumulated a small capital—but there was little chance to get ahead. In 1799 he made the decision to go out west and look the ground over.

It is about 180 miles from Suffield to what is now the town of Herkimer, but was then Fort Dayton—a nice morning's run by motor. It took Remington six days to make the trip. First he had to walk to Hartford where he picked up one of Mr. Beale's new stages for Albany and Schenectady. Nostalgic memoirs picture those old Concord coaches rattling along a fine white road with their four horses at a dead run and the coachman singing ballads for the edification of the contented travelers. Actually they went most of the way at a dead walk, while the clumsy vehicle lurched and groaned on the miserably rutted roads and the passengers cursed or prayed according to their lights. The only time there was any speed was just before arriving at an inn, when the coachman would whip up his flagging team and come careening down the village street to make a spectacular stop with brakes screaming and the horses sitting down on their haunches.

Mr. Beale's stage eventually deposited Mr. Remington at Mr. Beale's big tavern-hotel in Schenectady. Mr. Remington did not think he was going to like this country. "Snacady," as the inhabitants called it, was the dirtiest, most licentious town he ever had seen. Its excuse for existence was that here the rapids of the Mohawk stopped navigation and all goods had to be transshipped to Albany by wagon. Its only claim to the consideration of a good New Englander was the new Union College, founded by Jonathan Edwards, the Younger.

Mr. Beale's tavern was a godless place and Remington was delighted when the morning stage pulled out for Canajoharie. The road, winding along the north bank of the river, tended to confirm his low estimate of the morals of the people, for there was a grog shop or tavern every mile. However, the luxuriant fields that spread over the flatlands and crept up the sides of the valley confirmed Uncle Josiah's letter. Remington had a fine, big breakfast at the "Park," which had once been the manorial home of that black Tory, Guy Johnson, and was now a public house.

At Canajoharie, Remington found that the Utica coach would probably be a day or two late, so he hired a ride on a settler's wagon to Little Falls. As he approached slowly up the narrow road, it appeared the most awe-inspiring work of the Creator he had ever seen. The far walls of the valley here closed in until it was a mere fissure through the granite hills. Palisades of naked, ancient rock rose sheer on either hand, and the river broke in thundering splendor over the falls. It was as though God himself had hewn a narrow gateway through the mountain barrier so His children might travel to the vast, smiling lands to the westward.

Here, too, was an impressive work of man, the new canal and locks of the Inland Lock Company, by which the river traffic could circumnavigate the falls. It somewhat restored Remington's faith in these York Staters.

Carrying his gripsack, Remington walked the seven miles from Little Falls to Fort Dayton, through the pleasant fields where the Palatine Germans had settled early in the eighteenth century. It seemed to him impossible that this peaceful land had been a scene of utter devastation less than twenty years before. Again and again during the years of Revolution, Walter and David Butler, with their Tory Rangers and Senecas and Mohawks under Chief Joseph Brant, had swept through the settlements, killing and raping, roasting whole families in their cabins, smashing babies' heads against the log walls; and fleeing back through the northern woods with a string of fresh scalps to be sold to the British at the bounty price of eight dollars per scalp without regard to size. Some of the old farmers working the fields, who had miraculously survived an Indian tonsure, still wore skullcaps to cover the bare white bones where their scalps had been.

In Fort Dayton, Remington put up at the Talcott House, a big log-cabin hotel that was an overnight stop of the Mohawk Pike Stage

Company. The next day, he had himself rowed across the river to Mohawk, where stood the fortress church of Herkimer. It was a most unchurchly looking edifice with loop-holed, brick walls for defense, surrounded by an earthern rampart. He walked up the River Road past Shoemaker's Tavern, where David Butler was captured, and on through the German Flatts to a tiny settlement called London. Here he turned south up the wagon track which was to become more familiar than the lines of his own face, and where on another pleasant June day, he was to meet a violent death.

The road followed the creek in the bottom of the Gulph, a narrow crack in the hills which scientists have since decided was furrowed out by the great glacier that once had filled the valley level with the mountain tops, making a flat plain of ice.

Presently, the road forded the creek and climbed up the steep side of the Gulph between the tall trees, to run along a wooded plateau for a space, before it dipped again and reforded the creek. Remington marked the spot mentally, for it looked ideal to him. The huge trees that grew on the high ground were mostly chestnut, red beech and walnut, a sure indication of good wheat land—just as birch and pine indicated a poor sandy soil. The swift current of the creek would turn a mill wheel, and there was a fine place for a dam at the bend beyond the second ford. It looked good, and it smelled good, as the cool freshness of the stream mingled with the pungent, earthy aroma of the woods.

That night Remington slept with old friends from Litchfield in a log cabin near Crane's Corners. They showed him their blooming fields and told him of their triumphs and difficulties. In the days that followed they took him on long walks through the cultivated tracts and the untouched forest to get the lay of the land. In the evenings, it was often not too hot to sit around the fire in the wide chimney place, where the conversation was punctuated by Remington and his host hammering out nails on two little anvils on either side of the hearth—there could never be enough nails. On Sunday, they read prayers in the front room of the cabin since there was neither church nor preacher within ten miles, though occasionally a Methodist minister rode through on his circuit.

The longer Remington stayed the better he liked the vigorous life of this pioneer community. His cousin, Steven Remington, came over from Little Falls and talked of purchasing land in Litchfield Township, which he thought better than his father, Josiah's, holdings on the north side of the valley. Taxes were far lower than in Connecticut and a man could really get ahead. On cultivated land the rate was one sixth of one acre's produce for every hundred acres, and the tax on forest land was twelve cents per hundred acres.

Eliphalet ended with a consuming desire to buy himself a piece of wilderness, and more particularly that part of it he had marked as he walked through the Gulph. In all his ramblings, he had seen nothing so well suited to his purpose. He discovered that the land belonged to James Smith and was part of lot No. 85 of the Bayard Patent.

It wasn't cheap. There was a first-rate boom in forest land, and it was being taken up fast by settlers. Remington was hot for it, and he paid Smith $275 for fifty acres. Then he went back to Suffield to break the news to Elizabeth.

## Chapter 3

# Building for the Future

In terms of transportation the shore of the Atlantic is not a quarter as far from the Pacific, now, as Litchfield, Connecticut, was from Litchfield, New York, in 1800. The only practical way for Eliphalet Remington to move his wife and children and all his material possessions from one place to the other was in an oxcart, or, more likely, a couple of oxcarts. One can sympathetically picture Elizabeth's feelings on the day in the early summer of 1800, when the last bundle was roped on to the tail of the cart, and the little caravan crept slowly past the pleasant, solid, familiar houses of Suffield. Even Eliphalet must have had some pretty sober thoughts; and it is certain that the children—there were three of them by that time—were as cross as noxious beasts.

It must have taken a couple of weeks or more to make the journey, and since there is no record, one can only surmise what Elizabeth said to her Eliphalet when the carts finally groaned up the hill out of the Gulph and halted in the somber gloom of the forest at the spot that was to be their home.

The first house Eliphalet Remington built on his land was a log cabin. He had to have a home in a hurry, and a cabin could be run up almost overnight. Probably his Yankee friends from Crane's Corners pitched in and helped.

The cabin was very different from the white clapboard house he and Elizabeth had left in Suffield. It was made of interlocking timbers of beech with the chinks caulked tight with clay, and consisted of two rooms. The chimney was made of stones hewn out of the cliffs in the Gulph and the wide fireplace was built of stone and plaster. This was the most important part of the house since it was the source of all heat, most of the light, and was the only means of cookery. An enormous back log was necessary to hold the great fires that would repel the winter's frost. Remington and his friends got it in place by fastening a stout rope to it, and carrying the line in through the door and out of the back window of the cabin where it was hooked to a yoke of oxen. The beasts drew the log through the door, scraping over the plank floor, until it was directly in front of the hearth. Then the men prized it into place with crowbars.

In the slack season, when the frost stopped both the activities on the farms and the water wheels of the mills, there was plenty of labor available for a man with a little hard money in his pockets. Remington had no trouble getting men to help clear his fields so they would be ready to plant late the following April when the frost left the ground. He paid the hired choppers the regular rate of $7.50 an acre, for which they cut down all the trees, chopped the great trunks into fourteen-foot lengths and piled them with the branches ready for burning. The next summer he got a bumper crop of wheat and hay. The latter was clover and honeysuckle, which sprang up without sowing the moment the shadowing trees were cleared away.

For the next ten years the Remingtons lived happily in their cabin and prospered. In addition to farming, Remington found much work to do in his trade of carpentry. The fact that there was no church nearby troubled him greatly, and, as his first contribution to the community, he built a meeting house at Crane's Corners with the help of the neighbors.

There were, of course, no schools, but the Remingtons were people of considerable learning, and when the candles were lit in the evening, they taught Elizabeth and Lite and little Aphia in front of the big fire, or read to them from such of the classics as they had brought from Connecticut. Lite learned to write the graceful hand that was the mark of all cultivated men. He was quite proud of his penmanship, and would indubitably have been astounded had he foreseen that his own sons would foster the invention which made it virtually a lost art.

How well things went for Remington is indicated by his expanding acreage. In 1807, he purchased 195 acres adjoining his property from Samuel Merry for $585, and the following year he bought 71 acres more. In the autumn of 1809, he decided to build Elizabeth the kind of house she deserved.

They must have talked about it for years and, doubtless, Mr. Remington drew and redrew the plans a dozen times. In the winter of 1809-10, he began to quarry limestone from a cliff in the Gulph. Cold weather was the best time for that, because it was much easier to transport the stones from the quarry to the homesite by sled than wagon. As soon as the frost broke, Remington began digging the deep cellar, and by the end of the summer of 1810, the finished house stood proudly where the oxcarts had halted in the wilderness ten years before.

It was a home that even a man of substance living in an established city would be proud to own. The walls were two feet thick, made of beautiful, roughhewn stones, that were joined together as closely as bricks. In the front they were cut quite small and were set in a pretty design, curving in a graceful arch over the big front door, but in the side walls there were stones four feet long that weighed over two hundred pounds.

The lower floor of the two-story house had two large rooms on either side of a central hall, with a big kitchen across the back. The paneling in the hall and all the interior woodwork were dark polished walnut. The high windows were paned with the best glass, brought in Durham boats from Schenectady, and then up the Gulph in the two-wheel oxcarts that were the pick-up trucks of the period. All the other details of the house were equally handsome.

Remington did a great part of the work himself, while planning and overseeing everything. He was very proud of his fine house, and he had a right to be. For he built it so well that nearly a century and a half later it stands solidly triumphant over time, with never a crack or weakness in its structure.

Other factors joined to make Eliphalet Remington a contented man. His children were handsome, and good as well. Young Elizabeth was nearly as efficient a housekeeper as her mother. She could cook and spin and weave with the best, and would make some man an extremely satisfactory wife. Ten-year-old Aphia was a quick and merry child, who already did a fair share of the great amount of woman's work that was necessary in a time when every household was almost completely self-sufficient and you did not go to the store and buy things, you made them yourself.

Lite was the most interesting of all the children. Though a good worker, he was a romantic youth who daydreamed and wrote poetry. His mother was sure he had the makings of a great author, and encouraged his versifying. Indeed, for the whole span of his teens it was a toss-up whether young Remington would elect to drive a lathe or a quill. Surviving fragments of his verse indicate that he made a wise choice.

Apparently the Remingtons were not much interested in politics. Like most frontiersmen they were so preoccupied with their battle against the great enemy, the forest, that they had not much time to consider the issues of the day, and little information concerning them. However, events transpiring in the remote city of Washington, newly built in the swamps of the Potomac, abruptly focused the attention of the valley on current events.

In 1812, the uneasy peace between England and the United States broke down—so many issues had been left unsettled that could only be clarified by the decisions of war. The British could not quite believe that they no longer had proprietary rights in their former colonies; and the Americans were as touchy as gamecocks.

The moment President Monroe and the Congress defied the power of England, the Mohawk Valley ceased to be a one-way road to the West and became a likely route for invasion. Once again the American troops, in their smart new uniforms and visored kepis, marched up both banks of the river, their long bayonets glinting in the sun, followed by their supply trains which cut the new roads to ribbons.

Things did not go so well in Canada, and presently Commodore Perry and his odd assortment of sailors, shipwrights and carpenters went through to build a navy on Lake Erie. It looked as though the British were coming again, and the inhabitants nervously watched sweating boatmen row the cranky, deep-laden Durham boats upriver, with the horrid snouts of the big naval guns pointing over their sides at odd angles.

Then came the news of the victory that made the valley safe. Commodore Perry and his cocked-hatted, gold-laced staff sailed back down the river in a rolling barrage of wild acclaim, whose fervor testified to the anxiety he had relieved. The Remingtons surely went down to Mohawk to see the brilliant spectacle of bright uniforms, flags and bands, and to hear the crashing salutes of ancient cannon. Just as surely, they disapproved of the almost universal alcoholism which was the concomitant of victory.

The family's attitude toward the glories of war is accurately if naïvely expressed in Lite's poetical tribute to the signing of the Treaty of Ghent which ended the war:

> "Hale sacred peace, thy gentle reign
> Is now restored to us again,
> Thy radiant smiles and gentle voice,
> Bid every virtuous heart rejoice.
>
> "But can thy smiles disperse the gloom
> That reigns within the warrior's tomb,
> Can it assuage the widow's grief
> Or to the orphan speak relief?"

The most important event of Lite's life, prior to the making of the gun, was heralded by the arrival in Litchfield Township in 1809, of another Connecticut family, the William Paddocks. Mr. Paddock bought a parcel of land about a quarter of a mile south of the Remingtons. Soon after they moved into their new house, Elizabeth Remington made friends with the Paddock girls.

As Lite himself told the story to his grandchildren, he was sitting at home one evening when his father said, "It's getting dark. Walk over to the Paddocks and escort your sister home."

Somewhat unwillingly, for he was absorbedly reading "Paradise Lost" for the third time, Lite obeyed. All his life he remembered taking the short walk through the soft September evening, and knocking shyly on the Paddocks' back door. When it opened, he was slightly stunned by the burst of noise and gaiety that rushed upon him. There were twelve Paddock children of all ages, crowded into the three small rooms on the lower floor. But Lite really saw only one.

Abigail Paddock was then a girl of seventeen, almost exactly a year older than Lite. She had gone to school in Connecticut where education was on a far sounder basis than in the frontier settlements of New York, and she was well fitted to cope with the young man's somewhat precocious intellect. Besides that, she was a jolly girl, full of fun and spirit, and very pretty. Lite fell in love right there on her doorstep.

Their courtship was not as sudden as the smiting of young Remington. It lasted for five years, but it must have been quite pleasant. There were hay rides and picnics in summer, sleighing and chestnut roasts around the great fires in winter. Every Sunday they saw each other at the church in Crane's Corners. No doubt Lite was inspired to poetic rhapsodies, although luckily none of them have survived.

The outcome was almost as certain as taxes. On May 12, 1814, Abigail Paddock and Eliphalet Remington, II, were married in the church at Crane's Corners. The bridegroom was extremely handsome in his new black broadcloth tail coat, with gray striped trousers. Under it he wore an embroidered waistcoat and a fine white shirt, with cuffs showing through the slits in the lower part of the long coat sleeves, and a high black stock tied in an elaborate bow. The bride, in her straight, high-waisted gown of the mode of Napoleon's Court, was slender and dark and filled with love and laughter. The omens were justly auspicious.

After the gaieties subsided, the young couple went to live for a while in the elder Remington's new stone house.

## Chapter 4

# Plowshares into Guns

Though no exact date is given for the building of the Remington forge, it can be definitely placed between the years 1812 and 1814. The deed for the land on which it stood was not recorded in Mr. Remington's name until 1815, but in those pleasantly casual times, transactions were frequently not registered until several years after they took place. On the other hand, by 1816, the forge was doing such a thriving business that Mr. Remington had found it profitable to build the dam and put in water power and a furnace for smelting ore. He had, in fact, seen and capitalized on an urgent need of his upland community. The nearest blacksmith was Adam Starling way down in Mohawk. That hustling little trade center also had a plow factory, but it was totally inadequate to supply the area. Wars invariably increase the demand for ironmongery of all sorts, and the hostilities of 1812 provided the added incentive that decided Remington to put a long-considered plan into effect. But he never dreamed of becoming a maker of firearms.

Nor was the gun the first thing that Lite made in his father's shop. The poetic vein in his nature had precedence and, a year before, he had forged himself an iron flute and succeeded in tuning it correctly. However, that was virtually the final flourish of his romantic side. The gun inexorably conditioned his future.

It all began when Eliphalet entered a shooting match in the autumn of 1816. This was then the major sport of America. Tennis, golf and football were yet to be imported. It would be twenty years before the first baseball game was played at Cooperstown a couple of valleys to the south. True, the young men of the frontier had other amusements such as running races, wrestling matches and games of agility and luck, like trying to catch a greased pig. However, all these were minor accomplishments, good enough for a rough-and-tumble afternoon of fun, but no great shakes compared to the more important art of sending a bullet as straight to the mark as the vagaries of crudely handmade guns and highly variable black powder permitted.

Shooting for food and for survival was an essential element of life. Shooting for sport, a man might display the skill of which he was most proud. So these matches were held wherever a few young men—or old—could get together in freshly made clearings in the wilderness on the outskirts of growing villages or towns. And the best shots competed on a county-wide basis; the nearest thing to organized sport in that part of the new world.

It was a county match that Remington entered. He had practiced all through August and September and was rather pleased with his marksmanship and his gun. On that fine October day he found the crack shots and their fans gathered in a clearing near Crane's Corners. Some wore the buckskin jackets of the frontier, others workaday homespun shirts and pantaloons, while a few stood about somewhat self-consciously in black broadcloth and beaver hats. Lite was among the last.

There were in the crowd quite a few young women, who had come to watch the menfolk display their prowess. They wore long stout woolen dresses with sunbonnets or shawls on their head, and they chattered together like squirrels, for it was not too often that they got together for a purely social occasion. The men, too, were in high spirits, boasting of terrific shots at improbable ranges, like bringing down a running buck at 150 yards.

However, when the shooting began, the horseplay ended, and even the women stopped talking as everyone tensely waited for the earsplitting bang of those long, big-caliber rifles and strained to see the result of each shot through drifting clouds of smoke.

Remington seemed as calm as one of those expressionless wooden statues that amateur sculptors of the time liked to carve from tree trunks, but as he laid his gun in a forked rest and sighted along its brown barrel, his nerves were twitching. He was afraid he might make a fool of himself.

That he did not; nor did he win the match. But he placed second, which was not a small thing against the best shots in the Valley.

When it was over, the chronicles say that the county champion came over to congratulate Remington, and examine his gun. Then he asked leave to try it and shot better than he had in the match.

"Where did you get it?" was his next question; and one can hear Lite answering with proper pride, "Made it myself!"

It seems that Remington had some difficulty convincing the men who crowded around that he was not boasting. When they saw he was serious, they were really interested. The champ was the first to ask what Lite would charge for a barrel.

Remington did a rapid mental calculation—so much iron, use of the forge, three days' work, a trip to Utica for reaming, a fair profit.

"I figure I could do it for ten dollars," he said.

"A fair price. When can I have it?"

Again Remington calculated. "In about ten days," he said.

Other shooters wanted barrels or complete guns. Before Lite left the field, he was in the gun business.

Within four years Remington guns were known throughout the State of New York and beyond. This flash success was due not only to their excellence, but to the primitive condition of the industry in the United States. It was less than a hundred years old. The first all-American factory-made musket was produced by the Honorable Hugh Orr at his new foundry at Bridgewater, Massachusetts, in 1748. By 1816, the big government arsenals at Springfield and Harpers Ferry were turning out military muskets in considerable numbers. A few small private concerns were making firearms, and there were over seven hundred individual gunsmiths in America. However, most of the latter did not attempt to build complete guns; they bought barrels and fitted them with locks and stocks. At a time when virtually every man ouside of the large cities needed a gun, the meager supply of American arms was totally inadequate. The hiatus was partially met by importing gun barrels from England and Belgium—an expensive process. So when it became known that the Remingtons were turning out straight shooting barrels, orders came from individuals and gunsmiths all the way from New York to Buffalo.

In 1817, Lite Remington built a home for himself and Abigail down in the Gulph near the forge. It was made of white clapboard with many small-paned windows like the houses he vaguely remembered in Connecticut. At one end a large, oval dormer of leaded glass looked out on the forge and the big wooden barn, which the Remingtons had built against the steep hillside. The foundation of the new house was made of the same red sandstone from which the millstones were cut. On the ground floor were two very large rooms besides the kitchen. They had wide, hospitable hearths and were handsomely furnished.

It was a much bigger house than the young Remingtons needed, except that so many people were coming to have gun barrels made. If they were gunsmiths, they often stayed to help work on their barrels, in which case the Remingtons allowed them two or three dollars off as the value of their labor.

Lite and Abigail, and their baby son, Philo, moved into their house that summer and ran it as a sort of hotel—strictly temperance!

Making guns soon became the main business of the forge, though the Remingtons continued to turn out agricultural tools as well. Skillful metal workers were engaged to help, and a reamer and wood-turning lathe were installed. A little later a sawmill was built near the forge.

All this required a great deal of iron and scrap. The ore was brought from the mine in Frank Fort's Gulph and from Clinton, up beyond Utica, and smelted at the forge. The scrap was hard to come by. Before the Erie Canal was built, it cost ten times as much to transport material from New York to Utica as it does today, which ruled out the New York market. So Remington wagons were sent scouring through the countryside buying old pots and kettles, plow facings, used horseshoes and all sorts of worn-out metal objects from the farmers.

Lite tested the guns personally before delivering them. The black powder then used was far more sensitive and dangerous to handle than the smokeless powder of today; and it burned much more slowly in the barrel. Where a modern charge is completely consumed in a few inches of the barrel, it then took full forty inches to use up the powder. For this reason there was a tremendous strain through the length of the barrels as the powder burned almost all the way up to the muzzles. One way of testing the guns to see how big a charge they would take was to fire them over snow. If a black trail stained the white surface, you knew that you had used more powder than could be consumed.

A very hard-to-get item was lead. There were no known mines in New York then. The Remingtons used to meet ragged remnants of the formerly ferocious Mohawks and Oneidas at the Council Rock in the hills behind Mohawk and make known their needs. The Indians would disappear into the woods for two or three weeks, and return bringing lead. Where they got it is still a mystery.

As business increased, so did the variety of the guns made by the Remingtons. By 1820 they would supply any sort of barrel you desired, long or short, for rifles or fowling pieces: plain iron at $3.00, steel $6.00, and Stubbs twist barrels for $7.50.

The last, now called "Damascus," were made of iron and very fine steel which the Remingtons imported from England. Thin strips of the two metals were twisted together in a new machine called a wringer. These were then welded into the familiar spiral barrel. When hazel-brown was applied, the steel remained silvery and the iron turned a copper hue. Intricate and beautiful designs were thus produced, at first by accident; then, as the workmen became more skillful, in deliberately planned patterns. Two of the men, Sam Wagor and George Dygert, became so expert that they are said to have turned out barrels with "Remington" etched down their length in flowing, silvery script.

Even though the forge was now turning out two or three hundred barrels and finished guns a year, no compromise was allowed with quality. Each was wrought with the same care as that first rifle. Lite Remington was too busy selling his product, purchasing supplies and keeping accounts in his fine hand, to do much of the actual work at the forge, but he kept a microscopic eye on the operation and never a piece of work went out which he had not personally approved. And he still kept his hand in. When his sister Elizabeth was married to Alanson Merry in 1820, Eliphalet gave his son a handful of silver dollars and told him to take them to a silversmith to be made into spoons as a wedding present. Lite went to the silversmith, watched him at work, and once again decided he could do better. So he carried the silver dollars back to the forge and wrought them into graceful spoons, which are still the pride of the Remington family.

In those final years in the Gulph, the Remington forge—foundry should be its designation at this point—was a remarkably self-contained enterprise. It was, in fact, a miniature in one plant of the great vertical industrial organizations of modern times, and it did something that no single plant in the United States—perhaps in the whole world—can do today. It performed every operation of production, from the raw material of untreated ore and standing timber to finished guns.

## Chapter 5

# Down by the Canal

The forge in the Gulph had become too small to handle all the new business. When Ben Harrington came up from Morgan's Landing, as the settlement at the mouth of Staley's Creek was then called, to order two guns for his boys, he was told he might have to wait for months. Ben allowed that it was a shame to let good business go for lack of room. Why didn't they move down to civilization and build a bigger plant? The Remingtons had been thinking of this for some time.

It was not the lack of room that bothered them, it would be easy to run up some more buildings. But now that the Canal had really gone through, it was just plain foolish not to take advantage of the cheap, convenient transportation it offered.

The Erie Canal was, in fact, the key that opened the whole Mohawk Valley to industrialization, and changed its little mills and hand-work foundries to big businesses with national distribution. It had been a long time coming. Half the people thought it never would, while the other half prayed that they might live to see it finished.

As far back as 1809, Judge Platt of Oneida County had interested the farsighted DeWitt Clinton in the project for a waterway from Lake Erie to the Hudson and thence to the sea. The War of 1812, stopped everything, as wars do. But when it was over the Canallers moved forward vigorously. In 1815, Clinton, then Mayor of New York City, returned to his great dream.

It seemed a fantastic idea. Thomas Jefferson, no mean engineer, had said it would be impossible for a hundred years. Others, looking at the route through nearly three hundred miles of wilderness, swamps and mountains, heartily agreed. But the produce of the expanding West was piling up for lack of transport, and the settlers there were yelling for the manufactured goods of the East. To break a passage through the mountain dam for this two-way river of trade would be a splendid thing —especially for the people who did it. If the gamble was great, the stakes were fabulous. Clinton saw that success would mean that his New York would become the greatest port in America instead of being overshadowed by Philadelphia.

It was not easy. Legislators with small minds and big voices orated flamboyantly against "this waste of the people's money." The project was derisively nicknamed "Clinton's Big Ditch." But the people, who had more imagination then the orators, backed Clinton to the hilt. The Canal Bill was approved in April, 1817.

Before that, while Lite Remington was actually building the Gun, the first surveying party came through the German Flatts in August, 1816. They took their bearings with a hand compasss and blazed a trail through the swamps and woods. Then the chainmen followed, measuring, and drove their stakes. Levels were calculated roughly, and the party pushed on. At night they camped around the covered wagon that held their supplies.

Ground was broken at Rome on July 4, 1817. It was a grand and glorious way to celebrate Independence Day, and it was done in a highly festive manner. "Along the line of the Canal at convenient intervals were to be found barrels of whiskey, pure old rye, with part of the head cut out and a tin dipper lying by, and all were expected to help themselves."

"Let us proceed with the work," said Commissioner Young, and heaved up a shovelful of earth.

Everybody took a hand at digging that first day, while four-span ox teams dragged the big plows through to break the soil. After that, Irish immigrants did most of the digging, since native Americans are enthusiastic shovelers only when the bands are playing and the press is present. Though local contractors bid on the work in their respective sections, they had to rely mainly on imported labor. The big, two-hundred-man gangs passed through the little towns and villages like a riotous but good-natured army, leaving behind them a broad ditch forty feet across and four feet deep.

Ahead of them went the axmen, clearing the forest, followed by a gigantic stump puller invented for the occasion. Codman Hislop describes it in "The Mohawk"— "They swung an axle twenty inches in diameter, thirty feet long, between a pair of wheels sixteen feet in diameter. In the middle of the axle was another wheel, smaller, a mere fourteen feet in diameter. Paddy, the crew leader, would brace the outer wheels, wind one end of his chain about the axle, and lash the other end around his stump. Then the oxen went to work, dragging on a rope wound around the center wheel. Stumps came out of the ground like corks out of a grog crock."

The stump puller could handle full-grown trees as well. When the engineers needed a dam above Fort Plain to raise the level of the Mohawk nine feet to feed the Canal, they hauled great trees out by the roots and laid them lengthwise in the river, branches, roots and all. Then they piled rocks and dirt on top, and so built the dam in sixty days.

The canal gangs went through London and Morgan's Landing at the foot of the Gulph in 1819 like a swarm of locusts, consuming every bit of food to be found, drinking Cary's Grocery and Gillespie's Distillery bone dry, and probably eating the mash. The water came curling down the dry ditch a little later. By 1821, two hundred and twenty miles of canal were built and swarming with traffic.

But that was the "easy" central section. Nobody yet knew how it was to be finished, if ever. Black Rock and Buffalo were frantically vying to be the western terminus. Official opinion swung back and forth between them. When Buffalo got a favorable report the mayor would fire off a thirty-two-pounder cannon. But on the next veer of the political wind, it would be the turn of Mayor Fraser and the people of Black Rock to bang away with their ancient artillery.

The eastern end was as much in dispute, for the gorge and rapids of the Mohawk below Schenectady, and the Great Cohoes Falls above Albany were gigantic problems. To put his canal through, DeWitt Clinton had to get himself elected governor, replacing fuddy-duddy Governor Yates, who still went around in knee breeches.

The thing was done at last. Canvass Webb, the engineer of the Eastern Section, carried the Canal across the Mohawk on an aqueduct forty feet high to the easier north shore and dropped it down a series of locks that were as steep as a staircase to the Hudson opposite Troy. At the other end, Buffalo became the terminal, and the final mountain barrier at Lockport was conquered by another series of locks made of stones so beautifully fitted that they needed no masonry.

October 26, 1825, was the greatest day of Governor Clinton's life. Seldom does a man live to see a great constructive dream come true and still have strength to celebrate it with a colossal ten-day binge.

Early on that sparkling autumn morning, the Governor and his young wife boarded the canal boat *Seneca Chief,* which had been gaudily bedecked for the occasion. In its cabin he found a heroic painting depicting himself in a Roman toga in the company of a weary Hercules (who had just dug a canal) inviting Neptune to upper New York State.

Arrayed behind the *Seneca Chief* was a line of gaily painted canal boats ready for the great parade from Buffalo to New York. Even the disgruntled citizens of Black Rock had swallowed their grief and chartered the Canal Boat *Niagra* at the moderate price of $115 for the round trip.

At precisely nine o'clock, the *Seneca Chief* started down the Canal. As the three-horse tandem hitch took up the slack of her tow rope, a thirty-two-pounder cannon, which had taken part in the Victory of Lake Erie, roared a salute. Other naval guns, taken from the hulks of Perry's fleet, were placed at ten-mile intervals all the way to New York to telegraph the news of the opening. They were loaded to the muzzle by enthusiastic amateur cannoneers. Booming, belching and blowing up, they fired in turn, so the signal was carried to the waiting crowd at New York's Battery in one hour and twenty minutes.

Governor Clinton and his party set no speed records. Four miles an hour was the speed limit on the Canal and at every large town they stopped for a celebration. Enthusiastic local officials boarded the boats for short spans to point out places of interest. Schoolmaster John Taylor of Fort Plain was one of these. As the boat started off, he took up his duties, with the sententious phrase, "Your Excellency, it is a great honor and pleasure to instruct you in the historic places we are about to pass." And making a deep bow, fell into the Canal.

Traffic was thick, for once, on the Gulph Road as all the people of Litchfield Township poured down to see the Governor go by. The Canal ran right along the River Road which was carried by a low wooden bridge to its northern bank at Albert Baker's house just west of Morgan's Landing and recrossed to the south bank half a mile farther down. The best fun of the day for the Remingtons and their fellow townsmen came as the *Seneca Chief* approached the first crossing. "Low bridge!" shouted the red-coated postilion ahead with the horses. "Low bridge!" roared the captain, and blew a mighty blast on his horn.

There followed a hilarious scene as silk-hatted dignitaries and their ladies in full skirts and beribboned petticoats scrambled frantically down from the cabin roof of the *Seneca Chief* or dropped flat on their faces on her deck.

By the favor of the God of Rivers and the stamina of the Governor and his guests, the entire party reached New York safely on November 4, 1825. DeWitt Clinton poured a bottle of Lake Erie water into New York Harbor and spoke with the eloquence of real emotion of the wedding of the waters of the Great Lakes and the Atlantic which his romantic gesture symbolized. The Erie Canal was an accomplished fact, and the great days of the Mohawk Valley began.

The Remingtons, father and son, both knew that sooner or later they must move down to the Canal. The Cedarville Road through the Gulph had been improved, but it was still a weary, winding, uphill way from the landing to the forge. The Remingtons began to prepare for expansion as early as 1825. In Lite's ledger of that year, he notes the purchase of "four and a half thousand shingles—$9.00," and 7,350 bricks. The size of the business is also indicated by the items, "3,128 bushels of charcoal—$139.00," and "1,200 pounds freight to and from Albany—$12.00." The latter figure was at pre-canal prices. Once the waterway opened, the cost of moving a ton of goods from New York to Buffalo fell from $100 to $12.

Yet the Remingtons hesitated for another three years. This was not for reasons of business timidity—that was something they obviously had not. Rather it was reluctance to leave the quiet oasis of godliness, which the belt of untouched forest on the hills insulated from the roistering life along the Canal.

The Remingtons were sober folk—there is no trace whatever of humor in the family until Lite's son Samuel came along. Though they were cultivated men who loved music and good reading, they abhorred frivolity and had absolute integrity, both financial and religious. Indeed, they were the spiritual descendants of Cromwell's Roundheads. As such, they were very content in their upland pastures with a few neighbors who were of like mind—the Paddocks, the Samuel Merrys and their cousin Stephen Remington. Mr. Remington's beautiful stone house was a symbol of the solidity of their lives.

Lite and his father knew that their environment would be terribly different down on the Flatts. Though the villages were still small, they were kept restless by the tremendous volume of traffic using the new artery of commerce. Upward of two hundred canal boats passed through Morgan's Landing every twenty-four hours. All day and all night mule teams and horse teams jangled along the towpath while the teamsters cursed and the blasts of the captains' horns echoed back from the hills. In London there were already a warehouse and two teamsters' hotel-taverns that ran wide open all night. Gillespie's Distillery was thriving. So affluent was he that he printed his own money: "On demand we promise to pay to bearer Fifty—50—Cents in goods or current bills at our store in German Flatts." These shinplasters were the accepted currency of the district.

But if the Remingtons were of a puritanical strain, they were also good businessmen. To relinquish the opportunity, which they both recognized, for making a fortune, seemed a sort of cowardice, as though their moral fiber were too delicate to withstand contact with a tumultuous world. Thus it became a matter of conscience, as well as interest, to accept the challenge of business expansion.

Perhaps it was Ben Harrington's complaints about not getting his guns that finally made up the Remingtons' minds. In 1827, they began to look for a location. At first they thought of Frankfort, which was close to the iron mine. But they could find no land with adequate water power, so they began to dicker with John and Nancy Clapsaddle who had a farm where Staley's Creek foamed out of the Gulph. On the first of January, 1828, Lite Remington bought one hundred acres of land from them for $2,800. John Clapsaddle signed the deed in flowery script, but Nancy, being a mere woman, had to make her mark.

The land extended from the south bank of the Mohawk River back across the Canal and up the rise which was later known as

Armory Hill. The tract included most of what is now the business section of Ilion. From it John Clapsaddle, with Remington's willing consent, excluded two small islands of land, where stood the cooper shop of their friend Ben Harrington and Daniel Dygert's small warehouse. On the ground that Lite purchased in 1828 part of the huge modern Remington factory stands today.

No sooner was the deed signed, than the Remingtons began to build a stone drop forge. Winter was still the best time to move the material down from the limestone quarry that was part of their purchase. The stones were cut out by boring a rectangle of holes into the rock, filling them with whale oil and setting the oil afire. As the heat penetrated the intensely cold rock, it split off as neatly as though cut with a precision tool. Then the stones were dragged on sleds to the site of the new forge. In early spring men went to work fitting them into place. Meanwhile, Ben Harrington and Asa Sharp dammed Staley's Creek and built a stone raceway to carry the water to the big mill wheel at the rear of the forge. From there it flowed under the building, and—by arrangement with the state authorities—was dumped into the Canal as a feeder.

Though Lite Remington was conservative in his way of life, he was almost a radical in his approach to the processes of manufacture. Never satisfied with conventional methods he was always testing new ideas. During the years in the Gulph he improved the quality and design of his guns more rapidly than even he realized. On one occasion, he picked up a barrel which had been left unclaimed in the shop for two years, and was startled by its crudity compared to those he was currently producing. He was constantly trying different combinations of metals in his own smelter, and he even sent to the great steel makers of Europe for samples, and tested them in Stubbs twist and lap-welded barrels. When he found a steel that was particularly good, he imported it in quantity, regardless of expense.

It was Lite's nature to accept the ideas of other men as eagerly as his own. This open-mindedness, which became the living tradition of Remington Arms, was to attract innumerable inventors to Ilion. Any man with a new idea that made sense was welcome to use Remington resources to develop his invention. This policy, rather than mere business acumen, was what made the company live and grow.

Remington's industrial pioneering appeared in the equipment of the new shop. In addition to the grindstones, power-driven borer, the Whitney milling machine and rifling machines with which the forge was furnished, he installed a tilt hammer for working the iron and steel for the gun barrels. This precursor of the trip hammer was a heavy block of iron mounted on a wooden shaft. Attached to the shaft was a big wooden cam that traveled on a semicircular plank tilted sharply upward, thus lifting the hammer. When the cam reached the end of its travel, the heavy iron block fell with a shattering crash on the anvil beneath. Thus the picturesque but sweaty smith, laboriously swinging his sledge to forge the molten iron and steel, was eliminated from the armorer's craft.

Simultaneously with the building of the new forge, Mr. Remington began work on a house nearby for Lite. It was planned as a temporary expedient, for the younger man loved his house in the Gulph, and still regarded it as his real home, though he realized that he would have to spend much of his time on the Flatts.

Since building the first Gun, young Remington had almost imperceptably assumed the management of the business. His father continued to run the agricultural manufacture and to do most of the building. But the rapidly expanding gun business was in Lite's hands, and the decisions concerning it were his. Hence, Mr. Remington took charge of building the little frame house on what is now Otsego Street, which was to be his son's temporary headquarters.

All the lumber for it was carted down from the Gulph in big drays pulled by four powerful horses. Early on the morning of June 22, 1828, Mr. Remington superintended the loading of a dray, from the piles of twenty-foot planks that were stacked in the drying yard near the sawmill. Then he mounted to the top of the high, sweet-smelling load, while a young driver gathered up the reins. It was a hard pull up the hill, but the going was easier on the Cedarville Road. They passed the stone house and went down the hill into the Gulph again, and across the wooden bridge with the big, iron-tired wheels rumbling on the boards and the measured stamp of the horses' hooves like the rolling fire of distant cannon.

Where the gorge cut between the crests of the hills its walls were several hundred feet high and a scant two hundred feet apart. Here, the untouched forest still stood in its somber splendor, and the bright morning was dimmed to a dusk so deep that the teamster halted to light his lanterns. Their yellow light gleamed dimly on the huge boles of the trees, and threw fantastic shadows as the dray moved on.

Beyond the heights, the road pitched sharply downward, and the wheelers braced themselves against the breeching straps to hold back the load while the driver leaned on the long lever of his brakes. Jolting and swaying, they moved slowly down the steep hill until, where the road made an abrupt curve to follow the course of the creek, they came to a sink hole. As one wheel dropped into it, the strain was all one way on the piled-up timbers. They slid a little between the holding stakes, and the whole load canted suddenly, pitching Remington off and ahead. There was no stopping the slow momentum of four horses and a loaded dray. The horrified driver tugged frantically at the reins and braked with all his might, but, irresistibly, the equipage rolled forward, and a six-foot, iron-shod wheel passed over the dark body in the road.

Five days later Eliphalet Remington died in the fine stone house he had built in the wilderness.

Chapter 6

# Vulcan in Broadcloth

That summer of 1828, Eliphalet Remington II brought his family to live in Morgan's Landing. There were five children now. Philo was a strong young man of twelve who went to school at Cazenovia Seminary in the winter, but cared more about mechanics than book learning, and worked in the forge all summer. Then came Samuel, golden haired, blue-eyed and merry, who didn't take much interest in work at all; and the three little girls, Mary Ann, Maria, and Susanna. Eliphalet III was born that autumn.

The advent of eight Remingtons increased the population of the little village by exactly twenty per cent, since there were at that time only eight families, totaling forty people, living there. But they did far more than swell the roster of inhabitants. The new forge gave a tremendous impetus to the village. From April to December, Remington employed twenty expert machinists. Winter ice shut off his water power, but even then he employed quite a few workmen to put finished guns together from the extra parts manufactured during the open months.

It was easy, now, to ship the guns all over the state. They would wrap them securely in bundles, tag them properly and take them to the humpback bridge over the Canal. As one of the big, bullhead freighters passed slowly underneath, they passed the bundle down to a boatman, or simply dropped it on the cabin roof, which almost scraped the underside of the bridge.

The year after he moved to town, Remington built a small temperance hotel on the corner of Otsego Street and the River Road to accommodate his customers—he was not going to have them bedding down with the canallers at the gin mills in London. In 1832, he more than doubled the capacity of his works by erecting the first regular factory building, a large wooden structure on a stone foundation back up the hill from the drop forge. The raceway from Staley's Creek turned the wheel in this building and, passing on under it and down the steep hill, regained sufficient power to drive the forge wheel as well.

The spate of new business that flowed higher each year did not just happen. Remington no longer sat in the woods waiting for the world to beat that path. Leaving the works in charge of A. C. Seamans, his shop foreman, he began to travel afield, seeking new business. His lean, elegant figure in a flowing cape and a stovepipe hat became familiar in all the river towns and in many others beyond the valley. He often took Abigail with him, for she loved to travel.

The fine eighty-foot Canal packets like the *Victory* and the *Paragon,* pulled by relays of horses which were changed every ten miles or so, were the most comfortable and cheapest method of locomotion. The cost of traveling nearly three hundred miles from Albany to Buffalo was only $14.33 with all meals included; and the scenery was magnificent. Part of the way, the Canal passed between high dikes that cut off the view, but mostly it was carried above the level of the countryside, as where it crossed the Genesee River on an aqueduct eight hundred feet long, supported by beautiful Roman arches. The passengers lolled in easy chairs on the cabin roofs, floating high above the slow panorama of rich farmlands, backed by the forested hills.

But the "fast" packet took over four days to traverse the length of the Canal, and when Remington traveled alone, his driving energy seldom allowed him to indulge in such luxury. Usually he endured the miseries of John Butterfield's bucketing stage coaches to save precious time. Not that he did not like his comforts or was unwilling to pay for them. When he went to New York, he traveled down the Hudson in style in Daniel Drew's fast, cake-and-frosting sidewheel steamers, which were the last word in luxury liners; and his favorite hotel in the city was the elegant Hoffman House, which in later years proudly advertised that it was Remington Headquarters in New York.

Even outside of the area of business, the Remingtons had a terrific impact on Morgan's Landing. No sooner were they settled in their new house, than they began to make improvements. Like his father at Crane's Corners, Remington was most upset by the fact that the village had no church. In fact, it had no public meeting place at all. Business and politics were usually discussed in Cary's Grocery Store, where cracker barrels and kegs of whiskey were handy. The miniature schoolhouse of logs painted red, where Sam and Mary Ann were learning their letters from McGuffey's Readers, wouldn't hold even a tiny town meeting. Religion was on an extremely erratic schedule. When circuit-riding Preacher John Erkenbrack came around, he usually held services in the Stockade, a loop-holed log fortress behind a palisade of tree trunks with sharpened tops, which was left over from Indian times.

This state of things was a shame and a scandal, which no Remington would tolerate for long. The first regular Methodist Bible Class was founded in 1832, with John Hunt as Leader. In 1835, Remington built them a regular meeting house, and in 1842, the Union Church was erected at a cost of $1,500, "largely contributed by E. Remington."

Perhaps Remington's church building was spurred on by the visitation on the Mohawk Valley of the classic plagues, considered indicative of the Lord's displeasure. First came the locusts. In 1831, they swept down the valley in a horde that filled the sky from mountain ridge to ridge. The still surface of the Canal was encrusted by their dead bodies. No Indians ever wreaked such devastation on the fields.

The next year came the most dread plague of all—cholera. It started in New York and rode swiftly up the river and the Canal on the rodent stowaways that infested the shipping. Men and women who died aboard canal boats were hastily buried alongside the towpath; and the rats ran ashore at the ports carrying the sickness with them. Not being much of a port, Morgan's Landing escaped unscathed, except for the terror that spread far wider than the plague itself.

After the locusts and the cholera passed, the years went by serenely. Almost without realizing it E. Remington had become a citizen—in fact the leading citizen—of Morgan's Landing. Some people even began to call the place Remington's Corners, though Eliphalet was dead against that as he proved some years later, when, for the only time in his career, he allowed his temper to tamper with business.

By 1836, he had given up all ideas of returning to his home in the Gulph. The little forge by the creek was sold to the firm of Hawes and Haines, who manufactured carpenters' squares and edged tools. Abigail's family homestead burned down, and her father built a pleasant rambling wooden house by the banks of the Canal.

Remington, too, decided to have a new house, and drew the first rough plan for it on the back of a bill of lading which still exists. The house was made of brick with a hall running through the center and spacious rooms on either side. It stood on the River Road at the foot of Armory Hill, facing north toward the Mohawk and the Hasenclever Hills. There was a shady porch at the western end of the house on which the Remingtons loved to sit on quiet summer evenings, looking up the valley along the still surface of the Canal, which ran straight and level to the edge of infinity like a long narrow mirror, reflecting the improbably beautiful colors of sunset.

Around the house, Eliphalet planted an orchard of which he was immensely proud, and fields of corn in the land he owned north of the Canal. Very early in the morning, before he went to work, he liked to cross the bridge and walk through his fields, with his black cape slung across his shoulders and his stovepipe hat bobbing between the tall, spiked stalks of corn.

That first summer, 1836, he sat on his porch watching the rafts of one-hundred-foot logs being floated down the Canal for the railroad then building from Schenectady to Utica. Soon the Irish construction gangs were laying wooden rails faced with a thin strap of iron across the flats, and in no time at all the opening day was at hand.

The Schenectady and Utica Railroad was a vital link in the series of little railways that finally joined up with each other to form a through route to the West, and became the New York Central Lines. Remington was too good a businessman not to appreciate its value to the valley in general and his own business in particular—indeed, he invested heavily in its stock. Now he would be able to go to Albany in eight hours instead of two days. Now the freight could move throughout the long winter months when the Canal was frozen; and it would be handled faster and more efficiently. Already the Mohawk and Hudson Railroad from Albany to Schenectady was taking the local hauls away from the boatmen by undercutting their rates.

Though his works declared a holiday as did every other factory, mill, shop or school along the track, Remington did not propose to attend the opening ceremonies of the railroad. However, from his porch, he had a fine view of the first gala train. It was drawn by the famous old engine, DeWitt Clinton, an oddly ironical name, since it and its ever more powerful successors eventually made Governor Clinton's Big Ditch obsolete.

Heralded by a great plume of white wood smoke and the banging of bells and screeching of its whistle, the little train appeared far off in the flats. The children, frantic with excitement dashed across the bridge and over the flats with Abigail anxiously running after them.

Eliphalet went so far as to rise from his chair and stand at the edge of the porch looking on. The train crossed the flats at the then incredible speed of nearly twenty miles an hour. The engine looked like a long barrel laid lengthwise on a dray, with four enormous, wooden-spoked, iron-tired wheels that flashed around with alarming rapidity. In front was a stove pipe with a fancy crown top. The engine driver stood on the open platform at the back end of the boiler hanging on by one hand, and flinging billets of wood into the furnace with the other.

The next car was a platform with a wooden surrey top, loaded with barrels of wood. Then came five cars, which were simply stage coaches mounted on little iron wheels. The seats on top were crowded with gentlemen clinging to tall beaver hats, and ladies clutching their full skirts, which billowed and flapped in the wild wind of progress.

The whole contraption shivered and shook and rocked with speed. Every time the engineer threw more wood in the furnace an angry red shower of sparks belched from the chimney, and flew back upon the excited passengers, sometimes setting their clothes afire. Remington could see the men letting go of their hats to beat out the smouldering flames.

The spectacle careened past in a matter of seconds and vanished into the serenity of the western valley with a diminishing screech. Eliphalet sat soberly down in his chair aware that progress was not an unmixed blessing.

In his own business, Remington continued to push forward His new machinery included a turning lathe and four milling machines. In addition, he organized a shipping department under Seamans where a supply of locks, rough gun stocks, butt plates, patch boxes, and other trimmings were kept on hand so that orders from gunsmiths could be instantly met.

Since selling the forge in the Gulph, Remington had no facilities for smelting iron. So in 1839, he and Ben Harrington got together in a partnership that became a separate but allied business. They damned Staley's Creek again, farther up, to furnish power, and built a smelting plant to make bar iron from ore and scrap. There they also carried on the business of making agricultural tools and parts for grist and saw mills. A little later they built a saw mill of their own which was called the Harrington Mill.

It was also in 1839, that E. Remington recorded proudly in his ledger, "My son, Philo, this day entered the business." Samuel joined it a little later; but being a restless youth—and man—with an itchy foot and no fondness for parental discipline, he went adventuring for a while to the Far West—Ohio—where he worked at constructing railroads until a sudden pressure of business, in 1845, made his father write to him to come home and help run the family enterprise.

Philo had not been at work long when he contributed two Remington firsts to the gunsmith's art. This took quite as much courage as mechanical skill, for Eliphalet was just but stern, as the model Victorian father felt he must be, and he expected his sons to obey him without question. His receptivity to new ideas was all for outsiders; those springing from his own family were *ipso facto* suspect.

Being painfully aware of paternal prejudice, Philo said nothing to his father about his new notions; he just went ahead on his own.

One hot day, Eliphalet walked into his drop forge like Vulcan in broadcloth, pleasantly soothed by the miniature inferno it represented. Half lit by soot-stained windows, the cavernous room swirled with smoke through which the red glare of charcoal fires lighted the figures of the gunsmiths as they labored. Everything seemed perfectly normal until Eliphalet came upon Philo straightening a gun barrel at an anvil which he had moved near a window. Instead of testing it with the traditional plumb line, the young man raised it to his eye, sighting through it at the window. Then he placed it on the anvil and tapped it with his hammer.

"That's no way to straighten a barrel," Eliphalet yelled above the din of machinery. "I'll stand for no sloppy workmanship here!"

Philo's eyes blazed in his sweaty, soot-stained face but he said respectfully, "Will you inspect the barrels I have just straightened, Sir?"

With a snort, his father seized a barrel from the pile and dropped a plumb line down it. No scientist measuring the deviations of an atom ever gave his subject a more meticulous examination than Remington gave that barrel. He wanted to find something wrong with it. When he could not, he took another and still another.

Eliphalet was stern but not pig-headed; he could be convinced even by his son.

"How do you do it?" he asked.

"I catch the shadow from the cross bar of the window in the bore," Philo said. "If there is a deflection it tells me where the barrel is crooked. When there is no deflection, the barrel is straight."

With the addition of some gadgets for more exact measurements, that is the method by which gun barrels are inspected and straightened today. In fact, the most experienced gunsmiths dispense with the gadgets and straighten the guns just as Philo did.

Philo's second contribution to gunmaking was to put a steel facing on the trip hammers. This made for far more accurate workmanship than was possible with the easily pitted iron formerly used. While Philo and the workmen were fitting the steel into place, Eliphalet came up to see what was going on. This time, however, he did no bellowing, for Philo had won his respect. Nor did he verbally approve the change. He merely examined the work for a moment. Then he walked silently away.

To anticipate a little, the Remingtons and their gunsmiths shortly made a vastly more important forward stride in the making of guns. Until the 1840s, all gun barrels had been manufactured by either the same process young Remington had used in making his first gun or lap welding. Attempts had been made to drill cast-steel barrels but they were unsuccessful. Now the Remingtons succeeded in designing a drill that would bore a small-caliber hole through a round bar of solid steel four feet long. The device consisted of a stout, wooden frame, like the rifling machine then in use, and the drill was a small adaptation of the drills used for boring cannon. It was driven by a belt from the water-wheel and lubricated with oil which the operator poured on by hand.

Every so often he would stop the drill, and pull it out, thus removing the chips and shavings of steel.

It was exacting, laborious work, requiring a high degree of technical skill backed by exact calculations, but it paid off magnificently. For it resulted in an unwelded barrel of solid steel, the prototype of all modern guns.

Chapter 7

# The Shadow of the Gulph

Though they had been so happy in the Gulph, its somber depths held tragedy for the Remingtons. Once it had struck, and would again, almost as though the forest were still the great enemy to be conquered and subdued.

Abigail Remington was very gay on the morning of her forty-ninth birthday, August 12, 1841. Eliphalet and the boys came home for lunch, and all her daughters were there. After the meal, the men went back to work, and Abigail proposed to Maria that they go for a drive.

"I'd like to go up through the Gulph," she said, "and see the stone house, and our home by the creek where we all had such fun."

Maria thought it would be delightful. "It's so long since I've been there, I've almost forgotten how pretty it is," she said.

"I'll drive the phaeton," said Abilgail, "so we won't have a man along to bother us."

A stable boy brought the small open carriage to the front door, and stood at the horse's head while the ladies got in and settled their full skirts. Abigail expertly gathered up the reins and the whip; and Maria opened her small, beruffled parasol.

"Light the carriage lamps," Abigail said to the boy, "it's always so dark in the woods."

She held a taut rein on the nervous young horse, as the boy ran into the house for a lighted taper and applied it to the fresh candles in the shiny brass lamps on either side of the carriage. Then she gave the horse his head and they were off in a clatter of gravel.

Mother and daughter, in their light summer dresses and their big leghorn hats tied on with filmy chiffon veils, made a pretty sight as the smart trap rattled along the River Road at a fast trot. Even when they swung into the Cedarville Road and began the steep climb upward, the horse wanted to keep going and it took all of Abigail's strength to pull him down to a walk. At the slightest excuse, he started off again, his feet dancing on the dusty road.

In the deep cleft between the hills it was, as always, chilly, and the light was like the summer dusk. Marie closed her parasol and shivered a little. But Abigail did not notice the cold; she was too busy controlling her horse, which skittered and shied at the shadows thrown by the carriage lamps.

They went along the creek to the spot where the road turned right and forded it. The horse picked his way daintily across, hock deep in the swift current, and set himself against the collar for the steep upward climb. As they neared the plateau on which the stone house stood, the light grew stronger. Then the road leveled, the great trees broke away, and the summer sun struck them with a blast of heat.

Maria grabbed her parasol and opened it so quickly that the silk cracked like a pistol shot. The horse made one tremendous bound forward, tearing the reins from Abigail's hands. Then he was off at a dead run with the bit in his teeth and the reins trailing and catching under his hind feet.

Across the meadow he tore, with the light carriage swaying and leaping behind him. The fatal parasol flew out of Maria's hands, and both ladies clutched the slippery leather arms of the carriage, their faces taut with terror.

Never slackening, the horse bolted all across the upland stretch, and hurtled down the narrow, twisting road to the second ford. The darkness of the trees closed about him and he slipped and stumbled on the steep slope. Somehow he kept his feet, and, frantic now, increased his pace. The carriage teetered to the left on two wheels, recovered, swayed to the right and smashed to splintered wood, against a big oak tree.

Maria, sitting on the left, was thrown clear, landing unhurt on the springy forest floor, but Abigail pitched head first into the great tree.

They sent a messenger to the works for Eliphalet and his sons. The three men galloped madly up the Gulph, but they were too late. Five seconds would have been too late—for Abigail's head was crushed by the blow and she died instantly.

Remington jumped off his foaming hose, and ran to her, lying still on the pine needles. There, almost at the exact spot where his father had halted the oxcarts in the wilderness, Lite knelt, stricken and tearless beside the body of his wife.

His grandchildren say that Eliphalet Remington never smiled again.

## Chapter 8

# William Jenks and the U.S. Marines

In the 1840s breech-loading guns were made by Remington. To understand the consequence of this event, it is necessary to take a quick backward look at the history of firearms.

The Remingtons did not invent the breech-loading gun. Nor, for that matter, did William Jenks, the little, round-faced, dreamy-eyed Welshman whom they brought to Ilion to perfect his ingenious mechanism. But he and they did produce the first practical percussion-cap breech-loading carbine.

Breech-loading guns had been a long time coming—more than three hundred years. No important tool of the human race ever developed more slowly than firearms. Perhaps it was the resistance that the military mind had toward new ideas in the old times. Nowadays, when the generals stand behind the laboring scientists, waiting to snatch the latest invention, it is hard to conceive how adamant they were against innovations right up to the last decade. Whatever the cause, the guns were there and the inventions made, centuries before they were properly utilized.

Back in the Fifteenth Century, it was known that a spinning bullet traveled more surely to its mark than one from an unrifled barrel. The inventory of the Fortress of Guastalla in Italy, dated June 28, 1476, lists:

"Also one iron gun made with a twist like a snail shell." But rifling did not come into general use until about 1800.

The breechloader was invented by 1537. In that year, Henry VIII of England owned a harquebus with a good breech mechanism which resembled that of the comparatively modern Snider rifle. The English King, who was very foresighted, urged the excellence of the new arm on his generals. They would have none of it! Seventy years later, Henry IV of France tried to interest his military geniuses in a new French breechloader with the same negative result.

There the matter rested for a couple of hundred years. Breechloaders were actually used by the British in the American Revolution. Major Patrick Ferguson invented a rifled gun, which had a lever-and-screw action, drop breech. In addition, it was very light and was equipped with adjustable sights. He demonstrated it officially at Woolwich Arsenal in England, on June 1, 1776, firing six shots a minute in the pouring rain—at least three times as fast as a muzzle-loader could be fired. The British Brass turned it down.

But Major Ferguson was an Irishman who was not easily quashed. He had thirty guns made at his own expense, and equipped his company of riflemen with them. Washington Irving in his *Life of Washington* states that Major Ferguson's gun, "is said to have far excelled in facility and execution anything of the sort ever before known." According to Irving, the troops equipped with them outdid all others "in their adroitness and quickness of firing and in the certainty of hitting the mark, lying upon the back or belly, and in every other possible position of the body."

Incidentally, Ferguson's breechloader nearly altered the course of American History, or, possibly, brought it to an abrupt conclusion. He tells the story himself in his diary.

At the Battle of Germantown, Ferguson and his riflemen lay in front of General Kuyphausen's division. According to Ferguson's account, "A rebel officer in French hussar dress . . . passed within a hundred yards followed by another in blue, mounted on a good bay horse, with a remarkably high cocked hat."

Ferguson called to them. The officers stopped for an instant, and the one in blue regarded him haughtily. Then, ignoring the Britisher's shouts and signals, they continued nonchalantly on.

Ferguson was credited with being the finest marksman of his time—he could shoot the head off a small bird at thirty yards. He says quite truly, "I was in that distance at which in the quickest firing I could have lodged half a dozen balls in or about him before he was out of my reach."

But the gallant major belonged to the sporting English tradition that will not shoot a sitting bird. He put the sights of his rifle on the American, but could not bring himself to pull the trigger. It was too damned easy!

So he watched, while Generals Washington and Lafayette rode slowly past him into history.

The United States Army finally ordered some breech-loading carbines from John H. Hall in 1819. At that, it was the first army in the world so to equip its troops. But the Hall carbine, a flintlock, was unsatisfactory. It was a heavy gun, with a barrel that bulged as though an accident had already happened. The breech mechanism was crude, and so weak it had to be strengthened by wrought-iron straps bolted to the side. It was, in fact a typical country blacksmith's job, but it was the best we had until William Jenks came along.

The combination of Remington's first service to the United States Government and the production of a really practical breechloader in his factory was the result of the tensions of the times.

In 1845, the United States was faced with an almost inevitable war with Mexico. During the previous decade, Americans had thrilled vicariously to the immortal defense of the Alamo, and rejoiced when Sam Houston and his fellow Texans won their liberty from Mexico. Now Texas was begging to be annexed and a majority of Americans were unwilling to see that rich land go begging, even if it meant war with Mexico.

In addition to its claims on Texas territory, the Mexican Republic still held the whole golden Southwest, and left its fabulous resources totally undeveloped. If war came, everyone knew that California would be its glittering prize, and that, too, seemed worth fighting for.

In 1844, James Knox Polk was elected President on a platform declaring for the annexation of Texas. President Polk personally desired peace; but while he made considerable efforts to settle the trouble by diplomatic means, he was obliged to prepare for the ultimate resort to arms. And, as usual, the government lacked arms.

The main reliance of the infantry at this time was a percussion-cap, muzzle-loading, rifled musket known as "The Harpers Ferry Rifled Musket." The John Griffiths Company of Cincinnati, Ohio, held a contract to supply five thousand Harpers Ferry rifles to the Government. Griffiths lagged in their deliveries, and the Government needed those rifles. So the thought was unofficially conveyed to Eliphalet Remington that it would be very nice if he could see his way clear to doing something about it. Remington acted with his usual energy. He purchased the contract from Griffiths, with the Government's hearty blessing, evinced by an order for five thousand more Harpers Ferry rifles, and immediately set to work to expand his production.

His first move was to recall Sam from the West. Simultaneously he remodeled the old forge and began work on the big wood-and-stone factory building which remained in use until 1915, and was known as Armory No. 1. A new mill race was constructed to furnish it with power.

In addition to more floor space, Remington needed machinery. Some of it was built in the foundry of Remington and Harrington; but it could not supply all he needed. So Eliphalet clapped on his stovepipe hat and went traveling again, this time to buy, not sell.

He purchased edging machines and sent them to his armory to be adapted for cutting out gunstocks. Heretofore, the stocks had been rough shaped on Blanchard lathes and finished by hand. The use of the edging machines to cut them to the exact form required resulted in the first machine-made gunstocks. At the Remington works they also devised tools which made it possible to turn out the first machine-made gunlocks.

Remington's trip had an even more significant result. At Chicopee Falls, in Massachusetts, he visited the plant of the N. P. Ames Company. For many years Ames had turned out excellent swords, bayonets and other military ironmongery. Recently they had gone into gunmaking with a Navy contract for a new-fangled breech-loading carbine invented by William Jenks.

Mr. Ames was not happy with his latest experiment. He had no experience with the manufacture of firearms, and was rapidly acquiring too much experience with governmental red tape. He was ready to listen to a proposition.

Remington looked at the excellent Ames machinery and coveted it. He examined the Jenks carbine, and decided that it was a practical mechanism. With his inventor's perception, he saw that he could make it into the best breechloader yet seen. And he took an instant liking to William Jenks.

Jenks was a Yankee, of Welsh descent, with curly hair, round eager eyes, a straight chiseled nose, and a thin, unhappy mouth. He looked like a minor poet, but his appearance of delicacy was strangely deceptive. For Jenks had the fire and imagination of a true genius, and a resilient inner core that had enabled him to buck bureaucratic indolence and red tape for nearly a decade, until by sheer perseverance (plus the excellence of his invention) he had dragooned the Navy into ordering a few of his guns. In Remington, he saw a chance to realize his ambitious dreams.

The upshot of Remington's visit to Chicopee Falls was that he bought the whole Ames gun business including machinery, contracts, guns in all stages of completion and, most important of all, the services of William Jenks. The price was exceedingly moderate. In addition to a small down payment, Remington gave Ames two notes on the Phoenix Bank of New York payable in eight and ten months. Each note was for $1,290.50, making a total of $2,581.00.

The machinery and partly finished guns were shipped from Massachusetts to the Mohawk Valley, and installed in the new armory. William Jenks came along with his charming wife, and built himself a fine house down by the Canal.

The Harpers Ferry production was temporarily postponed, at the insistence of the Government, who wanted a hurry-up order of ancient flintlocks!—the last ever issued to American troops. But this was routine stuff, which kept the new machines going, while Jenks and the Remingtons, and their skillful old gunsmith, Riley Rogers, who had been with them ever since they moved down to the Canal, went to work redesigning the Jenks carbine.

There were plenty of improvements to be made. Sam Remington had already written to the Government on January 27, 1845, suggesting the use of cast-steel, drilled barrels. His proposal was agreed to, and the Jenks was redesigned with this innovation. The guns supplied to the Navy in 1847 were the first unwelded-steel barrels ever used by the armed services.

The actual breech mechanism was excellent and needed no improvement. It consisted of a sliding bolt linked to a hinged lever lying along the top of the grip. When you lifted the lever it pulled the bolt back. The paper cartridge could then be shoved into the chamber. When the lever was thrown forward again, it locked and sealed the breech so completely that it was the strongest part of the gun.

However, the first Jenks guns were old-fashioned flintlocks. In a later model made by Ames, the percussion-cap method of firing was used. In this, the fulminate of mercury cap was placed on a nipple with a hole running through it. When the trigger was pulled, the hammer fell on the cap, and the small blast of flame shot through the hole, firing the charge.

The Remingtons improved on this system by using Dr. Edward Maynard's new patent lock. For this the caps were made on a paper tape, exactly like those used in present-day toy pistols. A small pan with a hinged lid held a reel of the tape, which was threaded over the nipple, while the hammer had a cutting edge to sever the tape. This saved the time lost by having to fix a separate cap before firing.

As finally delivered to the United States Navy, the Remington-Jenks was a beautiful, if somewhat gaudy gun. The cast-steel barrel was brightly tinned for protection against salt water and the lock and breech were case hardened. The butt plate and trigger guard, the bands that clamped the barrel to the shining straight-grained wood, the sling rings, screws and other fittings were of brass, polished so highly that it sparkled and flashed in the sunshine. To make these parts the Remingtons set up a small brass foundry in their words. Such were the guns that went with Commodore M. C. Perry's Fleet to Vera Cruz in 1847, and were in the hands of his marines when they stormed into the Halls of Montezuma.

At this same time, the Remingtons made a cavalry model of the Jenks carbine. Compared to its naval cousin, it was as drab as a hen pheasant beside a cock. The barrel was finished in brown lacquer and the brass, which Navy specifications demanded because of its superior resistance to salt-water corrosion, was replaced by dull-finished metal. It was probably the best gun in the world of 1847 for cavalry use, but the dragoons sneered at it and the Ordnance Department turned it down.

This was done in spite of the fact that in 1845, a joint Army and Navy board had approved the Jenks carbine with the comment: "The board is of the opinion that this carbine combines in an eminent degree the two great advantages attending arms loading at the breech, that of propelling the ball with great force, and that of being loaded rapidly and easily in situations where the use of the rammer is inconvenient; the latter consideration would recommend it for use in boat service and the fighting tops of vessels as well as in the cavalry service."

It has been said that breechloaders were developed in spite of the best efforts of the Ordnance Department. There is plenty of evidence for this in the letters of Lieutenant Colonel George Talcott, a man of resolute stupidity, to the Secretary of War:

> A prejudice against all arms loading at the breech is prevalent among officers, and especially the dragoons. That the arm of Mr. Jenks, even if found better than others, can be introduced is not to be supposed. . . . As regards the arming of the Second Dragoons with them, Colonel Twiggs has protested in advance . . . against the use by his regiment of any breech-loading or patent arms of any kind whatever.
>
> There are now, Colts, Jenks, Hubbels, Nuttings and I know not how many other kinds of patent arms. . . . That they will ultimately all pass into oblivion cannot be doubted. . . .
>
> I am, Sir, etc.
> *G. Talcott*
> LIEUTENANT COLONEL OF ORDNANCE
>
> HON. WM. WILKENS
> SECRETARY OF WAR.

Even the determination of doughty Colonel Twiggs to keep his troopers fiddling with three-foot ramrods while they tried to control nervous horses did not discourage Jenks. He bought a hundred-acre farm at Arlington, Virginia, so as to be near the Capital and continued to plug his guns.

When General Winfield Scott returned from the wars full of enthusiasm for the Jenks carbine, things looked brighter. The General spent a lot of time shooting at the Jenks farm. His influence got Jenks another trial of the gun.

One of the conditions of the test was that Jenks must fire his gun 1,500 times without any noticeable deterioration in its performance. At about the 1,400th shot, the nipple on the firing mechanism broke, and the gun was turned down again.

When that nipple broke, so did Jenks' indomitable spirit. He gave up and went abroad to sell his gun. In England and France they welcomed him with glad cries and spirited bidding. That scared the Washington officials out of their somnolence. They begged Mr. Jenks to be a good patriot and come home. He was a good patriot, so he did.

In 1858, the Jenks carbine, with an improved breech designed by

J. H. Merrill at the Remington Armory to accept cardboard cartridges coated with beeswax and tallow, was tested once again. They fired it 126 times. Then they loaded it with a cartridge, held it under water for a full minute and set it aside. The next day according to the official report "the carbine was discharged, and though much rusted, I found no difficulty in firing fifty rounds with the usual rapidity."

So it passed at last, and was approved by the Ordnance Department.

Jenks did not long enjoy his triumph. In 1859, in curious coincidence with the death of Eliphalet Remington, the First, the inventor was killed by being brushed from the top of a hay wagon as it entered his barn in Arlington.

Compared to Colt and Winchester and Sharp, Jenks' name is virtually unknown. Yet his influence on the development of modern firearms was immense. Backed by the Remingtons through all his adversities, and guided by their technical skill, he produced the first really useful breechloader, which was a boon to sportsmen as well as to the armed forces of his country.

## Chapter 9

# Peace and Prosperity

Contrary to the general impression, the Remington Arms Company has always prospered more in peace times than in war. The wild flurry of war contracts, the extravagant expansion to fulfill them, the financial and mechanical risks which they enforce, the strain on men and machines alike, and the sacrifice of personal comfort and health, which patriotism prompts such men as the Remingtons and their successors to make, far outweighs the illusory profits, which are usually lost in the aftermath of reconversion.

In 1848, the southwest was opened to Americans, and the shimmer of gold in the California rivers set off a mass migration as the whole nation turned its face westward. Every one of those pioneers, who braved the perilous journey across the vast inhospitable plains, needed a gun to protect his life and supply his larder.

The Remingtons were mainly concerned with the production of sporting arms. Throughout the peaceful 1850s, they turned out all manner of guns designed for civilian use. There were beautiful fowling pieces with Damascus barrels and intricate engraving on the locks; muzzle-loading rifles of all calibers for every kind of game; and fine double-barrel combination guns in which one barrel was rifled and the other smooth-bored for shot, so the hunter need never be at a loss whether he started a deer in the woods or flushed a covey of quail in the open fields.

The advent of breechloaders brought additional interest in hunting for sport instead of just for food. Both sportsmen and pioneers took to the new guns with enthusiasm. A fine light rifle with the Jenks action was popular with them, and, somewhat later, the Merrill adaption was made into a sporting gun.

There was good reason for this eager acceptance of the new arms. Fictional tales of hunting in the old days seldom give any idea of the enormous difficulties involved. In the first place a sportsman with a flintlock rifle was burdened with a conglomerate collection of paraphernalia in addition to his gun. He must, of course, have a ramrod, a powder horn, and a supply of bullets. In addition he needed oiled patches for the bullets, made either of fine linen or chamois skin, extra powder and a supply of flints. Often he took along a forked stick for a rest, otherwise he must rest the barrel across a branch or a rock, for few men could hold a steady aim with those long, heavy, badly balanced guns.

Another item in the rifleman's equipment was a bullet mold to make his own ammunition, for in the days when guns were handmade, the caliber of each varied and the bullets had to be tailored for each individual rifle.

Picture the sportsman with this assortment of gadgets hung about his person, as the moment comes to load his gun. First he measures the charge of powder into the muzzle, then wraps the bullet in its oiled patch and rams it laboriously down the long barrel. Now he lifts his gun and, opening the priming pan, shakes a pinch of powder into it. If it happens to be raining, his difficulties are multiplied, for he must keep his powder dry by any means he can devise from holding his hat over the muzzle with one hand while he loads with the other to crouching under a projecting rock.

No matter how skillfully he worked, all this took considerable time. In effect it meant that he had time for just one shot at his quarry; and for practical purposes the game had to be standing still, because the long lag between pulling the trigger of a flintlock and the explosion of the main charge made it virtually impossible to shoot moving animals.

Incidentally, the accuracy of those famed Kentucky rifles has been grossly exaggerated. The tales of shooting the spots out of playing cards at fifty paces or hitting the bull's-eye ten consecutive times at a hundred yards are plain and fancy nonsense. The ballistic factors varied so with each charge, and the guns themselves were so eccentric, that it was a superb marksman who could place two bullets within a foot of each other at a hundred yards.

With the cards thus stacked against him, the sportsman who went out for big game, was a sport indeed. If his first shot failed, he got no second chance, and his very life depended no longer on his marksmanship, but on the basic factors of agility and speed in going away from there. Yet many a panther, wolf and wildcat fell to those intrepid sportsmen; and a standard barbecue dish of the era was "bear roasted whole, frontier style."

John Forsythe's invention of the percussion cap in 1807, was a great help, for it eliminated both the danger of wet priming causing a missfire and the time lag of the flintlock. Breechloaders were an even greater boon to the sportsman. For example, in loading a Jenks all one had to do was to flip open the breech, shove the patched bullet into the chamber, bite off the end of the cardboard cartridge, put it in place and close the breech. The Merrill breech was an even greater improvement, for its semi-waterproof linen cartridge contained both powder and ball, so that to load required only three motions.

For fundamentalists among hunters, the Remingtons manufactured a long, forty-four-inch barrel of remarkable accuracy for the time. Many of these long barrels were shipped to Kentucky where they were used in the so-called "Kentucky rifles."

In addition to complete guns, the Remingtons continued to do a great business in barrels, which were finished by other gunsmiths. In their catalogue for 1858, they state that:

> We have acquired a practical knowledge of the above business, especially in the manufacture of Barrels, which we believe few, if any others possess, having during that time (40 years) tested a great variety of iron for the purpose, but having mostly manufactured it ourselves expressly for our own use.
>
> We have also, for nearly thirty years, been testing the Steel of almost every manufacturer in the world, for our Cast Steel Barrels, and have for a long time had it made to our order expressly for that purpose.
>
> These repeated and long continued experiments, in pro-

curing the proper material for every variety of barrel, and an equally long experience in the various methods of working and annealing it, enable us to say, without boasting, that we are now prepared to make Barrels both of Iron and Steel in greater variety and perfection than any other Establishment in this country, if not in the world; having been first in successfully introducing Steel for Sporting Guns, and also for U. S. Rifles and Carbines, and having recently manufactured about 15,000 such for the U. S. Service.

It seems absurd to say that a blurb can have an emotional content; yet there is something a little touching in that naïve announcement, with its curiously placed capitals and stilted English. The pride of workmanship shines through it, and it is instinct with sincerity. Reading it, you know that E. Remington and Sons honestly believed that they made the best barrels in the whole world; and you feel that they were probably right.

Considering the workmanship and technology that went into them, the barrels were amazingly cheap. Some of the prices quoted are:

| | |
|---|---|
| CAST STEEL BARRELS | $3.00 each |
| IRON BARRELS | 2.00 each |
| STUBBS TWIST (DAMASCUS) | 4.00 each |
| MATCHED BARRELS FOR DOUBLE GUNS, CAST STEEL | $6.50 per pair. |

The Remingtons also imported and sold foreign gunlocks, and, reversing the process, shipped their own locks to England, and undersold the British manufacturers.

It is no wonder that the Remingtons' business boomed. Production figures show the rising graph. In 1850, they were averaging 588 barrels a month. By 1851, the number rose to 672 per month and 1,233 barrels were turned out in October. The total production for that year was 8,061. The year 1852 saw the average production rise to 835 barrels with a high of 1,475 barrels in August. The guns made from these barrels guarded the long slow wagon trains that were fanning out across prairies and deserts to civilize a continent.

At this time, Philo and Samuel became full-fledged partners and the firm name was changed to E. Remington & Sons. The money rolled in so fast that Eliphalet, who was no believer in stocks and bonds unless he could see the security as in the case of the Utica and Schenectady Railroad, was hard pressed to get it reinvested. Some of it was plowed back into the business. Two large buildings were added to the plant, and steam engines were installed to supplement the strictly seasonal water power. These were impressive affairs, with fat cylinders, huge flywheels, and flashing connecting rods, whirling governors and spinning cog wheels. They drove long shafts angled off from three-foot beveled gears, and power was transferred from floor to floor by means of leather belts eighteen inches wide.

The new engines were gaudy in bright red paint with gold trim, and they were decked out with ornamental ironwork, for the Victorians carried their taste for gimcrack ornament from their homes to their industrial machinery. Nevertheless they were splendid machines, built to last forever. Indeed, the 500 h.p. Corliss engine, installed in 1861, continued in operation at Remington Arms until 1935, when it was sold to another company. It is probably still running.

In addition to plant expansion, the Remingtons branched out in other directions. A big new foundry was built across the Canal in 1856, where machinery was manufactured for the Armory and other industrial establishments.

The Remingtons also sought other profitable side lines. For example, Linus Yale, had taken advantage of their hospitality toward inventors to carry on experimental work in the Remington shops, and now Sam Remington set up a company to manufacture his locks under license. From this Sam expanded to making safes and vault doors for banks. Remington steel doors were installed in the United States Mint at Philadelphia.

Other things made by the Remingtons at this time were telescope tubes, kaleidoscopes and the newly invented Sayre tooth for cultivators. A few years later the Rabeth cotton spindle, which revolutionized textile manufacture, was invented and manufactured at their works.

The Remingtons were not the sort of people to throw their money around in extravagant living. Eliphalet lived in simple comfort in his brick house, while Philo, Samuel and Eliphalet III, who had all married, lived in small frame houses on the same street. The time would come when the younger Remingtons would branch out in the lavish style of the nineteenth century, but not while their father lived.

Despite the complexity of his rapidly expanding interests, Eliphalet Remington did not neglect his home town. Due to the enormous increase in the Remington business, it had grown from a hamlet of eight houses, to a large and prosperous village; but it was still pretty primitive. Indeed, until the 1840s it did not have a post office of its own; it did not even have a name!

Long after the Remingtons had established their business at the mouth of Staley's Creek, their only regular communication with the outside world was via Mr. Luke, the letter carrier, who rode from Mohawk to Schenectady once a week to get the mail. Apparently few people along the river had any interest in national affairs. Once Mr. Luke embarked on a little business venture. He bought a packet of newspapers in Schenectady and tried to peddle them along his route for two pennies each. He ended the trip with most of the papers still on hand—the people just didn't care twopence for the news.

By 1843, the citizens of "Remingtons' Corners" were all riled up by their mail-less situation. The question of a post office was the main topic of conversation at the cracker-barrel meetings in the stores and around the firesides at home. But to get a post office, the village had to have a name. That started a real storm.

The area had had several informal designations. Part of it had been called London, another part Morgan's Landing; the Canal Company listed it as Steele's Creek, and since 1830, almost everybody had called it Remingtons' Corners. When the question of an official title came up, over thirty names were proposed. Popular among them was the name of Remington, which Eliphalet modestly declined to authorize. After hot and heavy debate the thirty names were boiled down to two—Fountain and Vulcan. A mass meeting was held in Cary's Grocery, and the friends of Fountain outnumbered the Vulcanites nine to one.

The petition for a post office was then handed to Congressman Charlie Benton of Mohawk. However, he did not like the name of Fountain, and even the people who had voted for it began to think it was pretty silly. So Benton, without a by your leave, changed the name in the petition to Remington, and it was approved by United States Postmaster General A. G. Wicliffe. David Devoe was appointed postmaster.

When Eliphalet learned that he was living in Remington, he went into a fine fury. Two things about the deal sent his temper to white heat. The first was the sneaky way it had been put over; and the second was that, in some curious way, it outraged his deep religious abhorrence of personal vanity. He was so angry that he refused to give his address as Remington, but dated all his letters "German Flatts," which resulted in important business letters addressed to him wandering all over the state, while harrassed postal employees endeavored to locate a non-existent community.

The situation was intolerable. Mr. Devoe, who had been reading Homer's Iliad, went to his old friend Remington and suggested the village be renamed after ancient Troy, as became a neighbor of Rome, Syracuse and Utica, New York. Eliphalet remarked that he thought it was somewhat presumptuous to name so small a town after the heroic citadel of Homer's epic, but he guessed it would have to do. Whereupon Devoe wrote to the Postmaster General, and changed the name. Thus it happened that the astounded citizens, whom nobody had consulted, awoke one summer morning to discover that they were residing, not in Remington as they supposed, but in Ilion.

Under all its names, the Remingtons were active in the civic affairs of the village. Eliphalet had previously given the Meeting House and the Methodist Church. In 1852, he built a fine temperence hotel, and founded the Bank of Ilion, of which he was the first president. Also in 1852, the Village was incorporated with Eliphalet Remington, Jr., as its first clerk.

Though he was its most active and prominent citizen, Eliphalet Remington never tried to impose his will on the people of Ilion, save only in the matter of using his name. Nor did he ever try to dictate to the workers in his factories, which would have amounted to the same thing since most of the town depended on him for their livelihood. Instead he managed his business on a plan designed to give him no personal authority over the men who worked for him.

The Remington system grew out of the practices of the Old Forge. Back in the Gulph, Eliphalet would pay a skilled workman, not for his time, but for so many barrels or locks or whatever the man's specialty happened to be. As the business expanded, these original workmen became contractors, who agreed to build so many barrels and hired other men to assist them. For example, in 1835, Eliphalet's ledger records a contract with Daniel Dygert for 1,500 barrels to be delivered in one year.

Under the Remington system the contractor was given the use of certain space in the factory, and the machines and tools that he required. He in turn agreed to produce a specified number of parts—or in the case of assembly contracts, of finished guns; and was solely responsible for engaging the labor force needed. So long as he lived up to his contract, and his product met the rigid standard of excellence, he was on his own.

This did not mean that the Remingtons stood aloof. On the contrary, they were constantly present with advice and technological assistance. But they did not try to boss the job.

As a result, Eliphalet Remington and his sons were in the position of impartial mediators between the contractors and the workers who trusted implicitly in their sense of justice.

The men were right to do so, for to be just and honest was part of the Puritan creed by which the Remingtons lived. There is no record anywhere that Eliphalet or his sons ever gave anybody a raw deal.

They also took a friendly interest in the people who worked in their plants and could be generous when occasion required. Generosity, however, did not imply a casual attitude toward money even in the smallest amounts. That same stern code which enjoined absolute integrity also demanded its just due to the last penny. In the 1840s, when he was handling great sums of money, there is an entry in Eliphalet's ledger; "Received from John Daniels (a timekeeper) $1.50 for the loan of a watch for 1 year."

The contract system was continued by the company through all the years that the Remingtons controlled it. That it worked well is evinced by the fact that there was never a strike against them. And so loyal were their people that, when the time of trouble came to Eliphalet's sons, contractors and workmen alike lent them money to keep the business going.

## Chapter 10

# Hand Guns for Gentlemen and Gentlewomen

From the long barrel of a Kentucky rifle, so heavy that it would stretch the muscles of Daniel Boone himself, to a tiny pistol less than two inches long is a considerable span in the manufacture of firearms. The Remingtons took the step in 1847.

That year Eliphalet Remington was looking for good gunsmiths to man his expanding armory. He found Fordyce Beals working for the descendents of Eli Whitney in their arms plant at Whitneyville, Connecticut, and engaged him as Superintendent of Manufacture. The fact that Beals had just patented a revolver did not escape the eyes of Eliphalet, who was looking for more worlds to conquer.

Samuel Colt had invented the revolver in 1836. The early Colt revolvers and revolving rifles had a cylinder with five or six chambers. Each of these had to be loaded by hand with loose powder and ball; a percussion cap was then placed on the shielded nipple of each chamber. When the hammer was pulled back to the cocked position, a central "hand," engaging a ratchet, turned the cylinder one sixth of a revolution, bringing a fresh chamber in line with the barrel.

These guns were the first practical, rapid-fire weapons ever made.

However, once the six shots were gone, you were through for the next three minutes while you laboriously reloaded each chamber.

Ten years after filing his patent, Colt had established a virtual monopoly of the revolver business. Eliphalet Remington decided to try to break it. The first Beals revolver was a poor instrument to this end. The cylinder was poked around by a three-pronged "hand," like a tiny devil's pitchfork. There was a shield back of the cylinder, which seemed like a fine idea, until the disconcerting discovery was made that it carried the flash of the cap to the other chambers which sometimes resulted in all of them going off at once, with disastrous results for the shooter.

This defect, also present in the early Colts, was remedied by removing the shield, and Remington began to manufacture the Beals revolver in 1849. However, it did not catch on until Beals brought out his greatly improved model of 1856.

This was a superb weapon, equal if not superior to the Colts then in use. The cylinder was revolved by a new type of "hand" located to one side of the lock under a sheath. Remington manufactured a great number of Beals revolvers in styles for all purposes. There was an Army model, and one for the Navy. These were .44- and .36-caliber guns with long barrels, some of them plated with gleaming nickel. Another style was made for police use, and there were small pocket guns and belt revolvers for civilians. They were offered in .31, .36 and .44 calibers and various barrel lengths.

Beals later developed a revolving rifle, with the same action as his hand gun, and a popular breech-loading rifle for sportsmen, in which the whole barrel slid forward to open the breech.

While Beals was perfecting his inventions, Eliphalet Remington brought in another hand-gun expert, Joseph Rider of Newark, Ohio. This was especially significant, because Rider was later the co-inventor of the most famous of all the guns made at Ilion, the Remington Rolling Block Rifle.

In 1856, Rider had invented a revolver with a curious mushroom-shaped cylinder, which he had sold to the manufacturing firm of Dill, Dean and Martin. Eliphalet thought so highly of it, that he bought them out, and gave Rider a new contract. He paid an odd price for Rider's remaining rights—twelve brace of revolvers and four hundred acres of land in Ohio.

Rider worked to improve his invention at the Remington Armory, and, in 1859, came out with a mechanism, the principle of which is, even today, the final word in revolvers. The new weapon was designed so that pulling the trigger turned the cylinder, cocked the hammer and fired the gun in a single motion. It was the first double-action revolver ever made.

Incidentally, Rider invented a four-shot magazine pistol in 1871, which used a metallic cartridge. It was two years before Colt brought out a metallic-cartridge revolver.

Rider liked to amuse himself by turning out odd types of pistols. One of these was a tiny thing about two inches long. The bullet was a BB shot, and the charge a single percussion cap. Another unusual weapon was a .22 caliber, single-shot pistol, only three inches long, which he designed so the ladies might protect their honor against those sinister mustachioed villans, who apparently lurked behind every gas lamp. It was one of the first of the so-called "muff guns."

In the next decade, the Victorian wolves must have grown both bold and numerous, for there was a regular boom in muff guns. The Remingtons did their bit for the protection of female virtue by producing the double Derringer, invented by William Elliott of Plattsburg, New York, in 1864. This was a .41 caliber pistol with under and over barrels which swung around and down to permit slipping cartridges into the breech. The deadly little Derringer, which was about four inches long, was popular with men as well as women and was made by Remington until 1936. The model for ladies of high degree had gold-plated barrels and a pearl-handled grip. A gentlewoman so equipped was quite safe from the advances of a too-eager escort.

Elliott had joined the Remington stable of inventors in 1861. His first contribution was a revolving pistol in which the five barrels rotated on their axis. Next to the double Derringer, his most popular product was the so-called zigzag pistol, which had four stationary barrels fired by an ingenious mechanism which traveled a zigzag course to each barrel in turn.

William Mason contributed another Remington first in 1866, when he invented the first revolver in which the cylinder swung out on a crane for loading.

With all these young wizards working at their benches in various corners of the Armory, the atmosphere was electric with the excitement of progress. It so stimulated John F. Thomas, the old master mechanic of the Armory, that he turned inventor, too, and in 1858 produced the most unusual weapon of them all. It looked like a perfectly ordinary walking stick; but if you slipped the ferrule off, you found yourself looking into a steel barrel. The gun was fired by pressing an innocent little button in the silver band under the handle. These cane guns became very popular with gentlemen who liked to combine sartorial elegance with a handy means of self-protection.

While his armory and foundry boomed, and new items were daily added to their production schedules, Eliphalet Remington continued to be his own best traveling salesman. His circuit had an ever-expanding radius. Still carrying his important papers in the crown of his high silk hat, he ranged from Ottawa to New Orleans, and from St. Louis to New York. In the latter city, he made a valuable new contact with the enterprising young firm of Schuyler, Hartley and Graham of whom more—a great deal more—later.

The indefatigability of Eliphalet on the road is illustrated by a letter he wrote to Philo at this time:

Galena, Ill. June 22, 1857

Dear Son:

I find we have thrown away two days and about ten dollars in pursuit of our *lame ducks,* at Joliet, as there is but little prospect of ever getting anything out of them. On my return I called on our customers at Ottawa, and Mr. Holland will take half a dozen pistols. I also found Volney Beckwith there (one of our old hands) who appears to be doing very well. The delay occasioned by this somewhat retrograde movement to Joliet has rendered it difficult to leave here until today. I now propose to go on to Galesburg this afternoon, and then proceed by way of Quincy and Alton to St. Louis. . . . I assure you I shall make no unnecessary delay, as I am well aware that our business requires my presence with you.

The weather has been rather wet and cold for several days, making fires in our rooms rather comfortable. My health continues good, and I remain

Truly yours,
*E. Remington*

In those lines is hidden a portrait of Eliphalet Remington in the final vigor of maturity. Though addressed to his eldest son, they are almost coldly formal. His mind is preoccupied with his affairs, and none are too small for his attention; no trouble too great to accomplish his purpose. But his only personal emotion is pleasure at finding an old employee doing so well. That is characteristic. For description, he can only talk about the weather.

Where, you might ask, is the ardent young man, who made a flute before he made a gun, and preferred poetry to practical matters? Is he buried so deep beneath the accumulated crust of success that he is lost forever?

Almost he is, for Eliphalet has not dared allow himself the luxury of emotion since Abigail died there in the Gulph. But there was one more poem that Eliphalet Remington was to write.

## Chapter 11

# The Civil War and Its Aftermath

Men were marching in 1861. On the elm-bordered commons of New England, in the flat dusty fields of the Midwest, and in the magnolia-scented parks of gracious Southern cities, perspiring civilians in blue or gray, and a whole rainbow of other fancy uniforms, marched and wheeled, shouldered arms and presented them, in obedience to the synthetically raucous voices of drillmasters who knew little more than they; while dashing officers, who knew least of all, cantered along the ranks, waving brand-new swords that were innocently bright and shiny.

Though the uniforms were gay, the hearts of thinking men were heavy as America moved toward the war, which at Gettysburg came within a few bloody yards of destroying her destiny. Despite the efforts of honorable and intelligent men in the North and in the South, men who spoke the same language, shared the same heritage and loved the same country, the tensions built up until they were resolved by the crash of a smooth-bore cannon, as General P. G. T. Beauregard jerked a lanyard and a shell arced over Charleston Harbor.

Eliphalet Remington watched the inexorable drift toward civil war with deep unhappiness. His sentiments had not changed from those of his youthful ode to peace in 1815; and the fact that, if war came, his armory would be a principal reliance of the Federal Government added an almost intolerable burden of responsibility to his unhappy musing.

But Eliphalet's mind held no question of the justice of the Union cause. He was a man of powerful convictions, who saw things in black and white, and whose patriotism was as profound as his faith in God. He had been an old-line Whig. When the Republican Party was founded in 1856, he voted for Fremont and Dayton. In November, 1860, he voted for Abraham Lincoln, and watched the triumph of his candidate with satisfaction untinged by elation.

The institution of slavery was completely abhorrent to Eliphalet Remington, and the destruction of the Union was unthinkable. Thus political ideals, love of country and religious faith all combined to strengthen his convictions. Only his horror of war was in conflict with them. Every day he knelt in prayer that it might somehow be averted. But if it came, he was resolved to spend his utmost strength in the service of the Union. And so he did.

The call came quickly. When Simon Cameron, Lincoln's first Secretary of War, took office on March 5, 1861, he found the War Department in chaos. In addition to the inevitable slackness of peacetime, Army leadership was riddled as Southern officers resigned to go with their states. Worse still, because of President Buchanan's anxiety to preserve the Union peacefully, preparations for war had been kept to a minimum lest they offend the Southern states, and reserve supplies of munitions in Southern arsenals had been taken over by the seceding states. In this way some of the Remington-made Harper's Ferry rifles fell into the hands of the Confederates. In short, Cameron found that the Army was almost disarmed.

In those days the War Department mainly relied for its rifles on the Government arsenals at Springfield, Massachusetts, and Harpers Ferry, Virginia. Springfield could turn out only a few thousand rifles a year, and the moment Virginia seceded, Cameron knew that Harpers Ferry would be lost. It was, in fact, destroyed in the first days of the war. So even before Beauregard pulled the fatal lanyard, Cameron summoned Eliphalet Remington to Washington.

Remington needed no salesmanship now. Rather it was a question of how many guns, or revolvers or bayonets, can you make for us? With all the daring of his imagination Eliphalet gave his answer. He accepted orders totaling millions of dollars—orders from the Army and Navy eventually amounted to $29,196,820.01. Then Eliphalet returned to Ilion to make the contracts good.

There was an enormous amount of work to be done. The main armory, built in 1845, was greatly enlarged and other buildings modernized. Two large new buildings were erected especially for the manufacture of Remington designed Springfield-type rifles ordered by the Army. Incidentally, these rifles were far better than regular Government Springfields, with many refinements in design. Contractor J. W. Kinney constructed the new buildings under Remingtons' direction.

The power plant was tripled by the purchase of the latest and finest steam engine then in existence, a 500 h.p. Corliss; and a vast network of power-transmission shafts and belts was installed. Looking along a one-hundred-foot floor of one of the new buildings was like peering into a moving forest, the trees of which were rapidly flowing leather belts, running from the overhead shafts down to dozens of machines. Beside some of these machines were individual stoves to heat the metal being processed by the sweating workers. Despite their sturdy, brick construction, the buildings shivered and shook under the vibration, as though in a man-made earthquake, and the whole town of Ilion was pervaded by the rumble and roar of the heavy machinery.

Still cramped for room, Eliphalet secured the old Hamilton Hotel in Utica, and tearing out the partitions transferred the pistol department there. At its peak, it had a production of two hundred pistols a day. Near the end of the war, capacity of Ilion was nearly one thousand rifles per day.

In addition to rifles and pistols, Remington drop-forged thousands of bayonets for Harpers Ferry rifles shipped in by the Government. Colonel Hiram Berdan invented an ingenious device for attaching the bayonets in such a manner that they could be shifted out of the way, so the guns could be fired without removing them.

Eighteen thousand Maynard percussion locks were built, and installed on the old Government flintlock muskets of 1842. A cartridge department was set up which supplied 9,759,750 cartridges to the Government. Other deliveries included 125,314, Beals .44 caliber

Army revolvers, 4,901 Beals .36 caliber Navy revolvers, and 20,000 Remington carbines. Bullet molds, reloading tools and all the other manifold accessories of firearms were also manufactured.

The plans for the great expansion of the armory with all the multitudinous details of machinery, power transmission, material flow and a four hundred per cent increase in personnel were drawn by Eliphalet with the aid of his three sons. In addition, he did most of the purchasing of the unheard of amounts of material needed—thousands of tons of steel and coal, of brass and copper and lead, and a thousand other items. He worked incessantly, hardly pausing to eat, and sleeping only from midnight to six A.M.

As April softened to May, and the sun of June blasted down on the buildings that were already suffocatingly hot from the forging fires, Eliphalet become more gaunt and grim. He drove himself as no man would for money, but only for passionate devotion to duty. Like most Northerners, he believed that this would be a short war, over when the thousands of volunteers pouring into Washington marched south to stamp out the rebellion. But *unlike* most, he worked as though the war would last forever.

July 2, 1861, ended those illusory hopes. On that day, the volunteer Union Army, bravely clad but totally untrained, met the Confederates, who were even more brilliantly attired, but hardly more experienced, at a little stream in Virginia, whose name became as symbolic of defeat as Waterloo. There was but one well-trained component in either army at Bull Run, and that one decided the issue. Confederate General Stonewall Jackson's brigade, first stopped the charging ranks of blue, then, with the piercing Rebel yell, charged from its wooded knoll. The Union Army broke and fled.

It was an utter rout. Citizen soldiers dropped their guns and trusted only to their legs. Some were so terrified that they climbed trees and clung like frightened monkeys, while the gray-clad Southerners ran screeching and whooping underneath, chasing the other Union troops back to Washington. Two nights later Confederate watch fires twinkled on the Virginia hills within rifle shot of the Nation's Capital.

The Battle of Bull Run ended any frivolity in the Northern attitude towards the war. Grimly the nation buckled down for the long agony ahead. It scarcely seemed possible that Eliphalet Remington could work any harder, but somehow he did. His tall figure became hardly more than a skeleton on which the fine black broadcloth suit, which he wore even in summer, hung like a shroud. The familiar silk hat surmounted a face in which the skin stretched tight over the fine bone structure, and the dark sunken eyes glowed with the light of fanatic determination.

No human body could stand the strain, least of all one that approached the Biblical term of three score years and ten. In the first days of August, 1861, Eliphalet broke under the load.

The doctors called it inflammation of the bowels. Today they would say, "appendicitis," and whip the appendix out in no time. But whatever name it went by, it was essentially the collapse of an overtaxed machine in which the weakest part breaks first.

As Eliphalet lay in the corner bedroom of his brick house on the River Road looking under the cool branches of his favorite tree to the still mirror of the Canal, he forgot all about business and guns and war. The encrustation of material matters peeled away from his mind, and, as in the freshness of his youth, it turned to poetry. To his daughter Maria, sitting beside him, he dictated:

In manhood's strong and vigorous prime
I planted a young linden tree
Near to my dwelling, which in time
Has spread its branches wide and free.

Oft have I viewed its healthful growth
With something like a parent's pride
Who sees the offspring of his youth
Grow to strong manhood by his side.

But now, old age had damped the flame
That glowed within me at that day
Energy and strength desert my frame
And I am sinking in decay.

But thanks! I've lived and long have shared
Health and vigor like this tree
And when I'm gone let it be spared
A mute remembrance of me.

On August 12, 1861, Eliphalet Remington died.

Eliphalet Remington's three sons carried on his work. The great machines in the armory stopped only long enough to pay respect to the

Founder as he was buried beside Abigail in the little cemetery on a hill back of Ilion. Then they started up again full force, making the guns that General George B. McClellan needed so desperately to rebuild the Union Army. Nor was initiative lost. None of the younger Remingtons possessed all their father's great qualities. Rather these were shared among the three, so that each took over one of the functions that Eliphalet had performed in his own person.

Philo, the eldest, was a handsome man with a massive head of curly graying hair, a full curly beard and a wide-flung mustache. His fine eyes were set well apart under strong level brows. He lived by the same stern moral code as his father, and was as strict a Methodist. Yet he was no bigot. Once, when one of his best workmen persisted in getting drunk, he went to see the man and urged him to reform. "Go to church," he said. "It will help you to overcome your weakness."

"But I wouldn't go to your church," the man said. "I am a Catholic."

A few days later, Philo sent the man a Catholic prayer book and a discourse by a Catholic Cardinal on alcoholic indulgence.

On another occasion one of Remington's contractors came rushing to him with the news that a gun had been stolen by one of the workmen. "And I know who did it!" he said. Philo shrugged him off with, "He only took *one* gun, didn't he?"

It was Philo who inherited Eliphalet's mechanical skill and organizing ability. He assumed the management of the Armory, and the purchasing of raw material.

Samuel Remington, who had a beautiful young wife, was himself broad-faced and florid, with twinkling blue eyes and a genial manner. He had the charm and salesmanship together with the daring vision to plan for the future.

Eliphalet III was the financial man, small and rather timid, almost lost behind a luxuriant beard. He was a bookkeeper born with a meticulous love of figures.

In some ways, he had the hardest task, for his father had never bothered with systematic accounting. Everything was still entered in leather ledgers, but a ten-thousand-dollar payment for one thousand tons of steel might be on the same page as an item of three and a half dollars received for one cast-steel barrel. At any moment the Founder could have told you the exact financial position of his company, but he carried it all in his head. A modern accountant would have run away screaming after one look at the books. Somehow, Eliphalet III got them in order.

One of the first things Philo did was to put in an adequate fire-protection system. A huge cistern was built on Armory Hill and water mains laid to every cranny of the works. The Armory Hose Company was organized with volunteers from the employees. This soon split, like an amoeba, giving birth to the Excelsior Fire Company No. 2. Finally the Ilion Steamer and Hose Company No. 1 was organized. The Remingtons equipped it with a magnificent Sillsbury Rotary Steamer that cost four thousand dollars.

Samuel and Philo continued the tradition of importing promising inventors. They induced Leonard M. Geiger to come to Ilion. Geiger's new breech-loading mechanism eventually became the basis for the famous Remington Rolling Block rifle. The Geiger gun had a curious split breech through which the hammer struck a rim-fire cartridge.

The Ordnance Department ordered twenty thousand short Geiger carbines. Since the Remington Armory was already awash with orders, these guns were manufactured by the Savage Arms Company of Middleton, Connecticut, under license from Remington, and with Remington-designed machines which were supplied to them under a sort of lend-lease arrangement. The guns were delivered early in 1865, and used with great effect in the battles before Richmond in the last days of the Civil War.

Some Geiger carbines were equipped with a unique kitchen gadget. The GIs of the Grand Army of the Republic used to grind their own coffee. So every fifth Geiger carbine issued to them had a tiny coffee mill attached to the stock. They must have been a great nuisance in battle, but a great convenience around a campfire.

In 1864, the end was not yet in sight. The huge Union armies, which were gradually crushing the Confederacy by sheer weight of numbers, required vast quantities of munitions. The United States Government piled orders upon orders with Remington Arms. To meet them, the Remingtons began another great program of expansion. Five new buildings were erected that year, and hundreds of pieces of machinery installed.

The new machines were just settling into their roaring stride in the spring of the following year, when early on the morning of April 10,

1865, Walter Baker rode wildly down the River Road, shouting hoarsely, "Lee's surrendered! The war's over!"

Citizens dashed out of their houses in nightshirts and kimonos, laughing, crying and leaping in the air. Al Brooks ran to a small brass cannon on the green, filled it to the muzzle with black powder, and stuck a cigar in the touch hole. The tremendous bang echoed up the hills to wake the sleeping farmers to the glorious news.

Nobody worked that day. There were parades and bands and devout prayers of thanksgiving in Ilion, as in every other corner of the Union.

Nobody worked on April twelfth either, or for a long time thereafter. On that day, the Government canceled all its arms contracts effective immediately. The fires were drawn in the great furnaces at Ilion. The new machines in their shining rows stood silent; and the workmen gathered in knots in front of the plant to talk gloomily of their uncertain future.

In their small office, with its roll-top desks and dusty files, the three brothers met in anxious discussion. The sudden cancellation of the Government contracts had left them owing large sums of money for the new equipment, which it was evident that they would not be able to pay immediately. Indeed, the Ilion Bank failed—though later the Remingtons met all its obligations from their personal fortunes.

Though the brothers were worried, they did not despair. The spirit of enterprise and determination which had carried Eliphalet from the forge to the great Armory on the River Road, burned brightly, as they planned a future for their company which would far outrun its past. They planned well, as subsequent events will show. For as long as all three of them lived, their combined talents made them a winning team. It was only when Samuel died, that the combination was broken and the great industry that Eliphalet Remington and his sons had built, tottered on the brink of ruin.

Remington Arms was saved by another pioneer industrialist, who resembled Eliphalet Remington in many ways, and shared with him the American common denominators of an enterprising spirit, industrial sagacity and absolute personal integrity. His name was Marcellus Hartley.

*Part* **2**

# Enterprise at Bridgeport

## *Chapter* 12

# *The Hartleys*

Great industrial companies are people—that is, they have definite personalities which develop through the years. Though management and ownership change, that personality persists. The same phenomenon can be observed in many other composite entities. Yale is no more like Harvard today than it was in 1752. Certain famous military units, such as the 1st Regiment of Marines or the 3rd United States Cavalry, retain their particular qualities of steadfastness or dash through successive generations, under many commanding officers, and in changing conditions of warfare. In the case of the 3rd Cavalry, the essential spirit of the regiment even survived the swap of horses for tanks.

The personality of a corporation is usually stamped upon it by its founders and their immediate successors. By the time it passes into other hands, its traditions and customs are often so strong that they bend men to their ways. Instead of the new president altering the character of a company, it insensibly changes him. This esprit, morale, ethos—call it what you will—appears to be an essential of survival. Without it any organization soon lapses into desuetude.

The Remington Arms Company has a particularly strong individuality because, for over a century, there was only one major change in management, and that a change of person but not of kind. Though Eliphalet Remington would be stunned at the sight of the great factories that bear his name today, and would only vaguely apprehend the uses of the thousands of machines which they house, he would be perfectly at home in the councils of the management, for they think as he did.

It was a fortuitous—and fortunate—circumstance that Marcellus Hartley, who founded the Union Metallic Cartridge Company, the more youthful but the dominant component of the combined companies which are called Remington Arms, was essentially the same sort of man as Eliphalet Remington. Indeed, the resemblance in their backgrounds, ideals and even in the places of their origin is so close as to be almost coincidental.

Marcellus Hartley, like the Remingtons, was descended from a Yorkshire clergyman, the Reverend David Hartley, who was Vicar of Armley in York in 1705. For a century, the Hartleys were a powerful influence in the intellectual life of England. The Reverend Mr. Hartley's eldest son, Doctor David Hartley (1705-1757), was outstanding in medicine, philosophy and metaphysics, and his "Observations on Man" were an eighteenth-century classic. His son, the third David Hartley, was the first member of Parliament to introduce a bill for abolishing the slave trade, and, with William Wilberforce, he pushed the crusade until there were no more slaves anywhere on British soil.

This David must have been regarded as a pretty radical fellow, for he also stood against the Tories as a fast friend of the American Colonies during the American Revolution. When we won our liberty, he was appointed by Lord North to sign the treaty by which England acknowledged the United States to be free and independent.

Benjamin Franklin's biographer, John T. Marse, says of David Hartley, "He was a man to whose memory Americans ought to erect statues."

Marcellus Hartley was descended from a younger branch of the family, which, though less spectacular intellectually, were successful merchants and devout churchmen. Isaac Hartley, Marcellus' grandfather, had a sensitive and imaginative mind, which made him the chosen schoolboy friend of the great English poet, William Wordsworth. And he had a venturseome spirit.

Isaac established a flourishing little woolen manufacturing business at Cockermouth in Cumberland, England; married a pretty Cumberland girl, Isabella Johnson; and begat four children, the youngest of whom was Robert Milham Hartley, the father of Marcellus. At thirty-odd, Isaac was apparently settled for life. Then, like the first Eliphalet Remington, he felt the urge for wider horizons. In 1797, he sailed for America to look things over. He must have liked what he saw, for two years later he sent for his wife and their four children to join him. Robert Hartley was just three years old, when the family embarked in a sailing packet for the turbulent two-month crossing of the Atlantic.

The Hartleys settled in the Mohawk Valley, near Schenectady. Young Robert may well have stopped his play to watch Eliphalet drive his oxcarts through in the summer of 1800. Whether he did or not, he grew up in the same general environment as the Remingtons.

Opportunity had beckoned to Isaac from the wooded hills of the frontier country; his country-bred son found his calling in the brash and bustling metropolis of New York. He went there and entered business in 1822. Two years later he married Catherine Munson, the daughter of Alderman Reuben Munson of New York, who was one of the fathers of the Bowery Savings Bank, and the Tradesman's National Bank.

Robert Hartley set the stamp of his personality on his adopted city in other than mercantile ways. He could not accept the many forms of vice and suffering that he saw in New York's proliferous tenements, and he devoted most of his life to combating them in highly practical fashion. He brought pure milk to tenement babies, founded the Association for Improving the Condition of the Poor, and sparked the founding of the Hospital for the Ruptured and Crippled.

Marcellus Hartley was born in 1827, the first of ten children of Robert Hartley. He was a wizened infant prone to colds and childish ills. His robust heritage, and a few summers on his grandfather Isaac's farm in Fulton County, New York, soon set that right. Those summers upstate, when he ran barefoot through the meadows and learned to swim in the mountain-chilled waters of Chuctenunda Creek set the foundation of his sturdy constitution, just as association with his father and grandfather laid the cornerstone of his character.

He was not a boy who rattled easily. Once he went with his uncle to the docks to watch a cargo of produce from the upstate farm unloaded. Skipping from barge to barge, he fell into the river and disappeared. There was consternation on the wharf as agitated gentlemen in claw-hammer coats and anxious longshoremen peered down into the turbulent water, prepared to dive to the rescue. They need not have worried. Marcellus was discovered swimming quietly downstream after his cap. When he had retrieved it, he swam back, and was fished out with a boathook.

Young Hartley got all his schooling in New York City, first at the classical academy which the Reverend Mr. Norton conducted in Military Hall at 193 Bowery and, when Mr. Norton retired, he was sent to private grammer school in the basement of the Methodist Church on Seventh Street.

His real education began when he went to Public School No. 15 on Twenty-seventh Street and Second Avenue. This was a remarkable institution. As the first experiment of the old Public School Society, it was under the personal direction of Anson G. Phelps, James Stokes and Peter Cooper. This eminent trio were determined to make it a model of modern education, and one or the other of them visited it almost every day.

It was almost like going to school in the country, for at that time Second Avenue ended in an open field at Twenty-eighth Street, and rail-fenced meadows ran from the school to the East River. On hot June days after school, the boys liked to dash down to the river for a swim, just as did the Dead End Kids a century later under appallingly different conditions. On one of these occasions Marcellus' ability as a swimmer again came in handy. One of the boys got too far out, and began to flounder and yell for help. Marcellus started to the rescue. Swimming a steady breast stroke, he swiftly reached the drowning boy. Seizing him by his lank hair, he started back.

Though the East River was far less turgid then, the tide was just as swift, the water as turbulent. Then, too, the breast stroke depends so much on the powerful sweep of the arms to maintain momentum while the legs draw back for the frog kick, and Marcellus had only one arm free. It was heavy going.

He had too much sense to buck the current, but quartered it, and fought diagonally toward the shore, towing the water-logged body of his friend. The salt waves slapped his face and his breath came hard as each stroke ended in a full stop. The tide was running in, and he saw the level beach give way to the cliffs of Murray Hill. There were sharp rocks in the tideway, that he managed to avoid, and then a smooth, small island of stone near shore. Desperately he kicked and struck out with his free arm. The current buffeted him away, then relenting, swirled him against the rock. He clung to its smooth side for a moment's rest; then plunged on the last fifty feet to shore.

The other boys had followed along the bank, running hard to keep pace with the tide. They formed a human chain and pulled the exhausted swimmers in. The rescuee recovered after being rolled over a barrel, and Marcellus was in fine shape after a few minutes rest. But it was a long, embarrassing walk back to Twenty-seventh Street and their clothes.

Marcellus Hartley's education ended when he was graduated from P. S. 15. But it ended only in the formal sense, for he was the sort of man who goes on learning all his life. Even a high-school student in those days acquired a considerable amount of classical knowledge, and Hartley knew both Latin and Greek in addition to what were considered the more lowly subjects of history and mathematics.

In 1844, at the age of seventeen, he took a job as a clerk in his father's business. But clerking under paternal protection was not for Marcellus Hartley; the future looked too limited, the present too cut and dried. After three years, he decided to get a job for himself, and his father applauded the decision. On February 8, 1847, Hartley went to work for Francis Tomes and Sons, importers of fancy hardware and dealers in fine guns and sporting goods. Thus he found his natural medium, and the destiny of Remington Arms was determined.

There is a daguerreotype of him taken then, a formal portrait, stiffly posed. It shows a young man in the inevitable black broadcloth and stiff-bosomed shirt, with a wide, black, bow-tied stock, and the white wings of a Daniel Webster collar lapping a round, firm chin. His hair is rather long by crew-cut standards, but there is power in the bold pointed nose and alert eyes. You can see him straining to hold still for the long ten seconds that the camera required; you feel the springs of nervous energy coiling tight, and know that the click of the closing lens will release them to action.

A young man as ardent as Marcellus Hartley is bound to shoot upward in any business except that of a father fearful of nepotism. Hartley had been with Tomes for only six months when he was given charge of the Gun Department. It was an exciting place to work.

There were beautiful English fowling pieces with Damascus barrels and exquisite engraving on the locks, long-barreled Kentucky rifles, big 8-bore double-barrel heavy-duty guns, small muzzle-loading carbines, and a new make of sporting rifle with an ingenious breech mechanism and a solid cast-steel barrel stamped "E. Remington." Hartley loved the guns, the sheen of smooth, cool barrels, the touch of straight-grained stocks and the silent precision of well-made locks. Loving them, he communicated his feeling to the customers and so became a splendid salesman.

In the slack season, Tomes sent Hartley on selling trips through the West. These excursions made him familiar with the raw, booming America beyond the Appalachians, and the sturdy men and women who were spearheading the westward surge of the nation. They also satisfied his appetite for adventure—sometimes they completely sated it.

There was the trip he made in 1851. His route took him up the Mohawk Valley by train and stage to Buffalo. There he embarked on the small, paddle-wheel steamer, *Mayflower,* for Cleveland. The voyage was shorter, but rather more hazardous, than that of the Pilgrims. He describes it in a letter dated December 19, 1851:

> Such a storm as we had beggars description. . . . I had given up all hope and was patiently waiting for the boat to founder. To give you an idea of the weather, the thermometer was fifteen degrees below zero, the wind blew a perfect hurricane, the sea went completely over the boat, the spray freezing as it rose in the air. . . . Food I never tasted for twenty-six hours until we struck the shore, which occurred at eleven o'clock at night.
>
> When we struck, nobody knew where we were, nor did we much care, for then we never expected to reach land. But when morning came we saw the shore some two hundred feet from us—a high bleak coast with a ridge of ice eight feet high all along the shore, the sea running mountains high,—we had hopes of reaching it, and with the assistance of some persons from shore, we eventually sent a line, and once more safely reached *terra firma.*

Young Hartley even managed to get his baggage ashore, with the precious catalogues and samples, but he was not safe yet. He walked a mile through deep snow, and rode a borrowed horse another twelve miles to the nearest stage depot. The letter continues:

> When I tell you that I came near breaking my neck twice you will think I am unlucky. We were upset twice in the stage

> and went over a bank some six feet high, the last time being about four o'clock in the morning. Cold! It was awfully cold. . . . We footed it through the snow some half a mile to a farmer's house who kindly gave us shelter and a fire until morning. Sleep! I had none since leaving Buffalo, three evenings before, until last night and but two meals in three days. Such, my dear friend, has been my fortune so far; and through it all I have came out, thanks to a kind Providence, with but a frozen foot, one finger frost bitten, and with my phrenological bump of veneration raised considerably by the upsetting of the stage.
>
> The writing you will please excuse as my fingers are somewhat frostbitten. . . .

That trip took Hartley on to Detroit, Chicago, St. Louis, Memphis, Montgomery and New Orleans, which is to say he traversed a large sector of the perimeter of the America of those days.

In 1854, Marcellus Hartley embarked on the classic adventure of American youth—he went into business for himself. It was a bold undertaking, since he had a minuscule amount of capital and no special influence. But he had gone about as far as he could with Tomes, and in seven years had learned all there was to know about the business of selling sporting guns and a good deal about importing. He had also made some valuable connections on his western trips.

Two young men joined him in the venture. J. Rutsen Schuyler and Malcolm Graham, both of Smith, Young and Company, a rival firm to Tomes. The three of them met for lunch one January day at Clark and Brown's Steak House and Tavern on Maiden Lane. They discussed their prospects with the iridescent optimism of youth, which turned out to be more than justified, and considered ways and means—mainly a question of how much money they could borrow. Thus was founded the firm of Schuyler, Hartley and Graham, Importers and Manufacturers of Guns, Pistols and Fancy Goods.

Schuyler, who was a junior partner in Smith, Young and Company, put up eight thousand dollars so his name was first in the partnership. Hartley advanced three thousand, mostly borrowed; and Graham contributed his services.

Because Hartley later bought out his partners, founded the Union Metallic Cartridge Company and saved the original Remington Arms from dissolution, that original three thousand can be considered the small stake he built into all the great capital assets, which Remington Arms represents. It is not the actual money that counts; were that all, it would be no more than figures written in a book. Rather it is the contribution to the real wealth of America that is important; the augmentation of her power for defense, the skilled workmen which it trained and the potential pleasure of millions of sportsmen who take the field with Remington guns and ammunition. To build so much from so little is an achievement that is unspectacular only because it has been done so many times that it is the accepted pattern of American life.

## Chapter 13

# Sporting Guns, Coral and Old Masters

Despite the steadying effect of fore and main topsails and a spanker on her mizzen, the new steam packet, *Baltic,* was rolling her gunwales under as she sped through a rough beam sea on a fast ten-day crossing of the North Atlantic. Two young men aboard her, watching her sharp bow slice the gray waves into crystal spray, gloried in her surge of speed under the combined drive of sail and steam, for they were in a hurry. Schuyler and Hartley were off to Europe to buy wares for their new business.

No grass had grown under their feet. The partnership was formally organized on March 1, 1854, and they sailed three days later, ammunitioned with a letter of credit on Brown, Shipley & Co. of London. They went first to England, where they called on the leading manufacturers of sporting guns, cutlery and other types of fancy hardware. Marcellus Hartley had a bit of trouble at first with the pompous magnates of British industry. Their greeting was apt to be, "Why doesn't your company send a senior partner? We are not accustomed to doing business with a junior clerk."

Hartley explained that he was a senior partner, but he realized that he did look tenderly young to be negotiating with the hoary heads of such ancient firms. It was then he decided that he must age quickly, and grew the fine, broad beard which he wore the rest of his life.

Despite the handicap of youth, Hartley negotiated contracts with most of the great gunmakers of England. He bought beautiful muzzle-loading fowling pieces with laminated steel barrels from William Greener, and Poultney and Sneider's new breech-loading shot guns. Enfield let him have the selling rights to their latest military rifle with a sword bayonet and elevated sights graduated to 1,000 yards. In addition he arranged to handle guns by Westley Richards, Moore & Harris, Purdy and half a dozen more. Then he went on to the Continent, where among others he secured Lefaucheux's exquisitely made breech-loading shotguns.

Meanwhile, Schuyler was signing up with manufacturers of other products. Shiploads of goods went back to Graham, who had opened the store at 19 Maiden Lane. He found a quick market for them, and when Schuyler and Hartley returned after four months abroad, their business was already showing a handsome profit.

After that Hartley went on a buying trip to Europe every year. In the spring of 1855, he visited the home of his grandfather in Cockermouth, and evidently came to the conclusion that the old gentleman had made a wise decision in leaving it, for he wrote to his sister:

> My first impressions of Cockermouth you no doubt would like to hear. I must say that they were very unfavorable. It looked like some old, worn out city. . . . The river, like all English rivers is very small, about the size of Uncle John's creek. . . .

Though he traveled so much, Hartley was incurably American in his point of view. In a later letter, written to his mother, he admires Venice but admonishes the Venetians thus:

> Sunday with the Venetians is a holiday and the sight from our windows was grand. . . . On the canal were hundreds of gondolas following a barge filled full of Austrian musicians, drawn by two gaily decked gondolas. It was about seven o'clock in the evening. All Venice had collected in their boats to take a ride and hear the music. We were not disturbed by the noise of horses and vehicles. It was as quiet as if you had been to sea in a calm. The sight was grand, yet turned my thoughts to my own country, where we venerate the Sabbath. I thought that had the Venetians attended more to the observ-

ance of the Divine Laws, they, in common with the rest of Italy, would have more to boast of at the present day than the ruins and dilapidations of their city, once the pride of the world.

While he was traveling that year, Marcellus Hartley was conducting a long-range courtship by letters, the stately prose and formal manner of which were typical of his reverent approach to the lady of his choice. Though they hardly rank with the amatory correspondence of the Brownings, the lady seems to have been able to discern between their stilted lines the genuine ardor of her suitor, for soon after Hartley returned from his second trip abroad she capitulated.

In the fall of 1855, Frances Chester White was married to Marcellus Hartley at the Madison Square Presbyterian Church, which both families attended. The bride belonged to one of the first York State families, being the daughter of Doctor Samuel Pomeroy White and a great granddaughter of Seth Jenkins, founder and first Mayor of the City of Hudson. Marcellus took his wife to live in his father's house for a little while, and then the young couple established a home in the fashionable northern fringes of the city on Thirtieth Street just off Fifth Avenue.

In the spring of 1856, Marcellus took his bride on a combined business trip and honeymoon to Europe. The elevating effect of feminine influence not only enriched his spirit by instructing him in the cultural beauties that he had been too hurried to enjoy before, but fattened his fortune as well, since it led him to embark on two profitable ventures, which were a long way afield from sporting guns.

The first of these began as he and Fanny stopped in front of a shop window in Florence, filled with excellent copies of Renaissance paintings. The Hartleys went in and inquired the price of their especial choice. The shopkeeper, scenting a chance to fleece some rich Americans, named an exorbitant figure. Hartley simply turned and walked out. The dealer followed him, dropping his price all along the way; but he still made no sale. Being a persistent man, he even pursued the Hartleys on to the next city and there made his final, very low offer.

"How many pictures have you in your shop?" asked Marcellus.

"Seventy-five of the first order," the man replied.

"What will you take for the whole lot?" asked Hartley.

The Italian's eyes stood out on stalks and his olive skin went green. Then he laughed tentatively. "Il Signore makes the jest," he ventured.

"I am not joking," Hartley replied. "I, too, have a shop, in America. I am asking a serious question."

"But if I sell all my pictures, *I* will have no shop."

"You can certainly order more. How much?"

The man reluctantly named a reasonable price, and Hartley closed the deal. He shepherded the pictures safely through the hazards of the voyage home, and they sold like hot chestnuts in a blizzard to Americans who were just becoming conscious of culture.

When the Hartleys got to Naples, Fanny was ecstatic about the coral jewelry which was a specialty there. "It's getting to be the rage at home," she told her husband, "and it's very hard to find good pieces. May I buy some?"

"We'll buy it all," said Marcellus. And, in fact, he virtually cornered the market in coral; with immensely profitable results.

Hartley made another trip abroad in 1857. He returned to find the country in the icy grip of panic. Business was blocked by frozen assets as eighteen banks failed in New York City alone, and bread lines formed along the Bowery. Nobody wanted guns or any other luxury items, and the young partners faced a precarious prospect. However, they had financed their business so soundly that it rode out the financial storm all snug and secure; and when reviving credit quickened the flow of commerce in the spring of 1858, Schuyler, Hartley and Graham were in a position to take advantage of the opportunities thus presented.

For the next few years Hartley remained at home, building up the firm's American connections. A most important one was established when a tall old man, wearing a flowing cape and a shining high silk hat, the crown of which was filled with important documents, came to call. He was a persuasive salesman and the integrity of his character so impressed Hartley that he placed a large order at once. Thereafter, Schuyler, Hartley and Graham always carried a big stock of sporting guns and other ironware made by E. Remington and Sons.

All those trips abroad, all the knowledge Hartley had gained of European methods of business and sources of supply, all the friendships he had formed, and the trust and confidence he had built up with his manufacturing connections there, promised well for the future of his growing business. That he had accomplished anything more than this Hartley was obviously unaware. Yet, as it turned out, he had incidentally been readying himself to be of unique service to his country in the greatest crisis she ever faced.

## Chapter 14

# *Mr. Lincoln Asks a Favor*

By 1860, just six years after it was started, Schuyler, Hartley and Graham had become the largest sporting goods company in America, with a branch at 31 Rue du Chateau D'Eau in Paris. After the election of Abraham Lincoln in the fall of that year, the prospect of civil war produced another cataclysmic contraction in the financial world; but it only served to boom the business of Marcellus Hartley's firm. As the political skies grew blacker, more and more people adopted a policy of personal preparedness by buying guns, pistols and other lethal equipment.

Throughout the pre-war period and during the confused beginnings of the conflict, Hartley was scrupulously careful that none of the arms he sold reached the Southern states, for he was a devoted Union man. It was lucky that he acted thus. Jealous competitors of the young firm did everything in their power to smear its reputation by circulating rumors that it was trading with the South. Hartley met their innuendoes with the indifference of a clear conscience. Then his enemies took drastic action.

On a summer day in 1861, Marcellus Hartley was astounded to see a line of policemen, sweating in their heavy blue uniforms and gray helmets, form a cordon in front of 19 Maiden Lane. A moment later, a group of detectives, with large tin stars glittering on their chests, burst through the doors and served summonses on the three partners, who had been cited before the grand jury for selling military goods to the South.

Consternation and rage were written on the faces of Schuyler and Graham, as customers scuttled through the doors and white-faced clerks began locking up the stock. Marcellus Hartley's anger was magnificent; his beard fairly crackled with high-tension emotion; but, by a tremendous effort of will, he forced his seething passion beneath a frigid mask of calm.

"We have nothing to fear, gentlemen," he said. "Our books are in order, our records are clear; and we know how loyal are our sentiments."

Then he took the company's books and went before the grand jury.

Fortunately, there was nothing haphazard about the accounting methods of Schuyler, Hartley and Graham, no carrying of papers in a high hat or indiscriminate entries in a single ledger. Hartley was able to prove conclusively to the grand jury, not only that he had never sold a single gun to the South, but that he had canceled every order, no matter how profitable, which bore the slightest suspicion of being intended for clandestine shipment to the arms-hungry Confederates.

The grand jury dismissed the case, and commended the firm for its scrupulous conduct. Much later, evidence was unearthed that the whole smear campaign was inspired by enemies of the Federal Government to embarrass the loyal states and make it more difficult for them to obtain arms for their troops. That the mud thus slung did not stick was proved by the extraordinary confidence soon shown by the President in Marcellus Hartley.

By the spring of 1862, Lincoln's government was desperate for guns. State and Federal armories had been swept as bare as Mother Hubbard's cupboard, and the government arsenals and private manufacturers such as Remington, Colt and Spencer could not begin to meet the enormous demands for arms, as McClellan in the East and Grant in the West gathered ever larger armies for their great campaigns. Meanwhile, the Confederates were bringing large shipments of European arms in from British Nassau in fast, specially built blockade runners, which ran circles around the Union warships trying to seal the Southern ports.

In this clutch, Lincoln and his new Secretary of War, Edwin M. Stanton, sought a means to divert these priceless guns to the Union. They asked the advice of Governor Edwin D. Morgan of New York.

Marcellus Hartley was sitting in his high-backed, horsehair-cushioned chair before the roll-top desk in his office, when an agitated clerk announced that the Governor of New York craved the honor of an interview. Right on his heels came the Governor, high hatted and portentous.

"Mr. Hartley," Morgan said, "I have just left President Lincoln. He wants somebody to go and buy arms on the Island of Nassau, and I have told him you are the man to do it."

Everyone thinks first of self, whatever sacrifice second thought may bring. "Why, Governor," said Hartley, "I have a business here."

Morgan waved this protest out of the window with a casual gesture. "I have told Mr. Lincoln," he repeated, "and he wants me to bring you to Washington this week."

Of course Marcellus Hartley went. He had time to do some hard thinking during the long train ride in the bucketing coaches of the Baltimore and Ohio, and, by the time he reached Washington, his plans were already formed.

Morgan took him in a hack to the White House, where they pushed through the crowd of place-seekers, soldiers' mothers, politicians, salesmen, cranks and curious citizens that always infested the entrance hall, and mounted the grand marble staircase with its worn red turkey carpet to the President's study on the second floor.

Abraham Lincoln untelescoped himself from a tall arm chair and gently brushed out a couple of importunate visitors.

"It is good of you to come here, Mr. Hartley," he said. "I suppose Governor Morgan has told you what we want."

Hartley braced himself against the impact of that House, and the personality of the man who carried the burden of a nation in agony on his angular shoulders. He knew how this thing must be done, and it was not the way the President had planned.

"Mr. President," he said firmly, "I am sorry that if you insist on my going to Nassau, I do not want to undertake this business."

Governor Morgan snorted violently. The President looked surprised but patient. "How would you do it, Mr. Hartley?" he asked.

"I should go straight to the source," he said. "The guns that are in Nassau are already consigned to the South and in the hands of Southern sympathizers. I can do nothing much there. I'd go to England and the Continent and buy the arms directly from their makers. I would corner the market for guns of all Europe."

Governor Morgan was fuming visibly. Now he burst out. "Mr. President, I will have nothing to do with this if you change from the plan of going to Nassau where all the arms from Europe are dumped."

The President smiled at the two men, both bristling now, like terriers on the verge of a fight. "I'm sorry, Governor Morgan," he said, "but I think this young man has the right of it."

Then he asked Hartley searching questions as to how he would go about this business, and what it would cost. Hartley had the plan ready in his mind, the names, production figures and costs were on the tip of his tongue. The President was convinced. He sent for Stanton and the plan was adopted. Hartley was given the rank of brigadier general. His salary was $2,500 a year. The credits placed by the Government in his name eventually amounted to many millions of dollars.

Taking his wife and their three small daughters, Marcellus Hartley sailed for England in July, 1862. He went first to the great banking house of Baring Brothers, where the United States Government had placed eighty thousand pounds to his credit—or so he thought. The Barings pretended not to believe he was an emissary of the United States, and made fun of him. The next day he went back. Mr. Baring roared down the echoing hall, "Mr. Hartley, we have no credit for you. Don't come in today!"

On the third day, they said with evident reluctance, "We have your credit, Mr. Hartley. It was lost in one of our drawers, misplaced."

So lame an excuse convinced Hartley that the credit had been purposely withheld to embarrass him. The truth was that Baring Brothers, like most of the bankers of England, had large investments in Southern cotton plantations—they wanted to see the North lose. This attitude of hostility was prevalent with most of the British aristocracy and industrial magnates. It greatly increased Hartley's difficulties.

Marcellus Hartley's grandson once said of him, "He was a ball of fire." Certainly he hit England like one. As soon as he had cleared his credit with Baring Brothers, he went to Birmingham, the industrial heart of England, and set to work with such energy that six days later he was able to write to Secretary Stanton that he had virtually exhausted his eighty thousand pounds and had acquired about thirty thousand guns, "nearly the whole produce of this market."

"Please lose no time in sending me an additional credit of at least £100,000," he wrote and added that he would soon be shipping six thousand stand of arms a week.

To accomplish this without sending the price of guns through the roof required the most delicate financial technique. Hartley played a tremendous game of economic poker in which the stakes were, in fact, the lives of Union soldiers, and his opponents were the hostile bankers of England, agents of the Confederate States, wily speculators who tried to jump on a rising market and even some of his own countrymen who were out for a quick turn. With the assistance of his partner, Rutsen Schuyler, and his former boss, Francis Tomes, who acted as purchasing agents while Hartley remained in the background playing the cards, he met trickery with chicane and succeeded in outmaneuvering and outbluffing them all.

He broke the power of the English Small Arms Company, which was a sort of cartel or trust, and, when Mr. Inman, the great British shipping magnate, refused to ship any more arms to America "because of the risk," Hartley arranged to charter steamers of his own and thus brought about cancellation of the order.

While he was in Birmingham, Hartley heard that Confederate agents had made a contract with some gun manufacturer on the Continent for many thousands of rifles. Immediately, he was off like a beagle on a hot scent. He did not know the names of the arms makers or even what country they hailed from, but he was determined to find out. By boat and train, traveling day and night, he rushed to Paris, Vienna, Frankfort and Budapest, but had no luck. Finally at Liege, the arms center of Belgium, he found his quarry.

The Belgians did not care who won a local war in the hinterland of North America, but they loved money. When Hartley upped the Confederate offer and promised immediate payment by sight drafts on London, they broke their contract with the South and sold to him.

Marcellus Hartley was genuinely sorry to have won this round. Though he could be Machiavellian in his country's service, he so hated dubious business ethics that he was genuinely shocked by the weakness of the men he had suborned. Also, if they fell once they could again, so he stayed right on the spot until he saw the guns shipped.

Even then he was in a tight place, for he did not have that much money or credit in England. He rushed back to London, pledged his own personal fortune partially to cover the drafts, and wrote frantically to the Secretary of War. Stanton backed him with immediate funds and he gratefully withdrew his neck from the financial noose into which he had patriotically thrust it.

The sequel to this episode took place years later at a large dinner given in New York by Mr. Charles R. Flint to a London banker. Passions of war had long since cooled, and one of the distinguished guests was George A. Trenholm who had been a resident agent in Europe for the Confederacy. After dinner Mr. Trenholm made a speech in which he alluded to the kindness and courtesy he had received among his former enemies, and complimented them on their sagacity and enterprise. Then he talked about the difficulties in trying to buy arms for the Confederacy abroad. "Once I thought, I had procured all we needed," he said. "Then some invisible force disrupted the whole deal. I never knew what happened."

"Tell us the details," urged Mr. Flint.

As Trenholm complied, Hartley realized that he was hearing the story of the Belgian business from the other side. When the Southerner finished talking, Flint said, "Now, Mr. Trenholm, I should like to introduce you to 'the invisible force,' Mr. Marcellus Hartley."

To the delighted amusement of everyone, Hartley told his side of the story and became the hero of the occasion. Trenholm bore no grudge and even joined in the cheers.

Having accomplished his mission, Marcellus Hartley returned to America in April, 1863. Just as he had promised the President, he had sewed up the English gunmakers, and virtually controlled the arms output of all the rest of Europe. Wherever guns, good guns that is, were to be had, there Hartley went. He left few loose ends as Trenholm testified. Before he left, he had shipped more than two hundred thousand stand of arms to the United States, and had contracted for hundreds of thousands more.

When Hartley saw the Secretary of War in Washington, after presenting his accounts, Stanton fairly beamed through his steel-rimmed spectacles.

"You have accomplished all, and more, than we hoped, Mr. Hartley," he said. "As for your accounts, they are the most complete and businesslike that have come before me during my administration. They are, in fact, a model accounting of fiduciary responsibility."

## Chapter 15

# Metallic Cartridges

In 1865, Marcellus Hartley was in a very strong position financially, but he was without any immediate objective. He had taken Schuyler, Hartley and Graham about as far as it could go. It was, perhaps, the largest sporting goods company in the world, with branches in England and France; but there was a sharp delimitation of demand which prevented its growing much bigger. Nor could such a limited business satisfy Hartley's ambition. He was only thirty-seven years old, and he felt that his capabilities had never been extended.

The coming of peace acted upon the business of the Nation like the breaking of the ice pack in a mighty northern river. The dammed-back torrent of economic expansion burst forth to flood the vast vacant lands of the West with new railways, factories and farms. Opportunity was fairly pounding on the door of every man with a little capital and the slightest degree of initiative. Hartley was keenly aware of this situation, and sought a great new venture on which to embark.

The answer came to him in the shape of a battered brass cartridge case, which he had picked up on a trip to the West some years before. It was a curiosity then, one of the first metallic cartridges ever made, for almost all guns still used either loose powder and ball, or unsatisfactory paper cartridges. Crude as it was, Hartley had seen its possibilities. He had filed it in a drawer of his roll-top desk, and he had filed an idea in the back of his mind.

Now, in 1865, he took that shell out and fingered it. He refurbished the old idea; and decided to enter the business of manufacturing metallic cartridges. Due to a combination of his own sound judgment and the luck which is a useful ingredient of any successful businessman, he had chosen exactly the right moment in history for his venture.

The history of ammunition is even longer and more curiously static than that of gunmaking. It goes back to the thirteenth century when Brother Roger Bacon, experimenting with new ways of making Greek fire, combined saltpeter, sulphur and charcoal, and blew himself out of his laboratory.

That gave the world gunpowder; and for six hundred years, until the invention of pyro-nitrocellulose, or smokeless powder, in the 1880s, the formula was hardly changed at all. For most of that time, even the method of loading guns remained the same. You shook a measure of loose powder down the barrel, dropped in a bullet and rammed it home. The charge was fired at first by a slow match and a little later by sparks struck by flint on steel—the flintlock.

The first real advance in ammunition in five centuries came when a French gunsmith named Houiller conceived the idea of making a handy package out of powder and ball. The early cartridges were much better than loose loading, but they left a lot of room for improvement. Made of various kinds of paper, cardboard or linen, they were easily broken or ruined by water. During the Civil War wastage from these causes ran 40 per cent.

Some of the early cartridges had to be bitten open before loading so that loose powder would spill out to receive the flame from the percussion cap. Good teeth were thus a military necessity. For many years the United States Army had such severe tests for occlusion that thousands of men were turned down because their teeth did not meet quite evenly. These standards were finally relaxed about the middle of World War II when some genius at the Pentagon suddenly realized that no one had to bite a modern cartridge.

The most notable advance in firing the charge was made by another ecclesiastic. In 1807, John Forsythe, a Scotch clergyman, invented the percussion cap, which was simply a pinch of highly volatile fulminate of mercury sandwiched between small copper disks. The cap was placed on a nipple outside the chamber of a gun. When it was struck by the hammer, the miniature explosion shot flame through the nipple and fired the gun.

All through the first half of the nineteenth century, men were working on the idea of combining the firing element with the cartridge. The Germans got there first with the famous needle gun, which was also the first bolt-action rifle. In the needle-gun cartridge the fulminate was put up in front against the bullet, which acted as an anvil. The firing pin was a long, needlelike affair which pierced the entire length of the cartridge to strike the cap.

The first metallic cartridge that was anywhere near successful was made by the Maynard Rifle Company in 1851, and consisted of an elongated bullet and a brass case containing the powder. A small hole was left in the base and it was fired by a separate percussion cap. At the same time, Smith and Wesson produced an equally crude metallic revolver cartridge. Volcanic Arms Company improved on these by making a hollow rim around the base of the cartridge and filling it with fulminate. This was the first practical rim fire cartridge.

The invention of the metallic cartridge finally and forever established the supremacy of breech-loading guns. It had been impossible theretofore to make a gas-tight breech with the result that anyone shooting such a gun took a beating from escaping jets of gas and flame. The brass cartridge, expanding from the pressure of the explosion, automatically sealed the breech tight.

Though the Civil War was fought mainly with muzzle-loaders, it proved that they were obsolete. Every soldier who had seen a Sharps or a Henry or a Remington-Geiger wanted a breechloader which used metallic cartridges. Marcellus Hartley, who knew perhaps more about the market for arms than any other man in America, recognized the trend; but he had no desire to embark on the manufacture of sporting guns. As he reasoned it, a man might buy one or two guns in all his life, but he bought ammunition every year. That was where the great demand would rise, and dazzling profits would come to him who was in a position to satisfy that market.

Following this line of thought, Hartley looked into the business of manufacturing metallic cartridges. Nobody so far had made much of a success of it, for it was a tricky and dangerous operation, and the demand had previously been uncertain. This did not discourage Hartley; for he saw that the tide was about to flood, and he prepared to ride it. For a comparatively small sum, he and his partners bought up two small New England cartridge companies, with all their machinery and patents—the Crittenden and Tribbals Manufacturing Company of South Coventry, Connecticut, and the C. D. Leet Company of Springfield, Massachusetts. Crittenden and Tribbals made rim-fire ammunition for the Spencer rifle, which Schuyler, Hartley and Graham sold.

Hartley closed up the Leet plant, and for a little while continued the business at Coventry. Then he moved the whole operation to Bridgeport, Connecticut, where he had previously purchased an ideal manufacturing site. On August 9, 1867, the well-tried team of Schuyler, Hartley and Graham, together with Charles H. Pond and Robert J. White, incorporated the Union Metallic Cartridge Company. Charles Pond became its first president.

For a while the new company had nothing but trouble. Making cartridges was an even chancier business than Hartley and his associates had supposed. The black powder with which they were filled was much more sensitive and therefore more dangerous to handle than modern smokeless powder, and it was difficult to get it in uniform quality. As for the fulminate which was used to fire the charge, that was so touchy that it seemed to explode if you gave it a cross look. As a result parts of the factory were always blowing up, and far more serious than the physical damage to the plant were the injuries to the workers.

For some time the Union Metallic Cartridge Company lost money rather faster than Schuyler, Hartley and Graham could make it. Then it had three pieces of good fortune which established it on a firm base, and set it on the road to becoming the leading cartridge company of the world.

The first bit of luck was when Marcellus Hartley secured the services of A. C. Hobbs, a mechanical wizard who could do anything possible—and some things that were not—with machinery. Hobbs had such sensitive finger tips that he excelled the mythical Jimmy Valentine in opening safes, though he practiced this art as a hobby, not a profession. On one occasion, the British Government offered a prize of one thousand dollars to anyone who could open a fancy new lock which had been designed for the vault of the bank of England. Hobbs accepted the challenge, and opened the lock after fifty-one hours of continuous work. He collected the thousand dollars and the lock, which he hung on the wall of his office as a trophy of his skill.

Hobbs had been Superintendent of the Howe Sewing Machine Company. He brought great ingenuity to the problems of cartridge-making, and was soon put in sole charge of the manufacturing end of the business, a position which he held for over twenty years. During that time he personally invented nearly all the complicated machinery which gradually took the production of cartridges out of the handwork class and made it an all-machine process, thus vastly increasing the speed and—more important—the safety of the operation.

The second break that Hartley's lively infant industry got appeared in the unlikely person of an Armenian gentleman known as Mr. Azerian, who wandered into Schuyler, Hartley and Graham and evinced interest in the purchase of cartridges in considerable numbers. He also expressed a desire to visit the Bridgeport plant. Hartley humored him to the extent of taking him down to Bridgeport and personally showing him around. After looking at the operation with his melting brown eyes, Mr. Azerian identified himself as a representative of the Turkish Government, and rocked the partners back on their heels by ordering ten million rounds of ammunition.

That was a colossal order for the struggling young company, so large that it could not handle it all, but farmed part of it out to the newly organized Winchester Arms Company. The Turkish contract not only put U. M. C. on its financial feet, but the surplus assured the success of Winchester Arms.

The third and most important even in the early history of U. M. C. appeared in the personable form of Colonel Hiram Berdan. The Colonel, who came from western New York, had made a great reputation in the Civil War. He was one of the best shots in the whole Union Army and, in 1862, had organized a regiment known as Berdan's Sharpshooters. No man was admitted who could not put ten consecutive shots within five inches of the bull's-eye at two hundred yards. The Colonel himself could do much better. His regiment, which derided the gaudy uniforms of the Zouaves and other fancy outfits, wore a green uniform in summer and gray at other seasons "to assimilate as nearly as possible with the colors of nature." They were armed with the improved Springfield rifle, made by Remington, with a plain silver pin sight at the muzzle and a notch—or for distance or darkness—a globe sight at the breech.

Berdan invented a special bullet for his men. It was conical in shape with grooves, and was reasonably accurate up to three hundred yards. The Colonel also invented a breech mechanism known as the "Berdan Slam Bang Breech." It was used by the United States Army after the war to convert muzzle-loading Springfields into breechloaders, and was also adopted as the standard rifle of the Imperial Russian Army.

Very elegant in a gray cutaway and a gray topper, the Colonel came to call on Marcellus Hartley early in 1867. It seemed that he had been doing some more inventing and held the patents on a new kind of cartridge. He was seeking a firm who had the plant and the ingenuity to manufacture it. When he showed his drawings to Hartley and Pond and Hobbs, all three realized that here was the thing which inventors had been seeking for fifty years—the authoritative answer to the problem of producing the perfect cartridge.

Colonel Berdan's cartridge had the ingenious simplicity of most great inventions, the sort of obvious rightness that put it in the class with such famous strokes of genius as placing the eye in the point of a sewing machine needle or the magnet on the receiver of a telegraph instrument.

With certain clever but not essential modifications, the Berdan cartridge looked like an ordinary rim fire cartridge. The vital difference was in the firing element. The rim of the shell, instead of being hollow and filled with fulminate, was a solid flange that gave great additional strength where it was most needed, and made it much easier to extract from the breech of a gun. The base of the shell was indented to form a hollow in the center of which was a tiny raised wedge to act as an anvil. On either side of the anvil were small holes to let the fire into the load. A miniature percussion cap was fitted and sealed into the depression in the base.

This was the first practical center fire cartridge, and it was first made by U. M. C. at Bridgeport. It was far superior to the Boxer cartridge invented in England at about the same time.

The obvious advantage of the center fire cartridge over rim fire was its enormously greater strength. The thin rim fire cartridge could take no more than fifty grains of powder without exploding in the chamber of a gun, while, because of its solid rim, the Berdan shell could take all the gun would stand. In addition, it used less than a quarter as much metal-corroding fulminate; it was more sure of firing, and far less apt to accidental discharge. The cap of the Berdan cartridge was protected by being recessed into the base. The comparative safety of the center fire principle is illustrated in the official report of the tests at the Frankford Arsenal on April 21, 1868.

> A wooden box ready for issue containing 680 metallic cartridges, caliber .50, in paper packages . . . was fired into from the 1 inch Gatling gun. . . . Three shots perforated the box and the upper layer of paper packages, destroying the upper half of the wooden box. . . . The damage done was as follows:
>
> 29 cartridges exploded, 97 badly crushed out of shape, but none exploded, 38 loose uninjured, 480 in paper packages uninjured. . . .
>
> The trial seemed to prove that the explosion of a caisson or an ammunition wagon is made impossible or robbed of its greatest terrors by being confined to only a small number of the few cartridges that may be struck by an enemy's shot.

Manufacturing the Berdan cartridge, which had an unwelded shell drawn from a sheet of brass, required the invention of several types of special machinery. Hobbs worked on the problem day and night and developed the machinery which was used for many years. The cartridge first took shape as a metal disk one sixteenth of an inch thick and about the diameter of a quarter, which was stamped out of sheet brass from the rolling mill. The disk was then cupped by a special type of press. After that, the embryo cartridge was heated (annealed) to relieve the stress which had been set up in its crystalline structure. As the white-hot shell was drawn from the furnace, it was quickly quenched in cold water, yet remained soft enough to draw out from a cup to a case an inch long. Repeated operations of annealing and drawing brought the cartridge case to its final shape, tapering from considerable thickness at the base to 1/100 of an inch at the mouth. A combination feed punch and a heading punch then formed the head with its folded rim and cup and anvil. Each machine could turn out sixty-five cases a minute.

Hobbs also developed a machine for loading the shells. The cases were placed on an endless belt, where they passed under a hopper which measured out a charge of powder. If the weight of powder was not just right a bell rang. Then the patched bullets were fed into the cases and a final process crimped the edge of the case tightly onto the bullet.

The loading machines were mostly run by girls, as Hobbs found that they were more dextrous and more careful than men. This was the most dangerous process and he devised elaborate safety precautions. Just enough powder was brought to each machine to fill one hopper. Each hopper and the tube to fill the shells were put behind a conical shield of boiler iron so that at most only three or four loaded shells were in the open. To make sure the shield would protect the operator, Hobbs deliberately exploded a full hopper containing two and one-half pounds of powder in the experimental setup. There was a horrible bang, but the shield stood and no damage was done.

Due to Hobbs' inventive genius and the terrific pace at which he worked, U. M. C. got into large-scale production only a few months after the deal with Berdan was consummated. The long lead they won in the manufacture of the prototype of the modern cartridge gave U. M. C., almost overnight, the commanding position in the small-arms ammunition field that it has held ever since.

Chapter 16

# A General, a Grand Duke and a Traveling Salesman

Unlike many inventions, the Berdan cartridge was an instantaneous success. The arms makers of America, and indeed of the whole world, immediately began to adapt their locks to use the center fire principle. This was especially true of the Remingtons, who had just produced the famous Remington Rolling Block rifle as will later be told. The combination of the new Remington breechloader and U. M. C. ammunition was unbeatable. Schuyler, Hartley and Graham became general sales agents for Remington. Thus began the close co-operation between the companies which eventually resulted in their merger.

The center fire cartridge freed sportsmen once and for all from the necessity of muzzle-loading with all its attendent delays and frustrations. Rim fire cartridges had been a long step in this direction, but because they would take only a comparatively weak charge, they were far from ideal for big game. Powerful loads, like the 44-90-400 used by the buffalo hunters of the West, made it possible to kill game at previously impossible distances.

However, sportsmen are a sentimental group. Even today a few of them use muzzle-loaders; and a much larger number take great pleasure in hand-loading their cartridges to suit their own particular ideas, even though a wide variety of calibers, bullet weights and powder charges are available in commercial cartridges.

Under the forcing process of intense demand, the Union Metallic Cartridge Company had one of the fastest growths ever recorded in American industry. In 1867, it had about thirty employees and one small factory. Four years later, buildings had sprouted all over the Bridgeport site, and production was over *four hundred thousand cartridges a day.*

To manage so rapid an expansion and yet keep the company on a firm financial base and the standard of quality at top level was no inconsiderable feat. That it was accomplished is due to two men, Marcellus Hartley and A. C. Hobbs, with an assist from General Gorloff of the Imperial Russian General Staff. Hartley handled the financial arrangements with meticulous integrity. Hobbs bent his geniuses to production, while Gorloff played a negative, but vital role.

Marcellus Hartley's primary purpose had been to manufacture ammunition for sporting guns, but he also accepted contracts from some foreign governments. Priority on the list was given Imperial Russia, which in those days had not flouted the comity of nations, but on the contrary, was eager to prove that she could be as civilized as the best. This priority was only logical, since Colonel Berdan's breech-loading rifle was standard equipment in the Russian Army, and the contracts had taken cognizance of this fact.

In 1868, General Gorloff arrived in Bridgeport, accredited by the Czar as chief inspector of the cartridges to be manufactured for Russia. He was a polished gentleman, but Russians who served their government then were almost as fear-ridden as Communists are today. Czars, like dictators, allow no second chance.

Gorloff had good reason to be nervous. Once a ragged Russian youth appealed to the General as a fellow countryman to find him employment at Bridgeport. Gorloff kindly recommended him to Hobbs, who gave him a job cleaning the offices and doing odd chores. He worked steadily for two months, then one day, he failed to appear at his usual early hour.

At about ten o'clock that morning, Gorloff was conferring with Hobbs, when a resplendent character appeared at the door of the manager's office. In a gray morning coat, and pearl spats, with a shining topper cocked jauntily on his head, the young Russian advanced toward his astonished elders.

"Good morning, General and Mr. Hobbs," he said. "I am indebted for your kindness. I leave today, and wish to say good-bye."

He was a nobleman's son, whom the Czar had sent to spy on his trusted General.

With the long-range eyes of the Little Father of All the Russias fixed on the nape of his bulging neck, Gorloff labored with the grim determination of terror. He frequently gauged the cartridges himself, rather than trust one of his numerous subordinates. When he had been in Bridgeport for two full years, he so far relaxed as to accept an invitation from Robert J. White, U. M. C.'s Treasurer, for an evening of gaiety. Under the stimulus of champagne and charming ladies, the General's iron manner softened. "Do you realize," he asked his host, "that this is the first evening of pleasure I have had since I came to America?"

"Why do you drive yourself so hard?" White asked.

The shadow fell again across the General's face. "Because I am personally responsible to His Imperial Majesty for the success of this contract, for every cartridge you send to Russia. If the contract fails, the best thing I can do is to take one of your excellent American revolvers and blow out my brains."

The contract did not fail. General Gorloff was able to report to his government that:

"There have been fired in our regular work 20,720 cartridges without one misfire, and 200 reloaded ten times, making 22,720 without a misfire, in the inspection of 2,000,000."

Marcellus Hartley was always willing to give General Gorloff part of the credit for the excellence of U. M. C. ammunition. The almost impossible degree of perfection demanded by the Russian set a standard that the company always afterward maintained, a standard that exceeded reasonable expectations. For example, the bark *Forya,* bound from New York to the Russian fortress of Cronstadt with 3,645,120 cartridges, was dismasted in a gale. Her deck was stove in, and the crew abandoned the water-logged hulk. Some days later, the S.S. *Iowa,* from Liverpool found the derelict barely afloat in the North Atlantic steamer lane. With salvage as their incentive, the officers and crew of the *Iowa* pumped out the *Forya,* and towed her back to New York. The ammunition, which had been under water for five weeks, was taken out of her and shipped to Bridgeport. Robert White officially reported on the tests then made:

"The wet paper boxes were removed and 10,450 of the cartridges were fired, proving them uninjured."

Twenty years later some more of this same lot were tested without a misfire.

An even more rigorous accidental test of U. M. C. ammunition occurred many years later. Everyone remembers how the U. S. battleship, *Maine,* was blown up in Havana Harbor in 1898. In 1911, her twisted hull was brought to the surface by naval engineers, and the U. M. C. small-arms ammunition aboard her was sent to Bridgeport for testing. Hundreds of these cartridges, which had lain at the bottom of a tropical sea for thirteen years were shot off without a single misfire.

Bridgeport was en fete. Everyone was wearing his best clothes, and from all the hotels and factories and many private homes the Stars and Stripes flew beside the white Imperial Standard bearing the angry black eagle of the House of Romanov. For on that summer day in 1872, Grand Duke Alexis of Russia had come to inspect U. M. C.

In these times, when kings hardly merit a passing glance and counts are as common as prairie dogs in Kansas, it is hard to remember the impact that even the minor aristocracy had on the romantic citizens of this great republic. As for genuine, certified, purple-blooded royalty from one of the greatest nations of Europe, the effect was almost too entrancing to be born. U. M. C. employees, especially the female ones, were virtually out of their minds. Many a girl spent more time, thought and money on her costume for the occasion than on her wedding gown.

When Marcellus Hartley, with an easy grace that was unaffected by the proximity of royalty, led his magnificent guest through the long aisles of his buildings, the grand ducal eyes were greeted by a sight that made them pop. Every machine was running full blast. Hundreds of overhead belts whirred, wheels flashed around, great presses rose and fell, and the air quivered with the rumble of machinery and the screech of tortured metal.

But it was none of these things that caused grand Duke to stare;

Alexis expected them. Rather it was the fact that the girls tending the machines wore fine silk dresses, replete with all the frills and furbelows, buttons and bows that fashion then dictated. The climax came when the inspection reached the building that contained the "grasshopper machines" for heading shells. It looked like a garden stricken with St. Vitus dance, for the girls had tied bouquets to the long, leglike rods, which gave the machines their name, and the flowers jigged madly up and down to the syncopated rhythm of production.

When he left the plant the dazzled Grand Duke said nothing of the miracle of manufacturing technique. Instead, he asked plaintively, "How can working girls afford all those silk dresses?"

One of the largest single orders received by U. M. C. in the early days traveled part of the way by air—in 1870! That was the year when Germany first sought the domination of Europe. Under the guidance of the ambitious Prussian Chancellor, Prince Von Bismark, she challenged the tinsel empire of Napoleon III of France. The French Army marched gaily off to the war with visions of another Napoleon's glory in their eyes, and the Emperor took along his little son to give him his *"baptême du feu."*

The Prussian needle gun was comparatively crude compared to the American rifles of that time, but it was far better than its poor relation, the French Chassepot, and plenty good enough to make French tactics obsolete. When the cruirassiers of the Emperor's Guard charged in the best Napoleonic manner, with brass breastplates glittering, horsehair plumes streaming behind crested helmets and sabers swinging, the deadly rapid fire of the German infantry piled them in pathetic heaps of men and horses and scrap metal. The French Army was defeated at Metz and destroyed at Sedan, where the Emperor gave up his sword. The Germans pressed triumphantly forward, and what was left of France rallied under the new republican government of President Louis Thiers and Premier Leon Michel Gambetta to defend their beloved Paris.

Gambetta was a dynamic man with more military sense than all the glittering marshals of France who had advised the ersatz Little Corporal. As the German Army coiled like a great blue boa constrictor around the city of Paris, he realized that the armies, which were forming in southern France to march to her relief, must be armed with better weapons than the Chassepot, or even the needle gun, if they were to have a fighting chance. The only hope was to get rifles from America.

Unlike most Americans, who had hastily left Paris before the German Army closed in, William W. Reynolds, Paris representative of Schuyler, Hartley and Graham, had elected to share the fortunes of war with his French friends. He knew Gambetta well, and the Premier sent for him to come to the Palace of the Tuileries. In a small, ornate room, still decorated with Napoleonic bees and eagles, Gambetta explained the situation. He needed one hundred thousand rifles and carbines and eighteen million cartridges. "Here is the order," he said, "and here is a draft on Lloyds for the money. I trust you and the integrity of your house. Send me the guns."

Reynolds sat for a moment listening to desultory cannon fire from the forts that guarded Paris, and the deeper, more distant boom of the German seige guns.

"How do I get out?" he asked.

"Buy a balloon," said Gambetta.

The balloon factory was a disused theater on the Grands Boulevards. On the dusty stage and in the orchestra pit, cleared of its seats, men and girls were sewing together pieces of gayly colored silk cut from the gowns which patriotic Frenchwomen had donated. Others were gas-proofing the seams with gum, or applying varnish to larger sections. From the flies hung the shapeless, gaudy folds of a completed gasbag.

Aided by a letter from the Premier, Reynolds negotiated the purchase of a balloon for $1,250 in gold coins, which he counted out of a canvas sack. Delivery was promised in a week. This speed was due to the urgency of Gambetta's letter, for balloons were at a premium. A few daring men slipped through the tight German lines, but, generally speaking, balloons were the only means of leaving Paris. All news from the outside world came by carrier pigeons taken out in the balloons.

On the day before Reynolds was to leave, Gambetta sent for him again. "I must get out to expedite the arming of our troops in the south," he said. "Nothing is being accomplished. You must cede me your balloon. They will make you another in a hurry."

The second balloon was built so quickly, that it was ready before the weather permitted Gambetta to leave. On the morning of October 7, 1870, the two gasbags were placed side by side in a green field on Montmart and inflated with hydrogen gas made by pouring sulphuric acid over iron filings. When Reynolds arrived at the field, they were already nearly full. The varicolored pieces of silk of which they were made gave them the appearance of bulbous patchwork quilts, and the small, frail wicker baskets beneath seemed weak vessels in which to essay the elements and cross the German lines.

As became his rank Gambetta, wearing a frock coat and the inevitable high hat, took off first to a cry from the crowd that was half groan, half cheer. Then Reynolds quickly climbed into the tiny basket. An instant later his young, amateur pilot ordered the ropes released.

The first moments of the flight were astonishingly serene. The balloon rose swiftly, smoothly, while the noise and confusion of earth faded below. In the absolute silence of free flight, Reynolds forgot to be afraid as he watched the walled city, halved by its twisting, silver river, open out beneath him. There was the Champs Elysées flowing down to the wide, bare Place de la Concorde. The ornate façade of the Tuileries rose from vivid green gardens. Beyond, were the Grands Boulevards and the Opera and Notre Dame on its island in the Seine.

As it rose higher, the balloon began to spin slowly, as spherical gasbags always do, and it seemed to Reynolds that the city with its ring of forts was revolving like a great misshapen wheel of which the broad boulevards were the spokes.

He saw the German entrenchments, small streaks of raw earth forced up by tunneling moles. An occasional puff of white smoke appeared. Then one whole line of trenches billowed out a white cloud, and the faint rattle of musketry was followed by the loud buzzing of bullets in the quiet air. Reynolds instinctively tried to duck into the basket, colliding with the alarmed pilot. In the other balloon, floating a few hundred feet away, Gambetta's anachronous hat was wildly agitated. German artillery opened up as well, but the guns could not be elevated sufficiently, and their shells arced harmlessly beneath.

Soon the balloons floated past the German lines, and the delicious silence fell again. But underneath them could be seen beetlelike objects scurrying along the straight white roads, German Uhlans galloping in pursuit in the hope that the aeronauts would be forced down. The luck held, and a freshening wind blew the balloons beyond pursuit.

Throughout that sunny afternoon, the two balloons drifted across France in a northwesterly direction. By chance, the air currents kept them close together which nearly brought disaster. As they floated above Criel, Gambetta's balloon began to sink rapidly toward an attempted landing. When it was only a few hundred feet above the ground, it crossed a Prussian camp. Troops poured out like angry ants, shooting as they ran. Reynolds could see Gambetta and his pilot throwing their baggage out of the basket. Their balloon shot upward. Reynolds, peering over the rim of his basket, saw the motley gasbag rising directly beneath him. It came up so fast that both pilots were helpless to get out of each other's way. For a few agonized seconds it seemed as though the only two machines in the whole vast empty ocean of air were going to collide. Then a chance gust changed Gambetta's course. As he passed Reynolds, about fifty feet away, he politely raised his hat.

Gambetta came down in a treetop at Amiens out of reach of the Germans. Reynolds kept on going and landed in a field near Ville Roy.

Schuyler, Hartley and Graham presented their daring salesman with the most magnificent gold watch money could buy. On the back of the case a balloon was engraved bearing the flags of America and France with the date "October 7, 1870." Above it on a scroll was the pious and exceedingly appropriate motto: *Dieu Protéges.*

## Chapter 17

# *Ammunition for Sportsmen*

The Union Metallic Cartridge Company was not shackled to any special type of arm like many gunmaking companies, but made cartridges for all. The catalogue for 1872 listed over thirty separate patterns, center fire, rim fire, and cap and ball, applicable to breech-loaders of all descriptions, revolvers, repeaters, pistols, carbines, and even the Gatling gun, which was the precursor of the modern machine gun and machine cannon. By the early 1900s, at the peak of diversity before the modern trend toward standardization began, the company was able to produce more than *fifteen thousand different loads,* varying from BB caps to 10-gauge shot shells.

This great variety of production was due to Marcellus Hartley's determination that there should be a U. M. C. cartridge for every type of gun that was made. This policy was not an arbitrary piece of corporate vanity; it was the result of Hartley's philosophy of business. He believed that the future of the company lay in producing ammunition for sportsmen. Military demand fluctuated wildly, and was in exactly inverse ratio to the peace and prosperity of the world, whereas American sportsmen presented a steady, constantly growing market. But their needs were infinitely more various than those of the soldiers.

To produce so many different kinds of cartridges required remarkable flexibility in the organization and unusual adaptability of the machinery. Credit for achieving this result belonged in the beginning to Hobbs and a little later to William Morgan Thomas, who in his fifty-four years in the company so identified himself with it that he was known as U. M. C. Thomas, and even used that as his signature.

Thomas was a Welshman. In 1865, at the age of seventeen, he boarded the sailing ship, *Harvest Queen,* to seek his fortune in America. Sixty-five days later, he tottered ashore at the Battery, wondering whether it was worth it.

His first job was with the Great American Tea Company in New York. In 1869, he went to work for U. M. C. in the Inspection Department. Within three years he was head of that department, which, since it impinged on all phases of manufacture and was responsible for the quality of the ammunition, was the most important in the company.

There was no rigid compartmentation of production in those days, so Thomas ranged through the whole plant. All the technical education he ever had was gained at the heading machines and draw punches, at the loaders and on the testing range of U. M. C. He had a natural genius for ballistics, and became a sort of minor Edison of ammunition.

When Thomas went to work for U. M. C., ammunition was just changing over from cap and ball to metallic cartridges. American sportsmen were keen for the new, easily loaded guns which were so much more powerful and sure fire than the old percussion lock arms. This was especially true in the West. A few conservative Easterners might still hold out for the kind of guns their fathers had used; but out on the Western plains and in the Rockies, where a man's stomach, and, indeed his very life, depended on his gun, there was no clinging to outmoded equipment. The little bands of men and women who were pushing the bridgehead of civilization into a vast and hostile land needed the best tools that skill and care could furnish them. Indeed, it is doubtful if they could have survived without the reliable type of ammunition pioneered by U. M. C.

It is probable that no other single individual contributed as much as Thomas to the improvement of ammunition. The span of his service with U. M. C. stretched all the way from cap and ball to the advent of the autoloader. Working with Colt, he helped to develop the famous .44-40, used in both their revolver and the Winchester '73 repeating rifle. This has been called, "The cartridge that won the West." He also helped Colt to design the .32 short, .38 long and short, and the .45. For J. Stevens of the Stevens Arms and Tool Company, he designed the .22 long rifle cartridge and he advised Smith and Wesson on a large variety of cartridges to fit their arms.

Later, he helped John Browning at Remington's Ilion plant to develop cartridges for the first practical autoloading rifles and shotguns ever made.

Inevitably Thomas' work with cartridges brought him in contact with the leading powder manufacturers of whom E. I. du Pont de Nemours was by far the most important. U. M. C. bought most of its powder from Du Pont, and relations between the companies were cordial. Thomas constantly advised with officials of Du Pont and other powder companies, and occasionally made technical suggestions which they adopted.

Another rapidly growing field of sport was target shooting. For many years target enthusiasts preferred muzzle-loaders, considering them more accurate than breechloaders. They liked to measure the charge and weigh the bullets themselves. This situation was considerably changed by Remington's special, breech-loading Creedmore rifle and the microscopically exact ammunition which Thomas designed for it.

Almost as important as the switch to metallic cartridges was the change in shotgun ammunition. In the '70s and '80s, the autumn skies were still full of ducks and upland bird shooting was in its heyday.

The development of the shotgun followed closely after that of the rifle. In the days of the flintlock, there was, in America, at least, no odium attached to shooting a sitting bird, because few marksmen could hold on a flying object while a gun took its own leisurely time about firing, though it was done in England. The quicker-acting percussion cap first made wing-shooting really practical, and at about the same time—the beginning of the nineteenth century—the method of joining two barrels together by a top rib gave sportsmen the double-barrel shotgun, which was almost universally used in wing-shooting for a hundred years until, in the first decade of the twentieth century, Remington brought out their famous autoloading and slide-action repeating shotguns.

Breech-loading shotguns came to America from the fine gunmakers of England and France in the 1850s. But these beautiful Purdays, William Greeners and Lefaucheuxs cost a small fortune, and so were a perquisite of the rich. Until the 1870s, American shotguns were almost all designed as muzzle-loaders.

However, it was not the fine gunsmiths of Europe, but an ingenious American sportsman, who made the greatest contribution to shotgun accuracy. Fred Kimble of Peoria, Illinois, conceived the idea of choke-boring. He started experimenting in Charley Stock's gun shop in Peoria. At first he used left-over Civil War muskets, which, as he says, "could stand a lot of boring." When he had worked out the principle of decreasing the bore near the muzzle to hold the shot charge together, he choke-bored a 6-gauge single-barrel muzzle-loader made by Joseph Tonks of Boston.

The results were startling. The ordinary cylinder-bored gun of the period was also well named a scatter gun, for it scattered the pellets all over the landscape. Less than 40 per cent would strike in a thirty-inch circle at forty yards. It was useless at any range over that. Kimble's gun put virtually its full charge into a twenty-six-inch circle at forty yards, and was good for single ducks up to seventy yards. Within a few years choke-boring was adopted by all shotgun makers. Nowadays the sportsman has a wide variety of chokes to choose from including improved cylinder, modified and full chokes, as well as various choke devices that give as many as nine degrees of choke on a single gun.

Incidentally, Fred Kimble must have been quite some shot. He tells of killing 203 mallards with his old muzzle-loader in a single day at Duck Island. On another occasion, shooting from a brush-covered boat anchored in the Illinois River only a hundred yards off the Peoria water front, he killed fifty-seven bluebills with fifty-seven shots. To those of us who hunt the wild and wary waterfowl of today, the fact that the ducks came in so close to a city seems extraordinary enough. But allowing that the opportunity was there, a run of fifty-seven straight is phenomenal shooting, and a remarkable proof of the prowess of the shooter and the accuracy of the first choke-bored gun in the world.

When the Remingtons and other manufacturers began to make comparatively inexpensive breech-loading shotguns in the early '70s, Marcellus Hartley determined to develop a vast new market for ammunition. His first move was to send A. C. Hobbs to England where paper shot shells were being made and sold—unloaded—to sportsmen.

Hobbs returned with all the latest information, a consignment of special paper, and a new English machine for making wads for shot shells. He and Thomas designed a center fire shot shell around the primer which Jerome Orcutt invented for them. The first of these shells were empty brass cases, primed and ready for hand-loading. Shortly afterward U.M.C. put out a much cheaper paper shell with a brass head and a further improved primer. These were immensely popular, but Hartley and his designers were still not satisfied.

In the late '70s, they contemplated the revolutionary step of making fully loaded shot shells for sportsmen. This had never been done because of the intricate technical problems involved. The first difficulty was the matter of making the shells so cheaply that sportsmen could afford to throw them away instead of reloading. Another was to get a uniform load that would satisfy the exacting demands of the crack wing shots. The third was to convince the customers. It was a tremendous gamble—the kind of considered risk that pays off big in business as in battle.

Hobbs and Thomas worked out the details of design with meticulous exactitiude. New types of loading machinery were developed, and another in the series of new primers was used. Then the shells were thoroughly tested under conditions of such severity as were never likely to be encountered in the field. Shotguns were banging away all over the range, as expert shots tested them for pattern against targets, and for effectiveness against birds on the wing at all reasonable ranges. Shells were dunked in water and fired, and exposed to extremities of heat and cold. When the experts were completely satisfied, the shells were put into production.

Then the advertising and sales people planned a campaign to introduce the radical innovation of loaded shot shells to what they believed would be a resistant market. However, no advertisements were released until U.M.C. had built up a stockpile of ten million shells which was reckoned to be enough to satisfy the first year's demand.

When all was ready, the advertisements appeared. The result completely confounded the company's officials. U.M.C. ammunition had established such a reputation for reliability that the public trusted their printed word implicitly. Loaded shells were just what they had been waiting for, and they rushed to buy. Within one week the ten-million-shell "year's supply," was gone.

To be first in the field is not to stay there, however. U.M.C. had lots of hot competition and had to be constantly on the alert to remain ahead. Winchester, its hottest rival, was soon in the field with their own shot shells. Through the years, right up to the present time, the two companies have waged a battle for advantage in excellence.

Progress is a fine thing but there will always be conservatives who must also be pleased. For example, in 1936, nearly half a century after the invention of smokeless powder, U.M.C. was still making its black powder shell in the well-known yellow case at the rate of forty million a year to please their customers in the swamps and bayous of the Gulf States and the individualistic Kentucky mountaineers, who firmly believed that a shell was no doggone good unless it went off with a terrible bang and billowing clouds of smoke.

When smokeless powder was first introduced, Winchester got a jump ahead of U.M.C. by putting out an inexpensive smokeless powder shell, colored a vivid blue. At a pigeon-shooting match in Macon, Georgia, U.M.C. Thomas had to take an unaccustomed back seat. After the first day's shooting, the Winchester representative took him by the arm. "Let's take a walk to the firing stand, U.M.C." he said jovially.

As they neared it, he pointed at the heaps of used shells. "Look at that beautiful blue color on the ground," he exclaimed triumphantly.

"It is very handsome," Thomas conceded glumly.

Seventy-five per cent of the used shells were Winchesters.

When he talked to the shooters, Thomas discoverd that the Achilles heel of the Winchester shell was its primer, which was slow by a vital fraction of a second. He hurried back to Bridgeport, and developed the famous U.M.C. "Nitro Shell," with special primer number 5, which was slightly faster than lightning. The shell case was a rich maroon color.

The next year at Macon, it was Thomas who took the Winchester man for a walk, and pointed to the ground near the shooting stand, which was a nice autumnal shade of maroon. "More suitable for the season than blue, don't you agree?" said U.M.C. Thomas.

## Chapter 18

# Sir Hiram Maxim and Mr. Wu

Marcellus Hartley was middle aged. The beard he had grown in order to look older had a silvery sheen. But his eyes, with all their youthful ardor, were always looking for more worlds to conquer. He was still "a ball of fire."

From Monday to Friday he was at the offices of Schuyler, Hartley and Graham throughout a long working day, managing the affairs of his different companies. On Saturday he got up before dawn to make the arduous train trip to Bridgeport, where he kept close tabs on every phase of U.M.C.'s expanding operations, and supplied the drive that kept them expanding.

For example, on one occasion, the new primers in a lot of several million empty shot shells, were found to be inadequate. Hobbs and Thomas immediately decided that they must be changed even though it involved great loss and considerable time. In their own words they were making "desperate haste" to reprime the shells, when Hartley arrived on his Saturday visit. He commended the decision to change the primers; there must be no quibbling with quality. But he differed decidedly on the definition of "desperate haste."

"Do it more rapidly!" he ordered. "Put benches in the storehouses. Get a thousand more girls if necessary. I want those shells reprimed!"

Though U.M.C. was thus commanded by a driving captain, there were virtually no labor troubles. This was due to the high wages paid and the superior working conditions in the factory. The different operations were let out on a contract system similar to that of Remington in Ilion, but Hartley personally saw to it that the workers were kept happy. In the great countrywide depression of 1873, when a third of the nation's labor force was in the bread lines, Bridgeport was one of the least affected cities in the United States. The steady wages paid by U.M.C., because of its foreign contracts, kept things going.

Of course, there were drawbacks. It was inevitable that, at a time when men were feeling their way toward new techniques of the manufacture and the handling of such a dangerous product as ammunition, there should be some disastrous explosions. Every once in a while the Bridgeport papers would carry startling details of explosions at the plant. However, because of the rule that only a small amount of powder and an even lesser quantity of fulminate should ever be in the factory at one time, and the system of compartmentalizing the loading process, the explosions were localized, and comparatively few employees were injured. Then, too, the cause of each accident was carefully studied and safety precautions taken to make a repetition impossible.

As a result of progressively more stringent safety measures and the continuing campaign by which day in and day out the company dins into its workers the necessity for extraordinary vigilence and care, insurance companies now rate Remington as one of the best industrial risks.

The biggest bang that ever shook Bridgeport caused no fatalities at all, though it wrecked a lot of fine plate glass. It happened that on a crisp October afternoon a local lad took his Remington-Lee Sporting Rifle and went hunting for deer in the hills back of Bridgeport. To say that his luck was out that day is either not true or a colossal understatement, depending how you look at it. At any rate he saw no deer.

As he trudged home at dusk, he took a short cut through a field, loosely fenced with barbed wire. Certain beehive-like structures, half sunken in the ground, aroused his curiosity and he paused to examine them. The idea then crossed his misguided mind that here was an excellent chance for a little target practice—the stone beehives would provide, he thought, a safe backstop.

He fastened a piece of paper to the wooden door of one hut, and methodically paced off a hundred yards. Then he set his sights at the correct elevation, made an allowance for windage, and taking careful aim, pulled the trigger. The earth split open and hurled its molten core at the sky, which vanished in a blinding flash of light.

When the youth came to in a hospital three days later, he learned that he had chosen one of U.M.C's powder-storage magazines as his "safe" backstop. All Bridgeport had shivered in the blast, and windows were broken as far away as Long Island across the Sound. That he survived was due to the capricious and still unknown laws of blast, which may blow the whole front off a building and leave the medicine bottles untouched on the bathroom shelf.

It was after this explosion that U.M.C. bought its present Powder Park, consisting of three hundred sixty-one acres. The powder is stored in many small underground buildings; the whole area is surrounded by an overhang, barbed wire fence, and is closely guarded. A pleasant piece of irony is the fact that, if a young sportsman could break into the Park today, he would find plenty of deer to shoot. About 1908, a herd of native deer charged through a gate into its Elysian glades. There they have lived ever since, growing fat and multiplying so rapidly that every now and then the company has to organize a hunt to thin them out. It should be noted for the sake of any nervous citizens of Bridgeport that the modern powder magazines are completely bullet-proof.

In addition to U.M.C. and Schuyler, Hartley and Graham, Marcellus Hartley embarked on other considerable enterprises. In 1878, he organized the Bridgeport Gun Implement Company to make all sorts of accessories for firearms. Until then, appliances for sportsmen's use had been made only in small quantity, and the varieties were limited to the requirements of certain makers of firearms, which resulted in their acquiring a virtual monopoly of the business. Hartley broke that monopoly wide open, and so successful was his new concern that it soon branched out into the manufacture of all sorts of sporting goods.

Electricity was the magic word of progress in the late nineteenth century. Edison's first lamps were glowing dimly in his laboratory, electric motors were just coming into general use, and in a bright but hazy future loomed the indistinct shapes of the electronic miracles of today.

Marcellus Hartley wanted to have a hand in shaping that future. To this end he sought out a young American inventor named Hiram Stevens Maxim, who was considered quite a wizard. That was before Maxim gained fame and a British knighthood by inventing the Maxim gun, and then dimmed his new luster by the "crazy" notion that he could build a flying machine.

Hartley considered Maxim's theories of electricity very sound, especially his radical plan of using an alternating current instead of the almost universal direct current. He bought in the patents on Maxim's dynamos and incandescent lights, and gave him a laboratory at Bridgeport in which to work out his ideas. During the summer, Maxim was invited to relax and think at Hartley's rambling country home in New Jersey.

To promote the Maxim patents and others which he acquired, Hartley founded the United States Electric Lighting Company with a capital of $1,500,000. Sub-companies were established in several large cities and plans were pushed forward with the usual Hartley energy. However, the new company struck many man-made snags.

The United States Electric Lighting Company was as near a failure as Hartley ever had. The great gas companies, seeing their lighting monopolies challenged, ganged up on him, and the Edison companies challenged the Maxim patents. The opposition was so powerful that it looked as though Hartley's venture would be scuttled by economic piracy. Just as it was about to go under, his friend, George Westinghouse, proposed a merger with the new Westinghouse Electric and Manufacturing Company. Hartley agreed and became vice-president of the joint venture.

The rest is history. The combined companies were strong enough to take on all comers in the financial Donnybrook Fair which characterized the era of industrial expansion. Westinghouse Electric prospered and grew great, while Hartley's foresight is demonstrated by the fact that today most domestic users of electricity rely on alternating current.

As his financial interests broadened and his companies rolled up profits, Marcellus Hartley became a very rich man. But he never became a stuffed shirt. Though he lived very handsomely in a big brownstone house at 232 Madison Avenue, and a sprawling, turreted, Gothic cottage on the brow of Orange Mountain, New Jersey, he managed to keep his simple tastes and his sense of humor.

The latter is definitely demonstrated by the visitation of Mr. Wu, the personal representative of the Dowager Empress of China. Compared to Mr. Wu, the Man Who Came to Dinner was a piker. When the Chinese first came to New York to buy arms for his august mistress, Hartley invited him to spend the weekend at Orange Mountain. Mr. Wu stayed for ten years. Then he made a trip to China and returned for a brief visit of two years more.

Since Wu always wore the splendid brocades and peacock-feathered cap of his native land, he was a distinctly exotic addition to life in suburban New Jersey. The Hartleys' more conservative guests would gasp faintly as a resplendent Oriental, clad in blue and rose and gold, strolled nonchalantly into the somber Victorian drawing room, but Hartley never offered any explanation of his presence—he enjoyed their mystification.

Mr. Wu had his Jeeves, a character who was known to all the Hartleys as John Chinaman. Like his master, John always wore his Chinese clothes: black seersucker trousers, a loose blue blouse and a round black hat from beneath which dangled a long pigtail. He was a friendly fellow, anxious to be helpful, but he had no truck with the protocol of servitude. In those days the heavy, lace-curtained doors of old New York were usually opened by prim parlor maids in dainty caps and trailing ribbons. A visitor at 232 Madison found the door flung wide by John grinning from ear to ear. If the guest happened to ask for the master of the house, John trotted to the foot of the great staircase and yelled up it, "Hey, Hartley, man come see you!"

A ten-hour working day no more than took the edge off Marcellus Hartley's energy. Every afternoon, when he got back to Orange Mountain, he mounted a horse and rode ten miles or more, no matter what the weather. In the evening he liked to visit with the neighbors and reminisce about old adventures. Most of the men who lived on Orange Mountain had good tales to tell. There was General George B. McClellan, who had commanded the Army of the Potomac in the first bitter years of the war, and General Randolph Marcy, who was Hartley's closest friend. Doctor Addams, who had married the Hartleys, contributed amusing stories of his long clerical career, and Hartley had his own dashing youth to draw upon.

Marcellus Hartley's family life was extremely tranquil and happy for many years, until, in 1881, tragedy touched it. He and Fanny had three charming daughters, Emma, and the twins, Grace and Helen. In 1880, Emma was married to Norman White Dodge. As a wedding present, her father bought the house on Thirty-seventh Street adjoining 232 Madison Avenue, and had it splendidly redecorated and connected with his own. It was a delightful arrangement. The two households mingled happily, while the young Dodges were free to live their own lives. The measure of their happiness was only a matter of months. On March 3, 1881, Emma Dodge died in childbirth.

The sorrow of Marcellus Hartley was at first but little alleviated by the child who had cost his daughter's life, his grandson and namesake, Marcellus Hartley Dodge. But it was not long before his life was virtually centered around the boy, who always lived with him, and became, in effect, the son he had never had.

Marcellus Hartley had a great capacity for love—he believed in it as the touchstone of life. Once, when he was discussing religion with a friend, he said, "Life is a mystery anyhow. The only thing to do is to play trumps all the time."

"What are trumps?" asked his friend.

"Hearts," said Marcellus Hartley.

Young "Marcy" Dodge was the recipient of the full force of that love, and returned it in equal measure. Meanwhile, neither sorrow nor the unexpected responsibilities of fatherhood slowed Marcellus Hartley's business pace. He shortly embarked on his fourth and last great enterprise.

# *Chapter* 19

# *The Remington Rolling Block Rifle*

We left the three Remington brothers on April 12, 1865, sitting in the cluttered little office that was an antiquated appendage of their great new factory. Outside the April sun shone brilliantly on the big brick buildings that housed long rows of beautiful machines equipped to turn out guns that nobody wanted. Hundreds of windows glinted vacantly, and the tall brick stacks of the powerhouses were innocent of smoke. The splendid Corliss engine stood still—the heart of the great Armory had ceased to beat. There is nothing in the world so eloquent of desolation as a deserted factory. . . .

Oddly enough, the atmosphere inside the stuffy little office was less gloomy than out in the spring sunshine, though it certainly was not gay. At the peak of prosperity Philo and Eliphalet Remington III were somber men; now Philo's face was craggy with determination and Eliphalet looked grim. Sam's ruddy, rotund countenance was hardly adapted to express stern resolution, but his spirit was equally firm. Lite Remington would have felt proud of his sons that day.

The discussion between the brothers was concerned neither with recrimination against the Government for its abrupt cancellation of the contracts, nor with their patriotic error in taking the risk of accepting them. They were exploring the future with Sam's agile mind setting the pace.

Even among the clouds of debt and loss and waste, there were a few bright spots. In 1864, they had had the foresight to convert the foundry on the other side of the Canal into a factory equipped to turn out industrial machinery, farm implements and other durable goods. This was a definite asset and they hoped it would become a greater one as the demands of peace replaced production for war. A million men in the North and South would be returning to their farms. Perhaps an ancient Roman could beat a sword into a plowshare, but no one could make a Springfield rifle into a hoe. Those boys were going to need all sorts of farming tools.

The Agricultural Works, a separate joint stock company under the name of Remington Brothers, was not affected by the debts of the Arms Company. The latter had been incorporated on January 1, 1865, with a capital of $1,000,000 and an asset value of $1,500,000. Philo Remington was its first president, Samuel was vice-president and Eliphalet III was secretary and treasurer. Because of its incorporation, the Remingtons were not personally responsible for the debts of E. Remington and Sons, Inc. They could have kept the Agricultural Works free and clear, and let the Arms go into bankruptcy, probably buying it back in at a low figure. But that was not their way of doing business.

Also they had an ace in the hole that might yet send beautiful black smoke pouring out of the disused stacks and set the idle machinery banging and buzzing and chattering in the delightfully discordant symphony of production. They were on the verge of perfecting the best breech-loading rifle yet made.

Back in 1862, Philo Remington, searching for an improved breech mechanism, had found a lock invented by Leonard M. Geiger, which seemed to him the best yet. He determined to have both the patent rights and the inventor. This required some complicated trading, as Geiger had sold part interests in his patent to A. C. Alger and C. C. Pond. A three-way royalty agreement was worked out, and Geiger came to Ilion. The result of his labors there, in co-operation with Joseph Rider, whom Philo had called back to the Armory to help him, was the Geiger carbine mentioned previously.

Though it proved terribly effective against Confederate troops armed with muzzle-loaders, the Geiger carbine was a long way from perfection. The action was simple and effective, but the curious, split-breech arrangement had unfortunate weaknesses.

Improved Geiger-Rider breechloaders were presented to a board of Army officers at the Springfield Arsenal in January, 1865, where they were tried against sixty-five other makes including Sharps, Roberts, Burnsides, Peabodys and Henrys. The job had been rushed too fast, and too many bugs were uncovered at the trials. The guns just did not stack up. Back to the factory they came, and Rider bent all his genius to eliminating the defects and simplifying the action.

By April, 1865, he had made such progress that success seemed close. The Remington brothers decided, almost literally, to bet their shirts on him. They were right. But it was not until the winter of 1865-66 that Rider produced the gun that became known throughout the world as the Remington Rolling Block Rifle.

Rider's Rolling Block breech was at once immensely strong, easy to operate and as nearly foolproof as a gun can be. The breech was opened by simultaneously cocking the hammer and rolling the solid breech block straight back with the thumb. The backward motion of the block ejected the empty cartridge. A fresh one was shoved into the chamber and the breech rolled forward (closed) in one continuous motion. A locking lever secured the hammer while the gun was open, and locked the breech after it was closed.

The firing pin operated through the solid breech block. When the trigger was pulled, the hammer struck against the back of the block adding its full strength to that of the breech at the moment of explosion. This arrangement provided an interlocking and bracing connection, the hammer becoming a fulcrum acting on the bearing of the breech piece. Due to the scientific relation of the two sectors of circles—the hammer and breech block—pressure only forced them more firmly together so that the greater the recoil, the more securely the mechanism was interlocked. Breech block and hammer were made of solid pieces of fine steel .69 of an inch thick. It was literally impossible, as was later proven, to blow out a Rolling Block breech.

Now, when the smoke of controversy and the confusion of partisan claims have long since vanished and the relative merits of the different competing systems can be viewed in the dispassionate light of history, authorities generally agree that the Remington Rolling Block was the best single-shot military arm ever produced. So few motions were required to load and fire that an expert could get off seventeen shots a minute. It was so simple that raw recruits could handle it, and so durable that it stood up under terrific abuse in all climates from the steaming jungles of Central America to the sub-Arctic mountains of Scandinavia.

The most rigorous formal test the Remington ever met was given it in Belgium. According to the report of Alphonse Polain, Director of the Proving-house at Liege, a .50 caliber Remington was loaded with 750 grains of powder (normal charge seventy grains) forty balls and two wads. It was fired, and, the report notes, "nothing extraordinary occurred."

A sort of postscript notation states, "The barrel could not have received a stronger charge as the last one filled its entire length, 750 grains of powder and 40 balls occupying 36.31 inches." Incidentally, the gun was not made to shoot balls, but an elongated bullet.

In Spain, where they were interested in its resistance to the tropical dampness of Cuba, they gave the gun a different test. It was soaked in sea water and set aside to rust. When they tried it the following day, every metal part was coated with a thick, red film of corrosion, yet the mechanism worked perfectly.

Examining boards in other countries thought up incredible courses of sprouts to test the new Remington. They fired it continuously 2,500 times; they took off the stock and fired the gun without it; they filed down the metallic cartridges so they would burst in the chamber, and they left a ramrod in the barrel, and shot it off. Never a breech failed, never a gun burst.

In addition, Remington barrels shot straighter than those of any other production gun. The *Iron Age* of March 7, 1872, states that:

> The excellent shooting qualities of the barrels, made at their establishment [E. Remington and Sons] have been, from the era of the founder, a proverb in mouths of wisest censure. The superiority has been, moreover, quite as generally observed in the barrels of military as of the sporting rifles. It is possible that a degree of this excellence may be due to the choiceness of material, but the extraordinary care given to the interior finish, the delicate gauging of the chambers, and the exact turning of the muzzles, and more than all, the patient and faithful straightening process, which is never neglected, are probably the general claimants in this instance. . . . The

> Remingtons, with an honorable pride in the excellence of their production, and correctly estimating the superlative importance of this quality in a barrel, have omitted no care, whether it concerns the experience and skill of artisans, or the severity of intermediate and final inspection, that will secure the merit of precision for their work.

In 1872, the Remington Armory was capable of turning out 1,500 guns in a single day; yet the unprejudiced statement in the *Iron Age* proves that they were just as exacting as to quality as Eliphalet in his forge.

Though the Remingtons knew that they had the best breechloader in existence, they had yet to prove it to the world. Meanwhile, they were in the clutch of financial stringency. If their creditors had so desired, they could have taken E. Remington and Sons over in that summer of 1865. But they knew they could not run it. Right here was where the Remington's reputation for integrity paid a huge dividend. All their largest creditors agreed to a postponement of payment dates.

Even so it was a "narrow ledge." As the Ilion Bank crashed and other debts mounted against expectations that were still merely "faith in their product," the brothers threw everything they had into the pot. Moneys earned by the Agricultural works went to pay workmen in the Arms. Small orders for guns helped out. Among these was a Government contract for converting muzzle-loading Springfields to a breech-loading system invented by Colonel Hiram Berdan of the center fire cartridge. The entire center sections of the Springfields were cut out and the Berdan lock substituted. In addition, some revenue came in for sporting guns, pistols and revolvers. Though this could nowhere near carry the debts accumulated (at Government insistence) to expand war production, the Remingtons somehow staggered through.

The first vital test of the new Remington rifles occurred on a wild, high plateau in Wyoming, where they saved the lives of a small band of pioneering cowboys. Young Nelson Story had struck it rich in Virginia City. Then he had ridden fifteen hundred miles to Texas and invested thirty thousand dollars (gold) in a herd of three thousand longhorn cattle. He had recruited a band of Texas cowboys—ex-Confederate Cavalrymen—to handle them. Following good grazing land, Story and his herd reached Fort Leavenworth, Kansas, in the summer of 1866. He was on his way to the green upland valleys of Montana, where were thousands of acres of the finest grassland in the world with never a cow to chew a cud. Gold and copper had brought plenty of people to Montana—over one hundred thousand of them—and Story figured that if he ever got his longhorns there, he could sell one thousand head for forty dollars or more apiece, and have two thousand left to start a ranch in the Galatin.

At Fort Leavenworth, Story got bad news. Chief Red Cloud of the Sioux was annoyed by the chain of forts the Army was building across Wyoming. The whole Sioux Nation was on the point of going on the warpath. Army officers said that no one but a lunatic would try to drive a herd of cattle fifteen hundred miles through those wild plains and mountains. Story decided to be a lunatic.

As counterbalance, he also got a break at Leavenworth. He was able to buy thirty brand-new Remington rifles, together with some thousands of brass center-fire cartridges. It must have been almost the first shipment to reach the West. In addition, his Texans were armed with Colt revolvers, and Story himself wore two big Navy Remington-Beals in his holsters.

In the August heat, they started—three thousand longhorns, a train of oxcarts and thirty men, following the Bozeman Trail across the prairie sea. They took it easy. The cattle fed on the lush buffalo grass and actually gained weight. The men lived well on slaughtered beef and the game they shot with their new Remingtons. As they mounted the immense sloping plain toward the uplands, the air grew cool and tangy. They rode, alert for hostiles, but never a Sioux showed his feathered head, though the towering pillar of dust, kicked up by twelve thousand hooves trampling the ancient turf, could be seen for fifty miles across the level plain.

So they came to Fort Laramie in Wyoming and, after a brief rest, pushed on over the roof of America, where the bare stone rafters of a continent showed through the thin thatch of turf. They had almost reached Fort Reno on the edge of the Wyoming Badlands when the Sioux first struck. It was not much of an attack. A couple of hundred braves galloping over a ridge, thundering down the slope, preceded by a cloud of ill-aimed arrows. They were met by an unexpected volume of fire. As ponies and warriors fell in tangled confusion, the Indians decided that something was wrong here, and fled. But the outer fringe of the great herd was a mile or more from the center of the fight, and, as they galloped away, the Sioux stampeded part of it into the Badlands. Leaving a small guard and two wounded cowboys, Story took his men after them. It was a short chase and a merry one. As soon as the Sioux saw the cowboys with their terrible guns, they scattered into the hills and Story retrieved his cattle. But one of his cowboys had been killed.

From Fort Reno, Story pushed northward to where Colonel Henry B. Carrington was building Fort Kearney, the Army's farthest outpost. When Story got there, Carrington forbade him to go on. Three thousand Sioux, Cheyennes and Arapahoes, under Red Cloud and Crazy Horse, were blocking the Bozeman Trail, he said. Twenty-seven men would not have even the shadow of a chance of getting through to Montana.

Story waited around for two weeks, hoping that Carrington would change his mind. The Colonel made him camp three miles from the great eight-hundred-foot-long stockade of Kearney so that his herd would not eat the safe pasture nearer the Fort. At that distance, Story was no safer than he would be on the trail, and he was not a patient man.

On the night of October 22, 1866, bullwhackers quietly yoked up their oxen, cowboys softly stirred up the longhorn herd, and Story's huge caravan slipped away, defying Colonel Carrington and the whole Indian confederacy.

The Colonel shrugged him off as a fool. Red Cloud reacted as you would expect. To him that vast, slow-moving herd of cattle was visible wealth more potent by far than gold, and the twenty-seven men, who rode beside it or drove the oxcarts, were arrogant in their temerity. The insignificance of their numbers was insult added to temptation. Red Cloud sent five hundred braves under Crazy Horse, the Indian Jeb Stuart, to wipe them from his land.

On a brilliant autumn afternoon, Story saw the Indian bands gathering on the ridges, contemptuous of concealment. He let his cattle roam and formed the classic circle of defense with his wagon train. They waited tensely, watching the distant bands of warriors signaling each other by the flash of pocket mirrors. When the Indians had formed into a single command, Crazy Horse waved his rust-red blanket, signaling the charge.

Down the long slope came a great flying crescent of warriors. It was a gay and awful sight. In the crystal clarity of slanting sunlight, barbaric colors throbbed and quivered: coppery, paint-daubed bodies stretched low on racing ponies, red and ochre of gaudy buffalo hide shields, war bonnets undulating like feathered banners in the wind; and, like the mounting crescendo of Wagnerian doom, the tympani of two thousand drumming hooves rolled before them, pierced by the thin savage screaming of the braves.

As the horns of the flying crescent drew in to close around the static circle, Story gave the order to fire. The Remingtons spoke in a staccato ripple, and then began a steady drumbeat of fire that ripped the Indian ranks. Warriors and ponies crashed in wild flurries of lashing hooves and flying feathers. The Indians circled, shooting arrows and muskets at full gallop, waiting, as was their tactic, for the slackening fire that meant the Americans were reloading, to close in for the kill.

But that moment never came. The deadly spurts of orange fire flickered through the billowing clouds of smoke in a continuous pattern of death. Story's men were pouring out a volume of fire never before seen in the West. Their guns were red-hot, but they poured water from their canteens over the barrels and kept on shooting.

At last the Indians had enough. They pulled back to what they thought was a safe distance to regroup. Reckoned by the range of a muzzle-loading Springfield they *were* safe, but the new Remingtons could shoot 50 per cent farther. Story's men merely raised their sights and continued the deadly rain of lead. It was too much for the warriors. The weak cohesive force of tribal allegiance broke, and in scattered bands, they bolted for the hills. Story told his smoke-blackened, grinning cowpokes to stop shooting, and counted noses. He had not lost a man.

The caravan continued on its way, marching at night when Indians won't attack, camping by day. Twice more they crushed large-scale attacks before the Indians decided it did not pay. So protected by the fire-power of his Remingtons, Story brought his herd to the green haven of the Galatin, and founded the cattle-ranching industry of Montana.

It was a matter of leadership—and guns! Back in Fort Kearney, Colonel Carrington's three hundred soldiers, armed with Springfield muzzle-loaders were corralled in their own stockade. A few weeks after Story left Kearney, Captain J. W. Fetterman led a scouting detachment of mixed cavalry and infantry out of the Fort. The Sioux cut them off and massacred them to a man.

After that, Fort Kearney itself was in danger. Nor was it considered safe until the spring of 1867, when fresh troops arrived armed with Springfields converted into breech-loaders.

Story, with thirty men armed with Remingtons, had taken a vast, unruly herd of cattle and a cumbersome oxtrain through the heart of the Sioux Nation with the loss of one man killed and two wounded.

## Chapter 20

# A Traveling Salesman in the Courts of Europe

Even after the orders from the Marines came in, and though, in 1869 and '71, Navy and Army boards had rated the Remington above all other breech-loading systems, there were insufficient American orders to keep the great plant in Ilion going. As an aftermath of the Civil War, the United States was loaded with secondhand guns—not very good ones, of course, but still shootable. The Army, hamstrung by the inevitable post-war economy wave, could only order a few conversion jobs on their ancient muzzle-loading Springfields. The sporting market was glutted with war-surplus guns.

Marcellus Hartley had foreseen this when he determined to specialize in ammunition. The Remingtons were also well aware of the situation. But if the American market was bogged down, the situation in Europe was very different. All the European general staffs had studied the Civil War and learned its lesson, that the muzzle-loader was as obsolete as the crossbow. But there was not a good breechloader on the Continent. The Prussian needle gun, for all its clumsy firing mechanism and paper cartridge, was the best they had. The French Chassepot, which leaked gas like a broken main, was a very poor second. Opportunity beckoned imperiously to the Remingtons.

They prepared to go more than halfway to meet her. All the

brothers agreed that Sam was their best salesman. He was a gregarious, polished gentleman, quick of wit, with a warmth and charm that were to make him fast friends among all nations and all classes from peasant soldier boys to kings, emperors and Oriental potentates. Equally important, he did not share his brothers' aversion to alcohol, nor their penchant for going to bed slightly ahead of the chickens.

He had married Flora Carver, daughter of Benjamin Carver. Mrs. Sam was a genuine beauty, with the willowy figure beloved by Victorian novelists and a lovely, laughing face. She had the distinction and social grace to hold her own at any court. Even though Philo and Eliphalet III puritanically disapproved of the Samuel Remingtons, they realized that they were the perfect emissaries to the "dessolute" capitals of Europe.

In order to give Sam the stature to deal with the European bigwigs, he was elected president of E. Remington and Sons in 1866, Philo taking a nominal demotion to vice-president. Sam sailed for Europe with Flora that summer and established headquarters in Paris, where he lived in great style. His carriage was drawn by high-stepping horses and there were always two men on the box.

The Remingtons were warmly welcomed in the gay, gaslit capital of France; and, indeed, at all the courts of Europe. It was an oddity of the structure of European society that, while tradesmen and industrialists were rigidly excluded from its aristocratic ranks, makers of firearms were excepted from the ban. This was due to the fact that the traditional perquisite of the nobility was bearing arms, and their favorite sport was hunting. Consequently, Samuel Remington became a familiar of the Tuileries, where Napoleon III's beautiful Empress Eugenie gave her splendid balls and soirées. He was elected to the best clubs in London, and welcomed at royal palaces from Stockholm to Madrid. Everywhere he went, he persuasively argued the superiority of the Remington Rolling Block. Since truth was on his side, and necessity stimulated demand, he lived in a salesman's paradise.

Amid his triumphs of salesmanship, Samuel Remington had several setbacks. The toughest piece of luck he had was in Prussia. German officers had declared that the Remington was the gun for them, when Sam was invited to attend the maneuvers near Potsdam. He turned out in a high silk hat and Prince Albert coat, mounted on a beautiful charger and carrying his trusty Remington.

At one point in the maneuvers, a brilliant group of officers, in silver cuirasses and helmets plumed like Indian war bonnets, galloped up, led by the King of Prussia, soon to become Kaiser Wilhelm I of Germany.

"My friend, Remington, the gun man!" exclaimed the King. "Now I should like to try your arm personally."

Sam was all smiling confidence. "Here it is, your Majesty. I am sure you will approve it."

He handed his gun to the King, who threw open the breech, nodded approval at its easy action, and closed it.

"Now what shall we shoot?" the King asked jovially. "That oak tree is about a hundred meters I should say."

He adjusted the sights, and taking careful aim, while his beautifully trained horse stood like cast bronze, he pulled the trigger. The hammer fell with a dismal click on a dud cartridge. One chance in ten thousand! All is lost; and there is no joy in Mudville!

The King's face turned imperial purple. He hurled the gun to the ground and, raking his spurs into his astonished horse, galloped furiously away, followed by his stony-faced staff. Left alone among a hundred thousand men, shunned like a mongrel in the American Kennel Club, Sam rode sadly from that stricken field.

Then the streak of bad luck broke. At the Imperial Exposition, held in Paris in 1867, the High Commission of Firearms, under the presidency of Marshal of France Canrobert and consisting of leading ordnance experts of France, England, Austria, Russia, Prussia, Spain, Italy, Sweden, Holland and Belgium, unanimously selected the Remington as the best rifle in the world. Samuel Remington, at his resplendent, genial best, received from Marshal Canrobert the Silver Medal of the exposition, the highest award for military and sporting arms.

Shortly thereafter the great Ismael Pasha, Khedive of Egypt, sent a commission to France to inquire as to what rifle they would advise him to provide for the new Egyptian Army, which was being reorganized for him by General Stone, formerly of the Confederate States of America. The Egyptian Commission called on Samuel Remington, who hotfooted it for Cairo to see Ismael Pasha.

During the negotiations and while an order was being filled, the relationship between Sam and the Khedive warmed from that of salesman and prospect to close personal friendship. Ismael Pasha presented his new friend with an exquisite scimitar of ancient Damascene workmanship. When the guns arrived on the exact date specified in the contract, the Khedive was so delighted that he made Remington a really magnificent, but highly embarrassing gift—a parcel of land in the most desirable residential district of Cairo.

When the Khedive gives a man a piece of land, he must build on it or else be guilty of grave discourtesy. Samuel was no piker. He built a small but exquisite marble palace on his land. But he never found an opportunity to live in it. After he died, it was sold to the British Government, who used it until 1952 to entertain V.I.P.s in Cairo.

Such contacts and the merits of the Rolling Block enabled Sam to place large orders for Remington guns in many European countries, including France and Spain.

## Chapter 21

# The Golden Age of Ilion

In Ilion the ten years from 1870 to 1880 were the Gay Decade. It was Boom Town by the Erie, but it boomed in a pleasantly genteel manner. There was no riotous living, no ostentatious flinging about of the money that poured in from distant parts of the world. The tone was set by Philo and Eliphalet Remington, who never relaxed their strict moral standards or changed their preference for simple living.

In the main, the Ilionites' new affluence enabled them to live the sort of life that nostalgic memoirs picture as typical of an American small town in the gentle years before the wars began. In the case of most villages, memory is tricked by time into a rosy picture that skips hard depression years and personal misfortunes, but in Ilion, the picture was a true one—while it lasted.

People amused themselves with picnics and outings on chartered canal boats, simple dances and lots of good eating. The loyal wives of Ilion prided themselves on being the best cooks in the country, and whipped up terrific nine-course dinners every time they had company. The bachelors did not fare too badly, either. At the Central Hotel they could get a simple little five-o'clock dinner, consisting of clam soup, roast pig, chicken, pastry, ice cream, fruit and coffee, for 25¢.

In the winter, there were sleigh rides and skating, hunting in the still wild woods on the hills, and coasting. Most fun of all were the bobsled races down the steep slope of Second Street Hill. The races were held at night, and teams came from all over the state to compete against the Ilion sleds. On coasting nights, all the town turned out to watch the sport and bet on their favorites. The beautiful nickel-plated coasters were upholstered in leather and carried banners bearing their names: *Red Cloud* (owned by Philo Remington), *White Cloud* (Fred Ingersall), *Comet, Flyaway, Nightmare, Tallyho, Red Jacket* and *Nancy Hanks.*

A reporter for the *Utica Globe* immortalized one such night. According to him the mile-long course had been flooded, and milk-white ice reflected flaring torches and strings of colored lights. A signalman's lantern, swinging at the top of the hill, announced the start of the first bob. It hovered an instant on the brink, then plunged downward, "like lightening." As it shot past West Street doing two miles a minute (the reporter's estimate) signalmen announced its safety that far. Now the crowd could hear the whiz of its runners and the captain's shout: "Lean!" as it flashed around a sharp turn.

Mayor Twiss of Ilion was standing importantly at the corner of Otsego Street. The coaster swung wide and for an instant tragedy loomed. But the Mayor, who was an agile politician, leaped into the air like an adagio dancer. The bob shot under him and he landed on the last crewman, rolling him into a snow bank. The only casualty was the Mayor's high silk hat.

Two thousand people often gathered to watch the sport. The lights, icing the course, teams to pull the sleds up hill, and signalmen were paid for by subscription of the leading citizens. Total cost for one evening—sixteen dollars.

In addition to those purely American amusements, an unusual international flavor was given the town by the delegations of foreign dignitaries who came to see the great Armory on which their countries depended for defense, or stayed to inspect the guns before acceptance. There were Frenchmen and Danes, Spanish cavaliers and ancient Chinese gentlemen in brocaded gowns. For a while, Ilion was almost as cosmopolitan as Cairo.

The boom went into high gear in 1870, when the Remingtons greatly enlarged the Armory. Numerous buildings were erected, and by the end of that year, there were nearly fifteen acres of floor space available. According to the *Iron Age* "Every feature of construction has here subsidized all that scientific and mechanical achievement can attain."

What the *Iron Age* refers to as "extraordinary results, results absolutely unique in the history of manufacture," were due to Philo Remington's engineering of the Armory and its production lines. In this he was aided by J. M. Clough, superintendent of the Manufacturing Department, and irascible old John F. Thomas, who still commanded the machine and repair shop with the ruthless drive and picturesque profanity of a Yankee skipper.

An example of the efficiency of the Remington Armory was the rolling mill where each of four furnaces turned out three hundred and fifty rough barrels a day at the hands of *only four men.* It took four hundred milling machines to finish the resultant output. The production per man at the Remington Armory exceeded that of any other firearms manufacturer in the world.

The Remingtons continued to operate under the contractor system. There were over thirty contractors now, and, at the peak of employment, fourteen hundred men worked under them. The monthly payroll was $140,000. Both contractors and employees were extraordinarily loyal to the Remingtons. To quote the *Iron Age* for the last time: "The great Armory at Ilion is, in fact, but a great family—and this, indeed, may be truly enough said of the whole busy village, every citizen of which owns an interest, at least of good wishes, in the general prosperity."

The employees' devotion to the Remingtons was actively demonstrated at the time of the French contract. Production was raised from five hundred stand of arms a day to an average of one thousand. But this was not enough. To meet the deadline set by the contract, the whole great organization turned to and performed an industrial miracle. For the fifteen final days they brought production up to 1,300 per day, and on each of the last three days they produced 1,530 guns.

As the Armory grew, the town grew up around it. From about two thousand people in 1860, the population increased to 2,876 in 1870 and four thousand in 1876. Besides, many workers commuted on foot or by boat and horse-drawn bus from Herkimer, Mohawk and Frankfort. To speed them back and forth the Frankfort and Ilion Street Railroad was incorporated in 1871, under the presidency of the Honorable A. C. McGowan. The first horse car, decorated with bunting and

American flags and loaded to the roof with leading citizens, rolled sedately up the tracks on July fourth of that year. In 1872, a steam trolley car, invented and built at Remington Brothers Agricultural Works, was substituted for horses. Of this short-lived adventure in transportation a contemporary account says, "It weighed about eight thousand pounds. The speed was all that could be required; the engine was very compact and not very noisy."

Perhaps the greatest civic improvement of the boom was contributed by Doctor Hamlin B. Maben, a fine-looking man with a cascade of curly whiskers and the alert eyes of a fox terrier. Maben decided that Ilion needed an opera house. At a cost of twenty thousand dollars he built a splendid theater to seat one thousand people. It was furnished with dressing rooms and the last word in scene-shifting devices. Maben's Opera House was completed in 1870, and attracted some of the most famous artists of the era. Among those who instructed or entertained the Ilionites from its elegant stage were Julia Ward Howe, Henry Ward Beecher, Mrs. Siddons, Queen of Tragedy; Hi Henry's Minstrel Show, the Fisk Jubilee Singers, Naughty Eva Tanguay, and Montgomery and Stone. Here also, as a momentous anticlimax, was shown the first movie seen in Ilion.

A less happy contribution to the architectural embellishment of Ilion was made by Philo Remington. Philo loved his little, red, frame cottage on Otsego Street. Though he had become a millionaire, he had absolutely no desire to dwell in marble halls—neither had Mrs. Remington. But people got after him to build a suitable residence. They pointed out that it was not proper or fitting for the president of the great Remington Armory to live in a cottage. What would the high muck-a-mucks from Europe, who were beginning to visit Ilion, think? To say nothing of where they would stay! The Osgood Hotel was a very comfortable caravansery for so small a town, but it was not at all the place to put even a middling muck-a-muck.

Philo yielded reluctantly to persuasion. But having agreed, he went at it on the Remington principal that if you did a thing at all, you did it amain. Unfortunately, his taste in architecture was not equal to his skill in industrial design. He placed himself in the hands of builders who designed for him what in heraldic terms might be called a castle rampant.

A monstrosity of pink and gray sandstone, which looked like strawberry ice cream, sprouted on Armory Hill. Its turrets and towers and ornate oriels were scrambled in reckless profusion. The porte-cochere was as massive as the main entrance of the Louvre, the fretwork as intricate as an Arabian mosque. Its grounds, enclosed by an iron picket fence, were elaborate with bright, formal flower beds, and gravel walks, centered on a large terraced fountain.

The interior was as handsome as money could make it. The halls were paneled in black walnut, and on the high ceilings were colored frescoes of fat cherubs and ample ladies in Grecian draperies. On the top floor was a ballroom all aglitter with crystal chandeliers and mirrored walls. This was reached by the grand staircase, which swept magnificently upward from the central hall and was embellished by a full suit of medieval armor at the first turn.

Inevitably, there was a music room with a grand piano and a Swiss music box, and a Turkish corner, where dim lights and rug-draped divans lent a deliciously Oriental atmosphere. The pride of the house was the Blue Parlor, the walls of which were sheathed in blue brocade with heavy satin draperies to match. Its floor was covered with a carpet of rose and cream on which stood a wilderness of gold chairs, sofas, fat hassocks and love seats.

Philo Remington moved into his palatial quarters in 1870. But neither the luxury of his surroundings nor the presence of an entourage of servants could affect his simple way of living. Every morning, dressed in formal broadcloth, with high silk hat and flowing cape like his father before him, Philo strode through the grounds and down the hill to his stuffy little office at the Armory. And every evening, when he had finished his ample five-o'clock dinner, he went early to bed. On all but special nights, when distinguished guests were being entertained, the lights went out at nine o'clock.

Even when European nobility were invited for dinner and the long table glittered with silver and crystal under pink-shaded candles, Philo abated not his stern moral principles. The unhappy Latins toasted their host and the success of their great ventures in lemonade.

The very apex of boom and glitter was the Spanish Ball given in honor of the Spanish Commission who had lived in Ilion while their huge contract was being completed. The gentlemen from Spain had endeared themselves to the Ilionites by a combination of courtly man-ners, good fellowship and a genuine enjoyment of American ways. Nor were the citizens ungrateful for the prosperity they had brought.

The *Herkimer Democrat* for December 9, 1874, announced, "A Grand reception and ball will be given to the Spanish Ordnance Commission by the gentlemen of Ilion at Maben's Opera House on the 18th Instant."

No expense or effort was spared to make the ball the most elegant ever seen in the Mohawk Valley. John Schmidt went all the way to New York to induce Pat Gilmore and his 22nd Regiment Band to come up and play. Gilmore was the Sousa of his day.

On the night of the ball the hall was decorated with massed Spanish and American flags. On the stage were Pat Gilmore and his men in brilliant uniforms, brass horns and silver cornets glittered in the gaslight as they blared out lively polkas and the new Strauss waltzes. The Spanish Commission, headed by Colonel Bermudez and Major Sanchez, were loaded with gold braid and adorned with rows of jeweled decorations, and the dark, vivid beauty of their ladies was framed in elaborate ball gowns straight from M. Worth of Paris.

The *Herkimer Democrat* describes "Senora Bermudez carrying a bouquet of pink and white camelias, a Mrs. Moore in red velvet with a high bustle accompanied by her little son in a black velvet suit with a deep lace collar, Mrs. Seward Merry in light blue satin with hair piled high, and Mrs. Charles Crandall in black and white grenadine.

"The whole affair was a combination of beauty, pleasure, music, mirth, fashion, fancy, and rare social enjoyment. . . ."

Even the *New York Graphic* was impressed. It opined that "It is a question whether the famed Brussels Ball, given on the eve of the Battle of Waterloo, excelled the Spanish Ball, except the former had the good fortune to be immortalized by one of England's greatest poets."

On the other hand, the Spanish Ball had the good fortune to take place ten years before the Remingtons met *their* Waterloo.

## Chapter 22

# *Buffalo Guns*

The Remington brothers, like Marcellus Hartley and those who have followed them, were well aware that the solid basis of their business should be the demand of sportsmen for their product. Accordingly, they consistently made strenuous efforts to capture this market. Sporting guns listed in Remington catalogues of the 1870s include the previously mentioned Beals revolving rifle of 1866; Beals sporting breechloader (1867) in which the barrel slid forward to open the breech; a cheap, single-barrel breech-loading shotgun which sold for $8.00, in 1870; and the beautiful breech-loading, double-barrel shotgun issued in 1873. The latter was the first American breechloader to challenge the supremacy of fine European shotguns, which held a monopoly of the American market. The plainest model of this gun sold for $45.00 compared to $125.00 for the lowest-priced foreign guns to which it was greatly superior.

However, the main reliance of the Remingtons was the rolling Block Sporting Rifle. Model No. 1 was issued in 1866. It was the most accurate single-shot sporting rifle of its day, and was soon extremely popular. For seven years Remington was supreme in this field; then the advantage was wrested from them by B. Tyler Henry's invention of the Winchester '73.

The Winchester '73 was a lever-action repeating rifle, the tubular magazine of which held fifteen shots. It was adapted from the repeating rifle invented by Henry for Oliver Winchester's New Haven Arms Company in 1860. Henry further improved this gun in 1866 and it became the first rifle made by the new Winchester Repeating Arms Company. The model of 1866 fired a .44 caliber bullet with a 28-grain, rimfire cartridge. The load was too light and, in consequence, the range too short for practical purposes.

In 1873, Henry produced his great gun. The principal improvement over the model of 1866 was its adaptation to the 44-40 centerfire Berdan cartridge. William G. Thomas of U.M.C. developed the cartridge with Colt that same year. He worked with Henry in adapting the gun to the cartridge. This was a brilliant conception on Henry's part, for it meant that the men who were winning the West needed only one type of ammunition for their revolvers and rifles.

Though the Winchester '73 achieved such a brilliant success, it could not compete with Remington in two important fields—big-game hunting and target shooting. For both of these sports, accuracy and range were more important than rapid fire. The Remington .50 caliber rifle with its load of 70 grains of powder outranged the Winchester by 50 per cent and was far more accurate. The later Remington buffalo gun, which fired a 44-90 cartridge with a bullet weighing 400 grains, was even better for stopping a charging buffalo.

The most interesting tribute to the virtues of the Remington as a big-game rifle came from no less a person than General George A. Custer. In 1872, having seen a consignment of Rolling Block rifles sent out by the Government to be tested by troops in the field, he ordered a beautiful sporting rifle of the finest (F) grade for which he paid $91.50. There was probably no better judge of a sporting rifle than the young general, who was a dead shot. That he felt he got his money's worth is proved by a letter he wrote to the Remingtons:

> Headquarters Fort Abraham Lincoln, D. T.
>
> October 5, 1873.
>
> MESSRS. REMINGTON & SONS:
>
> Dear Sirs—Last year I ordered from your firm a Sporting Rifle, caliber .50. I received the rifle a short time prior to the departure of the Yellowstone Expedition. The Expedition left Fort Rice the 20th of June, 1873, and returned to Fort Abraham

Lincoln, September 21, 1873. During the period of three months I carried the rifle referred to on every occasion and the following list exhibits but a portion of the game killed by me: Antelope 41; buffalo 4; elk 4; blacktail deer 4; American deer 3; white wolf 2; geese, prairie chickens and other feathered game in large numbers.

The number of animals killed is not so remarkable as the distance at which the shots were executed. The average distance at which the forty-one antelopes were killed was 250 yards by actual measurement. I rarely obtained a shot at an antelope under 150 yards, while the range extended from that distance up to 630 yards.

With the expedition were professional hunters employed by the Government to obtain game for the troops. Many of the officers and men also were excellent shots, and participated extensively in hunting along the line of march. I was the only person who used one of your Rifles, which, as may properly be stated, there were pitted against it breech-loading rifles of almost every description, including many of the Springfield breechloaders altered to Sporting Rifles. With your Rifle I killed far more game than any other single party, professional or amateur, while the shots made with your rifle were at longer range and more difficult shots than were those made by any other rifles in the command. I am more than ever impressed with the many superior qualities possessed by the system of arms manufactured by your firm, and I believe I am safe in asserting that to a great extent this opinion is largely shared by the members of the Yellowstone Expedition who had the opportunity to make practical tests of the question.

I am truly yours,

*G. A. Custer*

BREVET MAJOR GENERAL U. S. ARMY

Dashing General Custer of the golden curls and curly mustache and fierce blue eyes was possibly a better shot than a tactician. But though his impetuosity led him into the Indian trap on the Little Big Horn on June 25, 1876, the fatal massacre was not all his doing. His troops were still armed with converted Springfields using inferior ammunition which tended to swell and stick in the chambers, thus drastically slowing the rate of fire, while many of the circling Indians, who had bought their weapons from unscrupulous smugglers, were using Sharps, Winchester '73s and Remingtons. Had Custer's men been as well armed, they might well have stood off the attack until the relief column arrived on the scene late that afternoon.

The states east of the Mississippi were becoming thickly settled. Most people lacked the opportunity of their forebears to vary their diet by their prowess with rifle and shotgun. But if they no longer brought home the bear, Americans had not lost their appetite for the tangy taste of game. Indeed, one course of virtually every fashionable dinner was some form of game, with canvasback duck ranking as the greatest delicacy of all. This state of affairs produced the market hunter, a man who earned his living by shooting for profit. Since the north woods were still full of deer, and wild ducks rafted on the Chesapeake in almost their old-time millions, such pursuit could be a very good living indeed.

The market hunters played a great part in dangerously reducing American wildlife. Some of them followed methods that sicken us at the thought of the butchery involved, such as firing into rafting ducks with scatter guns that resembled small cannons.

On the other hand, the best of them scorned such methods, hunting cleanly for sport as well as profit. Many a young man, with his gun, earned the capital to venture in a small business; and others put themselves through college by their prowess in the hunting field. One of the latter was W. H. Foster, who became the editor of *National Sportsman* and *Hunting and Fishing*. He is known as "the father of skeet."

For such as these the new Remington guns were a great boon. Rolling Block sporting rifles were produced in numerous models and calibers designed for every form of game; and the beautifully made yet inexpensive breech-loading shotguns were ideal for wing-shooting. It was not at all uncommon for a good shot to bag 200 duck in a day; and Fred Kimble records that after he switched to a double-barrel breechloader, he once brought down 120 blue teal in 120 minutes.

The elite of all market hunters were the "buff runners." Although the slaughter of the vast herds of buffalo, estimated to number over ten million, that wandered over the grass ocean of the plains is sentimentally considered a sin and a shame, it was once regarded as a legitimate business and a public service. The business lay in supplying the market with buffalo skins and buffalo meat, while the public service consisted of depriving the savage Sioux, Cheyennes and Arapahoes of their mobile rations.

Though the destruction of the buffalo was never an officially announced policy, the Army felt so strongly that the Indians could never be confined to their reservations as long as the raiding parties, which swept out of the untamed hills to storm the wagon trains and massacre settlers in lonely cabins, were able to provision themselves on buffalo meat, that they gladly supplied the professional buffalo hunters with free cartridges.

Sentiment aside, the buffalo and civilization were absolutely incompatible. There was no way on earth to confine those shaggy survivals of the ice age to a range. Even if it had been possible to build a gigantic fence around, say, a thousand-mile-square reservation, the first stampede would have gone through it easily. Just as the great forests of the East were leveled by the scythe of civilization, so the buffalo had to be sacrificed if the West were to be settled.

"Running buffs" had the same adventurous appeal to the young men of the 70s as aviation does today, and the professional buffalo hunters were blood brothers of the boys who manned the Air Force and went on to pioneer the air lines of the world. It was also a very good living. The hides brought two or three dollars apiece according to the market. Extra fine ones, called "silks," were worth fifty dollars. Buffalo tongue was always a high-priced delicacy and the meat also could be sold. A good hunter might gross ten thousand dollars in a season.

But he needed a bit of capital to get started. First the hunter hired a cook and a couple of skinners—he lost caste if he wielded the knife himself. They traveled in a covered wagon on wheels with a nine-inch tread, pulled by a twelve-mule team. In this the hides were taken back to market. Another item was a good buffalo pony, worth from $250 to $500. Most important of all was the hunter's gun.

The Indians and the amateurs hunted buffalo by galloping alongside a stampeding herd, shooting wildly into the tossing sea of bodies. For such close work a Winchester '73, or even a bow and arrow, was adequate. But the professional hunters scorned such haphazard tactics. Their method was to stalk a herd, and pick the individuals off at so long a range that the report of the gun would not stampede them. And every shot had to be a kill. For that a man needed accuracy.

Though all sorts of guns were used from flintlocks to Sharps and Army Springfields, the acknowledged tops was the Remington. It was not only the longest ranged and the most accurate, but it could be fired almost as rapidly as a repeater. This was not important in the actual hunt, but it could mean the difference between life and death if a band of Apaches, who hated the buffalo hunters worse than they did the United States Cavalry, suddenly swooped down on a lonely hunter. The buffalo runners were so acutely aware of this occupational hazard, that they always carried a small glass tube of poison, fitted into a brass cartridge case, so that in the last resort they might escape the torture that inevitably followed capture.

Brazos Bob McRae, the greatest buff runner of them all, was a Remington man. His favorite rifle was a 44-90-400 Remington on which was mounted a Malcolm telescopic sight with plain cross hairs. With that gun McRae did some miraculous shooting.

On one occasion, he came upon a stand of fifty-four buffalo, quietly grazing on his favorite hunting grounds along the Brazos River. Taking cover behind the low rolling hills, McRae rode to within three hundred yards of the herd. There he set up the rest of crossed sticks that he used, and sighted his rifle as methodically as a crack shot on the Creedmore Range. The neck or the heart of the beast was his target, for no place else would produce a clean kill.

McRae fired just fifty-four shots, and killed fifty-four buffalo.

A peril less frequent but more terrifying than Indians was to be caught dismounted by a stampeding herd. One fine summer morning in 1873, Frank H. Mayer, an experienced buff runner, was loafing in camp, stretched out flat on his back. Lazily he noticed a humming in the ground. He lay there thinking about it for a little, then got to his feet to have a look around. The gentle swells of the prairie rolled toward the horizon as empty as a landscape on the moon and as silent as the day before creation.

But when he lay down again the rumbling was ominously louder. Frank put his ear to the ground and the sound was like thunder. He jumped up yelling to his men that a buffalo herd was coming their way. They swung the two wagons broadside on to make a flimsy barricade and crouched behind them—six men, all of them armed.

The stampede poured over the knoll in front of them, a roaring torrent of hairy brown bodies and wild-eyed, bearded heads. They flowed over the hill and down the slope like the bore of a flood when a great dam goes, and the thunder of hooves was like an earthquake in hell.

"Shoot into the middle and pick your buffs!" Frank yelled.

They fired and fired again. Through the swirling smoke, they saw the herd split in two, streaming to right and left of their barricade, and running together behind it so that their refuge was an island in the tempestuous flood. With the gun barrels burning their hands they poured in the fire, aiming always at the point where the tossing torrent parted as though split by an invisible prow.

When that frantic five minutes was over and the smoke blew down the plains, they stared dumbfounded at the instrument of their salvation. It was not fear of their guns that had split the herd—nothing will turn a stampeding buffalo—it was that they had built for themselves an impassable dam of dead animals, bodies piled on bodies until not even the mighty mass of five thousand charging buffalo could break it down.

When they went out to examine the kill, they found that thirty of the dead buffalo were rare "silks." Frank Mayer was in luck that day.

# Chapter 23

# Target Rifles

Shooting matches in America go way back into the morning mists of our history. Probably the Pilgrims indulged in them when they had any extra powder. The first rifle clubs came with the first rifles. The Swiss and German immigrants brought them over along with the heavy Jaeger rifles, which they evolved into the Kentucky rifle. Their clubs set the pattern for those of today.

As more and more Americans got hold of the straight-shooting Kentuckies, the sport became increasingly popular. We have seen how the Remington Arms Company started in business at a shooting match.

A favorite sport of early times was "shooting for the beef." A slaughtered steer was contributed by the promoter of the match, and the young bloods—and old gaffers, too—who fancied themselves as marksmen, generally paid a fee of from two bits to a dollar to enter the match. They shot at targets, the usual distance being a hundred paces, which was about as far as the guns they used would shoot with any accuracy at all.

Excitement ran high as each man stepped forward to the impromptu butts, and with infinite care measured out the charge and rammed the bullet down the long barrel of his muzzle-loader—skill in loading was quite as important as ability to hold on the target. Then, as he raised his gun, the tension gathered over the crowd like an electric charge, and the deep silence was only broken by the stertorous breathing of the onlookers.

The boom of the gun released shouts or groans as all eyes peered through the billowing clouds of smoke to discern the result of the shot.

The winner was customarily awarded his choice of forequarters of the beef. Second place took the other forequarter, and the remainder of the animal was apportioned to the shooters in order of the choiceness of the cuts.

Shooting for the beef has survived up to the present time, though not for beef at current prices, but in the form of a turkey shoot. Originally such a match consisted of putting the bird in a protected crate with only his head showing. Small-caliber rifles were used and the man who succeeded in knocking off that agitated noggin took the turkey.

Nowadays turkey shoots are generally matches at trap or skeet with the bird going to the man with the highest score. In the Southern states, however, there is a variation of this game. There they shoot with shotguns at a target. The bull's-eye is a dot on the target no larger than the head of a pin, and the winner is he who places a pellet nearest to the mark. Since no amount of skill can control the pattern of shot, the result is mostly a matter of luck, and every participant has a chance to win.

When the forests crashed down before pioneer axes and big game took to the more inaccessible hills, rifle shooting in the eastern part of the country declined sadly. American marksmanship seems to have reached its all time low just before the Civil War. In that conflict the shooting on both sides was terrible. Northern statisticians figured that the Grand Army of the Republic had 999 misses for every hit, and the Confederates were only a shade better. General A. E. Burnside, who had been a gunsmith before he became a general, complained plaintively that out of ten men who knew the manual of arms only one knew what the sights were for.

The European armies of the era, who had been holding target practice ever since Captain Minié of the French Army invented the accurate, conical Minié ball in 1847, had a much better record than the Americans. Such deterioration from the skill of our Revolutionary forebears, who had beaten the British by sharpshooting, hurt American pride and shook our confidence. Young men, coming out of the Army decided that something must be done. Sparked by Colonel William C. Church, editor of the *Army and Navy Journal,* a group of them got together to form the National Rifle Association of America in 1871. General Burnside was its first president and Colonel (later General) George W. Wingate became secretary.

The objects of the new association were to stir up the Army brass to improve the shooting of the Regular Army; and to foster target shooting for sport among civilians, so that the next time the President had to call for volunteers a reasonable percentage of them would have the traditional American ability to shoot. For eighty-five years the National Rifle Association has successfully pursued those objectives.

By dint of excellent planning and a very lucky break, the association got off to a slambang start. Colonel Wingate, who was a go-getter, made a flying tour of British and European rifle clubs and came back crammed with information on rifles, ranges, targets and rules.

Since there was no regular rifle range in America, Wingate's first job on his return was to build one. A site was selected on Creed's Farm in the flat Long Island plain, a short distance from New York. The State Legislature appropriated money to buy the land; and the National Rifle Association and the cities of Brooklyn and New York put up five thousand dollars apiece to build the Creedmoor Range.

Because there was no book of instructions for neophyte marksmen, Wingate wrote a manual in his spare time. It was the first such book published in America, and was adopted by the United States Army as the standard textbook for marksmanship instruction.

Late in the autumn of 1873, officials of the National Rifle Association read a very interesting advertisement in the New York *Herald.* In it the Irish Rifle Team—which had just won, at Wimbledon, the Elcho Shield, symbolic of the championship of the British Isles—challenged "any American team" to shoot a match in 1874 for one hundred pounds a side. There were to be six men on a team and three rounds were to be shot at eight hundred, nine hundred and one thousand yards.

At first the National Rifle Association was decidedly miffed. They felt that it would be undignified to pick up a match from an advertisement—the challenge should have been formally addressed to them. The Irish had intended no disrespect, it was just that they had never heard of the N.R.A. However, the members of the association were real sports who would not take a dare. They satisfied dignity by having a subsidiary organization—the Amateur Rifle Club—pick up the gauntlet. The match was on.

It looked suicidal for the Americans. The Irish had made a clean sweep of the British Isles, Canada and Australia, winning by the highest score ever made at Wimbledon up to that time. There was nobody left to shoot against over there, so they sought a new world to conquer. They were armed with beautiful, muzzle-loading match rifles especially made by John Rigby, the famous Dublin gunsmith, who was a member of their team. The guns were equipped with vernier elevation sights and wind-gauge scales. The Irish were veterans of many years of practice at long-range shooting.

By contrast, the Americans were mere rookies. They had only owned a rifle range for two years; they had no special guns and those they did have were innocent of vernier scales and wind gauges. They had never shot at ranges over six hundred yards, and they had no money to buy expensive equipment. But they did have plenty of nerve.

Few people believed that a breechloader could be made that equaled a muzzle-loader for accuracy. But the National Rifle Association decided to stake all on the American breechloader. They asked for help from E. Remington & Sons and the Sharps Rifle Manufacturing Company of Hartford, Connecticut. Both companies accepted the challenge. With enlightened self-interest they agreed to make the guns free, and they even put up five hundred dollars to make up the American side of the stake.

Philo Remington turned over the business of designing the gun to L. L. Hepburn, foreman of his Mechanical Department. Hepburn was not only an inventor but a crack shot. Lacking a wind gauge for his gun, he would take a hammer and tap the front sight just the right amount askew to allow for windage. The gun Hepburn designed around the Rolling Block action was eventually recognized as the best target rifle in America. Remington named it the Creedmoor Rifle.

Sharps also turned out a superbly accurate gun, which some people thought equal to the Remington. Both guns were .44 caliber and fired a 550-grain bullet, slightly hardened. The load was 90 grains of black powder.

The guns were delivered early in March, 1874. Throughout that spring and summer the Amateur Riflemen shot and shot, contesting for the honor of representing America. The team that was finally chosen consisted of Lieutenant Henry Fulton, using a Remington; G. W. Yale (Sharps), Colonel John (Old Reliable) Bodine (Remington), Colonel H. A. Gildersleeve (Sharps), L. L. Hepburn (Remington), General J. S. Dakin (Sharps).

On the Irish Team were Doctor J. B. Hamilton, John Rigby, Captain Walker, James Wilson, J. K. Milner and Edmund Johnson.

The match was held on a hot and hazy September day. James Gordon Bennett had been beating the drums for it in the *Herald* since early spring, and a vast crowd turned out. They came in coaches-and-four, family surreys, smart tandems, tallyhos and sea-going hacks jammed with enthusiastic Irish immigrants. The Long Island Railroad was completely swamped.

All across the continent, so lately linked by rail and telegraph, crowds stood in front of the bulletin boards, watching the score, hoping against hope, though they knew the Americans would surely be beaten.

Even the appearance of the teams, as they took their places in the shooting stands, emphasized the amateurishness of the Americans. The Irish wore rough tweed hunting clothes and deerstalker caps, or the pith helmets suitable for safaris in savage lands. The Americans were dressed in somber business suits and derby hats or toppers.

The team captains tossed for choice of stands and the Irish won. They surprised everyone by choosing stands 16 and 17, which were considered less desirable than 19 and 20, which went to the Americans. No. 18 was left vacant to avoid confusion. The squads took their places, marked for them by red flags, facing an immense rectangle of shaven lawn. Eight hundred yards away the targets, backed by massive mounds of earth, shimmered in a mirage of heat waves.

The targets were the English standard of that era, measuring 12′ x 6′. The square black bull's-eye was 3′ x 3′, the "center" was 6′ x 6′. This left a space 6′ x 3′ on each side called an outer. A bull's-eye counted 4, a center 3 and an outer 2. Thus the highest possible score for a round of 15 shots was 60, and a perfect score for a team of six was 360.

Neither team was in any hurry to begin. They stalled around, loading and firing their guns, waiting for the other side to start shooting.

Captain Walker of the Irish Team, a strapping six-footer, began the match. He lay on his stomach on the grass, grasping his rifle in his left hand with both elbows resting on the ground. The great crowd behind the ropes was utterly silent while he took aim, and the tension built up as the long seconds ticked away. At last the shot rang out, and everyone strained his eyes at target 16. No marker rose against its face, the captain had made a clean miss.

Tension broke in a groan among the New York paddies, who had come to watch their champions, and a cheer from the American part of the crowd. Colonel Wingate hastily quelled the discourteous applause, which was not repeated. Captain Walker stood up and quietly reloaded.

While all the excitement was going on, Doctor Hamilton was aiming. As he fired, the white disk went up over the bull's-eye. Now it was the turn of the Irish to cheer, and Captain Leach, the Irish substitute, shushed them.

Lieutenant Fulton was the first American to fire. A tall, thin man in a blue serge suit, he was evidently a contortionist. He lay on his back with his legs crossed and his right ankle hooked over his left leg. Turning slightly to the right, he placed the butt of the gun on his right shoulder with the barrel clamped in the V formed by his legs. Then he passed his left hand behind his neck, grasped the butt of the gun and pressed it against his cheek. His right hand was free to pull the trigger. Though Fulton's stance looked peculiar, it must have been useful, for he scored five bull's-eyes and a center with his first six shots.

The shooting was superb. Doctor Hamilton scored 13 bull's-eyes out of 15 shots, and J. K. Milner of the Irish team made 11 straight bull's-eyes. Fulton and Hamilton made the highest scores, with 58 out of a possible 60. When the score was finally totaled for the first round it stood:

| | |
|---|---|
| AMERICA | 326 |
| IRELAND | 317 |
| AMERICA | +9 |

The news flew over the telegraph wires across the wheat fields and the grass, and along the frail, single line that crossed the empty desert and climbed the far wild passes of the Rockies. Following it, rolled a wave of cheering that started in the flat Long Island plain and smashed its final echoes against the hills of the Golden Gate.

But the match was far from over—the Americans were expected to do best at the shortest range. At 900 yards it was another story. The Irish picked up two points, the score for the round being:

| | |
|---|---|
| IRELAND | 312 |
| AMERICA | 310 |

But it was at this range that the Irish had the worst break of the day. J. K. Milner had been shooting superbly, though his position was the most peculiar of all. He lay on his back with the butt of his gun resting on his armpit and the muzzle held between his toes. In that position his area of vision was the slit between his feet. When Milner fired his first shot of the nine-hundred-yard round, the white disk went up to mark a bull's-eye—on the wrong target. The shot was scored zero.

At one thousand yards the Irish had all the best of it. A big cloud swept up the sky, shutting off the sun and giving the Irish the clear gray light to which they were accustomed. Taking advantage of the familiar conditions, they fired rapidly, scoring bull's-eyes at almost every shot. When they finished they were well ahead, but Lieutenant Fulton and Colonel Bodine each had three shots left to fire.

The news of this crisis threw Fulton into a mild spin. He only got three centers. After Bodine made two bull's-eyes the total scores stood Ireland 931, America 930. It all hung on the last shot.

Before firing, Bodine asked for a sip of ginger beer. As he was opening the bottle, it exploded in his hand, cutting him badly. The crowd gasped. Ladies in beribboned bonnets turned pale as the Colonel's gore flowed over his starched white cuffs. His teammates turned pale, too, for a miss would lose the match.

Bodine pulled a huge white linen handkerchief out of his pocket and wrapped it around his hand. Then he lay down to shoot.

For an eternity, he lay there squinting along the barrel of his Remington through his blue spectacles, while all those thousands of people stood so still that the hawks came down out of the sky to look them over. Then there was a sharp crack, a spurt of smoke from Old Reliable's gun. On target 19, the white disk rose to cover the bull's-eye.

Final score:

| | |
|---|---|
| AMERICA | 934 |
| IRELAND | 931 |
| AMERICA | +3 |

The match at Creedmoor was too close to be decisive. After all, if Milner had not shot at the wrong target, the Irish would have won by one point. But it did prove that American marksmen could hold their own against the best, and that American breechloaders were equal to the best muzzle-loaders Europe could produce. Incidentally, the trio of Remington marksmen outshot the three Sharps shooters in the famous match by a score of 478 to 456.

A few people disputed the breechloaders' claim, because Lieutenant Fulton, who made the highest score of the match—an amazing 171 out of a possible 180, with 36 bull's-eyes and nine centers—loaded his Remington as a muzzle-loader: that is he rammed the bullet down the bore and then slipped the rest of the cartridge into the breech in the usual manner. This point was settled when American and Irish rifle teams met again at Dollymount, Ireland, in 1875, and during America's Centennial Celebration in 1876. On both these occasions the Americans won handily, with Remington breechloaders making the highest scores of the matches.

These victories brought about the great renaissance of rifle shooting in America. Clubs were formed in many parts of the country, matches were arranged and eagerly contested. The Remingtons moved to encourage the sport in many ways, among them by instituting a series of matches for the Remington Diamond Badge, which became one of the most coveted decorations a marksman could wear on his shooting jacket.

The special guns, which Hepburn had designed for the American team were produced as a regular model by Remington later in 1874. The Creedmoor Rifle was a beautiful gun. It had a heavy octagon barrel, equipped with vernier sights and wind gauges. The first model had a straight grip and the butt was curved like a horned crescent to fit around the shoulder. Later models had a pistol grip and slightly curved heel plate. The Creedmoor fired a specially designed 44-90-550 cartridge with a swaged and patched bullet.

The Remington Creedmoor sold for $108. It was the favorite gun of American marksmen for nearly a quarter of a century.

## Chapter 24

# A Writing Machine

Philo Remington was always harassed by the chancy nature of the military arms business. Indeed, when he was at the very peak of prosperity, in 1873, with all his debts paid and several million dollars in the bank, he wanted to retire and have done with it all. The only thing that prevented was his sense of responsibility to the workers at the Armory and the citizens of Ilion. If he closed his great factory, the skilled gunsmiths would be thrown out of work, and the whole thriving town would be doomed to desuetude; while if he sold the company, he could not be sure that the new owners would carry on the tradition of integrity and quality for which the name of Remington had stood for over half a century. Reluctantly, he and his brothers decided to continue.

Meanwhile they tried energetically to diversify their business by means of the Remington Brothers Agricultural Works. During 1865 and 1866, the Agricultural Works had carried the Arms. Throughout those years the business of making farm machinery was very profitable, as the brothers had foreseen. Mowing machines, and the Sayre cultivators were its principal products, with plows and such a minor department. But as factories sprang up in the Middle West, the leverage of shipping rates caused the Remingtons' business to dwindle, and they were put to it to keep the great foundry fully employed. In this attempt they sank a great part of the profits of the Armory.

The search for diversity carried them into many curious corners of industry. They made everything from cotton gins to fire engines, and the steam trolley car already described. The great iron bridges across the Mohawk at Fort Herkimer and Mohawk as well as the eight-hundred-foot span across the river at Schenectady were made by Remington Brothers.

Like Marcellus Hartley, they plunged into the field of electricity, making dynamos and other heavy equipment. Ilion and Mohawk sparkled with hissing arclights, supplied by the lighting company they organized. But larger competitions bore down, as they had on Hartley, and there was no George Westinghouse to bail the Remingtons out.

They backed inventors right and left. There was a reversible mower, the offspring of one J. F. Crawford, on which they took a $350,000 loss. The Scattergood cotton gin also failed to make good. More profitable for a time was the horse-powered fire engine, designed to obviate the expense, delays and other disadvantages of the heavy steam pumpers of the period, which careened through the streets with red-hot hissing boilers leaving a trail of smoke and sparks in their wake.

When the Remington pumper arrived at a fire, the horses were unharnessed and rehitched to a sort of capstan that worked a geared pump. Then they were driven around and around the machine, which delivered so powerful a stream of water that it was all two men could do to hold the nozzle of the hose.

The Remington sewing machine was another venture that promised great things, and produced great losses, which were no fault of the machine. It all started when T. J. Jones, formerly of the Singer Sewing Machine Company, came to Philo and Eliphalet Remington with some new ideas which he had been unable to sell to Singer. The Remingtons investigated them carefully and decided that they had great merit. Enthused by the fact that the demand for sewing machines was steadily growing, the Remingtons organized for production by contracting for the rights to use the basic patents held by Singer and by purchasing machinery. Combining the original patents with those held by Jones, they succeeded in producing an excellent machine.

To make a good machine was something that Philo knew how to

do. To sell it was another matter. Both Philo and Eliphalet III were somber men with no talent or inclination for selling things. And Sam the Salesman was still in England.

Recognizing their deficiency, the brothers sought someone to market their sewing machine, and found him—to their sorrow—in the person of W. H. Hooper. Hooper was a good salesman, but a dreamer of grandiose dreams, who needed a firmer hand on his fantastic imagination than Philo and Eliphalet, in their ignorance of sales techniques, could give. He persuaded them to form a sales corporation called The Remington Sewing Machine Company of North America. A majority of the stock was subscribed for by the Remingtons, but in their enthusiasm they also persuaded various local businessmen to take large blocks of stock.

With a million dollars' worth of capital in his hands, Hooper went berserk, opening offices all over the country and equipping them as lavishly as though he had heard of Hollywood in the world of tomorrow. The capital was exhausted before the sales could be built up sufficiently to carry the top-heavy establishment. As the new company crashed into bankruptcy, Philo and Eliphalet made the quixotic gesture of returning the money of the other stockholders and shouldering the entire loss themselves. It amounted to more than a million dollars.

The Remington Sewing Machine remained; and a new agency, formed by a group of hardheaded local businessmen headed by Charles Harter, Addison Brill and John Hoefler, marketed it successfully. But this, too, was lost to the Remingtons in the final debacle.

Though misfortune pursued them and bad judgment combined with super-scrupulous integrity multiplied its effects, the Remington foresightedness made a contribution to progress that changed all business procedure and revolutionized the economic position of women, not only in America but throughout the world. They perfected, financed and marketed the first typewriter.

Ever since the days of Queen Anne, when one Henry Mill patented "An artificial machine or method for the impressing or transcribing of letters singly or progressively one after another as in writing," men had been trying to invent a machine that would write. During the first part of the nineteenth century a variety of machines were patented which would write after a fashion. But they were huge contraptions, Goldbergian in operation, and fantastic in appearance. Ely Beache's mechanical writer in 1850 looked like a merry-go-round; and Samuel W. Francis patented one in 1857, that resembled a spinet. None of these machines could even approach the speed of ordinary penmanship. However, something was evolving.

The first machine that would write faster than a man was invented by Christopher Latham Sholes who coined a name for it—"Type-Writer." Sholes was a printer and newspaper editor of Milwaukee, Wisconsin. With his ascetic face, all enhaloed by silky white hair and a fine flowing beard, and his twinkling blue eyes, he looked like a saint with a sense of humor. Actually, he was a most unworldly man who eventually sold his royalty rights in his great invention to his partner, James Densmore, for twelve thousand dollars. A few years later he observed, "I have been trying all my life to escape being a millionaire, and I seem to have succeeded admirably."

Sholes did not benefit much by the experience of his predecessors. Indeed, the only writing machine he had cognizance of was a thing called a "Pterotype," invented by John Pratt, in which the type was printed from a wheel. The Pterotype was the ancestor of the modern news ticker, but contributed nothing to Sholes' invention.

Though Sholes did not borrow from previous inventors, he had considerable help from his friends. Carlos Glidden and Samuel W. Soule worked with him on the early models, as did Charles Schwalback, a mechanic in Kleinstanber's machine shop where they were made. Charles E. Weller, a telegraph operator, tested the machines for him and offered expert advice; while James Densmore, an early enthusiast, encouraged, exhorted and drove him on when he was discouraged by unexpected difficulties. Sholes even got an assist from his friend, young Tom Edison, who made some very pertinent suggestions.

Sholes had started inventing in 1867, and on June 23, 1868, he patented his first machine. It was even cruder than some of its predecessors and would only write a few characters. His second model, patented a month later, was a weird contraption with a maze of wires worked by wooden levers like a carillon player. Another had the type arranged on little metal fans. When you pressed a key one of the fans moved in front of the slot, and a hammer gave it a sharp tap. Between 1868 and 1873, Sholes turned out twenty-five different models. Each time he finished one, he said the nineteenth-century equivalent of, "This is it!" And within a day or two had a better idea.

Though he did not know it at the time, his model of January, 1873, was his last. It actually looked like a typewriter, and embodied many of the basic principles of modern machines. These included placing the type-bars on arms which rose from a semicircular bed to strike the paper at a common point; the traveling carriage for spacing the letters; and a line-spacing device on the cylinder. However, it would only print capital letters.

Densmore and Sholes gave a lot of thought to the arrangement of the alphabet on the keyboard. A controlling factor was the fact that letters close together were apt to stick when struck in rapid succession—they still do sometimes. The inventors tried to arrange them so as to make this as unlikely as possible, and, at the same time, to make the keyboard convenient for the operator. They succeeded in designing the "universal keyboard," which, with some minor variations, has been used ever since.

When Charlie Weller tested the new machine, he found that he could type as fast as he could receive on a telegraph instrument, which was a lot faster than handwriting. On the strength of that, Densmore told Sholes to stop inventing. Then he sat down at the new machine and wrote a letter to Philo Remington. After that things happened fast.

On a dreary day early in February, 1873, young Henry Harper Benedict, three years out of Hamilton College and already rising fast in the Remington Company, strolled into the boss's office. Propped up on the mantelpiece stood a queer sort of letter—it looked as though the address had been printed.

"What on earth is that?" Benedict asked.

"It's a letter," said Philo Remington. "Read it."

Benedict read James Densmore's letter and looked up full of excitement. "Have you done anything about this, sir?" he asked.

Philo shook his head. "No. What do you think we ought to do?"

"Of course we want to see this machine!" Benedict exclaimed. "It's a wonderful invention, if it's anything at all. We certainly shouldn't neglect a chance to look it over."

So it happened that a few days later, Philo Remington met Densmore in a parlor of the Osgood Hotel. To advise him, Philo brought

Benedict; Jefferson M. Clough, Superintendent of the Armory; and William K. Jenne, Assistant Superintendent in charge of the Sewing Machine Department. Densmore had brought his friend, George Washington Newton Yost, a high-pressure salesman traveling in oil, to do the talking. "He is Aaron to my Moses," said Densmore.

The six men played with the machine for an hour and a half, taking turns at the keyboard, while Yost talked furiously and Densmore demonstrated how fast an expert could make it write. Jenne was so excited that the little brush of hair on his bald head stood straight up. Clough was disinterested; Benedict noncommittal.

As they left the parlor to go down to the dining room for lunch, Philo pulled his young assistant aside. "What do you think of it?" he asked in a low voice.

Benedict was fairly fizzing under his calm exterior. "It's a crude machine," he answered, "but there is an idea there that will revolutionize business."

"Do you think we ought to take it up?" Philo asked.

"We must on no account let it get away," Benedict answered. Then he added cannily, "It isn't necessary to tell these people that we're crazy over the invention, but I'm afraid I'm pretty nearly so."

Late that same afternoon, Philo signed a tentative agreement with Densmore, which developed into the contract that gave the typewriter to Remington.

The Sholes model was very crude, as Benedict had said; it was impossible to manufacture it commercially as it stood. Because of his interest in the invention and his experience with sewing machines, Jenne was given the task of perfecting the machine and redesigning it for large-scale production. He also designed the machines for manufacturing it. These were made at the Agricultural Works.

Jenne worked with amazing speed. Remington Type-Writer No. 1, the granddaddy of all typewriters, came out of the factory in September, 1873. Jenne, who could not get away from environmental influence, made his product look like a sewing machine. It was mounted on an iron stand with the familiar grapevine pattern of the pedestals, and it even had a foot treadle which was hitched to the carriage return by a wire. The type arms were concealed in an ornamental iron case which had to be opened every time they stuck.

The first catalogue makes a point of the domesticity of its design!

"The Type-Writer in size and appearance somewhat resembles the family sewing machine. It is graceful and ornamental—a beautiful piece of furniture for office, study or parlor."

That statement is open to serious question. Nevertheless, it was a good machine that fully lived up to the further claim of its advantages over pen-writing of: *Legibility, Rapidity, Ease, Convenience* and *Economy*. With remarkable prescience, one of the woodcut illustrations depicts a woman working the machine. Incidentally, the first year's production was eight machines.

Refinements of design soon did away with the stand and treadle, but it was not until 1878 that the shift key was invented by Lucien S. Crandall and Byron A. Brooks working under Jenne. Remington Model No. 2 printed capitals and lower case from the same keyboard.

Again the Remingtons triumphed over mechanical difficulties only to fail in salesmanship—it was high time Sam came home.

Densmore and Yost were the first selling agents. Densmore was an eccentric who lived on raw vegetables and thought on an astral plane. Yost, like the unfortunate Hooper, was a persuasive salesman with more imagination than horse sense. They were both unfitted to build a sales organization on sound principals. Soon they were in trouble.

However, the trouble was not all their fault—the typewriter met unexpected sales resistance. The public, usually avid for new inventions —having snapped up the sewing machine, the electric light and the telephone as a seal snaps at liver—turned a cold shoulder on the typewriter. One great trouble was its price. One hundred and twenty-five dollars seemed a lot to pay when you could buy a pen for a penny. Another difficulty was that it took a long time to train operators—to sell typewriters successfully you had to supply a girl with each machine. Still another obstacle was the unexpected resistance of many people to receiving letters they could read easily. In the upper levels of society it was considered not quite genteel, and the annoyance of lesser folk was expressed by a Kentucky mountaineer who replied to a typewritten letter with the indignant comment, "You don't need to print no letters for me. I kin read writin'."

On the other hand, the typewriter got a boost from one rather eminent source:

Hartford, March 19, 1875.

GENTLEMEN:

Please do not use my name in any way. Please do not even divulge the fact that I own a machine. I have entirely stopped using the Type-Writer, for the reason that I never could write a letter with it to anybody without receiving a request by return mail that I would not only describe the machine but state what progress I had made in the use of it, etc., etc. I don't like to write letters, and so I don't want people to know I own this curiosity breeding little joker.

Yours truly,
*Saml. L. Clemens*

Clemens was walking down a Boston street late in the autumn of 1874, with his fellow humorist, D. R. Locke (Petroleum V. Nasby), when he saw a typewriter in the window of a Remington store; and promptly forked out $125 for it. He got the hang of "this new-fangled writing machine" very quickly. In the first letter he wrote on it to his brother, Orien Clemens, he said:

THE MACHINE HAS SEVERAL VIRTUES. I BELIEVE IT WILL PRINT FASTER THAN I CAN WRITE. ONE MAY LEAN BACK IN HIS CHAIR AND WORK IT. IT PILES AN AWFUL STACK OF WORDS ON ONE PAGE. IT DON'T MUSS THINGS OR SCATTER INK BLOTS AROUND. OF COURSE IT SAVES PAPER.

Clemens was so enamoured of his machine that he hired an operator to type his next book on it. So the first typewritten manuscript ever delivered to a gratified publisher was:

LIFE ON THE MISSISSIPPI
BY
MARK TWAIN

As Densmore and Yost sank into debt, the senior partner prudently pulled out, and fell back on the royalties he had purchased from Sholes. His place was taken by Mark Twain's friend, D. R. Locke. Locke, Densmore and Yost also failed, and, in July, 1878, Remington gave the selling agency to Fairbanks and Company, the famous scale-makers. They did a little better with it, but their greatest contribution to the commercial success of the typewriter was to appoint Clarence Walker Seamens to manage the business.

Seamens had started work with Remington in 1869, when he was only fifteen years old. In 1876, he took off on a silver-mining venture in Utah, but in 1878, he was back in Ilion. When Fairbanks inquired for a man to manage their new agency, George Yost proposed Seamens.

Philo Remington snorted, "Nonsense, why the boy is only twenty-four."

But Henry Benedict thought that youth was not a fatal objection, and so advised Fairbanks.

In 1881, E. Remington and Sons decided to take over the selling agency themselves, retaining Seamens as Sales Manager. That year they sold twelve hundred typewriters. It did not seem good enough to Seamens. He believed that the surface of demand had not even been scratched, and he thought he knew how that fallow field should be plowed.

Henry Benedict, always an enthusiast, thought so, too, and they found another true believer in William Ozmun Wyckoff, a court reporter from Ithaca. Wyckoff was a giant of a man, with courage and drive to match his great frame. When Remington first began to make typewriters, Wyckoff secured the selling agency for Central New York. He put a machine in his office in Ithaca, but his staff refused to touch it.

"Use it or quit!" thundered Wyckoff.

The three young men scraped together all the capital they had or could borrow, and on August 1, 1882, founded the historic firm of Wyckoff, Seamens and Benedict. Again the men and the moment met. The world was ready to be convinced that it needed the typewriter, and Wyckoff, Seamens and Benedict set out to convince the world.

Their energy and vision were rewarded by immediate success. They started in one corner of Remington offices in New York with a staff consisting of a few clerks and two or three mechanics. Two years later they moved into a large office of their own at 339 Broadway, and that same year, 1884, opened a Paris office, and began the sales conquest of Europe.

In 1886, as the tide of success began to flood, the partners were shocked by a rumor that E. Remington & Sons was in serious trouble and negotiating to sell their typewriter business. Henry Benedict caught the first train to Ilion.

As he walked into Philo Remington's familiar office, Benedict was saddened by the appearance of his former employer and long-time friend. Remington's round face was sagging and creased with lines of care. His eyes burned with fanatic fire. He moved feebly forward to greet the younger man.

When they were seated, Benedict asked, "Is it true, Mr. Remington, that you are thinking of disposing of your typewriter interests?"

"That is true," said Remington heavily.

"But why do you do this?"

"We need the money."

Benedict hesitated slightly, before he said, "May I ask for what purpose?"

"To pay our debts," said Philo.

Then Benedict proved that he had the same high order of integrity as his mentor.

"Mr. Remington," he said, "I was with you for thirteen years, and served you to the best of my ability. I was absolutely loyal to you, and I am going to be loyal now. My advice to you is not to sell your typewriter. The amount of money you would get would not go far. Ninety percent of your creditors would go unpaid, and they will be after you more savagely if you pay the claims of others and leave theirs unsatisfied."

Philo Remington thought for a long time. He knew that Benedict spoke truly, as a loyal friend. He had seen the rising graph of typewriter sales. But it seemed to him that at all costs he must save the Arms. A respite of even a month or two might make the difference. If the new Turkish contract came through. . . .

"Well, we think we'd better sell," he said slowly.

"Is that your final decision?"

"Yes, I think so."

"Very well," said Benedict, briskly now that his honor was satisfied. *"Now I want to buy the business."*

So it was settled between them in an afternoon. Benedict telegraphed New York for a certified check for $10,000 to bind the bargain. He had purchased the Remington typewriter for $186,000. It would be worth almost that many millions.

## Chapter 25

# The Crisis

Even while E. Remington and Sons slid toward bankruptcy, they continued to make the finest guns they knew how. No matter how desperate their financial condition, they never debased the coinage of their product. The best steel was purchased for their barrels; the standards of skilled workmanship and careful inspection were never lowered. And they continued to encourage and assist young men with new ideas. Thus in the very last years of their management of the business, the Remingtons made a magnificent contribution to the gunsmith's craft.

James P. Lee was one of the most brilliant of all the inventors who worked at Remington. He had been employed by the Winchester Arms Company, for whom, in 1877, he developed a refinement of the lever-action repeater which replaced the Winchester '73. But when he wanted to work out his own ideas for a bolt-action magazine rifle, he came to Philo Remington, who gave him a workshop in the Armory and all the technical assistance he desired.

The result was the Remington-Lee bolt-action, box-magazine repeating rifle. The advantages of a box magazine over the tubular type were considerable, especially from a military point of view. Once the cartridges contained in it were exhausted, it took a long time to reload a tubular magazine, whereas a soldier could hang loaded box magazines all around his belt, and reload by simply pulling the empty magazine off and snapping in a fresh one. Lee patented his box magazine in 1879.

Remington began to manufacture the Remington-Lee rifle in 1880. Extensive use of the early models uncovered a structural weakness in the breech, which occasionally blew the bolt back into the face of the shooter with uniformly fatal results. As soon as this state of affairs became evident, Lee improved the design, and made it one of the safest guns in the world.

At last the Remingtons had a good repeater. In fact they had two, for in 1876, they had brought out the Keene repeater, invented by James W. Keene, as a sporting rifle. However, the Lee gun was so superior to the Keene that the latter was soon abandoned.

At first the Remingtons made the Remington-Lee for the Lee Arms Company, which the inventor organized as a selling agency. However, this did not work out, and in 1884, Lee entered into an agreement with Remington to manufacture and sell the gun on a royalty basis.

Philo and Eliphalet III had great hopes of repeating the brilliant success of the Rolling Block with the Lee, and they came close to being justified.

In accordance with his contract, Lee recovered the rights to his gun when E. Remington and Sons went into receivership. How right the brothers were to back it, and how near the Rem-Lee came to justifying their hopes is shown by the fact that shortly afterward the British adopted the Lee system. The English version was the famous Lee-Enfield Rifle, which, with some modifications, was the standard arm of British infantry for more than fifty years—even into World War II.

They tell a curious tale in Ilion concerning James P. Lee. In 1878 and 1879, he lived in a room at the Osgood Hotel, and frequently took his drawings and models home with him to work on at night. The room above his was engaged by a German mechanic who also worked for Remington. The oldsters say that the German bored a hole in the floor of his room, and spent long hours flat on his stomach with his eye glued to the hole watching what went on below. The name of this enterprising gentleman was Mauser.

That Peter Paul and Wilhelm Mauser, the brilliant inventors of the Mauser repeating rifle, which became the leading military arm of Europe, profited by their American brother's alleged activities at the

Osgood Hotel is questionable. Certainly the design of their bolt action was entirely their own, having been invented long before Lee ever came to Ilion. In fact, in the case of the lock, Lee may have learned from Mauser. However, Lee was unquestionably the first to conceive the idea of the box magazine, and Mauser rifles were not so equipped until 1886.

The history of Remington Arms is ironically entwined with that of the Mausers. It was Remingtons' salesman, Samuel Norris, who first backed the famous German brothers.

In the summer of 1867, Marshal Count Bylandt of the Austrian Empire showed his friend, Norris, a new bolt-action rifle, which had been invented by a pair of obscure gunsmiths named Mauser, working at the Royal Firearms Factory at Obendorf in the Duchy of Württemberg. Norris saw that here was another of those simple basic inventions that might change history. A turning motion of the bolt closed and locked the breech, while a cam simultaneously cocked the hammer.

Though he had a boil on his leg, Norris took a train to Stuttgart; and a stage to Obendorf, which had no railway. He found the Mausers working at their jobs in an ancient stone building which had been converted from an Augustine cloister to an armory. The brothers were terribly discouraged because the invention of which they had such great hopes had been turned down by Württemberg, Prussia and Austria.

Norris took them to his hotel room and drove a hard bargain. For the sum of eighty thousand francs payable over a period of ten years, he secured the services of the Mauser brothers, the rights to all their inventions, and the rights to *all future patents* that they might take out in that period. For the first two years the annual rate of payment was three thousand francs or about six hundred dollars. Norris thought he was pretty smart when he slipped in a joker that he could discontinue the payments and forfeit the contract at any time.

Though Norris was an employee of Remington, he took out the contract in his own name. Sam Remington never quite forgave him for that, and the result was disastrous.

Soon after signing the contract, Norris had the Mausers meet him at Luttich in Belgium, the center of European experiment in firearms. The original Mauser had been designed to fire the paper needle gun cartridge. In Luttich, they redesigned it to use the new Berdan center-fire metallic cartridge. Norris took the model and drawings, made by "my German boys," as he called them, to the United States. So it came about that the first patent on the Mauser rifle was granted in America on June 2, 1868.

In 1877, Samuel Remington decided to come home. Since the simple life in Ilion bored him greatly, he bought a house in New York and a country estate at Cazenovia, but he continued to handle the sales and business affairs of E. Remington and Sons.

For five years more the company continued on a fairly satisfactory basis. Then, in 1882, Samuel Remington died. He was the only one of the brothers who had inherited either the salesmanship or business ability of Eliphalet the Gunmaker. Without him the remaining brothers were lost.

Philo and Eliphalet III never spent much money on themselves, but they were prodigal of it where others were concerned. We have seen them assuming huge losses on behalf of their fellow investors. They also loaned large sums of money to their friends, which were never repaid. Philo yielded to the desperate plea of his friend, W. S. King of Minneapolis, for a large loan, at a time when his own company was beginning to feel the financial pinch. And the brothers gave money away with both hands. For example, Eliphalet III helped to found Syracuse University with a gift of five hundred thousand dollars. When adversity hit the Arms, they had already dissipated most of their personal fortunes.

The years from 1882 to 1886 were a period of steady drain on the resources of E. Remington and Sons. There were no more great contracts with foreign governments, and the sporting arms business did not appear to be sufficient to carry the huge Armory. It would have been enough if the brothers had cut expenses to the limit, as they should have done. But without Samuel to advise them, they lacked business accumen.

Philo and Eliphalet III reasoned that, should they close a large part of the Armory and dismiss most of their expert gunsmiths, they might be unable to handle a contract satisfactorily if it did come through. An even more compelling reason was their sense of responsibility toward their old employees. If these men were dismissed, there would be nowhere else for them to go. For the world was moving into a period of profound peace—indeed, many people doubted if there would ever again be a great war—and gunsmiths were a drug on the market.

So the Remingtons hung on, giving ground inch by inch as the pressure of debts increased, instead of retreating quickly to a tenable position. Theirs was a very human error, since all but the shrewdest men let hope tip the scales of judgment; but it was fatal.

Realizing their limitations and bewildered by the maze of debt into which they had stumbled, they entrusted their financial management to John Brown, who, less competent than they, led them in a kiting downhill race.

The winter of 1885-86 was the time of crisis. The smokeless chimneys of the Armory looked bleak against the sullen sky, and in the long, silent buildings, broken windows and peeling paint proclaimed the lack of funds for proper maintenance. At these indications of decay, the creditors redoubled their clamor.

Meanwhile, Philo was desperately put to it to raise enough actual cash just to keep the Armory in limited operation. But loyalty begets loyalty in return. The contractors, many of whom had become rich, lent their savings to keep the Arms going. As a final measure of desperation the Remingtons were reduced to paying wages, not in cash, but in script redeemable in goods at the stores in Ilion.

The typewriter money did not even last a month. At this point John J. Hannas came up with a scheme to obtain an extension of time. In persuance of it, the Remingtons conveyed a majority of their stock to a committee of Ilion businessmen composed of Albert N. Russell, Addison Brill and John L. McMillan. The committee was to manage the affairs of the company, while Hannas stood off the creditors. The regency lasted only a few days.

When Philo saw that nothing more could be done, he asked Justice Pardon C. Williams to appoint Brill and Russell temporary receivers in bankruptcy. Later this appointment was made permanent. Creditors were then restrained from further proceedings, and, after a careful survey of the condition of the company, the court ordered the receivers to operate the works and to make and execute contracts.

Thenceforward there was nothing left for the receivers but to execute such minor orders as might be secured, complete the work in progress and realize on what assets they could. For two years they labored before the tangled skein was sufficiently unraveled to make a sale possible.

Philo Remington was not embittered by adversity. Mr. Russell records that, "He cheerfully rendered the receivers all the aid in his power in their endeavors to administer the estate in the interests of the creditors and of the people with them, and for whom, he had labored so incessantly."

But his body was less enduring than his spirit. When the job was done, the sudden relaxation of strain affected him as a diver, too suddenly released from the pressure of deep water, is stricken. It was a case of psychological bends. In the winter of 1888-89, he went to Florida in the hope of regaining his health. At Silver Springs on April 4, 1889, his heart suddenly stopped beating. On January seventh of this same year, a child was born who was destined to play a most important role in the future affairs of Remington Arms Company. He was christened Charles Krum Davis.

Eliphalet III lived in seclusion to the great age of ninety-four.

At first glance, the affairs of E. Remington and Sons would not have seemed too desperate. The assets of the corporation, as shown by an inventory based on cost with liberal deductions for depreciation, were $1,711,783.94. Liabilities amounted to $1,255,703.27, about $450,000 of which was due for labor. This sum was another amazing proof of the loyalty of Remington employees. Happily, the receivers were able to pay the labor accounts in full.

Since the figures show an apparent surplus of $456,080.67, it would seem that all liabilities could have been met. But a large part of the Remington assets was machinery adapted only to the very specialized business of making guns. It was of value only to men equipped with the knowledge and ability to use it. In those years of profound peace, when the frontier had at last been pushed to the Pacific and the security of the United States was assumed by almost all Americans to be inviolate behind her ocean barriers, there were few men who dared assume the risk of operating so great an arsenal. For a time it looked as though those splendid machines would be broken up for scrap iron, and the buildings sold piecemeal or let fall into decay. How great a loss that might have been no one could then know.

Marcellus Hartley, with an assist from Thomas G. Bennett, son-in-law of Governor Oliver Winchester, saved Remington Arms. Certainly his motives were not philanthropic. He saw an opportunity to acquire an excellent adjunct for U.M.C., which needed sporting guns to help the sale of its cartridges. Hartley knew the value of Remingtons' physical assets, but even more important to him was the name which for seventy years had been the guaranty of fine workmanship and top quality in the making of guns. He knew that he could acquire these great assets for a fraction of their book value, and he was confident that he could operate the company on a profitable basis.

But sentiment does creep into the calculations of businessmen, and Marcellus Hartley had no lack of that quality. He hated to see an enterprise built up so hardily through the years be lost in oblivion—it seemed such an awful waste. Though Remington had been the most powerful competitor of Winchester Arms, Bennett was of like mind.

So they banded together in March, 1888, to purchase E. Remington and Sons with all its physical properties and—especially—its reputation intact. The price they paid was two hundred thousand dollars. Thus, instead of an end, there was a beginning of great things.

***Part* 3**

# Remington Arms—U. M. C.

## Chapter 26

# The Renaissance of Remington Arms

Marcellus Hartley's particular genius was in organization and business methods. No enterprise with which he was connected had haphazard management or loose financial ends. As soon as the purchase contract for E. Remington and Sons was signed, he moved to reorganize the business and put it on a sound financial basis.

The name of the reborn company was changed to the Remington Arms Company. Hartley became its president, Bennett was vice president. W. W. Reynolds, the "ballooning" salesman of U. M. C., was elected treasurer and Wilfred Hartley became secretary. So, from the first, the new management was preponderantly a Hartley affair. A few months later, Hartley and Graham bought Bennett out. Since Graham had become increasingly inactive in the affairs of the parent firm, Marcellus Hartley was now, in effect, the sole owner of Remington Arms.

The company did not lose its individuality. Hartley was not one for mergers; as long as he lived, his four companies, Hartley and Graham, U. M. C., the Bridgeport Gun Implement Company and Remington Arms remained separate entities. The Hartley enterprises were not an industrial empire, but an economic confederation.

What Hartley did along the line of consolidation was to merge the sales department of Remington Arms with the splendid organization which already handled U. M. C. ammunition on a world-wide basis. Thus, for the first time since the death of Samuel Remington, the products of the company were expertly marketed.

At Ilion, Hartley pushed the reorganization with his still youthful vigor. Buildings were refurbished, machinery repaired or replaced by more modern tools. The operations were consolidated on a more efficient basis. Most important of all, Hartley's spirit of enterprise replaced the uncertainty and discouragement that the workers had felt throughout the years of failing finances and receivership. The enormous vitality of the man seemed to flow down through all echelons of Remington workers.

True to his belief that the needs of sportsmen should be the fundamental basis of the business, Hartley put the strongest emphasis on this aspect of Remington production. The Creedmoor and sporting rifles, and Remington shotguns became the primary products of the factory. Hartley's great experience and wide connections in the sporting market enabled him to sell these guns on a greater scale than ever before.

The traditional Remington policy of encouraging inventors to use the facilities of the factory was continued. In 1892, young Arthur Savage came down from Utica to experiment with a lever-action repeater which employed a revolving box magazine, and had a new type of hammerless, enclosed-breech firing mechanism. When his gun was perfected, Savage formed his own company. From this early association with Arthur Savage, Remington has a certain satisfaction in knowing that the first of the splendid line of sporting rifles produced by the Savage Arms Company was perfected in their factory at Ilion.

In order to utilize the potential of the great Remington plant, Hartley began the manufacture of bicycles. At the peak of the cycling craze the Remington Bicycle established itself as a popular favorite. Hartley's merchandising methods included such modern techniques as giving large cash prizes which brought the leading cyclists of America to race at Chismore Park in Ilion; and holding popularity contests among the young ladies of the Mohawk Valley with a Remington lady's bicycle as first prize.

As new life flowed into Remington Arms, the town of Ilion revived from the drab misery which had been its lot. The factory, though still well below its former peak, employed five hundred workers. Steady production on a smaller scale was far better than the wild cyclical swings of the 70s. In addition, Wyckoff, Seamens and Benedict, who rented several Remington buildings in which to manufacture typewriters, were doing a fine business. In 1889, they purchased the Remington Agricultural Works on the north side of the Canal and added a fine seven-story brick building.

With typewriter money pouring in from all over the world, the firm was able to equip its new plant with the most modern machinery. Production was pushed up to one hundred typewriters a day and eight hundred men were on the payroll.

Thus Ilion was a happy town again. Above the agreeable rumble of machinery from its two great factories, sounded the tinkle of Remington bicycle bells and the ring of the warning bells on Remington typewriters racing to record the orders that poured in. Once again there was money to spare and the heart to enjoy the simple gaieties of dances, strawberry festivals and picnics. The Sunday bicycle ride was as much a part of life as the Sunday automobile ride is today. A popular weekday pastime for the ladies was to catch the eight-thirty A.M. Canal packet to Utica. Still drawn by its three-horse tandem hitch, it floated serenely along the narrow ribbon of water taking three hours to make the ten-mile trip. There would be three hours for shopping and lunch in the metropolis before the two-thirty boat brought them back in time to get a sumptuous six-o'clock dinner ready for their husbands.

Meanwhile the Union Metallic Cartridge Company at Bridgeport was a scene of tremendous technological activity as it prepared to cope with the first major change in the propellant behind the bullets that had taken place in the six hundred years since Roger Bacon blew his eyebrows off in his laboratory at Oxford—the invention of smokeless powder.

Back in 1845, Professor Christian Frederick Schoebein of the University of Bale, Switzerland, produced a terrible concoction of nitrated cotton which he named "guncotton." At about the same time, Professor Ascanio Subrero of Turin, Italy, came up with nitroglycerin. Both explosives had terrific force and fired cleanly without smoke. A new era of explosives seemed about to dawn; and factories were built in England, France, Germany, Russia and Austria. They all blew up. The new stuff was too sensitive to handle.

In 1863, Emanuel Nobel and his famous son, Alfred, figured out a way to put nitroglycerin in cans for "safe" shipment, and to fire it with a fulminate detonator. That seemed to work for a time until people got careless and Nobel's "Blasting Oil" began blowing up ships, trains and people all over the world. The climax came when Nobel's own factory in Germany went up.

Alfred Nobel went back to his laboratory and discovered a way to dampen down the sensitiveness of his product by mixing it with a kind of earth called "kieselguhr." In this form the stuff was as tractable as a pet lamb. You could throw it around, and even set fire to it, without an explosion. But a fulminate-of-mercury detonator would produce an explosion twenty times as powerful as black powder. Nobel called his invention, "dynamite."

Dynamite had a terrific impact on the world of the 70s. Characters in de Maupassant's short stories sit around discussing its philosophical implications in exactly the same terms as those in which we talk about the atom bomb today. But the fact of the matter was that, while dynamite was fine for blasting, it was not usable in firearms. It still fired too fast to be a good propellant, and the few dynamite guns that were invented were failures.

Paul Vieille, a French engineer, finally invented smokeless powder in 1885. It was a variation of the thoroughly domesticated pyroxylin plastic used in babies' rattles and dudes' high collars, which James Wesley Hyatt had invented in 1870, and called "celluloid." Vieille's "Poudre B," named after French General Boulanger, was celluloid with the formula varied and ethyl alcohol added, which gave it a kick like Paul Bunyan's mule.

Poudre B was a single-base powder. In 1888, Alfred Nobel came to the front with a violent combination of guncotton and nitroglycerin (a double-base powder) which he named "Ballistite." Both types have been used ever since.

The moment smokeless powder was invented every army in the world demanded it, for it improved the performance of rifles by as much as 75 per cent. Muzzle velocities jumped from a maximum of 1,500 feet per second to 2,500, and have increased. This flattened the trajectory and extended the range enormously. The new powder burned cleanly at any desired speed, leaving no residue to foul the barrel. Finally, the vast, billowing clouds of smoke that blinded the riflemen and betrayed their presence to the enemy, vanished from the battle picture.

However, all the military guns in the world had to be redesigned. Smokeless powder raised internal pressures from about 20,000 pounds per square inch to about 50,000. The old guns just would not take it. First in the field was Captain Nicholas Lebel of France. The bolt-action 8-mm. Lebel invented in 1886, made every other military rifle obsolescent. It became the standard arm of the French infantry, who used it through World War I. In fact, a great many French soldiers still used this arm in World War II.

The first American smokeless powder was produced by E. I. du Pont de Nemours and Company, which even then was the greatest powder-making company in the world. Working at the Du Pont laboratory at Carney's Point, New Jersey, Francis I. du Pont and his young cousin Pierre, who was just out of M.I.T., developed a new smokeless powder in 1893. This first American smokeless powder was designed for use in sporting shotguns.

Du Pont immediately sent its new powder to U.M.C. and to Winchester. At Bridgeport, U.M.C. Thomas accepted the challenge with alacrity. First the loads had to be calculated to what the current shotguns would stand—it was no use making shells that no one could shoot. Then the machinery for making the shells required revisions. Finally, since smokeless powder was far less sensitive than black powder, a new and faster primer had to be invented. For this, Thomas turned to Jerome Orcutt who designed it. The first U. M. C. smokeless powder shot shells were ready for the hunting season of 1894. And the famous Nitro Shell with the No. 3 Orcutt primer was produced in 1895.

From there Thomas went on to develop smokeless powder cartridges for the new sporting rifles that quickly came on the market. Not only the gun but the bullet had to be changed, for a lead slug propelled at the terrific new muzzle velocities would be stripped and emerge without the spinning motion so necessary to equilibrium in flight. Lebel's rifle used a bronze bullet, but this was quickly replaced by the jacketed bullet. For sporting purposes the jacketed bullet posed a problem. Instead of mushrooming when it struck, it went right through an animal. So the designers went to work and produced soft-point and hollow-point bullets. These were more effective and much more humane, for they dropped the game in its tracks instead of merely wounding it.

Thomas also designed the world's first smokeless-powder revolver cartridge for the Colt .45, and the popular Long Rifle .22 caliber for the J. Stevens Arms and Tool Company of Chicopee Falls, Massachusetts.

The Spanish American War did not last long enough to have any important effect on Remington and U. M. C. However, as usual, the Government called on Remington to supply rifles, while U. M. C. made cartridges for the Army and brass cases for the 6-inch shells with which Admiral Dewey's fleet won the battle of Manila Bay.

In 1892, the Army had adopted as its standard arm the Krag-Jorgenson rifle invented in Norway. Very few troops carried them in Cuba in 1898, but immediately after the war, the entire Regular Army was supplied with them. The American Rifle Team for the Palma Match held in England, in 1903, decided to use the Krag. U. M. C. Thomas designed a special match cartridge and bullet for them, which was far superior to the regular ammunition. Using the new bullet, the American Team won the match against teams from seven other nations.

In 1903, the Springfield Armory produced the Springfield 30-03. This was a splendid bolt-action repeater, described by many experts—foreign as well as American—as the best non-automatic military rifle ever made. It fired a 30 caliber, 220-grain, blunt-nose bullet. The cartridge was changed in 1906, to a 150-grain Spitzer bullet—the 30-06.

U. M. C. made conventional cartridges for the Krag and both the Springfield 30-03 and 30-06. However, a group of young engineers under H. H. Pinney had recently come to U. M. C. With their slide rules and exact computations they decided that a better bullet could be made for sportsmen than those designed by rule-of-thumb methods of the older men, who wore high wing collars and derby hats even while sitting at their roll-top desks. The young engineers secretly started work on a bullet with a revolutionary pencil point. The experts held that such a bullet would be sure to "keyhole" (turn end over end), but when Pinney tested it on his new one-thousand-yard range, it outperformed any other bullet theretofore made.

Performance was one thing, but getting Thomas to accept it was another. That required tact. Pinney took the new bullet to his superior and said, "Mr. Thomas, will you test this for me? You know so much more about these things than I do."

Thomas took the bullet to the range. He came back with a glint in his eye, for he knew a good thing when he saw it. "This is fine," he said, "but it will be better if you slim it down a little near the point."

Pinney waited the four or five hours it would normally take to make the change. Then he brought the *same bullet* back to Thomas. This time the older man was really enthusiastic. "It's great," he said. "Now, Mr. Pinney, what are we going to call it?"

Pinney had an inspiration. "The Thomas Bullet," he said.

Old U.M.C. grabbed his hat. "I'm taking this straight to Camp Perry for the Government to test!"

So the first American sharp-pointed bullet was invented at U.M.C. The American Rifle Team used it in the Palma Match of 1907 at Ottawa, and again they won. Sharp-pointed bullets became standard for target shooting.

It is an interesting side light on history that, with all the great contributions which U.M.C. Thomas made to his craft, the one that was named for him was the one he did not invent.

Chapter 27

# The Boy President

Throughout the last decade of the nineteenth century, Marcellus Hartley continued to expand his interests; he was not a man who could stand still. His own companies were firmly established, so he took an increasing interest in the affairs of other great corporations. He had the ability to take in a proposition almost at a glance and say decisively, "This will work." Or, "It won't work."

He was idealistic in his own conduct, but he had a realistic approach to business. On one occasion a young clerk in Hartley and Graham started a letter to a dealer, who had treated the firm unfairly, with the words, "We are surprised at the position you take."

"Don't write that, young man," Hartley said, "and as long as you are in my employ, don't allow yourself to be surprised at anything. Just take people as you find them. Remember you are not surprised now; they have done just what you would expect rascals would do."

An honest man who cannot be surprised by ill fortune or rascality is an invaluable asset to any business. A great many companies wanted the benefit of Hartley's advice, and he went on the boards of such corporations as the Manhattan Railroad, the Western, Lincoln and German-American banks, the Mercantile and Fifth Avenue Trust companies, the American District Telegraph Company, the American Surety Company, and he founded the International Banking Corporation, which later became the Foreign Department of the National City Bank. He was on the powerful Finance Committee of the Equitable Life Assurance Society, where he wielded a considerable influence in building it to greatness.

Henry B. Hyde, the famous president of Equitable, was one of Hartley's closest friends. They made a sharply contrasting pair. Hyde was a two-hundred-pounder, standing six feet two in his silk socks; Hartley was one hundred and thirty pounds of vibrant energy. Hyde would often point to his friend and say, "I let that little fellow boss me."

In addition to his business interests, Hartley took part in many charitable activities, among them the founding of a settlement house on West Forty-sixth Street, New York, in memory of his father and his daughter, Grace Hartley Stokes, who had died some years before. Hartley House was opened in 1897 under the auspices of the Association for Improving the Condition of the Poor. The family has maintained it ever since, and today it is busier than ever, a gay place where neighborhood children play in the pleasant gardens or the recreation rooms, and read or study in the excellent library.

One of Marcellus Hartley's most important service to the city was in connection with the *New York Times*. The *Times* was in a bad way in 1896 as the sensation-mongering papers of the era cut into its circulation. In March of that year it was thrown into receivership. The way things looked, the *Times* would either have to lower its standards or fold up.

One day Marcellus Hartley was sitting behind his desk in his office at 315 Broadway when his secretary announced, "A gentleman from Chattanooga wishes to see you, sir."

"I have three engagements," Hartley said, "and cannot possibly see him. What does he want to see me about?"

"He wants to buy the *New York Times,"* was the answer.

After further pleading that it was out of the question for him to see him, his secretary said, "Mr. Hartley, I urge you to see this gentleman." The visitor from Tennessee turned out to be a man of medium height, with closely cut hair and penetrating eyes. He impressed his hearers with the soundness of his ideas and his ability to successfully carry them to fruition.

The Equitable Life Assurance Society at that time had so large an interest in the *New York Times* that it was essential to get their support to get control of the *Times*. Mr. Hartley was a member of the Finance Committee. As it turned out, Mr. Hartley not only saw Adolph S. Ochs, but was so fascinated with his plans, he missed all his meetings. "What do you propose to do with the *Times?*" asked Hartley.

"I want to make it as reliable a source of news as its great English namesake. Furthermore, I am sure I can make it pay. The people of New York deserve and will support a paper which will give them the news fearlessly and impartially."

Hartley asked Mr. Ochs what resources he had with which to acquire the paper. Mr. Ochs said he owned the Chattanooga *Times* and had some resources outside.

Mr. Hartley called up Hyde and told him of his interview with Mr. Ochs. Mr. Hyde said to Hartley, "We are representing widows and orphans, and with such limited resources, it is not possible to consider his proposal." Hartley asked Hyde to at least let Mr. Ochs talk with him. Ochs went to see Mr. Hyde and made a great impression on him. To make a long story short, the Equitable consented to assist in working out a plan to get control of the paper. The other stockholders were approached and controlling interest in the *New York Times* was placed in escrow. Ochs needed working capital and Hartley loaned him one hundred thousand dollars to assist him in carrying out his plans against stock pledged to secure the obligation. Over a period of years, Ochs acquired the stock set aside. What Adolph Ochs did with the *New York Times* is history.

Old age never caught up with Marcellus Hartley. Though his silky hair and beard turned frost-white, at seventy-five his small, spare body was full of youthful vigor, and his mind was as alert as when he had pitted it against the armament makers of Europe in the days of Abraham Lincoln.

He was hardly ever ill in his life. On the morning of January 8, 1902, he had a slight attack of indigestion, and stopped in to see his doctor, who pronounced him "as sound as a dollar."

"That's fine," said Marcellus. "Then I won't have to make my new will yet."

From there he went to his office. It was a routine day. At noon he attended a meeting of the Executive Committee of Equitable Life, and went on to lunch with his friend James W. Alexander. His first chore of the afternoon was a meeting of the Executive Committee of the American Surety Company.

Luncheon had been pleasantly prolonged, and when Hartley entered the walnut-panelled directors' room, his colleagues were already seated at the long table. He made the rounds, greeting them gaily; then took his accustomed place between his close friends, William A. Wheelock and R. A. C. Smith. They chatted a while longer, until the chairman called the meeting to order.

As the first of the reports was read, Smith noticed that Hartley's head was nodding. Other men might nap at board meetings and no notice would be taken, but Marcellus Hartley never!

Anxiously, Smith asked, "Don't you feel well, Marcellus? Are you faint?"

Hartley tried to answer but no words came. He fell forward with his head resting on his folded arms. Smith flung a protective arm around him, and Wheelock anxiously clasped his hand. So, within seconds, Marcellus Hartley died.

That day young Marcy Dodge, who was a junior at Columbia, was called from his classroom to the office of Dean Frederick P. Keppel. He could not remember having done anything to deserve such a summons, but it looked bad.

However, Dean Keppel was not angry. He put his arm around the young man's shoulders and said, "Marcellus, your grandfather has been taken ill. I think I will go home with you."

Even though no more was said on the long trip downtown, Marcy knew that his grandfather was dead. When he reached the big brownstone house at 232 Madison Avenue, where he had always lived, his suspicion was sadly confirmed. It was far more of a blow to him than would ordinarily be the case. His father had wisely decided to let the grandfather and grandmother bring up his motherless son. So Marcellus Hartley had been for him the source of all strength, protection and love. Quite suddenly Marcy became the one who must protect and counsel. For he was Marcellus Hartley's only living grandson, the head of the family.

Twenty-year-old Marcellus Hartley Dodge was almost a replica of his grandfather as a youth. He had the same slight frame, and the same nervous energy. Though he lacked the decisive judgment that hard experience had given Marcellus Hartley, he possssed the older man's strength of character, integrity and, especially, his warmth of heart.

The burdens that fell on his inexperienced shoulders were crushing. In addition to the four companies, which he owned and managed, Marcellus Hartley had the interests previously mentioned in other concerns. Marcy did not inherit all these investments immediately, though his grandfather had had the greatest love for him, and believed in him. Marcellus Hartley was too vital a man to give much thought to dying. He left an old will, which split his estate up into shares. Marcy inherited one sixth, the rest being divided between Hartley's widow, the other heirs of Grace Hartley Stokes, and his surviving daughter, Helen Hartley Jenkins, whose husband, George W. Jenkins, for a time played an important role in the management of the Hartley interests.

However, Marcy's grandmother and aunt regarded him as the head of the family and had full confidence in him. Through their generosity, he soon acquired a half interest in the Hartley companies. On his twenty-first birthday they elected him president of M. Hartley and Company, Inc., successors to Hartley and Graham. For two years, while the estate was being settled, Vice President George W. Hebard of Westinghouse Electric, who was Marcellus Hartley's executor, trustee and friend, served as president of the arms companies. Then he withdrew, and George W. Jenkins became President of Remington Arms while William J. Bruff became President of U.M.C. Marcy shared the responsibilities of management with these two men.

For more than a year after his grandfather's death Marcy continued at Columbia University until he was graduated in June, 1903. Throughout his last year at Columbia, he had spent every Saturday sitting behind his grandfather's big desk, making decisions as to the management of his company's affairs while he tried desperately to comprehend the intricacies of the business.

In addition to his work at M. Hartley and Company, Marcy, while still in his twenties, was elected a director of Equitable Life, to fill his grandfather's place.

One of the most important decisions Marcy ever made was forced upon him only a short time after he became President of M. Hartley and Company. It was, indeed, a decision which had been facing Marcellus Hartley the very day he died; a decision to secure the services of the gun-designing genius, John Browning.

That afternoon of January 8, 1902, two men were waiting in Marcellus Hartley's office. One of them was holding a handmade model of the first successful autoloading shotgun ever built, and the other had an autoloading sporting rifle, also the first of its kind. They were John Browning and his brother Matthew.

The Browning brothers had been waiting for nearly an hour when they heard the telephone ring in the inner office. A moment later, George Bingham, Mr. Hartley's secretary, came out of the door. His face was frighteningly white, but his voice was courteous and composed as he said, "I have sad news for you, gentlemen. Mr. Hartley died a few moments ago of a heart attack."

Bingham records the brothers' consternation. They had counted on Marcellus Hartley to forward their ambitious plans for their latest inventions. Now John stared at Matthew and Matthew looked at him. After a long silence, John asked, "What shall we do now?"

Matthew, the businessman of the pair, had an answer ready. "We can accomplish nothing here. We must go to Belgium and see what we can do there first."

"I calculate you're right," said John.

So it was decided, there in Hartley's office, that the original Browning Arms Company would be Belgian and not American. The brothers went abroad and entered into a contract with the Fabrique Nationale de Guerre at Liege which eventuated in the establishment of their famous factory. However, they only allotted the European rights to the Browning Company of Belgium, reserving for themselves the rights for the United States and other countries outside of Europe.

On their way back from Europe, the Brownings called again at M. Hartley and Company. The slim young man, who now sat behind the big desk, made no effort to conceal his eagerness to make the Browning guns in America. Matthew demanded an unusually high royalty, but Marcy Dodge felt that what the inventors had to offer was worth it. Bruff, whose excellent judgment Dodge trusted, was also enthusiastic about the Brownings, and urged the deal on George Jenkins and George Hebard, who finally agreed to come to terms with them.

With a contract in his pocket, which was to pay him more than a million dollars in the first ten years, John Browning went to Ilion to superintend production of the first semiautomatic sporting guns ever made in America.

Before he ever came to Hartley, John Moses Browning was famous for his work in the development of firearms. Captain John Houston Craige in his authoritative *American Guns* says, "Browning turned out to be the greatest designer and inventor of firearms that ever lived."

Back in the 1880s, Browning and his brother had a small gun shop in Ogden, Utah. There John worked out some revolutionary ideas for repeating rifles. Marcellus Hartley's rival, President Thomas G. Bennett of Winchester Arms "discovered" Browning. For Bennett, Browning designed the vastly improved lever-action Winchester of 1886, which replaced the Winchester '73, and the later Winchester '95 with a box magazine to handle the new high-power, smokeless-powder cartridges.

However, Browning was an eccentric individualist who would not be bound to one company. When he had a new invention on the griddle of his brain, he would retire to his shack in Utah, immuring himself for days with nothing but bread and water until he came out with a new gun. Though he worked for Winchester on repeaters, his real ambition was to invent autoloading and automatic guns. In 1889, Colt commissioned him to try.

Automatic guns were not a new idea. The Greeks had a machine that fired arrows like a machine gun, and multi-barrel guns were used in the middle ages. In the Civil War, right along with the muzzle-loaders, there was a sort of machine gun. This was the invention of Dr. R. J. Gatling of Indianapolis. It had six barrels which were revolved by turning a crank. Cartridges were fed from a hopper into the firing chambers as they went by. Gatling guns could fire up to two hundred shots a minute, and were used up to and including the Spanish-American War; but since there was always a sweating gunner turning the crank, they were not true automatic weapons.

Many others, in Europe and America, attempted to invent automatic weapons. Partially successful ones were designed by Sir Hiram Maxim in England and Ritter von Mannlicher in Germany during the 1880s. The autoloading feature of both these guns was actuated by the recoil of the barrel against a spring mechanism.

John Browning invented the gas-operated autoloading mechanism. His Colt air-cooled machine gun, produced in 1890, was the first practical gun to operate on this modern principle. In 1895, he invented the first automatic pistol for Colt, for which U.M.C. Thomas invented the cartridges. The model 1911 of this gun was the first automatic pistol adopted by the United States armed services.

John Browning was tired of inventing guns for other people. When he succeeded in producing his semiautomatic (autoloading) sporting guns, he wanted to have them manufactured on a straight royalty basis. That is why he went to Marcy Dodge, and so to Remington Arms.

The oldsters at Ilion remember John and Matt Browning, sitting at their work benches in the factory with the tails of their claw-hammer coats trailing on the floor and the naked electric bulbs glaringly reflected on their bald heads. Theirs was not a peaceable partnership. When a disagreement arose as to how something should be done, the brothers argued violently with each other, while fellow workers left their machines to gape in admiration at their sulphurous language.

It was different in the evenings when John and Matt retired to their room at the Osgood Hotel. Then John would get out his banjo and sing romantic, lilting songs like "O Promise Me," *Daisy Belle* and *After the Ball* while Matt joined in the choruses.

The first autoloading shotgun in America came out of the Remington plant in 1905, and the successful Remington autoloading rifle was produced in 1906. They gave Remington such a head start in the field of sporting autoloaders that no other American manufacturer ever quite caught up.

Another important inventor worked side by side with the Brownings at Ilion. This was John Douglas Pedersen, who came from Denmark by way of Wyoming. "J.D.," as everybody in the plant called him, was a theorist or laboratory man, as compared to John Browning who was a rule-of-thumb inventor. Remington's first repeating shotgun was produced from Pedersen designs in 1907. It had a slide (or "trombone") action and was introduced by Remington as their Model 10. This was the granddaddy of all those pump guns that are still the favorite weapon of some of the best clay-target shots in America.

In 1909, Remington produced its famous Model 12, a 22 caliber slide-action repeating rifle designed by Pedersen, and followed it in 1912 with Model 14, a high-powered slide-action rifle made in calibers up to 35 Remington. In *American Guns,* Craige calls the Remington Gamemaster (present version of Pedersen's M-14) "The most modern hunting rifle of the pump-action type manufactured today." And in the next paragraph Craige pays tribute to the Remington Woodmaster (based on the Browning patents) as "the most popular autoloading rifle in the hunting field."

## Chapter 28

# Remington Arms—U. M. C.

While things were going so well at Ilion, the youthful President of M. Hartley & Co., was having his troubles at Bridgeport. During the estate-settling regency, when responsibility for management was uncertainly divided, the Union Metallic Cartridge Company ran by its own momentum. The brilliant young men who had done so much to build it up were old men now. A. C. Hobbs was dead. U. M. C. Thomas and Jerome Orcutt were still vigorous enough to work a twelve-hour day by their own choice, and, despite their snow-white hair and Orcutt's white muttonchop whiskers, they seemed as alert as ever. But some of their ideas were now as old-fashioned as they had been progressive in earlier days. The truth was that Thomas and Orcutt, who was now General Manager and Superintendent, needed young assistants.

The old foremen of the departments were also set in their secret ways. They all had little black books of production figures which were for their eyes alone. The men in charge of gluing paper shot shells each had a little stove on which his own particular brew of paste bubbled and boiled, and none would tell another the ingredients of his jealously guarded formula.

As the plant coasted along, the workers, following the ruts of routine, grew too familiar with the deadly materials they handled; and custom led to carelessness.

The need for housecleaning was rudely brought to the attention of the management by a series of big blows. Bridgeport papers recorded them in scare headlines; the descriptions sounded positively atomic: "A cyclonic cloud with a long tail arose in the air. This funnel-shaped cloud kept its form for several minutes and was watched by thousands."

Probably the company was not at fault—certainly management was doing everything in its power to prevent accidents. But Marcy Dodge and William Bruff knew it must do more. Young blood was needed. Men trained in the new scientific techniques. At the suggestion of the well-known industrial engineer, Samuel Greene, they brought in a group of young engineers headed by Harry H. Pinney.

Pinney had served his apprenticeship as a foreman at the Pratt & Whitney Machine Tool Company in Hartford, Connecticut, and as Assistant Works Manager of the National Cash Register Company at Dayton, Ohio. He was a thin, nervous young man, whose hazel eyes sparked and snapped with the excitement of doing a job. There was a deeply sentimental streak in him, which made him at once intensely loyal to the management and immensely thoughtful of both the older men who were theoretically over him, and of the workers in the plant. But for all that, he would stand no nonsense. Pinney was a go-getter, and he had great mechanical imagination.

Dodge and Jenkins offered Pinney ten thousand dollars a year. His position was Assistant to Orcutt and his job was to invent and introduce new techniques, tactfully, without upsetting the older men.

Under Pinney the plant was thoroughly revamped. Power had been supplied by several steam engines operating in different parts of the works. Pinney put in a modern central power plant, which transmitted power to all the buildings by electricity. A scientific formula for shotshell paste was worked out, and it was all made in a big central vat and piped directly to the machines.

Most important of all were the safety measures which Pinney designed and installed. Under the old system, the powder was brought to Bridgeport by rail and trucked in horse-drawn drays through the city streets to the Powder Park. It was sent back to the plant in small quantities, and was distributed by men who carried the little two-pound cans of powder in a yoke over their shoulders, and handed them through the receiving windows, where other men opened them and poured the contents into the hoppers of the loading machines.

The first thing Pinney did was to enlarge the Powder Park to about four hundred acres and build new magazines. He had the New York, New Haven and Hartford Railroad build a siding directly to the plant and he got U.M.C. to build a private railroad from the Park to the plant. To haul the company's powder cars, he bought three tiny steam locomotives which had just been retired from service on the elevated railways of New York. When the powder reached the plant, it was stored in a bunkered magazine and distributed in aluminum cans through vacuum tubes to the loading machines. The operation was timed so that there was never more than one hopperful of powder at each machine.

The fulminate for the primers had always been the trickiest stuff to handle. It had to be moistened and mixed; then dried exactly the right amount before being loaded into the primers. The gray, pasty stuff was spread on big tables in carefully bunkered sheds and the drying process took from two to four days. During this period any rapid rise in temperature might produce a violent explosion. Because the sheds were almost buried in the ground, these blows were not fatal, but they caused serious losses to the company.

To correct this situation, Pinney designed an installation of vacuum dryers in which the fulminate was dried to exactly the right degree in a few hours. As a result of these improvements, statistics show that it became safer to work at U. M. C. than in the average industrial plant.

In 1908, a source of financial annoyance to U. M. C. was the high price of shot, of which the Company used up to one hundred tons a day. In Marcellus Hartley's time, the shot was purchased from the C. N. Marshall Lead Works at Granite City, Illinois. Thomas Fortune Ryan's National Lead Company bought Marshall in 1905, and combined it with other large companies. Then the squeeze went on. National Lead upped the price until U. M. C. was obliged to pay that company a net profit of six dollars a ton.

Pinney went to Dodge, and proposed that U. M. C. build a shot tower and make its own shot. That seemed a sensible way to save six hundred dollars a day; but shot towers are expensive and there were objections to obligating the company for what might prove a costly experiment. However, Dodge was convinced that Pinney was right; and he dared to go ahead on his own, putting up the money from his personal fortune.

The shot tower was begun in July, 1908, and completed seven months later, in February, 1909. Ten stories high, one hundred and ninety feet to the top of the flagpole, it dominated the Bridgeport skyline. Realizing that it might be either as beautiful as a campanile or as obnoxious as a gasometer, Dodge insisted that no expense be spared to give it that campanile look and make it an ornament to the city.

One of the few things that have changed scarcely at all in the industry since 1909, is making the perfectly round, smooth pellets that are the punch in a shot shell. The originator of the process is said to have been an imaginative German, who, watching round drops of water fall from his wife's watering can, was inspired with the notion that shot could be made by pouring molten lead through the equivalent of a watering can. But he realized that the shot must fall far enough to cool and solidify before landing in water which would cushion the shock. Hence the need for a high tower.

The shot tower at Bridgeport operates today very much as it did when it was built. At the very top are two huge kettles heated by oil furnaces. Each of them is capable of holding ten tons of molten lead—hundreds of thousands of pounds of metallic soup are brewed in them every working day. When the fires are roaring, expert mixers stand beside the kettles feeding them with the heavy gray bars of pure lead mixed with small amounts of antimony and arsenic. The proportions must be exactly right in order to form into perfectly round pellets. Art Hiertz worked in the shot tower from the day it was built and was in charge for many years before his retirement in 1955. He could tell immediately, by a sixth sense developed from long practice, if the proportions were wrong or if there was an impurity in the lead. Should such be the case, Art knew the right antidote to correct it.

The "soup" must be kept at 750°, give or take no more than 15°. The lead pouring out of small pipes in the bottoms of the caldrons looks like a stream of clear, cool water—it is too hot to smoke. It flows into steel pans like large skillets with pin-point holes in their bottoms. The size of these holes determines the diameter of the shot.

These colander pans are suspended directly over two shafts which traverse the length of the tower. On their undersides, the lead forms perfectly round globules, which fall 133 feet to wells of water about six feet deep. As seen through glass portholes near the base of the shaft, the falling shot looks like a gentle spring rain, but if you could put your hand through a port it would be torn from your arm, and the water at the bottom seethes and boils under that furious shower.

The shot is dredged from the bottom of the wells by buckets on endless belts which carry it to the highest floor but one, where it gets a preliminary polish. From there it travels downward again by gravity. The first stage sorts it for perfection. Two entire floors of the tower are filled with dozens of sloping triangular-shaped tables of glass. The pellets are piped to the narrow tops of the sheets of glass and cascade downward. At the broad base of each table there are two parallel gutters. Perfectly round shot, moving faster, leap the nearest gutter, and landing in the second go merrily on to completion. Imperfect shot trickle over the edge into the near gutter, and are returned to the kettles—there is no such thing as waste in making shot. There are repeated stages of sorting so that no imperfect pellets get by.

After sorting, the shot go on downward to be screened for size. They run through revolving wire sieves which exclude all but those of the right size. Those which fall into larger or smaller categories are automatically channeled off to the proper tanks, while odd sizes go back to the kettles. From the sorting machines, the shot passes through seven different types of rollers for cleaning, polishing and applying graphite.

After their long coast, the shot come to rest in the fat storage tanks in the lower floors of the tower. As orders come for shot of a certain size, a tank truck couples onto the hose of the proper storage tank and is filled up. It unloads in the same fashion at the hoists in the main building. These carry the shot to hoppers from which it is piped to the loading machines.

Art Hiertz figures roughly that the tower can make 1,200,000,000 pellets of shot in a day.

The people at Remington's Bridgeport plant are as fascinated by the shot tower as a small boy by an electric train. Throughout the years it has saved Remington literally thousands of times its original cost.

One of the most difficult decisions that Marcy Dodge had to make about the Union Metallic Cartridge Company concerned its name. As he became increasingly familiar with the business, young Dodge discovered that his sales force was at a disadvantage compared to their great competitor, Winchester. When a prospect bought a Winchester rifle or shotgun, the natural thing to do was to order Winchester cartridges to go with it. Chances were that he would go on using them all his life because he believed that they were best suited to his gun. There was no such obvious connection between Remington guns and U.M.C. ammunition.

The obvious answer was to combine Remington and U.M.C. under a single name. Yet there were powerful arguments against such a course. U.M.C. had been Marcellus Hartley's pride, and was the firm foundation of the Hartley fortune. It was known throughout the world as making the finest quality of ammunition. Remington had an even older name, it was true, but its business was far smaller. At this time the Ilion factory was doing a gross of little more than five hundred thousand a year, while U.M.C.'s business ran from ten to fifteen million. To put the name of Remington first seemed exactly like putting the cart before the horse.

George Jenkins was lukewarm to the idea, and the oldsters at U.M.C. were dead against it. But many of the younger men cogently argued its advantages. Marcy Dodge, himself still under thirty, listened to their advice. Though he, too, loved tradition, he was alert to opportunity and pervious to logic.

Having come to the conclusion that the move was a wise one, Dodge pressed the matter on Mr. Bruff and Mr. Jenkins. The latter yielded to the enthusiasm of youth, which in this case turned out to be wiser than the counsels of age.

The companies were called Remington Arms—Union Metallic Cartridge Company. It was a huge mouthful of a name, but Marcy was determined that U.M.C., even though behind the hyphen, should not be lost. Later logic and convenience prompted the change to the Remington Arms Company. But even today the Union Metallic Cartridge Company has a tangible remembrance. For on the head of each of hundreds of millions of rim-fire cartridges made by Remington Arms is stamped the letter U.

As Dodge gained in knowledge and matured through experience, his grasp of the affairs of the family companies became more sure. He was out of leading strings now, and he wanted the freedom to act as he thought best without the restrictions which divided counsels sometimes imposed. He was ambitious to build his prospering companies to the limit of their capabilities.

In 1912, he achieved this ambition. His grandmother had already presented him with her stock, and he had acquired all other holdings except those of Helen Hartley Jenkins. He made his aunt an offer for her stock, and she, generously, consented to sell—she wanted the business to remain in the family. Thus at the age of thirty, Marcellus Hartley Dodge became, like his grandfather, the sole owner and President of Remington Arms—U.M.C.

## Chapter 29

# The End of Peace

Hardly anyone now remembers how tranquil life appeared in 1912. Americans felt a sense of complete security; their land kept inviolate by two great oceans on which sailed a fine new Navy, which wore its peacetime coat of white paint. Even "The Great White Fleet," as it was affectionately called, seemed more like a gesture of national pride than a grim necessity of defense.

In the serene American economy Remington Arms—U.M.C. prospered pleasantly. Its youthful president was a happy man, absorbed in his business interests, and the charitable institutions—particularly Hartley House—which his aunt, Mrs. Jenkins, and he carried on in memory of his grandfather. On April 18, 1907, he had married Geraldine Rockefeller, daughter of William Rockefeller.

Dodge wanted nothing to do with military armaments. With the exception of a few minor government contracts for ammunition, all Remington's resources were devoted to serving American sportsmen. By way of publicizing its products, the company maintained a World Champion Rifle Team, and the Champion American Trap Shooting Team. The "Southern Squad," as it was called, was captained by Thomas Marshall and included among others, Colonel J. T. Anthony, whom the press always referred to as "the embodiment of chivalry." Though they sallied forth in business suits and derby hats, they were quite some shots. At Palestine, Texas, in 1904, the team made a world's record by breaking 488 targets out of a possible 500. Individual scores of 100 and even 125 straight were common. This squad's only defeat was at Memphis, Tennessee, where the winning team of amateurs all used U.M.C. Nitro shells.

The first decade of the century saw the heyday of the famous trick shots who toured the world giving exhibitions of their prowess. The best of them used Remington guns and ammunition. One of these was Annie Oakley, who was the only woman World Champion Shotgun Shot, and who beat the crack shots of all countries from the champion of England, to the Grand Duke Michael of Russia. Her match against the Englishman was shot at Easton, Pennsylvania. Using a little 20-gauge shotgun, she lost one target, and the Englishman five.

Annie was married to Frank Butler, a trick shot who became a Remington salesman. Naturally, she generally used Remington guns and U.M.C. ammunition, although the 20-gauge was made specially for her by a British gunsmith.

Annie was a whiz with rifles and pistols as well as shotguns. One of her tricks in Buffalo Bill's Wild West Show was to ride around the arena at full speed shooting glass balls, which Frank, riding ahead, threw into the air. To show her skill with a pistol, Frank used to throw six glass balls into the air at once. Annie would break them all before they hit the ground.

For perhaps her most famous trick, Annie shot the spots out of a playing card which Frank held up. This stunt put Annie's name in all the dictionaries of the English language. Because free tickets for a show are usually punched with a pattern of holes, such passes are called "Annie Oakleys."

Another amazing shot, who liked Remington guns, was Italian General Pisano. The General's favorite rifle was a model 24 Remington .22 caliber autoloader. Young Crawford Loomis, a gunsmith at Ilion, redesigned the guns especially for Pisano.

With his Remington 24, Pisano could play a tune on a pipe organ by shooting bullets at the keys. He also tossed cartridges into the air and exploded them by hitting the tiny rims. On a duck hunt at San Francisco, he killed more fowl with his rifle than all the rest of the party did with shotguns.

In Pisano's most hair-raising stunt—the phrase is used advisedly—he would shoot a small glass ball from between the heads of two assistants at fifty paces.

Besides the trick shots there were vast numbers of just plain sportsmen with wonderful tales to tell of feats performed with Remingtons. One of the luckiest of these was "Big Bill" Hillis of Alaska, a genuine pioneer from the last frontier. When Bill went hunting bear one day on Kodiak Island with a companion named King, he got considerably more than he bargained for. The two men were following a narrow ledge that skirted a sheer cliff overhanging the sea. Inching along in single file with Bill in the lead, they rounded a big boulder, and came face to face with a family of *five* huge Kodiak bears. The biggest, rearing up nearly seven feet high, looked like a monster in a caveman's nightmare, and he was clearly in a nasty frame of mind.

Fortunately, Big Bill was literally loaded for bear. As he put it, "If I hadn't had my Remington auto-loader and some of them pow'ful Remington bullets, I mightn't of come back."

He fired at the leading bear, while King dropped on his stomach and shot between Bill's legs at the second in line. Papa Bear fell dead, but his mate was only winged, and charged along the ledge bellowing with rage, followed by the rest of the family. The Remington would not have been much use if Bill had not been as cool as Malaspina Glacier. He fired four fast shots and four bears fell dead—making five bears with five bullets, since King's shot did nothing but exacerbate Mama Bear's disagreeable disposition.

Bill's modest comment was "Of course, I had the drop on them bears."

The happy days when game and glass balls and clay targets were the normal object of a bullet's flight were drawing to a close. The summer of 1914 was one of unusual tension. The war clouds, which gathered on European horizons in the hot months as habitually as thunderclouds on a summer afternoon in Indiana, seemed somehow darker and more menacing. A sort of sick pallor overcast the skies of international relations; and the diplomatic air had the electric quality that forebodes a tempest.

Despite the omens, nobody thought it would happen. Not even the principal figures involved, kaisers and kings, prime ministers and secretaries of foreign affairs, and the chiefs of the general staffs—not even they thought it could happen.

When Archduke Francis Ferdinand, heir to the double imperial crown of Austria-Hungary, was shot by a crazy Servian at Sarejevo, it just seemed a routine Balkan assassination—it was always the open season for crowned heads in the Balkans.

Then somehow things got out of hand. Austria mobilized against Servia, and Russia mobilized to protect the small Slav state. Germany, who had egged Austria on to punish Servia, called her conscripts to the colors, and France reluctantly countered with *L'Ordre de Mobilization.* Peace trembled on a razor's edge.

In the lucid light of history it would seem that nobody really wanted war—not even the German Kaiser. The pathetically ridiculous telegrams which the crowned cousins of Europe exchanged begging each other to stop the war, signed "Georgie" and "Willie," and "Nicky," had the ring of sincerity, even though they were frantically futile. But the momentum of men rushing to arms and the irresistible effect of decisions taken in anger and fear could not be halted. All along the borders of Germany and Russia and France, the pin-point flashes of rifles ignited the conflagration which was to destroy the peace of the world, not for the span of one war or even one generation, but for fifty years and maybe more.

Marcy Dodge, in common with many Americans, watched incredulously as the great conscript armies of Germany surged forward and flowed over neutral Belgium in repudiation of the solemn treaty signed by Germany. The black smoke billowing up from the ancient library at Louvain turned his incredulity to horror.

The Germans were halted at last on the Marne, a short taxi ride from Paris. The Allied governments took stock of their arsenals, and found a desperate need for guns and ammunition. In September, the Allied purchasing commissions reached America. One of the first places they went was to Remington.

Marcy Dodge had turned the Presidency of Remington Arms—U.M.C. over to Samuel F. Pryor, becoming Chairman of the Board of Directors. Pryor was a dynamic enthusiast who liked to do things in a big way.

The Allied commissions offered Remington enormous contracts, far beyond the capacity of its factories. To fulfill them meant a vast expansion, which would cost many millions of dollars. Pryor's imagination rocketed over all obstacles. Marcy Dodge took a more conservative view. He realized that this would be a tremendous gamble, and normally would have opposed it. However, like Pryor and many of his fellow countrymen, he had been appalled by the ruthlessness of the German military machine. It seemed to him that, if France fell and England were defeated, America itself would be in danger. Despite President Woodrow Wilson's injunction to be neutral in thought and act, Marcy could not be impartial in such a contest. He felt a moral obligation to give what help he could, whatever the risk. Thus he came to be of like mind to Pryor. It was not long before President Wilson and the great majority of Americans realized that neutrality was not enough.

The first contract accepted by Remington was to make a few thousand old-fashioned Lebel rifles for France. Then came the British. They desperately needed a million Enfield rifles, and perhaps a million more. At that time, capacity at Ilion was less than five hundred guns a day, at which rate it would have taken nearly six years to fill the contract. In addition, the new improved Enfield had never been manufactured in quantity anywhere—the machinery must be designed from scratch. It was chambered for .276 caliber cartridges—but the British had changed their minds and wanted it redesigned for their standard .303 caliber. It was up to Remington engineers to do this job as well, and to provide the 3,895 machines, 5,905 fixtures, 7,000 tools and 3,415 gauges necessary for a maximum production of 2,000 guns a day. Deliveries were to begin by January 1, 1916.

It was clearly impossible. So, with the approval of Dodge, Sam Pryor signed the contract in October, 1914. The first Enfields were actually fired at Ilion in October, 1915, exactly one year later.

The industrial miracle was accomplished partly by the lavish expenditure of money, but it was due far more to the tremendous cooperative effort of Remington officials, engineers, machinists and workers of all classes from Pryor and Works Manager C. C. Tyler, to the porters on the loading platforms, and the contractors, bricklayers, plumbers, painters and day laborers who put up the new buildings in record time. While engineers prepared the blueprints for making the gun, industrial architects drew the plans for the great new buildings. When these plans were still tentative roughs, the Stuart Construction Company's steam shovels were already scooping out the dirt for their foundations.

Because the hills rose abruptly behind the factory, Remington needed room to expand eastward along Main Street, as the River Road was now called. Mrs. John Hoefler's fine old Victorian mansion blocked the way. The eighty-year-old widow loved her home, and no amount of money would induce her to move; but she was a true Ilionite, and agreed to sell for the sake of the advantages the great new factories would bring to her native village. However, she was adamant on one condition. On her front lawn stood a tall ginko tree, imported by her husband from northern China. It had been his particular pride—the only one of its kind in the whole countryside. It was duly recorded in the deed that the ginko tree must be preserved, nor must any building be erected which in any way interfered with its soil, light or healthful environment. So it still stands, nearly one hundred feet high, waving its broad, spade-shaped leaves against the windows of the great factory buildings, which are pulled back out of line to give it room to breathe and flourish. Thus was production-line progress forced to bend before the strength of sentiment.

The new factory buildings ran down both sides of Main Street connected by overhead bridges. Those on the north dipped their foundations in the mirrored surface of a backwater of the Erie Canal like Venetian palaces.

The operation at Ilion was extremely successful from the first. Employment went from twelve hundred to 1914 to fifteen thousand in 1917. Peak production of Enfields was reached in March, 1917, just before the United States entered the war. That month the factory turned out sixty-one thousand British rifles.

In addition, Dodge and Pryor, joined with William Corey, of United States Steel, and Andrew Monel, of Monel metal fame, to set up the separate Remington Company of Delaware to manufacture still more rifles. Through the interest of President Samuel Vouclain of the Baldwin Locomotive Works they were able to lease a partly finished factory which Baldwin was building at Eddystone, Pennsylvania. This was converted to build rifles. To man it, every other skilled worker was taken from Ilion and replaced by a trainee. Four hundred and fifty thousand Enfields were built at Eddystone for the British.

Nineteen sixteen was the One Hundredth Anniversary of Eliphalet's first rifle and the founding of Remington Arms. It was celebrated at Ilion in lavish style, with parades and shooting matches, banquets and long laudatory orations by prominent personages. Among them were Major General Hugh Scott, Chief of Staff, United States Army, Governor Charles S. Whitman of New York, and a little-known but impressive-looking politician from Ohio, Senator Warren Gamaliel Harding.

Marcy Dodge seemed to be everywhere at once, hurrying to welcome a Very Important Person or darting through the crowds to congratulate one of the old gunsmiths on his length of service. His slim body, vibrating with energy, and his charming smile as he received the congratulations of the great, seemed properly proud and carefree. Actually, he was weighted with anxiety.

The great buildings trembling to the splendid thunder of machinery, the tall stacks flying the smoke banners of production, and the cases of finished rifles piling up on the loading platforms seemed to prove that all was going well. And so it was—at Ilion. But at Bridgeport, despite the best efforts of the men in charge there, unpredictable difficulties and delays, especially at the new rifle plant, threatened disaster. Losses were piling up at an alarming rate, while banks and bondholders, who had loaned the millions of dollars needed for expansion, watched with growing apprehension, ready to step in at any moment and take over.

As the Chairman of the Board stood in the August sunshine on the speaker's platform at Ilion, the congratulations and laudations had an ironic ring in his ears. For the whole great enterprise, which his grandfather had built up from scratch, and to which he had devoted his life, seemed about to fall into alien hands.

## Chapter 30

# America Calls on Remington

The Imperial Russian Government was the last of the great allies to come to Remington for help. But when they ordered, it was in truly imperial style. The contract, signed in 1915, called for one million Russian rifles and one hundred million rounds of ammunition. The guns could not be made at Ilion, which was overwhelmed by the British contract; and Bridgeport's remaining ammunition capacity was sufficient for only fifty thousand 7.62-mm. Russian cartridges a day. Whole new factories must be built in the face of rising prices and acute shortages of material.

Signing the contract exposed Marcy Dodge to grave financial dangers; but competent authorities assured him that the risk was not too great. And that spring the *Lusitania* had been torpedoed carrying hundreds of innocent men and women and children to their deaths in the icy Irish sea. To Americans, still unsophisticated in the ways of war, it seemed the ultimate outrage. Dodge felt that morality and patriotism alike compelled him to accept the Russian order. To finance the new construction, Remington Arms and U.M.C. were amalgamated in fact as well as in name. Dodge borrowed fifteen million dollars by selling gold bonds of the united company and fifteen million against his own preferred stock. In addition, he gave his personal notes to various banks for thirteen million more.

Luckily a plan for a rifle factory was ready at hand. Back in 1905, Harry Pinney had dreamed of moving the Arms Plant from Ilion to Bridgeport. At that time, he had worked with industrial architects on a blueprint for the most modern gun factory in the world. The final decision had been to keep the Arms in Ilion, but the plan was ready and waiting. Land was purchased north of U.M.C.'s original Barnum Avenue plant, Pinney's plan was expanded and construction started on the new factory. When completed, a little over a year later, it consisted of thirteen main five-story buildings, twelve service buildings, five forge shops, the power house and auxiliary buildings with a total floor space of over 1,100,000 square feet and a production capacity of five thousand rifles and five thousand bayonets a day.

Meanwhile the cartridge factory was more than doubled in size. It had consisted of 143 buildings in 1914. One hundred and sixty new buildings were erected, bringing the total up to 313 with an increase in floor space from sixteen acres to forty acres. To assist Works Manager Frank Hoagland, Pryor secured two experienced Army Ordnance officers, one from Springfield Armory and one from Frankford Arsenal.

Even this expansion was not enough to handle the Russian cartridge contract in addition to the large orders for British .303-caliber ammunition and 8-mm. Lebel cartridges for the antiquated French rifles. When it became evident that production was lagging behind schedule, Marcy Dodge said, "Send for Pinney!"

Harry Pinney had left Remington in 1910, to become Works Manager of the Chalmers Motor Company in Detroit. From there he had gone to the Presidency of the Metal Products Company, and was one of the founders of the Saxon Company. When the message came from Dodge, Pinney was recuperating from an operation which had nearly cost his life. His doctor told him that if he went to Remington he would come back on a stretcher. But Dodge sounded anxious, and Pinney liked a challenge. "I can't work more than three hours a day," he told Dodge, "but I can still think good."

Before he was strong enough to climb a flight of stairs, he had thirty-five thousand men working under him.

Pinney's first job was to report on the reason for lagging production at Bridgeport. After a tour of inspection, in a wheel chair, he reported to Dodge in his forthright language, "Bridgeport is like a cat chasing its tail. Also, you haven't enough space there. You have to build a new plant for the Russian ammunition."

"We have considered that," Dodge told him, "but the experts tell me that because of the present shortages of materials and trained men, it's impossible."

"Bunkum!" snorted Pinney. "For two million dollars I'll build you a plant in twelve months that will turn out two million cartridges a day."

"Go ahead!" said Marcy Dodge.

Pinney's plan was to build a factory to make cartridge cases, and send them to Bridgeport to be loaded. He had found the loading process there was operating very efficiently. To avoid construction delays, he looked around for a suitable factory and found it in a plant being built by the Hoboken Land and Improvement Company. He rented it and within ten months he had completed the conversion and was turning out components for 2,500,000 cartridges a day.

Meanwhile, Tyler had been brought on from Ilion to reorganize the ammunition operation at Bridgeport. Aided by Jarvis Williams, who later became Vice-president of Remington, he worked to such effect that by June, 1916, cartridge production of the Bridgeport-Hoboken operation had reached a peak of twenty-eight million a week. It was a remarkable accomplishment.

But a mere trickle of Russian rifles was coming out of the new plant at Bridgeport. It was losing several hundred thousand dollars a month. So Dodge and Pryor decided to ask Pinney to take it over in addition to Hoboken.

Pinney was still far from strong. In fact he had fitted up a rest room next to his office with a trained nurse always in attendance. When he had worked for three hours, the nurse would come into his office and say sternly, "Time is up, Mr. Pinney!" Obediently Pinney would go to the rest room for two hours and a half. Then he would go back to work.

Naturally he was very reluctant to take on this extra job at Bridgeport, but as he stated it, "There was that great, big beautiful plant like a ship on the rocks, so I decided to take the risk for Dodge's sake."

When Pinney walked into the new rifle plant, he found that they were turning out only 125 guns a day. The trouble was that the components of the rifles made according to Russian blueprints and Russian gauges would not fit together without being tailored by hand.

Pinney discovered that the Russian gauges, blueprints and the master model all differed. He locked a group of engineers in a room and told them not to come out until they had reconciled the differences and worked out the changes necessary to make the parts fit without handwork. When this was accomplished and the Russian Government had accepted the changes, production at Bridgeport went into high gear. In February, 1917, 5,000 Russian rifles came off the assembly line every day.

It was not done easily. The Tsar had sent no less than fifteen hundred inspectors to Bridgeport to make sure he was not cheated. They swarmed through the factory, getting under foot and inspecting with fanatic minuteness, impelled by the fear of death.

The most irritating of all the inspectors was a Cossack captain who strutted around in full regalia of astrakhan cap, full-skirted coat, crossed bandoleers, a gold-sheathed dagger and soft, red leather boots, just as though he were going for a gallop on the Steppes. His pomposity won him the nickname of Alexander the Great.

Alexander's particular fetish was an acute anxiety lest the rifles fire accidentally. He'd snatch a gun off the line, load and cock it, and bang the butt with all his might on the concrete floor. The rifles were too well made to jar off even under this heroic treatment, but stock after stock was split. Alexander wrecked as many as a dozen guns a day.

The officials could do nothing to stop this waste, but the gunsmiths got good and tired of seeing their work destroyed. They prepared a rifle especially for Alexander, filing down the lock mechanism until the trigger hung by a hair of steel. Then they maneuvered it into the Cossack's hands.

Alexander took the bait. All work stopped short, and the men watched breathlessly as he loaded and cocked the booby trap. Then he slammed it against the floor.

The crack of the rifle was multiplied a hundredfold by the confining walls, as the steel-jacketed bullet whizzed past his obtrusive nose. But the best was yet to come. The projectile pierced a four-inch pipe above Alexander's head and a solid stream of water under high pressure hit his upturned face, knocking him flat on his back. Weak with laughter, the workers dragged the sodden wreck of the half-drowned Cossack to safety.

The Russians were not the only source of worry to Remington officials—far from it! The Central Powers were frantic to stop production at Bridgeport, at any cost and by any means. German Ambassador, Count Johann Von Bernstorff, protested violently that Remington was "un-neutral," which it certainly was, though not in the legal sense. Then he screamed that Remington (and Winchester) were supplying the Allies with "dum-dum" bullets, which they were not. When protests failed, strikes were fomented against Remington, but failed to materialize. The company's employees were working an eight-hour day at good wages. Further, Remington undertook a three-million-dollar housing project to supply inexpensive houses for its workers, and provided dormitories for thousands of women workers who flocked to Bridgeport.

A little later saboteurs attempted to wreck the ammunition plant. Failure of a batch of British cartridges led to the discovery of "mysterious interference with metallic compounds for the bullets." Attempts were made to wreck machines and cause explosions. Remington took extreme security measures. Hundreds of guards were distributed throughout the plant, and the trolley cars, which ran down Barnum Avenue between the buildings, were locked in transit. A United States destroyer guarded Bridgeport Harbor. So effective were these measures, that no serious case of sabotage was ever uncovered in any of the Remington factories.

At this time, also, Marcy Dodge received a bona fide but mysterious offer of many millions of dollars for Remington Arms through a New York banking group. Heavy losses on the Russian contract were causing Dodge terrible anxiety. From day to day he did not know whether he would be able to withstand the financial strain, or if he would lose Remington and the greater part of his personal fortune to his creditors. Here was an easy out—a safe sure way to recoup his losses and free himself from the terrible load of debt which he had incurred.

It was, indeed, suspiciously easy. Marcy was sure that this was another scheme of the enemies of democracy to shut off Remington aid to the Allies. If that were so, then all the work that had been done, all the planning and accomplishments, the grave risks and inspired effort of so many good men would be cancelled out. He refused the offer.

More troublesome to Marcy Dodge than Cossacks or saboteurs was that problem of finance. In the summer of 1916, with the great new rifle factory virtually idle and expenses piling up, creditors and bankers became uneasy. An attempt was made by one group of creditors to take over the company.

At this critical moment in the history of Remington, Dodge appealed to William Rockefeller, his father-in-law, who sent him to his counsel, John W. Sterling, of the law firm of Sherman and Sterling, also counsel for the National City Bank, for advice. Sterling acted promptly. With the backing of Mr. Rockefeller, he instructed General Samuel McRoberts, Vice President of National City, to endeavor to form a creditors' committee to handle the affairs of Remington Arms. McRoberts obtained the services of such eminent bankers as Charles E. Mitchell and Charles H. Sabin. Samuel Pryor was a member of the committee. These men not only secured an extension of time from the company's creditors but received sufficient additional funds to tide Remington over until the Russian rifles came into full production. To act for the creditors' committee, Harry S. Kimball was put in as President of Remington Arms.

Things looked much better in February, 1917. In all the great Remington plants production was at new peaks—Ilion twenty-four hundred Enfields a day; Bridgeport Rifle Factory, five thousand rifles and five thousand bayonets a day; Hoboken and Barnum Avenue, four million cartridges daily. The millions spent so lavishly for the tools of production were returning the fruits thereof. More important still was the great flow of munitions to strengthen the sinews of the British battling desperately in Flanders, and the Russian armies clinging to a wavering line in the blizzards beyond the Carpathian Mountains.

At the moment of apparent success catastrophe overwhelmed Remington. The decadent government of Tsar Nicholas II, weakened by irresolution, gutted by corruption, unmanned by fear and riddled with superstition, completely collapsed. The whole great Russian nation disintegrated into chaotic fragments, over which the feeble republic proclaimed by the supporters of Alexander Kerensky exercised a nebulous authority in transition from one tyranny to another.

The first act of the new Russian Republic was to repudiate all contracts entered into by the Tsar's government—indeed, it did not have the financial means to carry them out had it so desired. The effect on the Russian Rifle Plant was something like an automobile hitting a telegraph pole at sixty miles an hour. One day it was running all out in the full tide of production. The next it stopped dead with the jarring dislocation of thousands of men thrown out of work, hundreds of thousands of unwanted rifles stocked in the warehouses, and the great capital investment apparently lost beyond hope of recovery.

Speaking of those weeks in March, 1917, Marcy Dodge, who had backed his company with everything he had, said, "Each night when I tried to go to sleep, I lay there thinking that I had nothing left of all I once had owned, and that I had no further employment for the thousands of men who had worked hard and loyally during the days of stress."

Remington was not alone in its difficulties. Other great arms companies were in a similar position. If they were permitted to collapse, America would lose a major element of the strength that everyone now knew she needed urgently. For the time of neutrality was almost past. The ruthlessness of the U-boats and the power of the Kaiser's army, had convinced the American people that a German victory would destroy democracy in Europe.

On January 31, 1917, Germany dramatically confirmed this opinion by declaring unlimited submarine warfare. Every ship that ventured into the zone of combat, which they arbitrarily designated, was liable to be sunk without warning and without regard to loss of civilian lives. President Wilson promptly severed diplomatic relations with Germany. The further sinking of unarmed American ships finally convinced him that America must intervene. On April 2, 1917, he asked Congress for a declaration of war, asserting that, "The right is more precious than peace," and pledging "Our lives, our fortunes and our sacred honor," to that cause.

Only then did the United States really begin to prepare for war. In his anxiety to avoid any imputation of aggression, the President had refused to permit the Army and Navy to move until war became inevitable. The Allies' situation was desperate. Submarine sinkings, averaging six hundred thousand tons a month, made it only a matter of time before England would be prostrate. On the Western Front, the French Army, with losses of over two million men, was discouraged to the point of revolt, while fresh masses of German troops, released by Russia's collapse, were about to be hurled against the bulwark of Verdun. If the war were to be won, America must arm four million troops in a matter of months.

The first step was to get the arms companies back on a firm financial basis. In the case of Remington this was done by government purchase of 600,000 of the 750,000 Russian rifles already manufactured. This reduced the company's loss from an estimated ten million dollars to about three hundred thousand. The rifles were later shipped by the Government to Vladivostok to arm the White Russian Army, which attempted to rescue that country from the Bolshevists.

Meanwhile Army Ordnance faced an apparently insoluble problem. At least 4,000,000 rifles would be needed within two years. There were about 700,000 Springfields in government arsenals, and total manufacturing capacity was 350,000 a year. The net deficit was 3,000,000 guns.

The Springfield, as then designed, was unsuited to production on a great scale. It would be years before they could be made in the quantities needed. Ordnance called on the great arms companies for a quick solution. Remington engineers brought the answer with them to Washington. It was a British Enfield which they had redesigned and chambered to take the Springfield 30-06 cartridge. The British order had been nearly completed at Ilion, and their own factories could take care of their further requirements. The U. S. Enfield, as it was called, was a far simpler gun to make than the Springfield and could be turned out in huge quantities at Ilion and other arms factories.

Rival companies reacted violently to the Remington proposal. "We had a cat-and-parrot time in Washington." But the opposition had nothing as practical to propose. The new rifle was officially adopted by the Ordnance Department as U. S. Rifle, Model 1917. The Ilion factory was retooled to make it, and other arms manufacturers also received large orders. By December, 1917, production at Ilion was 3,000 M17s a day, and by June, production peaked at 4,000. Total production at Ilion was 545,541, Eddystone produced 1,181,908 M17s. When the war ended, 1,000,000 M17s were stored in Government arsenals. These were the guns which were shipped to England after Dunkirk in 1940, and were a major factor in saving her from a Nazi invasion.

Meanwhile the Russian rifle factory at Bridgeport was converted to make Browning heavy machine guns, Browning automatic rifles, Colt automatic pistols and Very signal pistols, as well as five thousand bayonets a day. Simultaneously the ammunition factories at Bridgeport and Hoboken were converted to make the 30-06 Springfield cartridge, while a new plant was set up at Swanton, Vermont, to manufacture four million French Lebel cartridges weekly.

The Springfield cartridge was much more of a precision job than the Russian ammunition. For example, the tapering of the case toward the bullet was limited to 3/1000 of an inch, plus or minus, against a tolerance five times as generous in the Russian cartridge. The Springfield primer had to be right within 1/1000 of an inch. Despite these exacting standards, production at Hoboken-Bridgeport rose to forty million cartridges a week of which thirty million were Springfields and the remaining ten million were for such machine guns as Browning, Vickers, Lewis, Colt, Marlin Aircraft and the French Chauchat, as well as automatic pistols and 7-mm. cartridges for Servia.

Remington's record in World War I proved that a company which relied for its existence on making sporting arms and ammunition had become one of the greatest industrial factors in the defense of the United States. In Remington factories were made 69 per cent of all rifles manufactured for the American troops and over 50 per cent of all small-arms ammunition made for the United States and her Allies.

In addition, *all the ammunition* used by the gallant little Belgian Army, which for four terrible years clung to the last thin strip of Belgian territory, was made by Remington.

## Chapter 31

# Old Hats and New Primers

When the armistice stilled the guns on November 11, 1918, the whole world rejoiced in the belief that permanent peace had come at last. Their joy, though premature, was justified by the appearance of things. The democratic nations were completely victorious, and there remained no despotic power strong enough to threaten their security anywhere in the world. The only great country outside of the comity of free nations was Communist Russia. But the Bolsheviks were involved in so desperate an internal struggle for power that they appeared to most observers unlikely to survive for more than a year or two—a regrettable miscalculation.

Americans turned gladly to the normal ways of peace. None were happier to settle down to peacetime production of sporting arms and ammunition than Remington officials. War had been no boon to the company which had been subjected to great stress and hazard. Marcy Dodge, Sam Pryor and the other top men sincerely hoped that they would never have to make another military weapon.

As they took stock of the situation in December, 1918, they found that the huge factories, built for the necessities of defense, had a production capacity far beyond any possible peacetime employment. The first thing to do was to trim them down to size. The Hoboken Plant was returned to its owners, Swanton was closed down, and the Russian Rifle Plant at Bridgeport was sold to the General Electric Company.

At the same time the name of the company was also trimmed by leaving out the words Union Metallic Cartridge Company. It became the Remington Arms Company, Inc., as it is today. C. L. Reierson was elected President, and Pryor became chairman of the Executive Committee.

Even after the disposal of the three war plants, capacity remained far above the most optimistic estimates of the demands of sportsmen. In an attempt to utilize those long rows of buildings at Bridgeport and Ilion, Remington branched out into new fields. A line of beautiful steel cutlery was manufactured in part of the Barnum Avenue Plant. It included everything from sporting knives to household utensils. Remington cutlery won a deserved reputation for quality, and the company continued to manufacture it until the needs of national defense once again forced it to concentrate on military production.

Less fortunate was Remington's venture into making cash registers at the Ilion Plant. There was nothing wrong with the Remington cash registers; they were as good as any on the market. But other manufacturers were so firmly established that Remington found it impossible to put the business on a paying basis. In 1931, Remington sold the assets of its cash register business to the National Cash Register Company at a heavy loss.

These ventures were but excursions afield; sporting arms and ammunition remained the primary concern of Remington. Though small compared to the massive requirements of war, the demand for sporting rifles, shotguns and ammunition was bigger than ever before. Four million men had learned to shoot in the Army. Many of them considered target practice the one enjoyable feature of an otherwise unhappy experience. They wanted to go on to the greater pleasure of field shooting.

The popularity among them of Remington ammunition is shown by the fact that in a single day in 1922, fifty-one carloads of shot shells and rifle cartridges were shipped from Bridgeport. The cars were consigned to forty-one cities in seventeen states and contained 17,166,000 shot shells and 10,154,000 cartridges. It was the largest single day's shipment of sporting ammunition ever made up to that time.

These ex-doughboys wanted a bolt-action repeater like the U. S. Enfield they had used in the war. Remington was in the field with one in 1921. Models 30 and 30S were high-power bolt-action sporting rifles chambered for the famous 30-06 Springfield. For these guns Remington also made its own "Hi-Speed" game cartridge with a bronze-pointed expanding bullet weighing 150 grains and a muzzle velocity of 3,000 feet per second. Another popular cartridge was the Remington "Hi-Speed" with mushroom bullet weighing 110 grains. This was the highest velocity sporting cartridge successfully produced up to that time, with a muzzle velocity of 3,500 feet per second.

Other new Remington guns of this era were Model 24, the first autoloading rifle to handle successfully either 22 short or 22 long rifle cartridges, and Model 25, a slide-action repeater for calibers 25-20 and 32.

In addition, the standbys of the Remington line from the big Model 8 high-power autoloading rifle to the single-shot "Boy Scout" with the safe old Rolling Block breech were made in quantity. Special rifles and ammunition for crack target shots were also turned out.

The manufacture of ammunition was greatly simplified and improved from the 'twenties on, by the simplified practice recommendations of the United States Department of Commerce. The Simplified Practices Division of the Department was organized by Herbert Hoover when he was Secretary of Commerce. It applied to all industry, but was particularly valuable to the sporting arms and ammunition manufacturers. Its recommendations to this industry were drawn up in consultation with the Sporting Arms and Ammunition Manufacturers Institute, in the organization of which Remington officials played a leading role.

S.A.A.M.I. (familiarly known as Sammy) had its basic objects the safety and convenience of the consumer and establishment of uniform fair standards in the industry. The first consideration of the Division of Simplified Practices Recommendations—to which all the leading manufacturers of sporting arms agreed to adhere—was safety. For this reason rigid requirements were set for all cartridges on pressure and bullet-weight combinations. Standards on sensitivity were imposed for safe handling.

Next came the matter of simplification in order to make the process of manufacture less costly and more efficient. As a result of cooperative effort in this direction the number of different shot shell loads manufactured by Remington was gradually reduced from 4,067 in 1925 to 117 at the present time. Metallic cartridges were also greatly simplified.

Competition for accuracy was keen and in this field there was a constant battle for excellence. Regular hunting cartridges were steadily improved, and special target ammunition became incredibly accurate. Through constant research and development Remington maintained its leadership in this field. For example, in the 1930s, Remington 30-caliber ammunition held all the long-range center-fire rifle shooting records from one hundred to twelve hundred yards.

However, the trend was away from large-caliber match rifles—target shooters had come to prefer small bore. By far the most popular target ammunition throughout the whole world was the precision-built Remington "Palma Match" 22 caliber long rifle, made with infinite care for this purpose, and Remington Palma Match pistol ammunition.

As early as 1912, Palma was firmly established when Alfred P. Lane, shooting Palma pistol cartridges in the Olympic Games at Stockholm, was the only participant in this field to win three gold medals. In the World Small-Bore Rifle Championship matches held in Helsinki in 1937, with twenty-one nations represented, Jacques Mazoyer of France scored 1158 out of 1200 to win the world individual championship with Palma; and the United States Team, of which Remington's Advertising Manager, Frank J. Kahrs, was a member, won the Team Match, while Palma was used by the winners of every other event in the Meet.

The British National Championship at Bisley was won for ten consecutive years with Palma, and it was only natural that many of the five thousand shooters in the great annual rifle matches at Camp Perry used Remington ammunition. In 1934, at Camp Ritchie, Maryland, in the "Swiss Match," which is a miss-and-out proposition, Thurman Randle made a world's record of 212 consecutive bull's-eyes at two hundred yards, using Palma. In an impromptu test of the uniformity of this ammunition, Gail Evans, Remington's Assistant Director of Sales, once mixed together cartridges made in three different years. With this scrambled lot he made four perfect scores in succession. Even a microscopic deviation in the amount or quality of the charge would have produced a considerable error; this is an amazing tribute to precision manufacturing. Incidentally, as a boy, Evans was the youngest contestant ever to be on an international team, having shot for America against England at the age of sixteen. Others who established records with Remington's famous cartridges included Major John W. Hession, World Champion Rifle Shot, former U. S. Congressman Thomas Marshall and George W. Maxwell, the great one-armed trapshooter.

Though rifle shooting had received a tremendous impetus from the war, shotgun enthusiasts were just as numerous and their numbers were increasing. This was partly due to the ancient and honorable pastime of trapshooting (and later skeet) which had become one of the great American sports.

The "Old Hats" started it in England back in the days when Beau Brummel was making bon mots for the Prince of Wales, and the flintlock fowling pieces fired with a delayed action that must have made calculating the right lead a matter for an algebraic equation. The "Old Hats," were more formally known as the Hurlingham Gun Club of Fulham, England. In the slang of the day, an old hat was a good guy. The name had a double meaning for it was the quaint custom of these gentlemen to put live pigeons under a row of battered old beaver hats to which were tied pieces of string. At the classic command, "Pull!" a small boy jerked one of the strings. Over toppled the hat; off went the pigeon; and boom went the gun! If, when the smoke cleared away, there was a dead pigeon on the lawn, the shooter won his bet, usually a good stiff one.

The picturesque bell-shaped toppers soon gave place to little iron traps that collapsed at the jerk of the string; but the Hurlingham Gun Club remained the arbiter of the sport, making the rules for England, America and the Continent for a hundred years. The breed of pigeon they preferred was called Blue Rock, a slate-gray bird with a jato take-off. Today the targets made at the Remington trap and target plant at Findlay, Ohio, are called "Blue Rocks."

Some gentleman in Cincinnati, Ohio, formed the Sportsmen's Club and brought the sport to America in 1831. They must have been terrific Angolphiles, for they sent all the way to England for a shipload of Blue Rocks. When the travel-worn British birds were used up, the Sportsmen's Club settled for wild pigeons, dove and even quail.

The Cincinnatii had started something. The next organization formed was the Long Island Gun Club. Then came the New York Sportsmen's Club, and after that clubs sprang up all over the country.

Following the Civil War, with game taking to the remoter hills and conservation laws setting seasons, trapshooting got a tremendous boost, and new types of guns speeded the sport.

In 1826, a sportsman with the appropriate name of Samuel Woodcock had invented the shot cartridge, which was simply a paper package of powder and shot to be poured down the muzzle of a fowling piece. The beautiful breech-loading shotguns which came from England and France in the 1850s helped to push the sport along, and the comparatively inexpensive Remington double-barrel breechloader of 1873 was an even greater factor in popularizing it. Most important of all was the development of ready-loaded shot shells by U.M.C.

In the last decades of the nineteenth century, trapshooting was put on a uniform national basis by the organization of the Inter-State Trapshooting Association. This was succeeded by the American Trapshooting Association which evolved into the Amateur Trapshooting Association which presides over the sport today.

Things looked black for trapshooting in the 1890s. Henry Bergh, founder of the Society for the Prevention of Cruelty to Animals, took a dim view of the wholesale massacre and maiming of pigeons, and started a crusade against it. Popular sentiment backed him, for, though Americans love to hunt, they traditionally like the game to have a sporting chance.

Bergh got unexpected support from the shooters themselves, who felt that pigeons were too temperamental to be a fair test of skill. A lucky series of slow, straight-flying birds might let a poor gun win over a crack shot. And it was not always a matter of luck. In that era of uninhibited gambling, betting on the shooters was almost as popular as playing the ponies. With large sums of money changing hands, birds were tampered with despite the watchfulness of the committee. Some were doped so they would be slow and stupid. Others had their feathered control surface mutilated to produce eccentric swoops and tumbles. It was all most unsatisfactory. The obvious answer was a uniform, straight-flying target.

Artificial targets had been used as far back as 1866, when Charles Portlock of Boston produced a machine that pitched glass balls through the air. Charlie Portlock filled his balls with feathers so that the diehards could "see the feathers fly." But glass balls were a poor substitute for live pigeons.

About 1879, George Ligowski was watching some boys skimming clamshells over the water when he had a really bright idea. His brain wave produced the first clay pigeon complete with a gadget for skimming it through the air, which was the granddad of the modern spring-operated trap. Ligowski's invention was first exhibited at the conclusion of the New York State Shoot at Coney Island in 1880.

Ligowski's skimmer had a limited success, but the target was too fragile and the trap too crude. Fred Kimball of Peoria, Illinois, produced a better bird made of pitch, plaster of Paris and fine river sand. The "Peoria Blackbird" foretold the shape of things to come. "Clay birds" were eventually standardized. The modern specifications are: weight 3.4 ounces; diameter 4-1/4 inches; height 1-1/16 inches; height from rim 15/32 of an inch. They must be strong enough to stand shipping and the jerk of the trap; and fragile enough to break if hit by no more than two or three pellets.

The first Grand American Handicap Trapshoot was held at Dexter Park, New York in 1893—with live birds. This national championship proved so popular that it was repeated annually. The live-bird boys began to waver in 1900. That year the Grand American was first shot with inanimate targets at Interstate Park, Long Island, with seventy-four entries. It was won by Rolla Heikes of Dayton, Ohio, who broke 97x100. To please the conservatives a live-bird Grand American was held simultaneously, but since 1902, only clay pigeons have been used in this contest.

The Grand American grew and grew. In 1930, fourteen-year-old Rufus King of Wichita Falls, Texas, won it from a field of 960 entrants by breaking 97x100 from the sixteen-yard mark. Since 1924 it has been held at the home grounds of the Amateur Trapshooting Associaiton at Vendalia, in the Miami Valley of Ohio, which is right and fitting since in that state the sport was first practiced in America. All sorts of events have been added to the original match, and the tournament now lasts for a week.

The A. T. A. grounds are a tremendous sight on Grand American Day. Across the close-cropped emerald turf in front of the comfortable clubhouse stretches the long firing line—a quarter of a mile of traps which can accommodate 180 shooters simultaneously. Spectators are strung along behind the squads of shooters and cluster like swarming bees behind the center shooting stands. On either side of the clubhouse are rank on rank of parked automobiles. A little farther out are the rows of trailers in which many of the participants and their families live. Some of the trapshooting nomads, who are hunters or fishermen as well, acutally pitch their tents on the grounds and camp there for the entire week.

Over two thousand shooters usually participate in the Grand American. There are men, women and children ranging in age from eighty-odd to twelve years old, for here is a sport in which a man may participate from the time he is strong enough to lift a gun until he dies. More than once a fourteen-year-old, shooting in the Sub Junior Championship, has made as good a score as the winner of the Grand American itself.

During that fabulous shooting week, the thirty-six traps used at Vandalia, hurled 1,200,000 targets into the air, of which over 1,000,000 were broken by that straight-shooting group.

The greatest nuisance to sportsmen of all kinds from trap shots to elephant hunters, was the havoc wrought in the bores of their beautiful guns by the residue corroding their polished perfection. Unless guns, particularly rifles, were cleaned almost instantly after a day's shooting—or even after a single shot—the shining bore would be pitted and possibly ruined forever. The damage was not caused by erosion of the bullets or the totally consumed smokeless powder, but by the chemical action of the mercury fulminate and potassium chlorate used in the primers. Potassium chlorate was the real villain of the piece. It was used in *all* primers, even those which contained no fulminate. When a gun was fired, it left in the barrel a residue of potassium chloride which is akin to plain table salt. Like salt it absorbed water so quickly that even a minute grain would instantly begin a rusting process and eat a tiny hole in the steel. The only sure way to get rid of it was by pouring boiling water through the barrels, and drying and oiling them with the greatest care.

In 1926, when John B. Smiley was President of the company, Remington freed gunners forever from the tyranny of rags, cleaning rods and powder solvents, by perfecting the noncorrosive, nonerosive "Kleanbore" ammunition, fired by the first primer ever made in the United States which contained no corrosive element.

The development of Kleanbore began with a bang—or rather, six bangs. Egbert C. Hadley and E. E. Witsil of Remington's technical staff were sitting in their office one winter day in 1924, when their friend, James E. Burns, who had recently left the United States Cartridge Company, dropped in to pay a call. They knew Jim Burns as a lively character who loved to put on a show. He was also an imaginative chemist.

Jim chatted for a while about his plans for a trip to Florida. Suddenly a wild light flashed in his eyes. He pulled out a revolver and began to shoot up the office. People came running from all over the building. When the six-shot fusillade ended, the technicians somewhat sheepishly realized that Burns was shooting primed, but empty, cartridge cases.

Jim handed Hadley the gun. "Lay this away someplace where it's good and damp," he said. "And forget about it. I'll be back from Florida in about a month."

In due course, Burns turned up again. "Let's take a look at that gun," he said.

They had taken him at his word and put it in a very damp place indeed. The bluing on the outside of the barrel showed streaks of red rust. Burns ran a dry rag through the barrel and squinted along the bore. Then he grinned and handed it over.

What Hadley and Witsil saw upset them more than the original shooting. The bore of that small gun shone with all its pristine brilliance. It was a chemical miracle!

"Hey!" shouted Witsil. "What's in that priming stuff of yours?"

"That's for you to find out," laughed Jim.

"Oh, no, it isn't," said Hadley. "Because I think you're going to be working for Remington from now on."

Burns had discovered a substitute for potassium chlorate in primers. However, it took two years of intensive experimentation before Remington was ready to go on the market with their new, noncorrosive primer. The formula finally used contained lead styphnate which was manufactured experimentally by Du Pont in America and commercially in Europe. Allen A. Dicke and Dr. J. F. Hutchinson were sent abroad to look into the processes used there. Patents were purchased and several European experts headed by W. E. Brun were brought back to set up a plant to manufacture lead styphnate at Remington—the first time it was done commercially in America. They also made tetrazene, a sort of exciter for the styphnate.

After a completely reliable primer using these materials had been developed, came the time of testing, first in Remington laboratories and then by arrangement with shooting galleries in New York. Literally millions of rounds were fired in these really acid tests.

The guns in which the ammunition was fired were put through a rigorous program. Some were left uncleaned for eighteen months after firing anywhere from twenty-five to twenty-five hundred shots. Throughout the years guns, fired from thirty thousand to one million times, without cleaning, have shown no sign of corrosion or erosion.

Others were put in the laboratory humidifier where the wetness was 90 per cent and the temperature 120°. Guns were left in the annealing rooms of the plant where clouds of steam swirled as in a Turkish bath. The outside of the barrels of the guns so treated became encrusted with rust, but in every case the bore came through bright and clean. So it was conclusively proved that the benefits of the new priming mixture were not only negative, but positive. The "stuff" not only did not corrode but actually protected the bores of guns through which it was fired.

When the time came to market noncorrosive ammunition, Remington held a contest to choose a name for it. Two men a thousand miles apart had the same bright idea. W. A. Robins of Jonesboro, Louisiana, and Nelson K. Starr of Goshen, Indiana, both suggested "Kleanbore." They each received a prize.

All the great cartridge companies now make noncorrosive ammunition, but, as in so many other improvements, Remington pioneered this ultimate answer to a sportsman's prayer.

## Chapter 32

# The Sick Giant

Viewed through the lens of history, the year 1929 wears a sinister aspect. It was in October that the great panic on the New York Stock Exchange presaged the breakdown of the inflated economic structure and the coming of the world-wide depression. However, the crash came so late in the year that its effects were not immediately apparent on general business. For Remington, as for most of American industry, 1929 was a banner year.

But, as the depression deepened through the following years, Remington was hit harder than most. The national income sank from $69,000,000,000 a year to the starvation figure of about $32,000,000,000. Most of us had to do without everything but the bare essentials of life, and sales of ammunition fell off sharply. In addition, the Cash Register Company showed a terrific loss.

In 1929, Remington's sales amounted to $21,670,770; by 1932 they had fallen below $8,000,000. At that figure the Company was losing money at the rate of nearly $1,000,000 a year. Something drastic had to be done.

Dodge, Pryor and Saunders Norvell, who became President of the Company in 1927, conceived the idea of offering a controlling interest in Remington to E. I. du Pont de Nemours & Company of Delaware, with the thought that Du Pont capital and Du Pont know-how would reorganize the business and put it once again on a paying basis. The decision was especially hard for Dodge to make because it meant giving up control of the great corporation which his grandfather had founded and which he himself had helped guide through war and peace, good times and bad, to its eminent position in the field of sporting arms and ammunition. However, the circumstances were such that he felt obliged to take any course which promised to put the company back on its feet.

He could not have made a wiser decision. The little powder mill, which an enterprising French immigrant, Eleuthere Irénée du Pont, had built by the banks of the Brandywine near Wilmington, Delaware, in 1802, had grown into one of the principal pillars of America's economic strength. The vigor of Du Pont was primarily based on three constituents, diversity of products, sound financing and, above all, imaginative research which has kept it in the forefront of industrial and technical progress for a hundred and fifty years.

With its variety of basic products and its sound financial structure, Du Pont was in a position to rescue and reinforce Remington, if it would. But the question of whether to venture into what was a new field, and take on an operation which was basically mechanical—rather than chemical—was a matter for grave consideration by Du Pont directors.

In one sense it was a logical move. Ever since the days when Eliphalet Remington had bought powder from the Brandywine mills and Marcellus Hartley's new Union Metallic Cartridge Company had sought the finest powder for its cartridges, there had been continuous business relations between the companies. After exhaustive studies Du Pont decided to go ahead.

In the spring of 1933, the Du Pont directors voted, not unanimously, to accept Dodge's offer, and on May 24, 1933, the deal was consummated. Du Pont acquired a controlling interest of Remington common stock.

However, Remington remained a separate company and kept its strong individuality. Dodge was chairman of the new board which was strengthened by the addition of some of Du Pont's ablest men. On

June 2, 1933, the new board elected Charles Krum Davis President and General Manager of Remington Arms.

Marcy Dodge often says, "There are three key men in the Remington story—Eliphalet Remington, Marcellus Hartley and C. K. Davis." By an interesting coincidence, the forebears of all three were born in England within one hundred miles of each other. And all established homes in New York State. The comment by Mr. Dodge is justified by the fact that under the leadership of Davis, Remington rebounded from its depressed condition to the greatest achievements of its long and honorable career.

However, nobody, least of all C. K. Davis, would give all the credit to any one man. The results could not have been achieved without the counsel and guidance of many Du Pont officials and members of the Remington Board of Directors, and the co-operation, loyalty and teamwork of the employees.

Davis is a big man. His powerful frame is packed with energy and vitality. He was born in Lebanon, Pennsylvania, and spent four years in early childhood in Wilmington, Delaware, but for most of his youth, he lived in East St. Louis, Illinois. After graduating from high school there in 1905, he obtained a job in the chemical laboratory of the Aluminum Company of America and the following year he went to the American Steel Foundries in East St. Louis in a similar capacity. After a year's study of chemical engineering at the University of Illinois, we next find him working in the laboratories of the Baltimore plant of the American Smelting and Refining Company where he later became foreman in charge of refining gold, silver, platinum and palladium, and the recovery of selenium and tellurium.

Adventure beckoned with the offer of a job as chemist, draftsman and general foreman of the Braden Copper Company's great plant in Chile. Davis spent nearly four years with Braden. In 1915 he decided to return to the United States. A fellow engineer, R. E. T. Haff, who had been in Chile, wrote him that they were looking for men at Du Pont's Smokeless Powder Plant in Hopewell, Virginia. Davis applied for and landed a job as shift supervisor of guncotton. From this position he was advanced to that of chief supervisor of Guncotton Lines in the "A" plant and later became superintendent of plants "A" and "C."

Early in 1919, Davis was transferred to the Pyralin Department of the Du Pont Company in Arlington, New Jersey, formerly the Arlington

Company, manufacturers of pyroxylin plastics, which had been acquired by Du Pont in 1915. In May, 1925, he was transferred as general manager in charge of Production and Sales to the Leominster, Massachusetts, works of the Viscoloid Company, which had been consolidated with Du Pont's Pyralin Department. In 1928 he was advanced to the position of Assistant General Manager of the Du Pont Viscoloid Company and became President and General Manager and a director of that company in February, 1929, at the age of forty.

In the meantime Du Pont had acquired the Roessler and Hasslacher Chemical Company which manufactured electro chemicals, sodium, ceramic colors and peroxides. In 1932, Davis was given the opportunity of heading this company which is now the Electro Chemicals Department of Du Pont.

A little more than a year later, Mr. Davis began his long association with Remington.

At the same meeting which elected Davis, E. E. Handy, from Du Pont's Explosives Department, was made vice-president of Remington in charge of sales. Appointed as treasurer of Remington was one of Du Pont's best financial men, Walter U. Reisinger. In July, Davis brought young Donald F. Carpenter over from Viscoloid to be director of Remington's manufacturing department. George Bingham, who was associated with Remington for the astonishing total of sixty-two years, remained as a vice-president.

C. K. Davis did not know of the acquisition of Remington until one day Du Pont's Walter S. Carpenter, Vice-chairman of the Executive Committee and later President and Chairman of the Board of Du Pont, called him and told him of the tremendous new job they wanted him to fill. A Du Pont-trained executive readjusts fast. Because of his previous experience, an intensive study of the Development Department's report gave him an immediate grasp of the problems ahead.

In the first week in June, C.K. walked into the Remington offices at 25 Broadway, New York, and was introduced to Marcy Dodge, the new Board of Directors and key officials. His first act was to move the offices to Bridgeport in order to bring management close to the main operation. His office in the plant commanded the inner courtyards of the long range of brick buildings and a fine view to the shot tower. It was in the heart of the great plant. Satisfied, C.K. rolled up his sleeves and got to work. He had need of all his reserve energy in the hectic months that followed.

That was the summer of "Roosevelt Recovery," when the New Deal was new indeed. It was the era of General Hugh Johnson and the National Recovery Act. Everything was to be neatly codified and the Nation's business men gathered in Washington to try to write the complex codes which were required to implement NRA. As president of the largest ammunition company in the world, Davis was appointed chairman of the Industry Committee on Codes. Supported by old-time Remington experts, he spent half his time in Washington helping to write a code for an industry he had entered only a few weeks before.

When he was not in Washington, Davis was working fourteen hours a day remaking Remington. The problem was to bring it in line with the type of organization that the vast experience of Du Pont had proved to be most successful without destroying its fine traditions and the loyalty of its employees.

The workers and the managerial personnel were C.K.'s first concern, for their skill and integrity were Remington's most valuable asset. Their morale, he found, was very low. The wage cuts and reduced employment enjoined by shrinking business had produced a devastating effect. The news that Du Pont was backing Remington had produced a noticeable lift in their spirits, but much remained to be done. On July 1, 1933, all wages were raised approximately 10 per cent and the workers were put on a forty-hour week.

The Board of Directors promptly adopted Industrial Relations Plans, some of which were at that time far in advance of general industry, but already in effect in the Du Pont Company. Perhaps the most constructive of these steps were the adoption of a sound bonus plan and a pension and retirement plan which had been lacking at Remington, though, in some cases, pensions had been granted. By 1953 the Pension Reserve Fund, started twenty years earlier, had grown to more than ten million dollars.

Another of the original plans provided for paid vacations for wage-roll employees, almost unheard of in Bridgeport industry at the time. Others that followed throughout the years included incentive bonus plans and payments for valuable suggestions, company-paid Group Life Insurance, Hospital and Surgical Insurance and Disability Wages. The latter protected eligible wage-roll employees against loss of income during periods of nonoccupational illness or injury. These benefits replaced the limited and informal plans formerly in effect at Remington. Twenty-five Year Clubs were inaugurated at Bridgeport and Ilion for all employees who had been with Remington for that length of time. Over nine hundred employees wear the Club ring indicative of more than a quarter of a century of Remington service.

Davis also made a point of getting to know the personnel of the company to the greatest possible extent. He was concerned that good men be not lost in the new shuffle, but given every opportunity to rise in the organization. Furthermore, he wanted them to know him as a friend, anxious to help them. Within a short time he was known throughout the whole great organization as "C.K." Most important of all to the workers on the production lines, was the new sense of continuity and progress, and the assurance of stability that the vast resources behind their company gave them.

Employee relationship was only one of the things the new management tackled in those strenuous days of the summer of 1933. The physical properties of Remington needed revamping. The buildings showed deterioration due to lack of funds for proper maintenance. Paint was peeling, machinery wearing out—some of it was over fifty years old! Don Carpenter headed a comprehensive program of engineering study, plant renovation and redesigning of production lines for greater efficiency.

Ilion had been especially hard hit by unemployment and low wages. H. A. Brown, an experienced production man who had joined Remington in 1932, was appointed plant manager. Engineers were assigned to assist him in a careful study of plant layout and methods of production. As a result of this survey some of the old buildings were torn down—in one of them, Remington machine #1 was found, an old lathe—and the plant was completely rearranged in the comparatively new buildings erected in 1915. As soon as the remodeling was completed, production and employment began to rise, and morale improved.

Meanwhile Walter Reisinger was at work, putting in Du Pont methods of accounting and financing. First he pruned the figures on inventories and assets to give a realistic picture of the company's financial situation. In 1934, funds raised by a bank loan were used to buy out the bondholders, and in 1936, new preferred stock and common stock were issued to improve the financial structure of Remington.

Since 1936, no new stock has been issued, but the working capital of the company has been increased many times.

At the same time "Ras" Handy was revamping the sales department and building an aggressive sales organization. Du Pont was well aware that one of the most valuable assets of Remington was the extraordinary loyalty of its wholesalers, dealers and the sportsmen of America who had known and relied on Remington excellence for six generations. Handy built his sales policy around this heritage of good will.

After 1934, Handy was greatly assisted by the ideas and enthusiasm of Bernard E. Strader, who came to Remington when the Peters Cartridge Company was acquired, and shortly afterward became Director of Sales. He was the spark plug of the sales campaign. In 1944, Strader was made a vice-president.

Upon his death, in early 1949, he was succeeded by R. H. Coleman, who had come to Remington from Du Pont in 1937 as advertising manager. Vice-President Coleman was advanced to the post of Assistant General Manager in 1954 when Max R. Warden was elected President and General Manager. At this time Dewey Godfrey succeeded Coleman as Director of Sales and also became a vice-president. Gail Evans was named Assistant Director of Sales.

In the meantime the sales department was thoroughly revamped and new policies adopted to effect closer company-customer relationships and better service to the consuming public. The new policies were effectively implemented by such sales division heads as F. E. Morgan, J. D. Mitchell, J. J. Callahan, P. B. Patteson, and D. S. Reynolds. District sales offices were established in fifteen leading cities with experienced managers in charge.

Another project of C. K. Davis' looked to the distant future. Remington had never had a real research and development department. Now he installed one that was like the great Du Pont Research Department in miniature. Like their Du Pont colleagues, Remington researchers were not confined to projects that immediately concerned the making of arms and ammunition, but were encouraged to use their imagination in any related field, or to experiment in the domain of presently impractical theory. In World War II, Army Ordnance officers were astounded by the scope and character of the Remington research organization.

The infusion of new energy into Remington management showed

amazingly fast results. Nineteen thirty-three actually closed with an operating profit, though this was obliterated by Reisinger's financial surgery. His adjustments for obsolescence and write-down of inventory showed an accounting loss for the year. However, in 1934, Remington had a net profit of $142,589, and in 1936, with sales nearly doubling the depression low, the directors were able to pay a dividend of thirteen cents a share on the common stock. Although dividends had been paid regularly on the preferred stock during the 'twenties, this was the first dividend ever paid on the common stock of the present Remington Arms Company. Remington has never failed to pay a dividend since.

## Chapter 33

# Skeet and Ducks

The ingenuity of a Yankee sportsman and a magazine editor, neither of whom had any connection whatever with the company, also played a part in the rapid recovery of Remington. They were Charles E. Davies, who invented skeet shooting, and William H. Foster, who made it popular. It was the greatest innovation in shotgun target shooting since Ligowski invented the clay bird. Skeet began in 1915, with Charles E. Davies putting a trap in a field at the Glen Rock Kennels near Reading, Massachusetts, and walking around it to get shots from all angles—incomers, outgoers, cross-shots and quartering. He called it "Clock Shooting." The game was greatly improved by putting two traps in a "low house" and "high house" facing each other across the chord of a semicircle and placing seven shooting stands at intervals around its perimeter and one on the line between the traps. Station No. 1 is right under the high tower, No. 2 is 1/5 of the way around, No. 3 is 2/5, No. 4 is at the exact center and No. 7 beside the low tower. No. 8, the last station, is directly between the towers. At No. 8 the birds are bunged out of the slots directly at the shooter. The rule is that he must break them before they pass over his head. Since the targets are traveling at eighty feet a second and he is sixty feet away, he has less than one second to aim and fire. In addition to the single targets, doubles are thrown at stations 1, 2, 6 and 7. These, too, put a premium on speed.

The New Englanders kept this delightful sport all to themselves for eleven years. Then, in 1926, *National Sportsman* and *Hunting and Fishing* magazines simultaneously told the world of sportsmen about it. W. H. Foster, who was editor of both magazines, is justly called "The Father of Skeet." He helped to christen it as well, for so far it had been a game without a name. Foster ran a contest for the best name and got ten thousand answers. Mrs. Gertrude Hulbert of Dayton, Montana, won by submitting "Skeet," which is the ancient Scandinavian word for shoot. Roy C. Swan of Remington, who set up Lordship, was second only to Foster in popularizing this new sport. For many years he was ammunition sales manager of the company.

Skeet soon became a major shooting sport. Within ten years several thousand skeet clubs were formed, with the National Skeet Shooting Association as the presiding genius of the sport. Two great national tournaments were inaugurated—the Great Eastern Championship and the National Championship. The National is now held at a different club each year. Odis Walding, who won it at Detroit, made a record of 452 targets without a miss, using Remington ammunition.

The Great Eastern is the older of the two tournaments, having been inaugurated in 1929. It is held at Lordship, built by the Remington Gun Club near Bridgeport, Connecticut, and now operated by the Lordship Recreation Center, Inc.

Lordship is on a point that projects like the turf-covered bow of a ship into Long Island Sound. Around its edge nine skeet fields are arranged so that there is no danger from cross fire. Every year hundreds of skeet shooters gather there to compete in the Great Eastern Championship, the Lordship Cup Championship for teams of five, and in four other title events.

Because of the rigidly enforced safety rules, skeet is one of the safest sports in the world. Accidents on recognized ranges are so rare as to be almost negligible. Perhaps the most dangerous position of all is that of referee, as Ralph Scott found to his dismay when he was officiating at the National in Tulsa, Oklahoma, in 1938.

Scott was refereeing the All Indian Squad. The first man up was a huge, nineteen-year-old brave named Harry Bolton. On Bolton's first double, Scott sang out, "Lost and Dead." The next instant he went down under 290 pounds of irate Cherokee. Another crash flattened him further as 180-pound Bo Stanton joined his brother tribesman in protest.

Afterward, Bolton said, "The only reason we didn't scalp Scotty is that he is bald as an eight ball. He wouldn't make a good trophy."

The popularity of skeet in the 1930s brought a fresh demand for Remington guns. Though many trapshooters used the Remington Model 10T (Target Grade) slide-action repeater with its special 30-inch barrel topped by a ventilated rib, one of the most favored guns for that sport was the Parker single-barrel breechloader—there was no point in having a repeater when all the shots were singles. But the coming of skeet changed all that. For the quick work needed to get off the doubles, sportsmen turned with enthusiasm to the autoloader and the slide-action repeater.

However ingenious target-shooting games may be, they can never equal the thrill of hunting. There is no mechanical substitute for ducks coming over in a perfect vee on a frosty morning and peeling off to swoop down on the decoys while your gun barks twice for a neat double. But in the 1930s it began to look as though such delights might be lost forever to American sportsmen. The long drought, overshooting and lack of intelligent care for the breeding grounds had reduced the duck population of America from a plentiful 150,000,000 in 1920 to a pitiful 30,000,000 at the low point in 1935. At this rate ducks would have been virtually extinct by 1940.

Other game had suffered in proportion. J. N. (Ding) Darling, the brilliant cartoonist, who loved wildlife so well that he accepted the post of Chief of the United States Bureau of Biological Survey (now the Fish and Wildlife Service), tried desperately to stem the tide.

For many years Remington had contributed heavily to National Wildlife Conservation programs. In 1935, the management realized the situation was desperate. If the game disappeared, the sporting arms industry would be ruined, for target, trap and skeet shooting together accounted for only a small percentage of its sales. Spurred by this crisis, as well as the instinct of a sportsman to preserve the thing he loved, C. K. Davis got busy. He called on Remington's Henry P. Davis (no relation) to help solve the problem. Henry Davis, who was a leading authority on conservation, produced a plan upon which he and other experts had been working for years. Henry's program was revamped in consultation with C.K., such top conservationists as Senator Frederic G. Walcott of Connecticut, former Senator Harry B. Hawes of Missouri, Carl D. Shoemaker and Marcy Dodge. This plan became the basis of the American Wildlife Institute and, later, of the National Wildlife Federation. Ding Darling gave it his enthusiastic support and contributed very valuable suggestions. To launch it he gave a dinner at the Waldorf Hotel in New York at his own expense to which the leaders of the industry were invited. Nothing was too much trouble to make it a success. Darling even drew place-card cartoons for each guest. The American Wildlife Institute was founded at that dinner.

With such backing and the co-operation of the Federal Government, the conservation movement made tremendous strides. An annual Wildlife Restoration Week, proposed by Frederick F. Jordan, was sanctioned by the President of the United States and public interest was aroused. Congress passed the Pittman-Robertson Federal-Aid-to-Wildlife Act which allocated the excise tax on arms and ammunition to expand greatly the activities of the Federal Fish and Wildlife Service. The program of the Institute, including the formation of nine research units to study and develop scientific game management practices, were financed by the sporting arms industry with Remington as the heaviest contributor. Public awareness was further stimulated and more money raised by the sale of the beautiful conservation stamps, depicting various forms of game in North America, to wildlife lovers throughout the country. C. K. Davis wrote the slogan for the stamps which pithily expressed the purpose of the movement:

"For uniting the efforts of all friends of outdoor America to the end that future generations shall have their rightful heritage of wildlife."

Much of this research work is now conducted by the Wildlife Management Institute financed by the sporting arms industry, while the original Institute has evolved into the American Wildlife Foundation to promote conservation work in much the same manner as other great foundations advance the cause of public health or education. Remington's initial contribution to the Foundation was one hundred thousand dollars.

Working on parallel lines, Ducks Unlimited, financed by individual sportsmen has restored thousands of acres of the Canadian breeding grounds. The Isaak Walton League and the National Audubon Society are also important factors in the conservation movement.

Most important of all, the weather improved. The long drought broke and the world became again a fit place for ducks.

That is the story of how one of the great natural resources of America was saved for future generations. Shooting, with twenty million devotees, is second only to fishing (twenty-five million) among American sports; and the pursuit of waterfowl along the salt marshes of the coasts and on the lakes and prairies of the great inland flyways is one of the most popular forms of hunting. Few, if any, sportsmen wanted to destroy the thing they loved. All they needed was intelligent leadership.

The results tell the story. The whole dismal trend toward extinction has been reversed. From its nadir in 1935, the game population has risen steadily, and millions of future Americans will thrill to the sight of the southbound flights of ducks and geese etching victory Vees against the gray skies of autumn.

## Chapter 34

# Happy Days and Headaches

Though reorganization had been the first step, the new management's plans for Remington were not confined to reducing, pruning and revamping. They envisioned expansion in certain directions to give the company a balanced line of products. To this end Remington purchased the Chamberlin Trap and Target Company as early as August, 1933.

Chamberlin was one of the oldest concerns in this field making the famous "Blue Rock" targets and the Leggitt "Ideal" traps. It was a comfortable little company with a factory at Findlay, Ohio, which operated only in winter; in summer the plant was closed down so the employees could work their farms. Clay for the targets was dug from adjoining fields, and, originally, the factory operated on natural gas from seven wells on the company's property. As the wells began to fail the switch to electricity was made.

Chamberlin had been largely a handwork operation. The targets were even painted by hand, and they were shipped in handmade barrels packed in straw. Each barrel held six hundred birds. The company had suffered even more severely than Remington in the depression. Its equipment was old and inefficient and its manufacturing methods were positively hoary.

Remington and Du Pont engineers designed new machinery and production lines. Their most important contribution was a machine which eliminated the necessity for hand-dipping boiling pitch into the target molds. Even the most stalwart workmen found this operation trying in winter and absolutely unbearable in summer, which had been another reason for the seasonal shutdown. The Leggitt trap was improved and new machines were designed to make it.

With the new machines, and with Chamberlin products backed by Remington prestige and pushed by the Remington sales force, the factory was soon running on a year-round basis.

After acquiring Chamberlin, the next step in rounding out Remington production was the purchase of the Peters Cartridge Company in May, 1934. Peters had been an honorable rival of Remington ever since it was founded in 1887 by Gersham M. Peters, a Baptist preacher who liked to invent things. Gersham Peters' contributions to the industry bring to mind the surprisingly high incidence of churchmen in the history of ammunition—Brother Roger Bacon, of course, the Reverend Alexander Forsythe of the percussion cap and, finally, Peters, who invented the "Round Table" automatic-loading machine, which was the prototype of those used almost universally today. The particular slant of Peters' inventive genius was doubtless due to the fact that his father-in-law was J. W. King who owned the King Powder Works on the little Miami River, twenty-three miles northeast of Cincinnati, Ohio.

Backed by his proud parent-in-law, Peters built a shot shell plant across the river from the powder works, and made his brother, O. E. Peters, president of the new company. The mechanical advantage of Peters' loading machine, plus careful workmanship and intelligent management, got the Peters Cartridge Company off to a flying start. In 1895, it built a fine shot tower which dominated the Miami Valley.

When Remington bought the company, it had fallen on evil days like so many of its competitors, but the plant was up to date and the operation was efficient. More important still, as later events proved, was the acquisition of Peters' skilled workers, who for the most part lived in the model village of Kings Mills, and the well-trained executive personnel, many of whom became invaluable to Remington.

Though Remington built the finest autoloading and repeating shotguns in the world, it did not have a modern double-barrel gun. Right after the purchase of Peters, Remington remedied this by buying the Parker Gun Company of Meriden, Connecticut, on June 1, 1934. The Parker was the finest handmade gun in America. People called it "Old Reliable."

The evolution of the Parker was rather like that of a caterpillar into a butterfly. It all started with a coffee mill. Charles Parker, a broad-beamed, spade-bearded Yankee businessman, founded the company in 1832, to make his patent coffee grinder. The machine with its ornate cast-iron crank and fine wooden box, depicted in a catalogue over a century old, brings back nostalgic memories of the strong, sweet smell of freshly ground coffee ready to be boiled—not perked!—in an old-fashioned pot on the back of the stove, with an eggshell thrown in to settle the grounds. At the outbreak of the Civil War, Parker began to make Springfield rifles at the request of the Government. In 1868, the firm was reorganized by the three sons of the founder, Wilbur, Dexter and Charles Parker, and that year they brought out the first of their famous double-barrel shotguns.

From that time on Parker guns were an institution among American sportsmen. The brothers introduced many new features in shotgun design. In 1889, they produced a hammerless lock mechanism, and in 1902, added an automatic ejector. They produced the first 28-gauge shotgun ever made in 1905. The single-barrel Parker of 1917, with a ventilated rib running along the top of the barrel, became the favorite arm of American trapshooters. In 1926, Parker produced the first double-barrel gun to have a ventilated rib.

"Old Reliable" was famous all over the world for its beautiful workmanship. Parker guns contained the finest materials available and were handmade. Volume production was achieved by a unique method of preparing the component parts for the fitters by machinery, leaving an ample margin for fitting. The final process of assembling the guns was performed by master gunsmiths who fitted the guns with meticulous accuracy, so that every joint exactly met and the actions worked with silent precision.

For a time Remington continued to make the Parker at Meriden. Then the operation was shifted to Ilion, but the same high standards were maintained until the demands of World War II forced a suspension of production. As in the case of Peters, the purchase of Parker brought into the Remington organization a group of highly skilled artisans who were invaluable in the strenuous days ahead.

Meanwhile, Remington's management did not neglect their old friends, the rifle-shooting fraternity. Rifle design and methods of manufacture had remained almost static since the invention of the autoloader in 1906. Remington decided that the gun picture was badly in need of a new approach.

Throughout the 'thirties, engineers were hard at work designing new models and refining old ones. They produced Model 141, the "Gamemaster," in 1935, the only high-power rifle made with the fast slide action. It was chambered for caliber .30 and caliber .35 Remington center fire cartridges. The following year saw Model 81, "Woodsmaster," a high-power autoloading rifle chambered for the 300 Savage and the .30 and .35 caliber cartridges. The Woodsmaster was the only high-power autoloader that locked the cartridge in the chamber until *after* the bullet had left the muzzle.

In the field of .22 caliber, rim fire rifles, Remington brought out the autoloading 241, in 1935; the slide-action 121, in 1936; and Model 37, "Rangemaster," in 1937. The latter was a bolt-action, box-magazine rifle, designed for crack target shots, with a heavy, 28-inch barrel especially rifled for accuracy.

Though these guns were a great advance on all previous models, Remington engineers were thinking far ahead to envision a revolutionary advance in the manufacture of firearms. This was no less than a plan to produce a family of guns for all sporting purposes, many of the parts of which would be interchangeable. If it could be done, the parts could be mass-produced in quantities which would be impossible if they were used in a single model. Ray Crittenden, who became an outstanding creator in firearms design, was loaned to Remington by Du Pont to help with this project. He worked on it with Kenneth Lowe, a local Ilion boy, whose father had once been plant manager. In 1939 and 1940, Remington produced the first guns of the famous 500 series of .22 caliber rifles. These included Model 510, a bolt-action single shot; Model 511, a bolt-action repeater with a box magazine; Model 512 which has a tubular magazine and Model 513T, a special target rifle.

In 1941, Model 550 was added to the growing family. It was an autoloading .22 caliber rifle with a tubular magazine; the only one made that would shoot 22 short, long and long rifle cartridges interchangeably without adjustment.

The demands of defense then halted further development of Remington plans. They were put aside to wait until men could turn again to the pursuits of peace. When that time came, the plans were expanded and with remarkable ingenuity and scope.

Though the 'thirties showed a rising graph of production and a satisfying record of achievement, Remington officials did not escape some acute headaches. There was one in particular, which, though it only lasted a short period, caused intense anxiety. On October 3, 1934, a thief, with more cunning than sense, somehow eluded the guards and broke into a magazine in the Powder Park. The enterprising burglar helped himself to ten two-pound cans of what he evidently believed to be comparatively safe smokeless powder.

Shortly before seven o'clock an almost incoherent guard telephoned direct to President Davis' home at Fairfield. In a hoarse voice he gasped out the news that someone had broken into a powder magazine and stolen ten containers of polnol used in the primers. Until it is tamed by the proper processes, polnol is just about the most erratic and dangerous substance on earth. It is so sensitive that a harsh word might set it off, and so powerful that twenty pounds could devastate a large area. Such was the stuff that was at that moment, perhaps, jouncing through the streets of the city in the trunk of an old sedan.

While guards and officials fine-combed the Powder Park in the vain hope of recovering the polnol, an alarm went out to the Bridgeport police, to the fire department, the Connecticut State Troopers and the F.B.I.

The morning papers carried huge advertisements addressed to the reckless miscreant. In banner headlines Remington warned him of the fearful nature of his theft. Let him not touch the stuff himself, they pleaded. Only inform them where it was, and all would be forgiven.

Three days later, Stratford police and Remington guards found the ten cans of explosive hidden in two rock ledges near the Powder Park. The sensitive stuff had been hauled out of the magazine, dragged through a high wire fence, cleverly concealed in the obscure ledges and covered with underbrush. Somewhere in Bridgeport the luckiest man in the world was no doubt wiping the cold sweat from his forehead and making fervent resolutions to follow the straight and narrow path thereafter.

The other major headache of 1934, was the Nye-Vandenberg investigation of the munitions industry. It all started with the publication of a magazine article, which implied a combination for promoting war among the arms makers of America. In a time when idealistic hopes for peace had swung the balance of public opinion beyond the traditional American policy of armament for defense only, to the naked folly of pure pacifism, the article produced a terrific furor.

Senator Gerald Nye and Arthur H. Vandenberg immediately headed a Senatorial Committee to investigate the allegations. Other members of the committee included Senator Bennett Clark of Missouri, son of famous old Champ Clark, and influential Senator George of Georgia. The counsel for the committee was a man named Alger Hiss. At one time or another nineteen top members of the Remington management were called to Washington to testify. So were the high echelons of Du Pont. The investigators particularly concentrated on members of that famous family, and Pierre, Irénée, Lammot and Felix du Pont were grilled for hours.

Heavy fire was directed at Remington President, C. K. Davis, who had not been with Remington in World War I. Day after day he sat in the crowded committee room while senators, Government officials and even junior clerks hurled accusatory questions at him. There was one young upstart from N.R.A. who tried to prove that Remington had failed to co-operate wholeheartedly with that agency. It was too much for C.K. who had devoted months of strenuous work and thought to making the codes work. "Young man," he rumbled, "how long have you been in N.R.A.?"

"Two weeks," was the reply.

Davis' magnificent wrath burst out in a bellow that made the tall windows rattle and the microphones dance on the desk. "*I've* been working for N.R.A. for TWO YEARS!"

The final questioning of Davis concerned a letter he had written, stating his refusal of a large order for military ammunition from the Bolivian Government, because he felt it would not be in the interest of the United States Government, although no arms embargo was then in effect. Just before he was excused from the witness chair, Senator Clark commended Remington's President in these words: "I wish to express the opinion that that was a highly creditable attitude for you and your company to take, Mr. Davis."

Despite the smog of innuendo, the sensational accusations and questions slanted toward implications of guilt, the Nye-Vandenberg Committee was basically fair-minded. And the facts were incontrovertible. It was shown that for the past fifty years Remington had invariably lost rather than gained in time of war, and that it had been guided by patriotic motives rather than self-interest in making military arms. The sum total of the testimony of all parties conclusively proved that the company was interested only in manufacturing sporting arms and ammunition. The report of the committee completely cleared Remington Arms of warmongering in any form.

However, vindication never makes as good headlines as vilification. An undeserved stigma had been cast on the American arms industry. As for Remington officials, their comment that they had "a rough time" was quite an understatement.

Imagine, then, their feelings when only two years later, while bruised egos still hurt and the mud of slander still clung, the Ordnance Department approached Remington with a request for co-operation in drawing up a unit plan for building plants for the production of 30 and 50 caliber ammunition in the event of a national emergency. The idea was that if war came, the plants, each capable of producing one million rounds of ammunition a day, should be built in whatever number of units should be deemed necessary.

"Hold on to your hats, boys, here we go again!" just about expressed the sentiment of Remington officials. But their response was, nevertheless, wholehearted. Only one condition was made in the interest of self-preservation. The Government wanted Remington to do the whole job, but Davis insisted that Army Ordnance co-operate.

So for some months the best Remington engineers worked with an officer from Frankford Arsenal, planning the perfect cartridge plant. The plan developed building layouts, a catalogue in which the necessary machinery was listed, and a huge tome containing the whole intricate range of data. It was due to this plan, to the foresight of the Ordnance Department and the skill of Remington engineers, that late in World War II, Major General L. H. Campbell, Jr., Chief of Ordnance, could write to President Davis: "There has been no time, nor will there be such a time in this war, when a single American soldier will lack enough ammunition."

## Chapter 35

# England Alone

Nineteen thirty-nine was one of the black years of history. It started fairly enough. The conference at Munich in September, 1938, which threw Czechoslovakia to the Nazis, had eased the European tensions for a little while. In the United States, prosperity seemed to have permanently returned and the New York World's Fair expressed American aspirations for the World of Tomorrow—the bright tomorrow that never came.

Remington Arms, hitting a new high in the production of sporting arms and ammunition, envisaged a prosperous future if only the international situation remained on an even keel.

Though everyone feared that war would come, it was a stunning blow when the Wehrmacht crashed across the Polish Border in the dawn-red light of September 1, 1939. As the Stukas dove screaming down to destroy the Polish Air Force between sunup and darkness of a single day, and the armored divisions fanned out across the Polish plains to conquer a great nation in the space of a summer holiday, the world got a quick preview of modern war and German might.

When the Panzers rumbled through the smoking ruins of Warsaw and the Russians advanced to seize their prearranged slice of Poland, a queer quiet settled over Europe. The period of the "Phony

War" was more dreamlike than actual conflict. Millions of men in arms stood behind the Maginot Forts and the Dragon Teeth of the Seigfried Line while hardly a shot was fired. German trains puffed peacefully along the east bank of the Rhine in plain sight of the great French forts across the river, which made no effort to stop them. The Nazis were equally reticent about engaging in offensive warfare. Some skirmishes at sea were the only real indication that the world was at war though Russia enlivened the lull by attacking her small neighbor, Finland.

The weird quiescence threw confusion into the Allied councils, which was part of the plan—the Nazis, of course, knew exactly what was going to happen.

The outbreak of war in Europe had, at first, virtually no effect on the affairs of Remington Arms. The strict neutrality laws, which the Congress had enacted in the hope of keeping the United States out of European conflicts, precluded accepting any foreign arms contracts; nor did Remington management have any such desire. When an Englishman named H. E. Clive dropped in at the Bridgeport plant, and asked for permission to see the facilities for manufacturing military types of ammunition, he was politely told that the company was not interested and was refused a pass. Later Ted Clive worked very closely with Davis and Carpenter and was decorated with the Order of the British Empire for his outstanding services in building up ammunition production in America for the Battle of Britain.

However, American opinion grew that the Neutrality Act was not neutral at all, but gave a tremendous advantage to Hitler, who could draw supplies from Russia while the Allies were estopped from obtaining desperately needed arms from America. The law was modified to permit European purchases of munitions on a cash-and-carry basis. Immediately, the French and British Purchasing Commissions called on Remington Arms, and, in December, 1939, the State Department urged Remington to accept all the Allied orders it could handle.

Negotiations with the French came to nothing. Their commission reflected the confusions of their government, and did not know what they wanted or if they really wanted anything. The British, on the other hand, seemed to mean business. They wanted large quantities of .303 caliber Enfield ammunition. This could be made with machinery which had been stored in the Bridgeport "morgue" since 1919, but it would need reconditioning. Remington immediately made arrangements with several machine-tool companies to do this work as soon as the orders were confirmed.

Then the British began to back and fill—the phony war psychology made them uncertain what to do. One day Remington's management would get word that the ammunition was desperately needed; the next it would hear that it was not wanted at all. The machine-tool companies could not hold the capacity reserved for the overhaul of Remington machinery, and in January, Davis sent word to the British that unless they gave a definite commitment in two weeks, he would be obliged to give up his reserved position. On the last day of the stipulated period word came from the British that they did not intend to order ammunition from Remington or anyone else in the United States. So the reservations were given up, which cost England dearly when the time of crisis came.

Thus it happened that for the first nine months of World War II, Remington had no military contracts except for a small quantity of .45 caliber ammunition for the British. Then the big rush came.

In April, the Nazis invaded neutral Norway and Denmark. On May 9, 1940, the Phony War gave way to shattering reality. Holland and Belgium were suddenly engulfed by the mechanized Nazi hordes. Then came the fatal blow. At the ill-omened city of Sedan, the German armor pierced the patched-up Maginot Line, cutting off the flower of the French Army and the whole British Expeditionary Force, which had been sent forward to defend Belgium. It seemed that all was lost.

Not quite all! In the fire-shot fog of Dunkirk, English sailors and civilian mariners saved most of the valiant British Army, but all their equipment was lost; tanks, guns and great dumps of ammunition were left in the smoking wreckage of retreat. On June 17, 1940, feeble old Marshal Pétain offered to surrender France.

Staring at the stark situation across the Atlantic, Americans realized their own danger. It did not seem possible that Britain could stand alone against the conquering Germans. She was virtually disarmed by the debacle in Belgium. In all England there were but a few light tanks, less than one hundred field pieces, rifles enough to equip about two divisions and less than one million rounds of ammunition.

President Roosevelt went before the Congress to ask for unprecedented rearmament for defense. Then he sent to England most of the material stored since World War I, including nearly a million U. S. Enfields made by Remington. It was only a stopgap.

C. K. Davis acted promptly. He put all Remington production, actual and potential, at the disposal of the Government, and stated that he would accept no contracts not authorized by the War Department. Word came back to give the British anything they wanted.

Late in June, Davis got a telephone call from his old friend Arthur Purvis, formerly President of Canadian Industries Limited and connected with the British Purchasing Commission. Under his quiet English voice was the rough edge of strain. "We want to talk to you about rifles," said Purvis. "We need your help, desperately."

"You'll get it!" answered C.K.

He sent Don Carpenter to Washington that night.

Prime Minister Winston Churchill had sent his personal representative, Sir Walter Leighton, to Washington to get rifles at any cost. At a meeting at the Office of Production Management, attended by Owen D. Young, representing the United States Treasury Department, the Chief of Army Ordnance and other top American officials, Sir Walter told them of England's desperate need for several million Enfield rifles. The American officials urged that everything possible be done to meet England's needs. But what they wanted was technically impossible. All the machinery to make the new British Enfield must be designed and built from scratch. American machine-tool makers were jammed with orders. Even with top priority, the best Carpenter could promise was that large-scale production would begin in two years. That, he knew, was too late.

However, he had an alternative to propose. The United States Government had machinery for making Springfield rifles at the Rock Island Arsenal. If they would lease it to Remington, production of *Springfields* for the British could begin at Ilion within a year. The British objected volubly—they did not want Springfields. But they agreed to think it over.

After several weeks word came to Bridgeport that the Ordnance Department would lease the machinery. Then a query from the British: Could not the machines be altered to produce Enfields?

At this point Remington's President took a strong stand. It would be unpatriotic, he declared, to change the machines. Even though the official U. S. Rifle was now the Garand, most troops were still armed with Springfields. If the machines were altered, they would not be available to make spare parts if required. And in an emergency the Government might even need more Springfields. It was a wise decision as events proved.

Final agreement with the British was not reached until January, 1941. A group of engineers under Charlie Green had already inspected the machinery at Rock Island. The machines, protected by a thick coating of grease, were in only fair condition. On April 6, 1941, the first of more than fifty carloads of machines were shipped to Ilion where they were set up in the World War I buildings. Thirty-seven days later production was begun and in October, nine months after signing the contract and three months ahead of schedule, Springfield rifles began coming off the assembly line.

But they were not delivered to the British. During the interval, the necessity for arming millions of American troops had made it impossible to supply them all with Garands, and the United States Government took over the British contract. Had it not been for C. K. Davis' stand against retooling for Enfields, the GIs would not have had those guns.

The operation at Ilion was a tour de force of industrial ingenuity. Previously, the Springfield had been produced by the Government in such comparatively small quantities that it was virtually a bench-made job. To attain the daily production desired by Army Ordnance, Remington undertook extensive design and process changes. To the outstanding staff of Remington technicians belongs the credit for a remarkable feat of engineering. Of the ninety-one parts in the standard Model 1903 Springfield, twelve were completely eliminated in the new Model A-3. Twenty-three parts, previously requiring forging, were redesigned so they could be stamped by presses, and only twenty-four parts remained unchanged. Remington also developed a specially designed extra accurate Springfield for snipers, the Model A-4.

All these changes resulted in a better, lighter gun, a substantial reduction in labor and material costs, and a tremendous speeding up of production with consequent large economies for the Government and incalculable savings of that most precious commodity of all—time.

Under the direction of Works Manager George O. Clifford, and later of William T. Wood, employment at Ilion rose from nine hundred to nine thousand,—all those men and women had to be trained—and production at the peak was three thousand rifles a day. In addition, barrels and other parts for Thompson sub-machine guns were turned out as well as thousands of shotguns and .22 caliber rifles for use by the Army and Navy in marksmanship training. In all, 1,084,000 guns were made at Ilion to arm American troops.

Great as was Remington's rifle program, it was small compared to the production of ammunition. Long before any contract for guns was signed, the production of ammunition at Bridgeport was zooming. As early as June, 1940, the British had indicated their intention to place orders which would oblige the plant to increase its production of .30 caliber ammunition by 600 per cent and of .50 caliber by 2,000 per cent. Day and night sessions were held with Teddy Clive and other British experts to establish exact specifications and inspection procedures. Maximum production capacities had to be determined according to the amount of machinery available and the amount that could be secured, raw materials, additional building space, requirements of power, water, transportation, fire protection, guards, and, above all, manpower, skilled and unskilled.

As plans crystallized, contracts were discussed but there was no time to work out a formal agreement. The British offered a letter of intent which promised to cover expenses if work was started immediately.

"All right," said C.K., "we'll go ahead on that basis provided it is understood that capacity so built can be used by the United States Government any time they need it." The British agreed and the job was started.

The Works Manager at Bridgeport was James H. Chasmar, a veteran Remington man, with an imaginative grasp of the problems of production. None knew better than he that the making of ammunition is not to be undertaken lightly. Not only would the slightest variance of micrometric specifications result in inaccurate cartridges, but the ever-present danger of handling explosives could only be met by eternal vigilance by management and employees alike and by long-range planning of safety precautions.

Under Chasmar's experienced direction, blueprints of buildings, production lines, layouts, tools, roads, fences, barricades and hundreds of other facilities were rushed through the drafting rooms. As new production came in, working hours of office personnel normally eight to five, lengthened so they lasted until six, seven, eight and nine o'clock in the evening. Management often worked all night. It was a difficult task, accomplished with efficiency under Chasmar's leadership.

In industry as in life people are more important than machines. All the great expansion of the Remington plants would have been useless without trained men and women to man them. The people were there, long lines of workers formed in front of the employment offices at Bridgeport, but training them was the great problem. In fact, it may be said that the key to the success of Remington's entire war effort was the training school set up at Bridgeport under the direction of William E. Creadick.

Using real assembly lines as its classrooms and experienced technicians as teachers, the school trained the key workers, not only for the Bridgeport plant, but for the great plants that were later built, manned and operated by Remington for the United States Government. In addition, workers were trained for other large companies such as the United States Rubber Company, which were also operating ammunition plants for the Federal Government.

At its peak the training school had more students than Amherst or Williams. Bill Creadick was jokingly referred to as the "President of Remington University." The spirit and loyalty of old and experienced Remington workers made this great training program possible.

A special project that early got top priority was the English super-secret incendiary bullet. Those days of August and September, 1940, were the time of the Battle of Britain when a few hundred Royal Air Force Spitfires turned back the massed might of Hitler's vaunted Luftwaffe and, holding the English sky against incredible odds, saved England from invasion. To aid them, R.A.F. engineers had developed a laboratory model of a bullet with an incendiary core. That summer, the British entrusted Remington with their precious secret and asked them to redesign the bullet for mass production in calibers .30 and .50. The tricky part of the job was that the incendiary bullet had to have exactly the same ballistic characteristics as both the ordinary lead-core bullet, and the tracer bullet; otherwise it would be erratic. The job was turned over to two young engineers, Joseph Hodgson and Philip Burdett. In less than a month, they developed a working model of the bullet, which was put into large-scale production. This accomplishment was described by the Army Ordnance Department as "one of the vital factors in winning the Battle of Britain."

## *Chapter 36*

# *In Abundance and on Time*

By August, 1940, it seemed that Remington management was stretched to the limit of its physical capacity. The rapid expansion had loaded key men, from the president down to assistant division managers and even shop foremen, with so much extra work that they were pushed to the limits of human endurance. Key officials were working fourteen and sixteen hours, seven days a week. In fact, during the next two years many of them had only two days off—the two Christmases. In the light of later events, they thought that they had been loafing.

It was in the middle of the month that C.K. got a hurry call to Washington. Taking Don Carpenter with him, he went to meet the heads of Army Ordnance. The story was that vastly greater production of small-arms ammunition was needed—production far beyond the capacity of all the existing arms factories in the United States. Ordnance had decided that huge new plants must be built. They proposed that Remington should take responsibility for locating, designing and operating the plants, subject only to approval of important phases by Ordnance. A contract would be negotiated which would provide that the Government would advance adequate funds, would reimburse Remington for its expenditures, including the training of employees, and would pay a small fee for engineering, production and administrative services.

It looked utterly impossible. Where were the engineers, the managers, superintendents, draftsmen, foremen and the thousand of trained workers to come from? In the spring of 1940, there were in the whole Remington organization only three hundred and sixty men including skilled workers who had any experience with military ammunition. Forty times that number would be needed at Bridgeport alone. It was clearly impossible to stretch the administrative capabilities of the small group of Remington officials any further.

The Ordnance people said, "The plants must be built. You are the company we want to do it."

Davis answered, "O.K., we will!"

On the way back in the train, Carpenter and Davis began to plan the great program. They decided to divide the manufacturing activities of Remington into two divisions; the company-owned factories to be handled by one, while the other managed the construction and operation of the new Government plants. The first thing they needed was men—trained men as a nucleus for the great organization to come. Don Carpenter jumped off the train at Wilmington to see what help he could get from Du Pont.

The help they gave him was invaluable. Although Du Pont was itself overloaded with war work, they let Remington take some of their best men—eventually over five hundred supervisory personnel went to Remington. Du Pont also gave Remington a list of plant sites previously surveyed, and advice on purchasing and engineering. Despite ever-increasing commitments to the Government, Du Pont continued to help Remington throughout the war.

There was another reserve of trained men to draw upon—veteran Remington men who had been pensioned at the compulsory retirement age of sixty-five. They responded eagerly to the invitation to return, and throughout the next tough years worked with as great endurance and enthusiasm as any of the bright young men.

In less than two weeks Remington men were back in Washington with a list of plant sites. This time they met with Colonel L. H. Campbell, Jr., who because of his great ability rose to become a Lieutenant General and Chief of Ordnance; and Major—later Brigadier General—

Guy Drewry. Both of these men provided highly intelligent co-operation. Another Army go-getter was stocky redheaded, Major F. C. Shaffer, who became known to everyone at Remington as "Red." Shaffer was the kind of man who would stick his official neck way out to help get things going. Cutting red tape was his specialty. Instead of waiting for official sanctions he would give vitally needed authorizations on his own hook, trusting to the common sense of his Army superiors to ratify them later.

In Washington, it was decided that Remington should build one of the new plants and the Western Cartridge Company another. The unit plan, drawn up in 1937, was to be the basis from which to work.

After that things shaped up rapidly. Under Production Manager Charles Green's over-all direction, A. E. Buchanan, formerly head of Remington's Research Department, was put in charge of the Commercial Division, consisting of the company-owned plants, while Jim Chasmar was made head of the Military Division, which must be built up from scratch.

Chasmar set up offices in the basement of a disused church at Frankford Arsenal, and with the Government experts and engineers from Western Cartridge, the unit plan was revised to give more flexibility and larger production. Meanwhile a site had been chosen at Lake City, twenty-six miles from Kansas City. The architect-engineers were Smith, Hinchman and Grills of Detroit, who were directed by F. J. Van Poppelen.

Lake City was the first modern factory to be designed and built for the express purpose of making military ammunition. Eventually it consisted of three units for .30 caliber cartridges, two for .50 caliber and one for .30 caliber M-1 carbine. Each building was a complete manufacturing plant in itself, equipped with every element including its own power plant and administration office. Raw material went in one end, finished cartridges came out the other.

The design was daringly new. Each unit was a one-story building, laid out as a long rectangle with bulges here and there to suit special purposes. The machines for drawing the cartridge cases were placed in long lines across the room in progressive order—the first draw, second draw, third draw and so forth. Above them, on a mezzanine built of subway gratings, were the furnaces and machines for annealing, pickling, washing and drying the cases. The products of the first draw on the ground floor were taken on a conveyor belt to the side of the room, then up in a boot conveyor to the mezzanine, back across it, and down again to the second draw. Thus manufacture of cases was a continuous process with the work moving in a huge spiral down the long room.

It was the first time in history that ammunition was made in a closed cycle, continuous process. Remington engineers recognized the difficulty of this innovation—it meant that if, through carelessness or mechanical difficulties, a lot of defective cases got into the works, the whole process of production must be stopped until they were cleared out. In practice this only happened once. Chasmar says, "Our people had a deep sense of their great responsibilities and took extraordinary pains that nothing should go wrong."

From the sides of the main building wings were run out in which were placed the assembly lines for incendiary and tracer bullets, and the operations of priming and loading. These areas, where there was danger of an explosion, were so designed that behind every machine there was an exit with panic latches on the doors.

In the whole of World War II there was only one serious explosion at a Remington plant. This occurred in a small storage warehouse at Bridgeport. A hurry call for ammunition had come from the Navy; it swamped the regular packing department. In desperate haste to fill it, men had been set to work nailing up cases of primers in the warehouse. Someone, it is thought, drove a nail into a primer.

Despite the blast of the explosion, roaring flames and a convoluted column of black smoke a mile high, there was no panic in the great plant. Employees were evacuated from nearby buildings while the plant fire department and emergency equipment from Bridgeport and New Haven fought the blaze, and Joseph Kavanagh, Chief of Remington Protection Forces, threw a cordon of guards around the scene. In other buildings, the work for defense went on.

The explosion cost the lives of seven people. From that time forward, Remington refused to compromise safety on Government orders no matter how urgent. As inflated rumors of the damage reached Washington, the telephone lines got red hot with anxious officials asking how great a delay would be caused in deliveries. To all of them Remington officials were able to reply: "Production schedules will be met."

In October, 1940, the Board of Directors* met in the Empire State Building to approve the Lake City contract. It was a long session, for hundreds of clauses, worked out with Government officials, had to be considered. There was great anxiety. All the men present were wondering if the plant could be put in operation on time; whether inexperienced personnel could be trained; if the rigid Government standards could be met; whether the costs had been figured correctly, and whether there was enough capital to finance so huge an undertaking.

Late in the afternoon, it was moved, seconded and passed that the President be authorized to sign the contract. Almost like a stage cue, the closely guarded telephone rang. Don Carpenter answered it. Red Shaffer was on the line.

"Has your Board approved the contract?" Shaffer asked tensely.

"Yes. Just now."

"That's fine. We've just had a big jump in our requirements, and we'll have to build another plant big enough to make four million caliber .30 cartridges per day. We want you to handle it. It's to come into production right after Lake City."

Carpenter hung weakly on the ropes. "Good God! Red," was all he could say.

When the Board heard the news they were grimly silent. Each man there was facing the impossible, wondering how it could be done. Finally J. Thompson Brown spoke to C.K.. "Can you handle it, Charlie?"

Davis looked at Carpenter who nodded. Then he made his decision. "I think so."

"Well," said Brown, "if they have to have it, I guess it's up to us."

In the dairy lands and cornfields outside of Lake City, ground was broken on December 26, 1940, by the Junior Senator from Missouri, Harry S. Truman. Before the first shovelful was turned, Ordnance had stepped up its demands once more. There must be three more units. The plant must be finished in November, three months ahead of schedule. Generals Campbell and Brehon S. Somervell, Chief of Procurement and Supply, came out themselves to insist on the earlier date. So urgent were they that it was decided to put the construction

* See *Note 10,* Appendix I.

workers on costly overtime pay. When the contractor heard of this, he protested against the apparent waste of money. "What is the use of paying through the nose to get the buildings ready, when you know the power plant can't be delivered?" he asked.

"We'll go ahead anyhow," was the answer. "Perhaps we'll get a break!"

The units were finished before the power-plant boilers were ready. Remington officials hired a flock of old steam locomotives, ran them up on the new sidings and used them to power the machinery. The first lot of ammunition was produced at Lake City on October 12, 1941, less than ten months from the day of beginning.

Meanwhile "Buck" Buchanan had been recruiting workers. They streamed into his small office in Kansas City—bank clerks and butchers, gas-station men, chain-store managers, taxi drivers, saleswomen, farm girls, elevator operators and debutantes, people of every conceivable occupation and background. Whenever Buchanan heard of a group of available workers in some other city, he would open up a temporary office in a hotel—at Boise, Omaha, Topeka, and St. Joe. So twenty-one thousand workers were recruited to man the Lake City plant.

Though Lake City was in operation, all did not go well at first. The new machines kept breaking down or would not function at all. To meet this situation, Remington inspectors were sent to the machine-manufacturing companies to make sure that all machines were perfect before they were shipped. This system worked so well, and the method for purchasing was so efficient that, eventually, the Government put Remington personnel in charge of scheduling, expediting and inspecting all machinery for the *entire small-arms ammunition industry,* as well as that for shipment abroad under Lend-Lease. Remington's procurement activities involved, in all, approximately 27,300 machines worth $200,000,000 and countless other equipment from lock nuts to locomotives.

Another crisis came in the production of perishable tools. The punches and dies, and many others of the 150 different tools needed to make a cartridge, wore out quickly under the pressure of making millions of cartridges a day. One pair of tools—die and punch—was good for about one hundred thousand strokes, then it must be replaced. Since there were seventy-five operations, each requiring a pair of tools, making one million cartridges used up fifteen hundred tools. At full production, Remington plants wore out thirty thousand tools a day.

At first it was planned to make these small tools in the plants, as was done at Bridgeport in peacetime. But this proved impracticable. Fortunately many factories had tool shops, and small businesses all over the country, such as bicycle shops and jewelry manufacturers, had capacities for making them. It was a question of organizing them and teaching them how to meet the exacting specifications of tolerances as fine as 1/10,000 of an inch. Largely through the efforts of Ferris Rieves, Remington purchasing agent, and Albert French, who had been connected with Remington sales for thirty years, 480 suppliers—called "trained vendors"—were recruited. Through these manufacturers, many of whom converted their facilities to the production of perishable tools and gauges, more than fifty million dollars' worth of these badly needed items were purchased, inspected and approved by Remington personnel.

Meanwhile the pressure to get the Western plants into operation was tremendous. As early as September, 1941, C. K. Davis was called to Washington by Under Secretary of War, Robert P. Patterson, who painted a gloomy picture of the small-arms ammunition situation.

"All the ammunition from existing plants is needed to supply the British and other countries under Lend-Lease," he said. "The United States Army is wholly dependent on the new ordnance plants, particularly Lake City and Denver. Right now the Army has practically no stocks of small-arms ammunition for training purposes.

"The other day," he added, "I talked to a boy in training who told me that in six months he had fired on the rifle range just once."

At C.K.'s request, C. M. Green, Remington's manager of production, outlined to Secretary Patterson an estimate of the production that could be expected from the two plants for the next six months. The figures ranged from 15,000,000 rounds in October, 1941, to 152,000,000 in May, 1942, an encouraging picture. Under the constant drive by Remington's management, the critical situation did not long endure.

As the kinks were ironed out, Lake City went into high gear. At its peak, the great plant, on its reservation of thirty-eight hundred acres, had twenty-five miles of road, 236 major buildings, eleven miles of railroad track and parking space for five thousand automobiles. It had its own hospital, fire and police departments.

The original plans called for a daily capacity of 2,000,000 caliber .30 cartridges and 640,000 caliber .50. This was stepped up to meet

Ordnance requirements until, at the end, capacity was 8,900,000 cartridges per day.

Denver, Colorado, was chosen as the location for the second plant. The best site was a piece of land three miles long and three quarters of a mile wide, running right through Hayden Ranch from the suburbs of the city to the foothills of the Rampart Range. It was perfect except for the fact that there was no railroad near it. However, the trunk lines serving Denver were willing to co-operate. They got together, formed a company and built a new railroad to the site.

Remington was learning fast at Lake City, and the Denver plant benefited. Ground was broken on March 3, 1941. Production of cartridges began a little over seven months later—five months ahead of schedule. At peak production, the five units of the Denver plant turned out ten million caliber .30 cartridges each day.

Meanwhile, the military situation in Europe grew ever darker as the Nazis took Greece, Crete and Yugoslavia; and were joined by the rest of the Balkan countries. In June, 1941, Germany attacked her erstwhile ally, Russia, and as the Wehrmacht's armored columns romped across the fertile Ukrainian plains, it looked—for a time—like another Hitler hayride. On the far side of the Pacific, Japan was slowly swallowing China, and obviously preparing an attack against Indo-China and Malaya.

Under these circumstances Army Ordnance once more stepped up requirements. This became known as "the second wave." Another great cartridge plant was ordered, and Remington picked Salt Lake City in Utah as the site. This time the main difficulty was finding a range to test the ammunition. A hill was needed as a backstop for the high velocity bullets and there was not even an anthill on those level plains. Eventually Remington acquired a four-mile strip of land ending at Great Salt Lake over which spent bullets might whiz harmlessly.

Upon Remington fell the task of building the Utah plant. The Du Pont Engineering Department was called on to furnish engineering management for the design and construction phases of the job. Headed by Maxwell R. Warden, construction began on July 21, 1941, and the plant was run up in the record time of six months from ground-break to finished product. As it neared completion, Warden telephoned C.K. that a works manager must be appointed. "You take it!" answered the

President of Remington. However, he had to use all his powers of persuasion to induce Du Pont to part with Warden.

Warden had no previous experience in making ammunition, but he was a first-class executive and he soon had Salt Lake running like a gigantic watch. He went on to become Assistant Manager of the Military Division, and ultimately Vice President and Assistant General Manager. In 1954 he succeeded Davis as President of Remington Arms.

In addition to the Utah plant, the Ordnance Department's "second wave," included a contract with the United States Rubber Company to build a similar plant. In this case Remington was called upon to teach the difficult techniques to U. S. Rubber. Over one thousand key personnel for U. S. Rubber and other manufacturers were put through the Remington training school.

The great Bridgeport Works was the heart and center of the Remington organization. It was expanded and expanded again, and then again. The executive offices were yanked out of the plant to make room for production lines and established on three floors of the Hotel Stratfield. As management personnel expanded, Remington had offices scattered all over Bridgeport in buildings owned by the Cadillac-Oldsmobile Agency, the Packard Agency, the D'Elia Electric Company and the Seaside Club. Bridgeport was constantly called upon to contribute heavily to the whole tremendous war program, since it was the chief source of the Remington know-how, which was diffused through the company's rapidly expanding ranks and passed on to the entire industry. Bridgeport provided much of the top supervision and repeatedly loaned groups of veteran machinists, tool setters and other skilled workmen to assist in setting up new operations.

By 1943, over fourteen thousand people worked at the plant on Barnum Avenue, and it was unique among ammunition plants for the variety of calibers and types manufactured for the defense program. The list included ball, armor piercing, tracer and incendiary cartridges in standard military calibers; a wide variety of primers; shot shells and .22 caliber cartridges for training; and several other calibers for special purposes, including such oddities as .45 caliber revolver cartridges full of bird shot for airmen who parachuted into the South Pacific jungles, and frangible bullets so that soldiers in training could fire live ammunition at an airplane for test purposes without endangering the pilot.

Bridgeport was the first non-government plant to prime and load 20-mm. shells, the cases for which were made by the Bridgeport Brass Company with advice from Remington. In all, more than one hundred companies were given assistance through visits to the Barnum Avenue plant and the distribution of extensive technical and operational information.

Remington licensed the United States Government and all designated maufacturers without charge, under all Remington patents and know-how. In addition, Remington made its splendid Research and Development Department under Buchanan and E. C. Hadley available to the Government. They worked on a wide range of projects for a number of Government agencies and private manufacturers. Among the things they developed were a grenade launcher for the Garand rifle, super high-speed artillery projectiles, electrically fired primers for machine guns, a 12-gauge shell to start torpedo gyroscopes, new ballistic instruments, and dozens of other devices in fields far removed from their regular business.

All this shows clearly enough why Remington was the Government's chosen instrument to run the great new cartridge plants and to disseminate its know-how to other companies. Another evidence of the wisdom of that choice is the vital little matter of meeting the Ordnance Department's rigidly high standards of acceptance for military cartridges. These standards were set up back in the leisurely days of peace to apply to Government arsenals operating on a small-production basis. Even at that time, the commanding officer at Frankford Arsenal complained privately that the Ordnance Department's ideas were unrealistic. When the same standards were set for the huge mass-production operations at Bridgeport and the new plants out West, they were regarded as too extreme. The very men who drew them up said frankly, "We thought we would have to retreat from our standards. We were just giving you something to shoot at."

Colonel Wallace L. Clay, U. S. Army, Retired, who knows all about Government specifications and methods of inspection, set up the Remington system of standards and inspection. C. K. Davis called him "our guardian of quality." Clay's interpretation and clarification of Government procedures was of great value in orienting Remington people to Ordnance Corps methods. In addition, he made Remington standards even tougher than those of Ordnance. As a result Remington not only met the "impossible" Government specifications, but in some instances raised them even higher.

The remarkable thing is that all this was done—the basis laid for the huge expansion and the vast training program, the setting of standards, the development of new types of ammunition, the improved Springfield rifle, the complex organization of machine-tool and perishable-tool procurement, and the arrangements for obtaining the incredible masses of raw material that the huge plants consumed—all this was planned and most of it was functioning before Pearl Harbor.

## Chapter 37

# From Pearl Harbor On

War came to most Americans on a quiet Sunday afternoon when their radios shouted the stunning news of blast and flame and death, of planes with strange, red sun symbols on their wings, flashing through the oily smoke from dying battleships, that was Pearl Harbor. It came to them in the solemn words of the President as he told of the events of the "date that will live in infamy." It came to them in Hitler's tirade as the arch-Nazi declared war against the United States; it came in the news bulletins of Japanese troops swarming against Malaya, Indo-China and the Philippines. But on December 7, 1941, the men and women of Remington had already been working under wartime tensions for eighteen months.

That first crowded day of war showed the face of the future. Men who had worked at the utmost limit of endurance must find the strength to work still harder. Somehow they did. The problem was not to spur them on, but to hold them within the limits of human capacity. Remington officials, as they traveled on inspection trips through all the plants, kept alert for signs of strain, ready to issue peremptory orders to this man or that to quit and take a rest before he dropped.

When they talk about those strenuous days, the men who went through them seem to glow at the remembrance of a splendid experience

—the experience of living to the hilt, inspired by selfless patriotism. Idealism and self-abnegation may seem odd ingredients of that materialistic world of machines and production, but they were present there as surely as on the fields of combat. In plain truth, those men were a dedicated lot.

The declaration of war brought on the third wave of Ordnance Department requirements. This consisted largely of stepping up production in the new plants. By a sort of scientific wizardry—increased efficiency of operations, the streamlining of assembly lines and the addition of some new machines—the capacity of the new plants was almost doubled. For example, production in the units designed to make 1,000,000 caliber .30 cartridges a day was raised to 2,000,000, and .50 caliber units designed for a maximum daily production of 640,000, were stepped up to 1,000,000.

The fourth wave followed quickly after the third. This envisaged the purchase and adaptation of existing industrial plants to the manufacture of ammunition. For this purpose Remington found a cotton mill with fine concrete and steel construction at Lowell, Massachusetts. It was converted to manufacture cartridge cases, but since it was located in the heart of the city, the explosive work—priming and loading—was done in new buildings erected on the old proving ground of the former United States Cartridge Company just outside of town.

The Lowell job was almost completed when the acute shortage of copper caused the Government to clamor for steel cartridge cases. Remington researchers had been working on this problem for some time. Great difficulties were involved, for steel was basically ill-suited for this purpose. They were eventually overcome and Remington produced 3,500,000,000 rounds of steel-cased ammunition. Most of this work was done at Bridgeport and Denver, but the Lowell plant went into production of both brass and steel cartridge cases.

In the fall of 1942, the Peters plant at Kings Mills finally went into military production. The delay was caused by a confusion of councils between the British Purchasing Commission and the Ordnance Department, as to what type of ammunition should be made there. On June 8, 1942, the plant was ordered to make .30 caliber carbine ammunition.

The final order stuck, and Kings Mills went into production on

November 10, 1942. At its peak, the following summer, Kings Mills was producing 2,000,000 cartridges a day. In addition, 125,000,000 shot shells were made for the Government training program.

Even little Findlay contributed its share. It was at first closed down. Then the Air Force discovered that one of the best ways to train aerial gunners to lead their fast-flying targets was to teach them to shoot skeet. A hurry call went out for traps and targets. High priorities were assigned, and the lights burned all night long in the little factory, where the toys of sport poured out for the uses of war.

Incidentally, wartime skeet shooting was a very different proposition from the sport as practiced at Lordship. The favored guns were the Remington Model 31, (slide action) and Model 11, (autoloader) and the Winchester Model 12. They were equipped with ring sights—like machine guns—and the gunners were taught to lead their target by "half a ring" or "a ring and a half." They learned very fast by this method, though it sometimes threw crack skeet shots for a loss when they tried to combine the ring-and-a-half system with their natural swing.

When the trainees got good enough, they were graduated to simulated airplane turrets, where the shotguns were placed on fixed mounts and swung just like the tail gun of a B-17.

Never in history have so few guns fired so many rounds. They were going all day long, firing so fast that if you spit on a barrel the stuff would jump off boiling. Forty million shot shells were fired at Laredo Army Airfield alone. Major Lee Braun, a crack skeet shot who was an Air Force instructor, personally fired four hundred thousand rounds from his Remington 31. In the course of duty it needed repairs only once—a broken action bar. Braun's gun is still usable.

As things turned out the battle of small-arms ammunition was won before ever America went to war, which is the way things should be but seldom are. Hardly had the great new ammunitions plants gone into full production before the Army found itself snowed under by cartridges. As early as July, 1942, Ordnance began shifting emphasis away from .30 caliber ammunition, and by the summer of 1943 cutbacks of production werc ordered. On December 31, 1943, five months *before* D Day, the great Utah plant was orderd to terminate operations and was placed in standby condition. Operations at Denver ended on July 31, 1944, and the plant was converted to make fuses for artillery projectiles. At the other plants the pressure for production gradually eased off. Thus were all requirements of the Ordnance Department met not only in full, but quite literally, overflowing.

The Government was quick to recognize Remington's outstanding services. On August 24, 1942, the Army-Navy E, with a white star, was awarded to the Lake City Plant. Denver got it on September first, and the Bridgeport Works on September fourteenth of that year. Ilion received its award on November 9, 1942. Utah was honored in September, 1943, and little Findlay was given the right to hoist the Pennant of Excellence on August 31, 1944.

The proud pennants flying over their factories and the E pins they wore in their lapels were a source of great satisfaction to Remington personnel and management. They took an equal pride in the extraordinary safety record they hung up. In evaluating this, it is necessary to understand the problems that were solved—first in designing safe facilities for the mass production of ammunition on an unprecedented scale, and then of training thousands of inexperienced workers to handle the hazardous materials that make up a cartridge.

Many American companies expanded 100 per cent and even 500 per cent to meet defense requirements; few if any, expanded over 2,000 per cent as did Remington. In 1939, there were fewer than 4,000 people employed in all its plants; at the peak in 1943, Remington personnel numbered 82,500. In addition over 15,000 Remington employees joined the armed services, and replacements were trained for them.

Now look at the safety record. In 1939, the major injury rate was 1.07 per million man hours worked. It rose sharply in 1940 to 1.72; then, as safety measures were redoubled, dropped even more steeply. In 1942, the rate was only 0.88 and in 1943 it dropped to 0.67. Remington-operated plants stood first in point of safety among small-arms ammunition plants generally, and the latter, in turn, ranked far better than the average of general industry. Both the Lake City and Denver Ordnance Plants achieved safety records which are among the best all-time performances in the history of industrial safety. When it is considered that the plants and machinery were of new design, the scale of production vast beyond any experience, and the employees virtually all newly trained, the result seems incredible.

Statistics are ordinarily dull, but these are offered without apology for they are thrilling. Add to them the fact that Remington manufactured 1,084,000 rifles and more than 16,000,000,000 cartridges for the Government during World War II. The latter figure represented 41 per cent of all the small-arms ammunition used by the United States for its own forces and for Lend-Lease.

Such a record was possible only because of the intense loyalty of the whole Remington organization. During the entire war program no production was ever lost because of lack of co-operation between labor and management. The Labor-Management Committees, which were organized at all Remington-operated plants worked together selflessly to speed production and insure safety of operation. They well deserved the tribute paid them by General Campbell, who wrote to C. K. Davis:

"All of you should be very proud of your fine record. Will you please convey to your loyal American personnel . . . our appreciation of their contribution to a speedy solution of the small-arms ammunition production problem. You and your people have helped to win a vital battle."

# Chapter 38

# The Breakthrough in Guns

There have been many dramatic improvements made in the manufacture of American sporting firearms and ammunition since the infancy of the industry at the beginning of the nineteenth century. From the crude muzzle loaders of the early 1800s to the precision rifles and shotguns of today, these changes have reflected the ever-improving technology of an industry that has geared itself to meet the needs of America's sportsmen.

Among the most dramatic of these advances was the development of metallic cartridges in the middle of the last century, which opened the way for the design of the first really practical breechloading guns. Later improvements, such as center-fire cartridges, loaded shotgun shells, choke boring of shotguns and the introduction of smokeless powder, were equally important to the development of modern sporting firearms and ammunition as we know them today.

As a result of all the advances made in the last hundred years, in a field in which improvements had been relatively slow in coming for several centuries, it seemed to many people that the development of sporting firearms had reached its zenith by the late 1930s.

However, in the years since World War II, there have been even more startling improvements, which have helped the industry to keep pace with the tremendous surge in popularity of hunting and shooting. These improvements have included a parade of new models, new calibers and new production concepts that, taken in the whole, represent a major breakthrough in sporting firearms design and manufacture.

Remington Arms Company has been one of the chief contributors of new design concepts during this period. Starting with the first of its postwar models in 1948, Remington has gone on to design and produce a complete new "family of guns" that has captured the imagination of the shooting public. Included in the Remington line today are bolt-action center-fire rifles, automatic and pump-action shotguns, slide-action high-power rifles, gas-operated automatic high-power rifles, automatic .22 caliber rim fire rifles, slide-action .22 caliber rim fire rifles and bolt-action rim fire rifles.

Before actual designing of these guns was started, Remington interviewed thousands of shooters to find out what they wanted in the way of new models. As a result of this survey, the company had a firm foundation on which to build plans for the future.

In designing new models to meet the needs found in this and subsequent surveys, some entirely new concepts in manufacturing were used. For example, the demand for lighter-weight guns in combination with heavier loads necessitated a search for new materials and new methods for containing the higher impact stresses. As a result, in shotguns the actions were redesigned so that breech bolts could be locked up more securely, using a barrel extension made of tougher high-strength steels. The closer tolerances possible also opened the door for barrel interchangeability, eliminating the need for hand fitting, should a shooter decide to use a different type of barrel.

In Remington's center-fire high-power rifles, the bolt heads were redesigned to provide a hardened steel shroud and thus give greater support to the base of the cartridge, with a resulting greater strength and safety. This was made possible with the design of a novel "wrap-around" extractor of spring steel that fits snugly in a circular groove enclosed within the bolt shroud.

The aluminum alloys, now available in abundance, provide a lightweight and rustproof material for many gun parts. Used in combination with steel, where high strength is a factor, these new lighter-weight metals are found in most trigger guards and many gun receivers.

Without a doubt, the most revolutionary breakthrough in materials for sporting firearms was signaled by the Remington "Nylon 66" automatic rifle. Performance standards for this new model were the highest ever set for an automatic .22 rifle. They were so high, in fact, that any use of wood in the stock would have left it short of these standards. A new material was needed that would be capable of meeting the following exacting specifications:

Ability to assume a shape consistent with that of the finest stock design.
High tensile, impact and flexural strength.
High abrasion resistance.
High resistance to heat distortion.
High resistance to cold temperatures.
Absolute resistance to most solvents; mild acids; alkalies; fungi; rodents.
Easily repaired finish.
Lightweight.
Permanent color.
Absence of corrosive effect on metals.
Dimensional stability.
Self-lubricating.

The search led to structural nylon. In every test, it stood out as the ideal material for holding to the standards set out for the gun. In the course of its development, early models were thoroughly checked and found to meet each of the exacting specifications. The result was a gun that has won universal acclaim from shooters for its lightness, ease of handling, accuracy and ruggedness.

Another very important phase of designing that contributed to Remington's major breakthrough was the development of parts that had a high degree of interchangeability. This has enabled Remington to produce "families of guns," guns of the shotgun type, guns of the high-power rifle type and guns of the low-power (or .22 caliber) class, all with a similar look and "feel." With these gun types, the parts can be replaced, with no factory fitting, in guns of the same model or class, thus making repairs much easier for owners.

Continued study of new processes and materials has enabled

Remington to produce guns of lighter and more compact design. Increased use of new welding techniques and lighter metal as well as explorations and research into the very nature of metal itself have revealed new ways of forming gun parts.

Another factor that has contributed to the quality built into every Remington gun is high-speed photography. To produce a gun that will perform as designed requires continuous study and testing of the pilot models. Since the reaction of the critical area of design, particularly in autoloading shotguns, is too fast to evaluate with the naked eye, a cutaway model is made, loaded and fired under the critical scrutiny of a high-speed camera. The action can then be slowed, studied and, if necessary, traced on actual charts for evaluation. Bulk of parts quite frequently can be eliminated in this fashion if the study warrants.

Any study of modern gun manufacture would be incomplete and any story of a breakthrough in the gunmaking field would be worthless were the more than one hundred fifty years of gunmaking experience by Remington not considered. The combination of father-to-son tradition coupled with modern research methods and advanced development creates a certain pride in accomplishment. Such a combination of heritage and talent has been the key to Remington's success in presenting to the gun-owning public the finest products of the gunmakers' skill.

# *A Remington Pictorial Essay*

Eliphalet Remington II.

The Remington Homestead, Ilion, New York. The birthplace of Eliphalet Remington II.

The first home of Eliphalet and Abigail Remington at Ilion "Gulf."

The old Remington forge, the birthplace of Remington Arms.

Ilion, New York, as it appeared in 1883. The Remington Armory and agricultural works are at the left.

The Remington Armory at Ilion. This building was erected in 1835 and dismantled in 1913.

THE MECHANISM: the first Remington rifle made by Eliphalet Remington in 1816.

THE MAN: an old photograph of Eliphalet Remington II.

The first woman's bicycle in Ilion, New York. This model was popular around the turn of the century. Remington Arms manufactured many products other than firearms and cartridges.

A photograph of the model '97 Remington bicycle. During the late 1890's some eight hundred Remington employees commuted to work on bicycles made by the company.

Remington's first production-model typewriter.

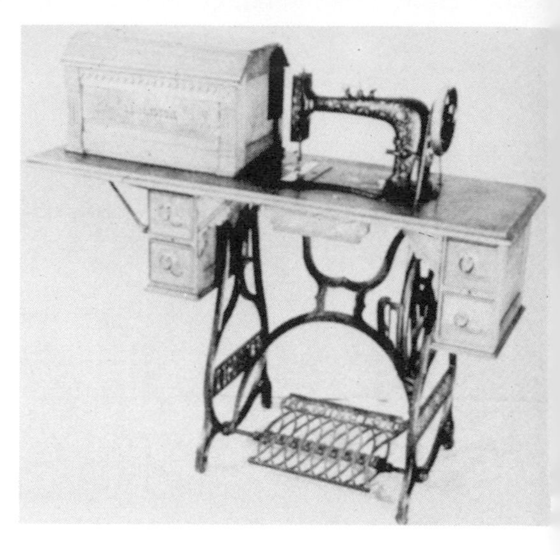

The Remington sewing machine.

Remington firearms have played an important part in the growth of the United States. The company has been called upon to aid our Armed Forces in five wars.

A consignment of rifles destined for the Czarist Russian Armies.

MANUFACTURERS OF

**REVOLVERS, RIFLES,**

MUSKETS & CARBINES,

For the United States service. Also,

POCKET AND BELT REVOLVERS,

Repeating Pistols, Rifle Canes, Revolving Rifles, Rifle and Shot Gun Barrels and Gun Materials, sold by gun dealers and the trade generally. In these days of house-breaking and robbery, every house, store, bank and office should have one of

**REMINGTON'S REVOLVERS.**

Parties desiring to avail themselves of the late improvements in Pistols, and superior workmanship and form, will find all combined in the New Remington Revolvers.

Circulars containing cuts and description of our Arms will be furnished upon application.

E. REMINGTON & SONS, Ilion, N. Y.

MOORE & NICHOLS, Agents, No. 40

July 6—4m Courtland-st., New York.

The Van Buren Press.

VAN BUREN, ARK., NOVEMBER 9, 1866.

D. C. WILLIAMS,

STAPLE DRY GOODS,

GROCERIES,

SHOES and BOOTS,

HARDWARE

DRUGS & MEDICINS,

GARDEN SEEDS,

PAINTS & OILS,

COAL OIL,

PATENT MEDICINES,

Old Drug Store,

VAN BUREN, ARK.

NOTICE.

U. S. Mail Lines

U. S. Mail Line from Ft. Smith and Van Buren to St. Louis.

THROUGH IN FOUR DAYS.

The Quickest Route to Saint Louis.

Little Rock and Van Buren Stage Company.

THROUGH IN 44 HOURS.

O. TULLER & CO., Proprietors.

HIRAM BRODIE, Agent.

REARDON'S BOOK STORE

REVIVED!

STATIONERY, BOOK-BINDING AND

Blank-Book Business.

POETRY.

MISCELLANY.

A Reminiscence.

TERRIBLE EARTHQUAKE ON THE MISSISSIPPI IN 1812.

A Remington advertisement of November 9, 1866. This ad appeared in the VAN BUREN PRESS, Van Buren, Arkansas.

# The Peters Cartridge Co., CINCINNATI, OHIO.

PETERS' NEW REINFORCED SHELL IS THE STRONGEST, SAFEST AND HANDSOMEST.

LOADED with "King's Smokeless" powder. Scientific tests have proven them to develop far greater velocity with less strain on the gun, and better pattern than can be obtained by any other loads whatever. Almost absolutely smokeless and clean. The crack of the gun and the pulverizing of the target are almost simultaneous.

Paper inside and high brass outside.

"QUICK SHOT" LOADED SHELLS

ARE unexcelled by any Black Powder loads ever made. Great penetration and velocity, fine pattern, accurate and sure fire. After hard shooting the gun may be wiped clean with a dry swab.

PETERS' METALLIC CARTRIDGES FOR GALLERY AND TARGET PRACTICE.

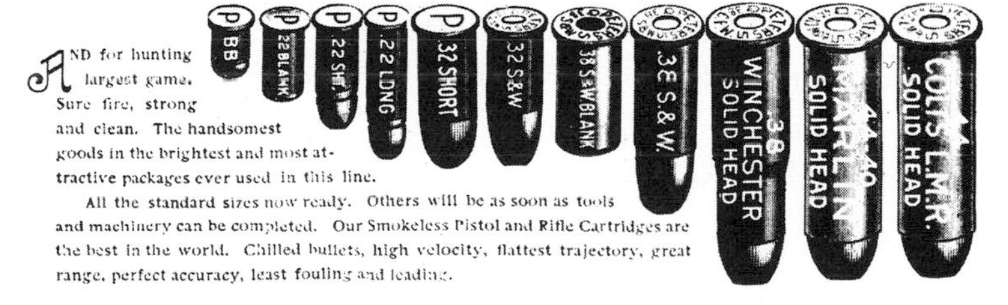


AND for hunting largest game. Sure fire, strong and clean. The handsomest goods in the brightest and most attractive packages ever used in this line.

All the standard sizes now ready. Others will be as soon as tools and machinery can be completed. Our Smokeless Pistol and Rifle Cartridges are the best in the world. Chilled bullets, high velocity, flattest trajectory, great range, perfect accuracy, least fouling and leading.

# The King Powder Co., CINCINNATI, OHIO.

TRY THE NEW KING'S SMOKELESS—THE MOST WONDERFUL NITRO POWDER YET PRODUCED.

IT is made under the personal supervision of Milt. F. Lindsl inventor and late manufacturer of American Wood Powder; latest formulas and processes being employed, as well as the m improved machinery and apparatus. It is the only Nitro pow made by a mechanical process similar to that of black powd which it closely resembles, and is, therefore, capable of perf regulation, hence remarkably uniform and stable.

It is not a diluted form of Gun Cotton, Nitro-Glycerine or Picric Acid, nor possessed of their treacherous and dangerous properties.

It is hard grained, and will not swell or shrink after loading.

It is clean, free from smoke and offensive and injurious gasses.

Has the *highest velocity, greatest penetration, lowest pressure*, therefore, *safest*, creates no excessive heat, even in the hottest weather: neither does the coldest weather affect its velocity. It is equally good for rifle or shot gun use.

**QUICK SHOT** has no superior as a Black Powder at the trap or in the field. It is celebrated for its strength, velocity, cleanliness, quickness of ignition, and freedom from foul smoke.

OUR NEW BRAND "RETRIEVER" IS THE BEST OF STANDARD POWDERS.

All these brands, as well as all kinds of blasting powders, are manufactured by above company.

# A. L. PETERS,

General Agent and N. W. Supply Depot for all above Goods.
391 E. THIRD ST., ST. PAUL, MINN.

Write for Circulars and Price Lists.

Peters advertisement which appeared in the initial volume of FIELD & STREAM magazine.

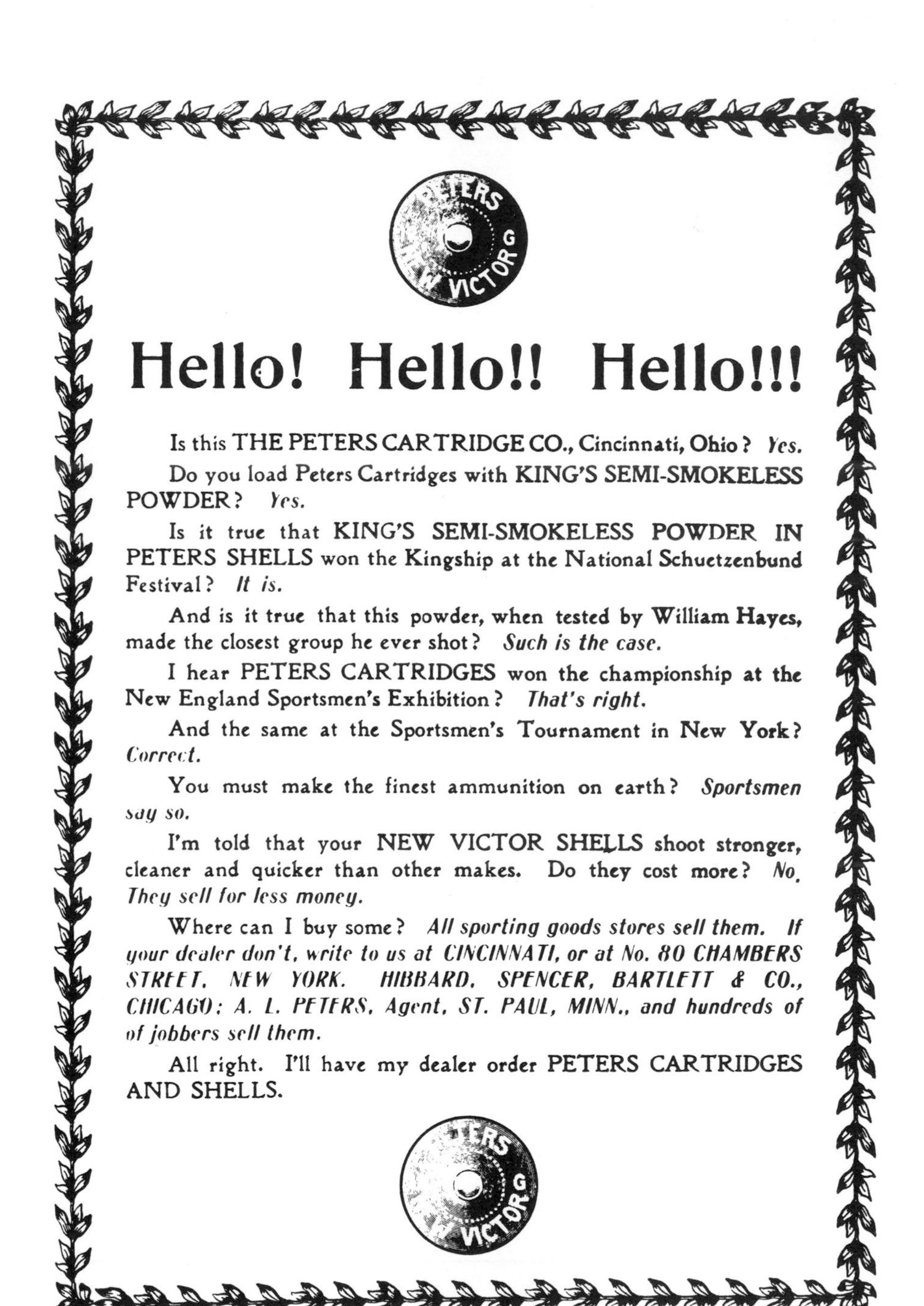


An unusual ad which appeared in 1899.

Trouble Bruin between the Remington Cubs.

*"There's often a quarrel over whose turn's next!"*

The graceful lines—the clean cut beauty of a Remington-UMC .22 Repeater—make you so eager to shoot it.

And it's as accurate as it is attractive.

The Remington-UMC .22 Repeater is rifled, sighted and tested by the most expert gunsmiths in the world—has the famous pump action—takes down in a twinkling, your fingers are your only tools; cleans from the breech—and the simple safety device never fails to work, so accidental discharge is impossible.

It shoots short, long and long rifle cartridges without adjustment, mix them in the magazine as you will.

Ask your dealer to show you this elaborate Christmas package—a reproduction of the most expensive type of a pigskin gun case. It will tickle any man or boy.

Drop in as you pass to-day. The cost of many healthful holidays in the open—of pleasurable hours at target shooting the year around—is less than you think.

**Remington Arms-Union Metallic Cartridge Co.**
299 Broadway, New York City

A Remington ad of November, 1912.

A contemporary advertisement of the Remington Arms Company.

One of the canal barges of Eliphalet Remington and Son. These barges were used to transport Remington products on the Erie Canal.

A photograph of the Erie Canal taken near Ilion.

An interesting view of the Remington Arms plant at the corner of First and Morgan Streets, Ilion, New York. The Remington Mansion can be seen on a hill in the background. This photograph was taken in the 1880's.

World War I construction at Ilion. This photograph was taken in 1914.

A 1915 view, showing the expansion of Remington's Ilion facilities.

The Ilion plant in full operation, Spring, 1916.

The Remington office building, East Main Street, Ilion. This structure, originally erected as the village residence for Eliphalet Remington II, was utilized for some years as Remington's office headquarters.

The Union Metallic Cartridge Company, 19 Maiden Lane, New York.

An interior view, Schuyler, Hartley & Graham.

FAMILY CRAFTSMANSHIP: The Howards—Grandfather, Father and Son. This picture was taken some years ago. These three men combine sixty-nine years of service to Remington Arms, from 1869-1912. Here, they are shown fitting Remington model 17 Shotguns.

An early gun line display shipment for one of the many expositions to which Remington has sent its products and from which the company has earned more than twenty awards for quality, craftsmanship and design.

A float which appeared in the Centennial parade in Ilion, marking one hundred years of Remington's service.

A view of the parade.

Another group of marchers in the Centennial parade.

Ceremonies marking the end of the Centennial celebration.

Left to Right: C. K. Davis, M. Hartley Dodge, Marcellus Hartley (Photo), Eliphalet Remington II (Steel engraving), Franklin Remington (Grandson of the founder) and Henry B. DuPont.

;amuel Remington's children in England. An 1878 photograph.

Elizabeth Remington Merry.

R. H. Coleman, President, 1963——

C. K. Davis, President, 1933-1954.

M. R. Warden, President, 1954–1963.

M. Hartley Dodge, Honorary Chairman, Board of Directors, at the time of his death in 1963.

A recent photograph of the Remington Arms plant at Ilion, New York.

A recent aerial view of the Remington Arms plant at Bridgeport, Connecticut.

A photograph of the Shot Tower, Bridgeport, Connecticut. This structure, which is 167 feet high, is used for the manufacture of Remington shotgun pellets.

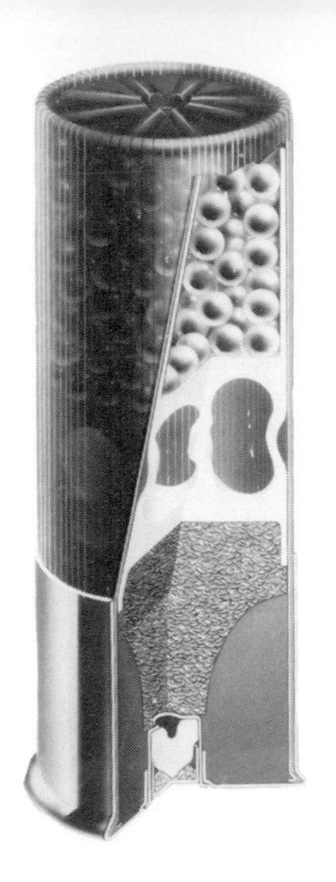

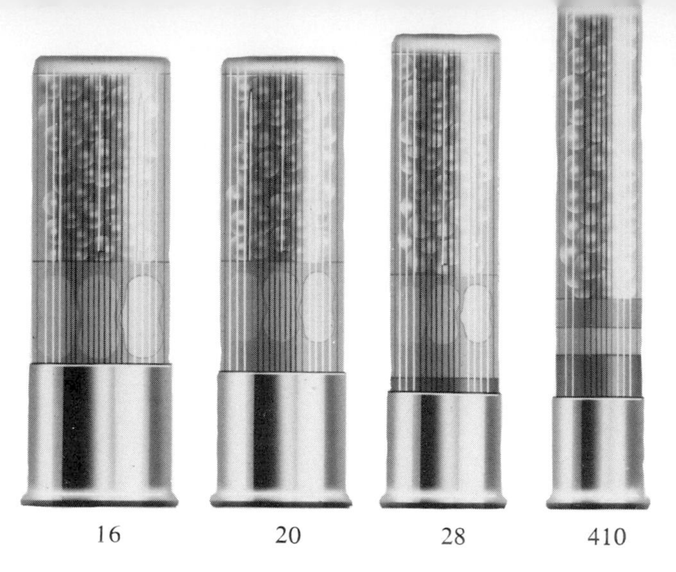


Left: Cross-section of Remington shotgun shell (enlarged) showing plastic body successfully introduced by Remington in 1965. To right are 16, 20, 28 and 410 gauge plastic-bodied shells.

The shot pellets form at the bottom of the shot pan and drop into a water tank over 100 feet below, in which they cool. (See shot tower on preceding page.)

DATES OF MANUFACTURE

## SPORTING RIFLES AND CARBINES

Sporting Rifles and Muskets Prior to 1846 (Unlisted)

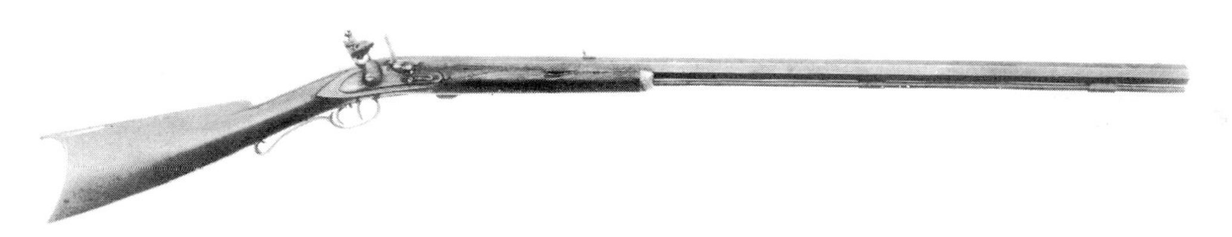

Flintlock rifles, muzzle loading. Flintlock rifles, Kentucky type. Flintlock muskets, muzzle loading. Miscellaneous calibers. Also, iron, steel and Stubbs twist barrels. Marked *E. Remington*. Also locks. 1816–1846

Percussion Lock Rifles, muzzle loading. Kentucky type Rifles. Mark: *E. Remington*. Late models marked *Remington*. Also percussion locks. Also barrels of all types. 1835–1861

Sporting Rifles from 1846 (Listed)

1847–1858 *Remington-Jenks Sporting Rifle.* S.S. B.L. Maynard type lock. Round, cast steel, drilled barrel, 24″. Caliber 52 marked: *Remington's, Herkimer, N. Y.* Later models *Remington's, Ilion, N. Y.* Barrels marked *W. Jenks.* Weight about 6 lbs. Wrought brass Trigger Guard.

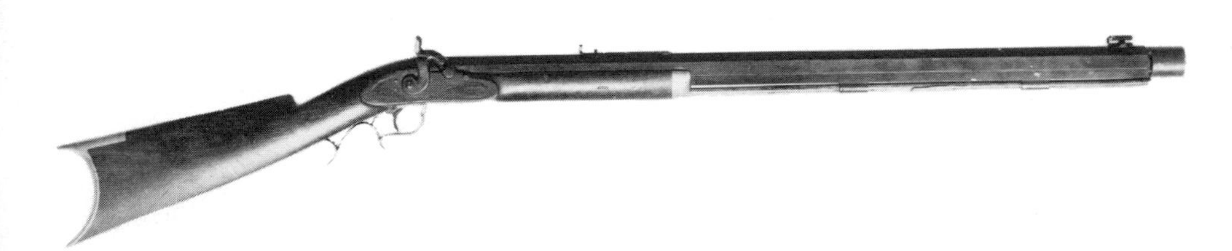

1850 (Circa) Percussion Lock Match Rifle, muzzle loading. Caliber 40. Barrel marked *Remington cast steel.*

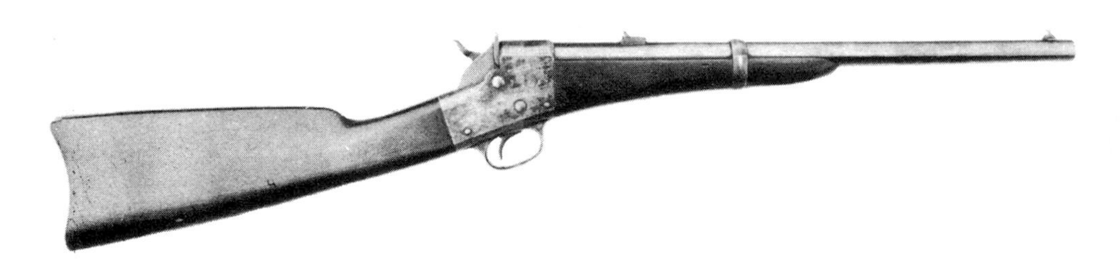

1865–1867 *Remington Geiger Rolling Split Block Breech Loading Rifle.* Calibers 40-44-50. Carbine style — 20″ round barrels — approx. 6 lbs. Other styles — 27″ octagon barrels — approx. 8¼ lbs. Marked *Remington's, Ilion, N.Y.* Pat. Dec. 23, 1863, May 3 and Nov. 16, 1864.

*Remington Beals Patent Sporting Rifle.* S.S. B.L. Calibers 36, 38 rim fire. Beals patent breech opened by sliding barrel forward. 24″ half-octagon barrel. Wt. about 5½ lbs. Marked *E. Remington & Sons, Ilion, N. Y.* 1866–1868

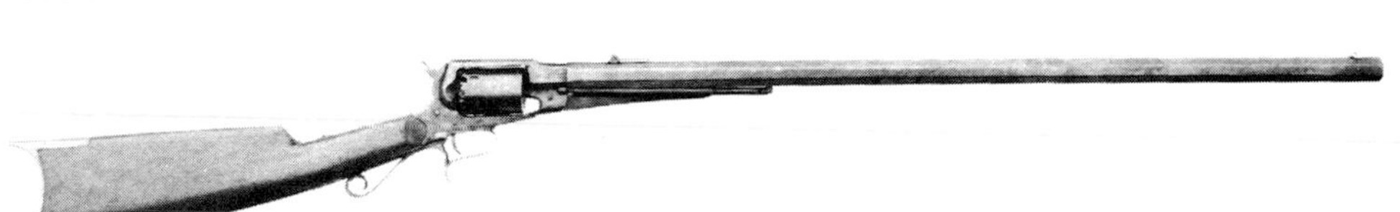

*Beals Revolving Rifle.* 6 shot cap and ball. Cast steel octagon drilled barrel with folding rear peep sight. Calibers 36 Percussion. 38 R.F. Wt. about 7½ lbs. Brass trigger guard and curved brass butt plate. Marked *E. Remington and Sons, Ilion, New York USA New Model.* Pat. Sept. 14, 1858. 1866–1872

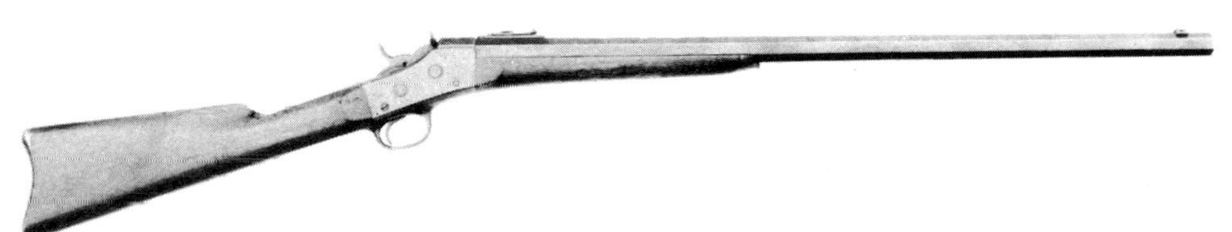

*Sporting Rifle No. 1.* S.S. Rolling Block. Calibers 22, 32, 38, 40, 44, 45, 50, 58. Rim or center fire. Octagon barrel. Miscellaneous lengths. Weight — 8 to 12 lbs. Marked *E. Remington & Sons, Ilion, N. Y.* Later models, *Remington Arms Co., Ilion, N.Y.* (The first and most famous Rolling Block sporting rifle. Made on Geiger-Rider Patents.) Pat. markings: May 3, 1864, May 7, June 11, Nov. 12, Dec. 24, Dec. 31, 1872, Sept. 9, 1873. 1867–1890

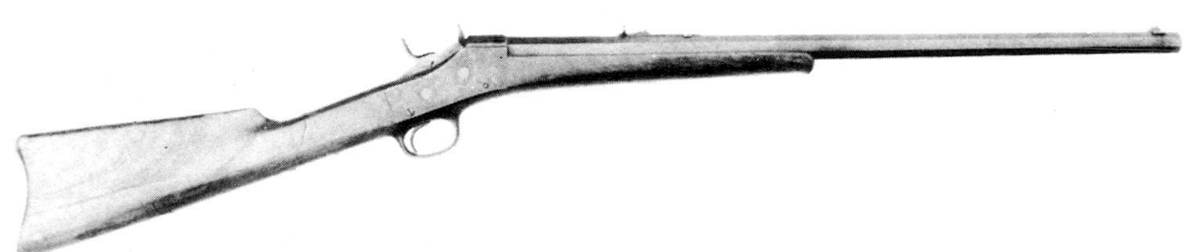

*Sporting Rifle No. 1½.* S.S., Rolling Block. Light Version of Model No. 1. Made in calibers 22 to 38 in both C.F. and R.F. Markings same as Sporting Rifle No. 1. Wt. 7½ lbs. 1888–1897

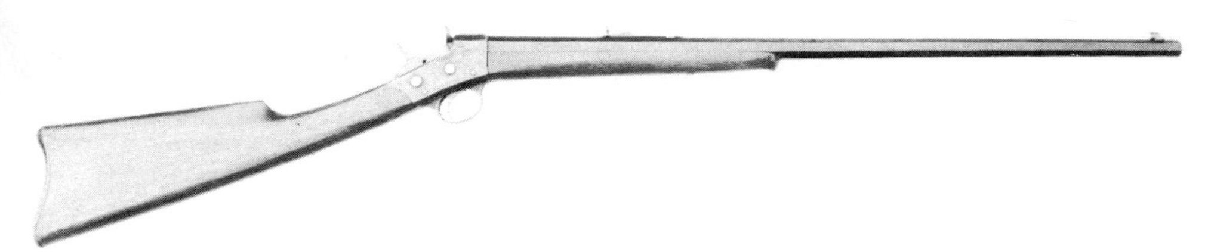

1873–1910 *Sporting Rifle No. 2*. S.S., Rolling Block, Calibers 22, 32 rim fire. 32, 38, 44 center fire, 25/20 and other variations of 25 caliber, 44/40, 38/40, 32/20, Octagon barrel miscellaneous lengths. Straight grip, walnut stock. Curved butt plate. Improved sporting and rear sights. Weights 5¼ to 6 lbs. Marked *E. Remington Sons, Ilion, N. Y.* Later models marked *Remington Arms Co., Ilion, N.Y., U.S.A.*

1872–1890 *Remington Buffalo Rifle*. S.S., Rolling Block. Calibers miscellaneous from 40-50 Sharps to 44-90-400 and 50-70 Govt. Octagon or round barrel 30″. A heavier version of Deer Rifle. Markings same as Remington Deer Rifle. (Not illustrated.)

1872–1890 *Remington Deer Rifle*. S.S., Rolling Block. Caliber 46 long rim fire. Octagon barrel, 24″. Straight grip stock. Similar to Sporting Rifle No. 1. Weight about 6½ lbs. (Not illustrated.)

1873–1890 *Remington Creedmoor Rifle*. S.S., Rolling Block. Caliber 44-90, 44-100, 44-105. Octagon barrel, 32″. Vernier and wind gauge sights. Pistol grip stock; early model horseshoe shaped, brass-faced butt plate. Later models shotgun type butt stock. This rifle specially designed by L. L. Hepburn for first International Rifle Match.

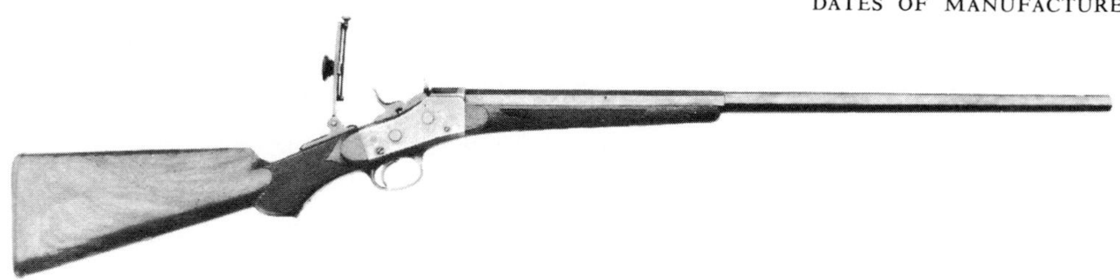

*Remington Mid-range*. S.S. Rolling Block. Version of Model No. 1. Calibers 40 to 50-70. Half octagon barrels 28″ and 30″. Otherwise same as Remington Short Range. Markings *E. Remington & Sons, Ilion, N. Y.* Weight about 7½ lbs.

1875–1890

*Remington Short Range*. Version of Model No. 1. Half octagon barrel 26″. Calibers 38 ex-long to 46. Rim and center fire. Peep and open sights or Vernier sights. Plain or Creedmoor stock. (Otherwise same as "Midrange") (Not illustrated.)

1875–1890

*Remington Black Hills Rifle*. S.S., Rolling Block. Version of No. 1 Rifle. Caliber 45-70 center fire. Round barrel 28″. Straight grip stock. Weight about 7½ lbs. (Not illustrated.)

1877–1882

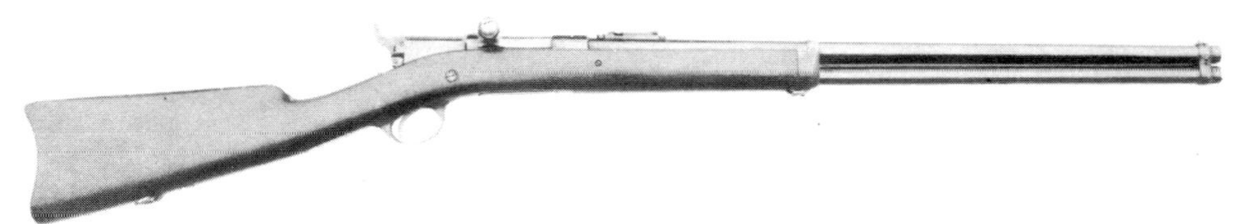

*Remington-Keene Repeater*. Tubular magazine. Bolt action repeater. Caliber 45–70. 24″ round or octagon barrel. Weight about 8½ lbs. Markings *E. Remington & Sons, Ilion, N.Y.* Pat. Feb. 24, March 17, 1874, Jan. 18, Sept. 26, 1876, March 20, July 31, 1877. Also chambered for calibers 40 and 43.

1880–1883

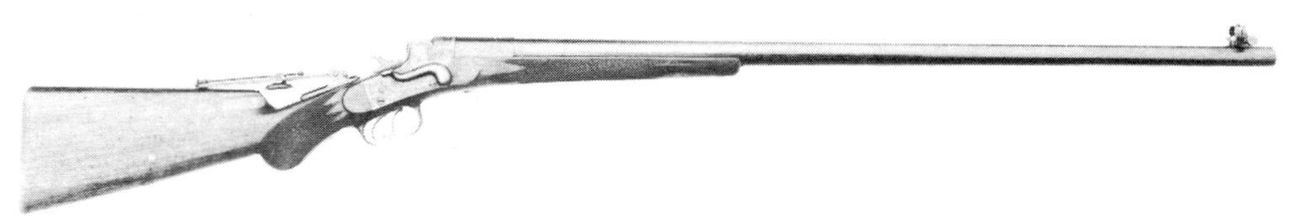

*No. 3 Improved Creedmoor*. (Remington Hepburn.) S.S.B.L. Hepburn Falling Block side lever action. Full octagon and round barrels 34″. Calibers 38, 40, 45 and others. Vernier and wind gauge sights. Pistol grip. Some with cheek piece stock with nickel-plated Swiss butt plate. Some with set triggers. Marked on top of barrel, *E. Remington & Son, Ilion, N. Y.* On frame Hepburn Pat. Oct. 7th, 1879. Weight about 9 lbs.

1880–1907

1883–1907 *Remington Hepburn No. 3.*
*Long Range Military Creedmoor.* Similar to the Long Range Creedmoor but was chambered for the 44/75/520 Remington straight shell. Round 34″ barrel. Fine grade oiled walnut stock, checkered and full length with sling swivels. Vernier and wind gauge peep sights with spirit level front sights and steel ram rod fitted under the barrel. Illustrated model is nickel-plated. Weight approx. 8½ lbs.

1880–1907 *Remington-Hepburn Number 3 Rifle.* S.S. B.L. Side lever action and rebounding hammer. Half-octagon or full-octagon barrels 26″, 28″ or 30″. Calibers 22, 25, 32, 38, 40 and 45 regular and various other calibers made to order. Pistol grip checkered stock, blade front sights with buck horn rear sights regular. Weights 8 to 10 lbs. Marked on top of barrel *E. Remington & Son, Ilion, N.Y.* On frame Hepburn Pat. Oct. 7th, 1879. Later models with barrel marked *Remington Arms Co., Ilion, N.Y. U.S.A.*

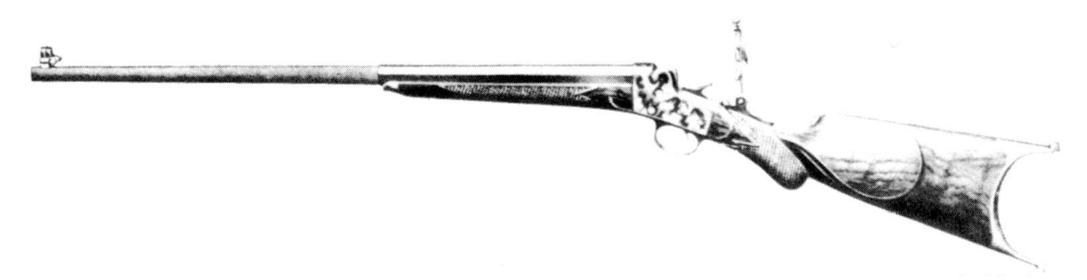

1883–1907 *Match Rifle No. 3.* S.S. B.L. Mid-range version of No. 3. Half octagon barrel 28″, 30″. Miscellaneous calibers 25-20 to 40-65. Center Fire Marking same as No. 3 Improved Creedmoor. Weights 8½ to 9 lbs.

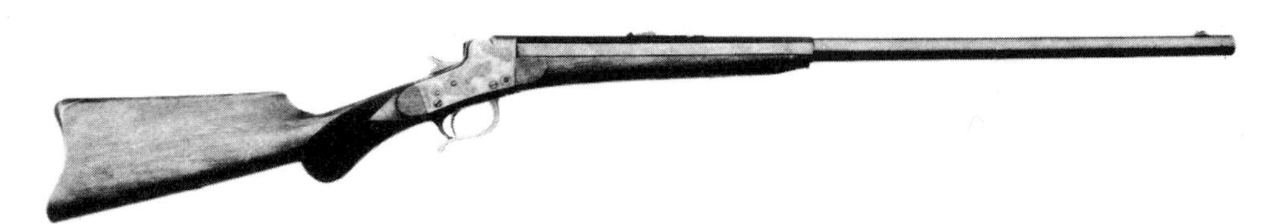

*Hunter's Rifle No. 3*. S.S. Breech loading (hunter's version of the No. 3 Hepburn) and with special under lever modification designed by L. N. Walker. Half octagon barrel 26", 28" and 30". Miscellaneous calibers from 25 to 50. Plain open sights, checkered pistol grip stock with curved butt plate. Weight about 8 lbs. Markings same as other No. 3 rifles. 1883–1907

*Remington Light "Baby Carbine."* S.S. B.L. Rolling block action. Round barrel 20" (some nickel plated) Caliber 44 C.F. (WCF-44). Total weight 5½ lbs. Straight Grip stock. Either blue or nickel-plated finish. Marking on tang *E. Remington & Sons, Ilion, N. Y., USA*. Pat. May 3rd, 1864, May 7th, June 11th, Nov. 12th, Dec. 24th, 1875. Dec. 31st 1872, Sept. 9th 1873, Jan. 17th, March 18th, 1874. 1890–1908

*Remington No. 3*. High Powered. S.S. B.L. New version of Remington-Hepburn Hunter's Rifle. Chambered for straight shells of miscellaneous calibers up to 45-90 and 45-105 Sharps. Full octagon barrels 26", 28" and 30". Approx. weight 8 lbs. Double set triggers to order. 1893–1907

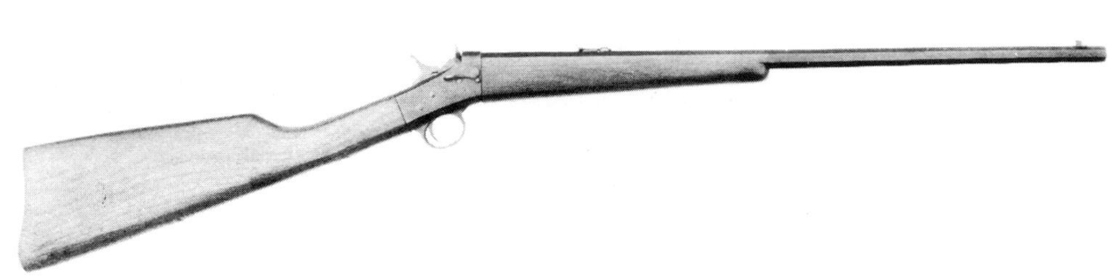

1890–1933 *Remington No. 4 Rifle*. S.S. Rolling Block. Automatic ejector. Octagon barrel 22½", 24" ("Take Down") Calibers 22 R.F. to 32 R.F. Straight grip walnut stock. Houghton and Simpson patents. Marked *Remington Arms Co., Ilion, N. Y.* Some marked *Remington Arms — Union Metallic Cartridge Co., Remington Works, Ilion, N.Y. U.S.A.* (One of the first models to be marked with the Remington Script Trade Mark.) Weight 4¼-4½ lbs.

1898–1905 *Remington No. 5. Special High Power Rifle*. S.S. R.B. Round "Smokeless steel" barrel 24", 26", 28". Sporting sights. Calibers 30-30 Smokeless, 7 mm., 30 Govt. 303 British 32-40 H.P., 32 Winchester special, 38-55 H.P. and others. Straight grip oiled walnut stock. Weights 7 to 7¼ lbs. Marked *Remington Arms Co., Ilion, N. Y.*

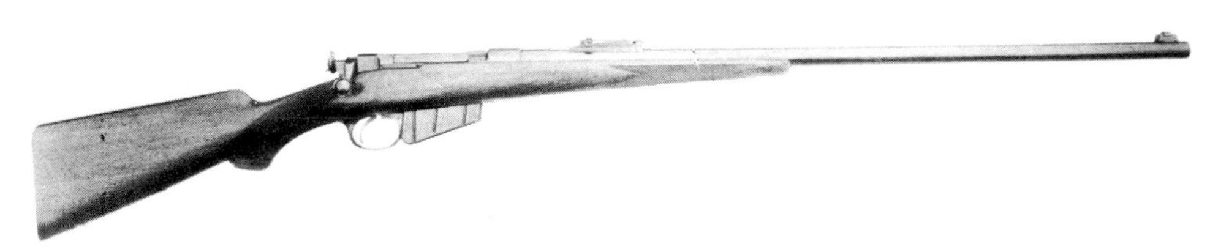

1899–1906 *Remington-Lee Sporting Rifle*. 5 shot. Bolt action box magazine repeater. Round barrel 24", 26", 28". Improved sporting sights. Calibers 6 mm., 30-30, 30-40 Govt., 7 mm. 32 Winchester, 35 Remington, 32-40 h.p., 303 British, 43, 44, 45, 7 mm., 7.65 mm., 38/72, and others. Half pistol grip walnut stock, marked, *Remington Arms Co., Ilion, N. Y.* Weight 8½ to 9 lbs.

*Remington No. 6 Rifle.* S.S. B.L. Rolling Block Light Weight "Take Down." Round decarbonized steel barrel 20″. Open sights. Also fitted with tang peep sight. Calibers 22 R.F. and 32 R.F. Straight grip walnut stock. Weight about 3¼ lbs. Marked *Remington Arms — Union Metallic Cartridge Co. Remington Works, Ilion, N. Y. U.S.A.* Patented July 22, 1902. Early models marked Patent Applied For. 1901–1933

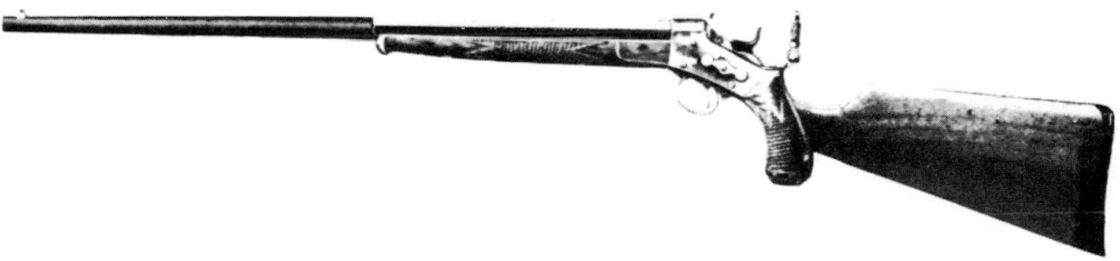

*Remington No. 7 Rifle.* S.S. Rolling Block, Half octagon barrel 24″, 26″, 28″. Lyman combination rear sight. Beach combination front sight. Calibers 22 short 22 long Rifle, 25-10 R.F. Also, miscellaneous in custom models. Exaggerated pistol grip walnut stock. Rubber butt plate. 1903–1907

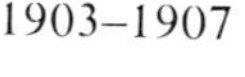

*Remington-Schuetzen Match Rifle.* A modification of the standard Remington-Hepburn action, utilizing an under lever sliding breech block. Double set triggers, special rear wind-gauge sights, Vernier peep sight on tang and hooded front sight. Specially designed Schuetzen-Swiss type butt plate. Barrels 30 or 32 inches, half octagon. 28″ barrel furnished on special order. Weights from 11 to 13 lbs. Special palm rest. Calibers 32/40, 38/40, 38/50 and 40/65. 1904–1907

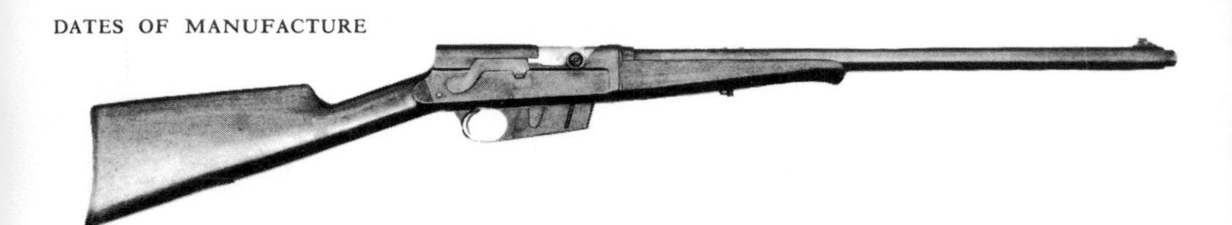

1906–1936 *Remington Model 8 Autoloader.* 5 shot. Box magazine. Recoil actuated mechanism Browning patent. "Ordnance" steel barrel 22", Calibers 25, 30, 32, 35. Straight grip or half pistol grip walnut stock. Made in A, C, D, E and F grades. First successful autoloading High Power Rifle in America. Weight about 7¾ lbs. Barrel markings: *Remington Arms — Union Metallic Cartridge Co. Remington Works, Ilion, N.Y. U.S.A.* Browning's Patents Oct. 9, 1900, Oct. 16, 1900, June 3, 1902. Later models with Patent Markings added May 14, 1907, Feb. 14, 1911, and the Union Metallic Cartridge Co. name eliminated.

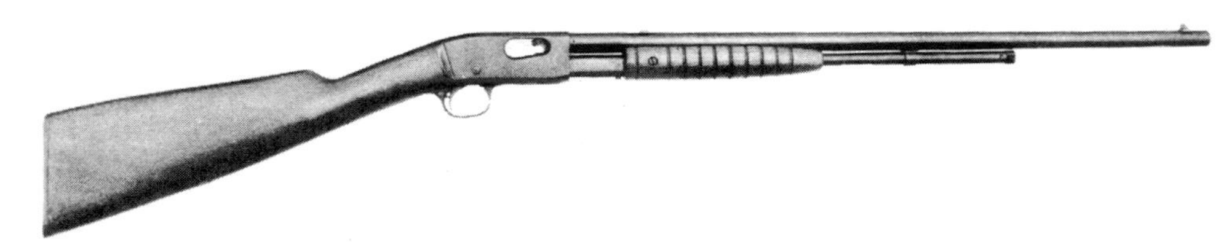

1909–1936 *Remington Model 12.* 10 shot to 15 shot according to size of cartridge. Slide action repeating rifle. Tubular magazine. Round steel barrel 22". Calibers 22 short, long and long rifle. Straight grip walnut stock. Also made in N.R.A. Target Grade C with 24" Octagon barrel and half pistol grip stock and in grades B, CS, D, E, F, DS and FS. Weight about 5½ lbs. Barrel markings: *Remington Arms Co. — Union Metallic Cartridge Co., Remington Works, Ilion, N.Y. U.S.A.* Pedersen's Patents Jan. 5, 1909, Oct. 12, 1909, Mar. 8, 1910, Nov. 21, 1911, April 16, 1912. Later models eliminated use of the Union Metallic Cartridge Co. name on the barrel marking.

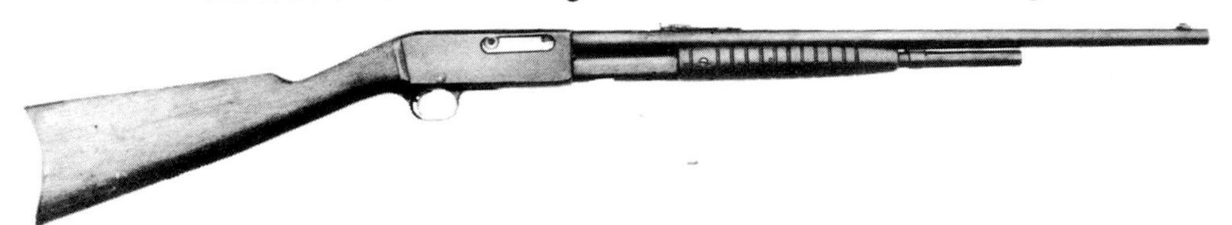

1912–1935 *Remington Model 14.* 6 shot. High power slide action repeating rifle. Tubular magazine. "Ordnance" steel barrel 22". Calibers 25, 30, 32, 35 Hi-speed and regular. Straight or half pistol grip walnut stock. Made in A, C, D, and F grades. First successful slide action high power rifle in America. Weight about 6¾ lbs. Barrel markings: Same as for Model 12 except Patent Markings: Pedersen's Patents Oct. 12, 1909 and July 5, 1910.

*Note:* A "UMC" style of cartridge base is located in the left side of the receiver to identify the caliber.

*Model 14R*. 6 shot, carbine with 18½" barrel and straight grip stock. Otherwise same as Model 14. (Not illustrated.) 1912–1934

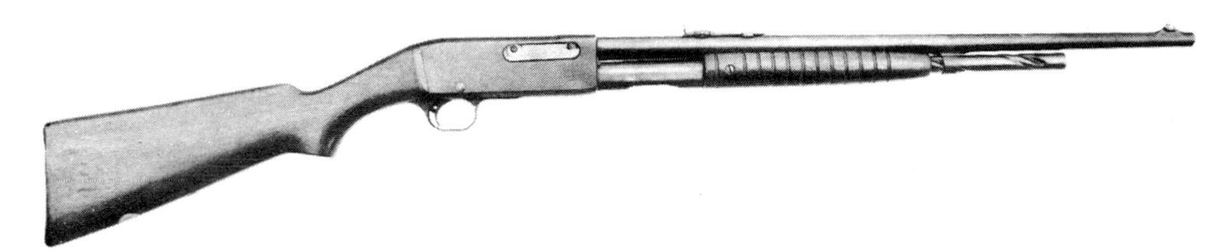

*Remington Model 14½*. Similar to Model 14 except chambered for calibers 38 and 44 W.C.F. 1912–1925

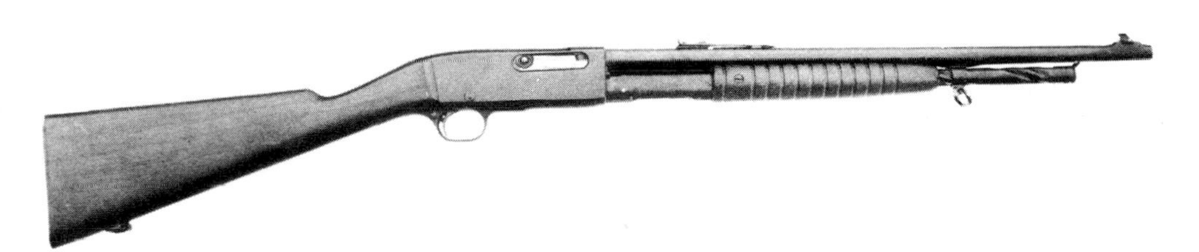

*Model 14½R*. Carbine version of Model 14½. 1912–1925

*Boy Scout Rifle*. (Model 4S) S.S. R.B. Round steel barrel 28". Calibers 22 short, long and long rifle. Straight grip walnut stock. Sling strap, stacking swivel, and small scout "bayonet." Weight approx. 5½ lbs. Barrel markings: *Remington Arms — Union Metallic Cartridge Co. Remington Works, Ilion, N.Y. U.S.A*. Patent July 22, 1902. 1913–1933

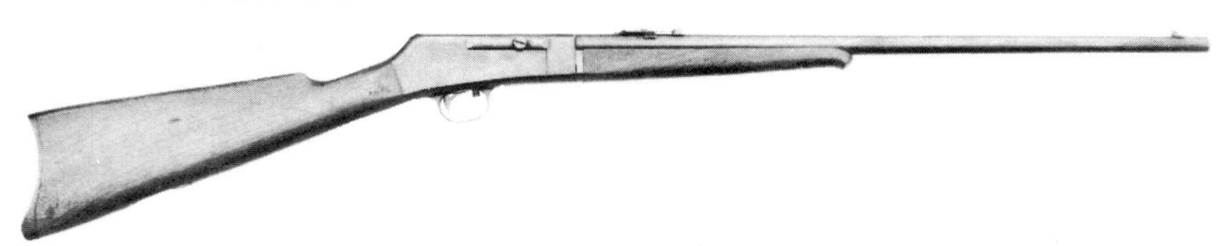

1914–1928 *Remington Model 16*. Autoloader, 16 shot. Tubular magazine in stock. C. H. Barnes patents. Round steel barrel 22″. Caliber 22 autoloading. Also made in C, D and F. Weight about 5½ lbs. Barrel markings: Same as Model 4-S except "Pat'd. Mar. 10, 1914." (Chambered only for special "Remington 22 Autoloading" cartridge.)

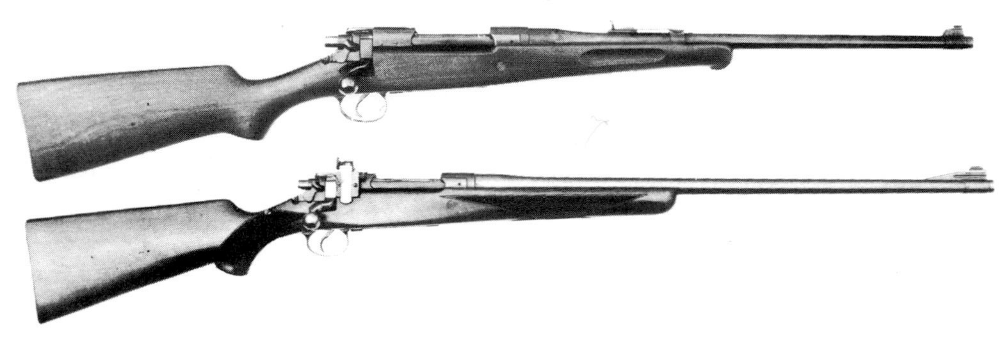

1921–1940 *Remington Model 30 and 30S*. 6 shot. Box magazine. Bolt action high power repeating rifle. Barnes and Loomis patents. Tapered, high pressure steel barrel 28″ to 32″. Calibers 25 to 35. New model sporting peep rear sight. Half pistol grip walnut stock. Rings for sling strap. Also made in F grade and with telescopic sights. Barrels marked: *Remington Arms Co., Inc., Remington Ilion Works, Ilion, N.Y. Made in U.S.A.*

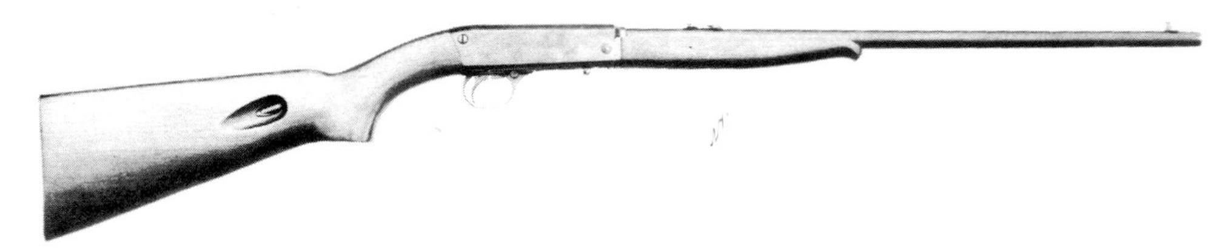

1922–1935 *Remington Model 24*. 22 Caliber Autoloading, Tubular Magazine. 19″ round barrels, chambered for 22 short or 22 long rifle cartridges. Quick take down action with over-all take-down length of only 19″. Magazine in stock — capacity 15 shorts or 10 LR cartridges. Supplied in regular or fancy grades. Weight 4¾ lbs. Barrel marked: *Remington Arms Co., Inc. Successor to the Remington Arms — UMC Co., Inc. Remington Ilion Works, Ilion, N.Y. U.S.A.* Browning's Patent Oct. 24, 1915. Early models marked: *Remington Arms — Union Metallic Cartridge Co. New York*. Browning Patents June 24, 1913, Jan. 6, 1914 Belgium.

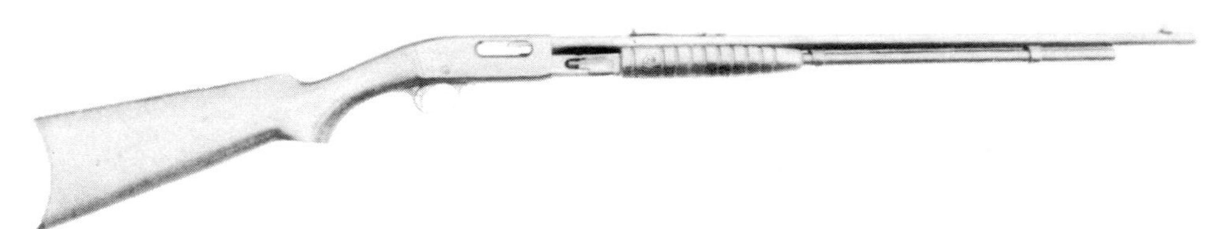

*Remington Model 25*. 10 shot. Slide action repeater. Pedersen & Loomis Patents. Tubular side-loading magazine. Remington steel, round barrel 24″. Calibers 25-20, 32-20. Weight about 5½ lbs. Regular and fancy grades. Half pistol grip walnut stock. Barrel markings: *Remington Arms Co., Inc. Remington Ilion Works, Ilion, N.Y. Made in U.S.A.* Pedersen's Patents January 5, 1909, July 5, 1910 and others pending. 1923–1936

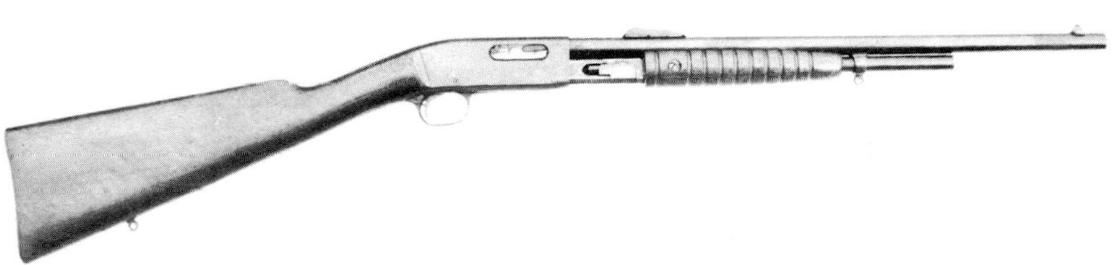

*Model 25R*. Carbine version of Model 25. Barrel 18″. Straight grip stock. Weight about 4½ lbs. 1923–1936

*Remington Model 33*. S.S. Bolt action. C. C. Loomis Patents. 24″ round steel barrel, calibers 22 short, long, long rifle. Pistol grip walnut stock. Weight about 4 lbs. Barrels marked: *Remington Arms Co., Inc., Ilion, N.Y. Made in U.S.A.* U.S. Patent Numbers 1,908,035 and others. 1931–1936

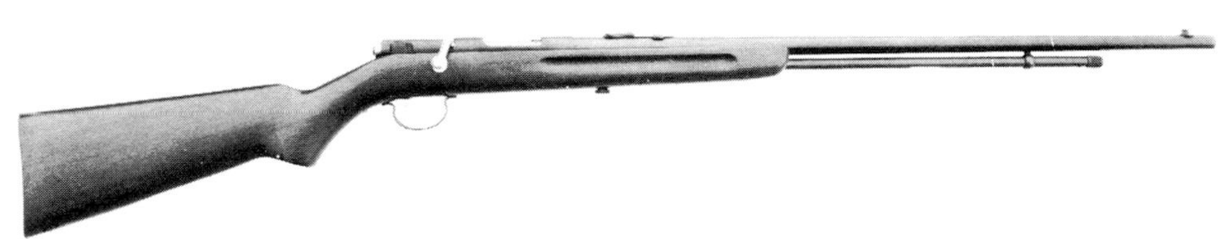

*Remington Model 34*. 22 Caliber. Bolt action repeater. Tubular Magazine, 20 short, 15 long or 14 long rifle. Weight about 5½ lbs. Otherwise same as Model 33. 1932–1936

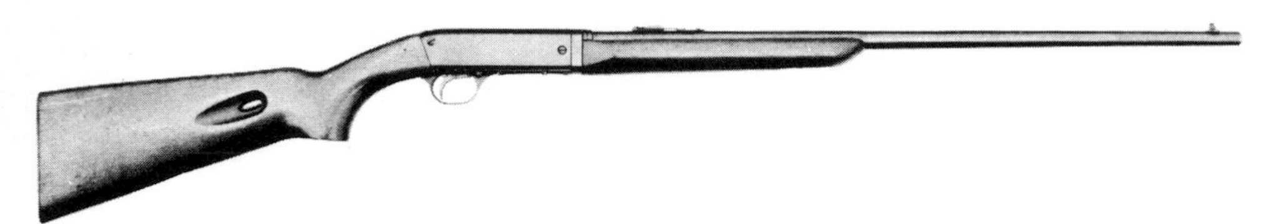

1935–1951 *Remington Model 241.* 22 Caliber. Autoloading. Improved version of the Model 24 with barrel length extended to 24 inches and beaver tail fore end. Adapted for standard and high speed 22 caliber rim fire ammunition. Supplied in regular and fancy grades and also a gallery grade. Barrel markings: *Remington Arms Co., Inc. Ilion, N.Y. Made in U.S.A.* Browning Pat. No. 1,372,336 — 1,381,448. Also Pat. No. 1,740,187 — 1,889,099.

1936–1954 *Model 121 Fieldmaster.* 20, 15, or 14 shot. Slide action repeating rifle. Tubular magazine. Round, tapered barrel 24″. Caliber 22 short, long and long rifle. Half pistol grip walnut stock. Adjustable rear sight. Made in all grades. Weight about 5¾ lbs. Pedersen, Garrison & Loomis patents. Barrel marking: *Remington Arms Company, Inc. Remington Ilion Works, Ilion, N.Y. Made in U.S.A.* U.S. Patents 1,481,638 — 1,628,548 — 1,682,704. *Model 121S.* Chambered for 22 W.R.F. Model 121SB. Smooth bore.

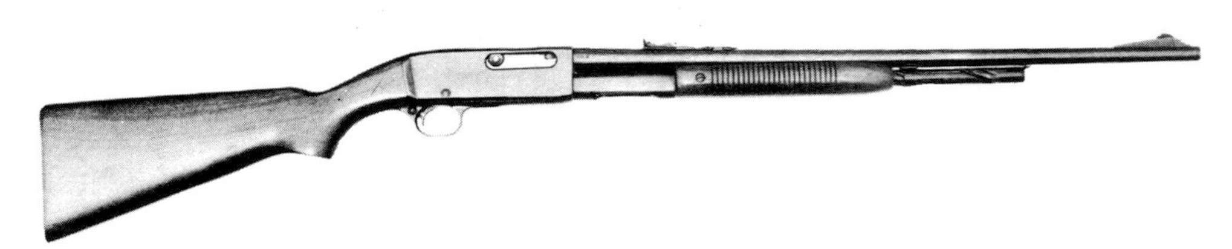

1936–1950 *Remington Model 141 Gamemaster.* Slide action high power rifle. Improved version of the earlier Model 14, 6 shot with tubular magazine. 24 inch round tapered barrel. Calibers 30-32 and 35 Remington C.F. Half pistol grip stock and fluted fore end. Ramp type front sight. Made in "A" Grade regular and "R" carbine. Also high grades "B" (Special), "D" (Peerless) and "F" (Premier). Weight about 7½ lbs. Barrel markings: Remington Arms Co., Ilion, N.Y. Made in U.S.A. — U. S. Pat's. 1,043,354 — 1,044,568 — 1,071,173 — 1,072,982. Also caliber marking on top left side rear and test and proof mark ("REP") right side rear.

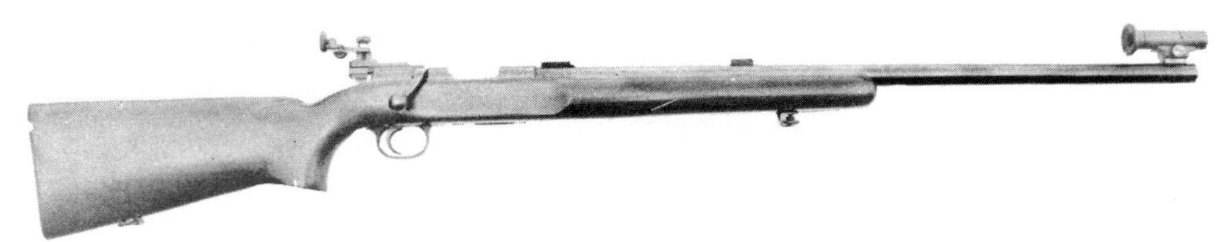

*Model 37 Rangemaster*. Bolt Action Target Rifle. Specially rifled round barrel 28", semi-floating, double countersunk at muzzle. Caliber 22 long rifle. High comb pistol grip stock. Sling strap. Loomis & Lowe patents. Barrel markings: *Remington Arms Co., Inc., Ilion, N.Y. Made in U.S.A.* Patent Numbers 2,005,866 — 2,007,019 — 2,125,350. Model name and number on top rear, caliber on left rear. Serial numbers stamped on front of receiver. 1937–1954

*Remington Model 41*. S.S. Bolt Action 22 Caliber R.F. rifle, 27" round barrel. Half pistol grip stock. Barrel markings: *Remington Arms Co., Inc., Ilion, N. Y.* Manufactured in grades A — regular, "P" (with peep sights), AS (chambered for 22 Remington Special or 22 WRF cartridge), 41SB (Smooth Bore). 1936–1940

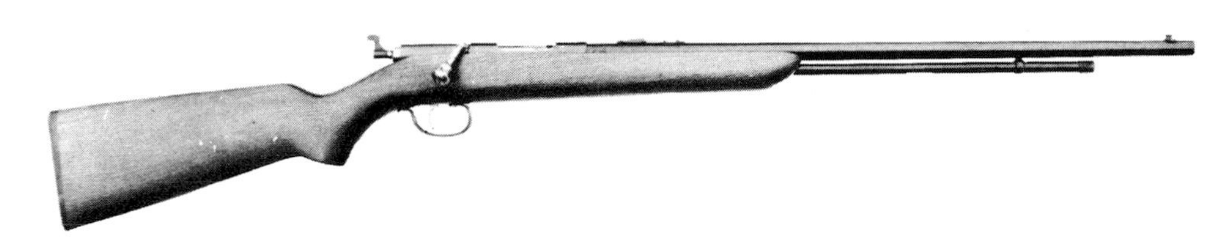

*Remington Model 341 Repeater*. 22 Caliber bolt action tubular magazine. Similar to Model 34 with improved larger stock and semi-beaver tail fore-arm. Barrel round — 24" long. Manufactured in A grade (regular open sights) and P grade (peep sights). Weight 5½ lbs. Barrel markings: *"Sportmaster" Remington Arms Co., Inc. Ilion, N.Y. Made in U.S.A.* U.S. Patent Numbers 1,908,035 — 1,913,840 — 1,924,692. 1936–1940

1936–1950 *Model 81 Woodsmaster*. Autoloader. 5 shot box magazine. Single column. Round steel barrel 22″. Step adjustable rear sight. Calibers .300 Savage, 30, 35 Remington and 32 Remington. Semi-beavertail fore-end. Half pistol grip walnut stock. Made in A, B, D, and F grades. Browning Patent. Barrel markings: *Remington Arms Co., Inc. Ilion, N.Y. Made in U.S.A.* Browning Pats. 658,507 — 659,786 — 701,288 — 853,438 — 964,263. Caliber designation marked on rear of barrel extension.

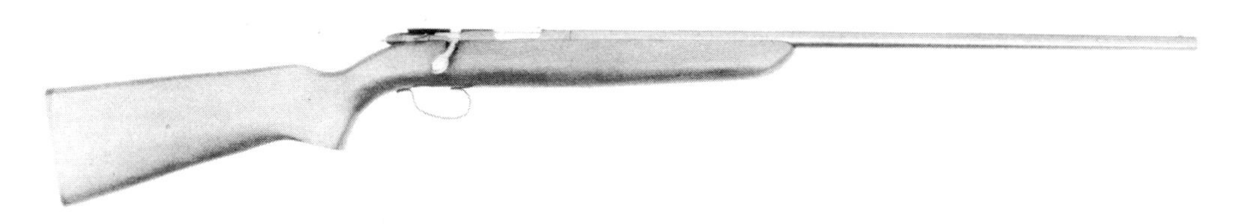

1939–1962 *Model 510 Targetmaster*. S.S. Bolt action. Round tapered barrel 25″, crowned at muzzle. Streamlined, self-cocking bolt. New design top loading platform. Calibers 22 short, long, long rifle. Pistol grip walnut stock. Semi-beavertail fore end. A.P. and S.B. grades. SB grade smooth bored. Barrel markings: *Remington Arms Co., Inc., Ilion, N.Y., Made in U.S.A.* Patent Numbers 1,908,035 — 1,913,840 — 2,356,257. (Model name, number and cartridge designation rolled on top rear.)

1939–1962 *Model 511 Scoremaster*. 22 caliber. 7 shot. Box magazine. Bolt action repeater. Steel tapered barrel 25″ crowned at muzzle. Streamlined, self-cocking bolt. Other details similar to Model 510, A and P grades. Barrel markings same as Model 510 except for model name and number.

*Model 512 Sportmaster*. 22 caliber. 22, 17 or 15 shot tubular magazine. Bolt action repeater. Otherwise same as Model 511. A and P grades. Barrel markings same as Model 510 and Model 511 except model name and number. Also, Patent Number 2,369,244 instead of number 2,356,257. 1940–1962

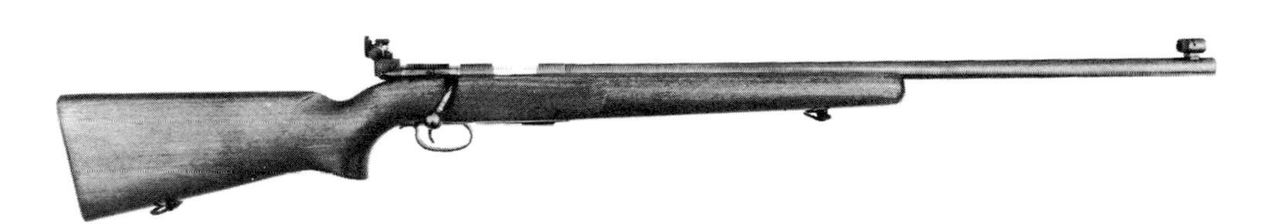

*Model 513T Matchmaster*. 22 caliber. 7 shot. Box magazine. Bolt action repeater. Semi-floating, specially bored barrel, 27″, countersunk at muzzle. Adjustable trigger stop and trigger pull. Target version of Model 511. Barrel markings same as Model 512, except for model name and number, and Patent Number 2,351,405 instead of 2,369,244. 1940–1969

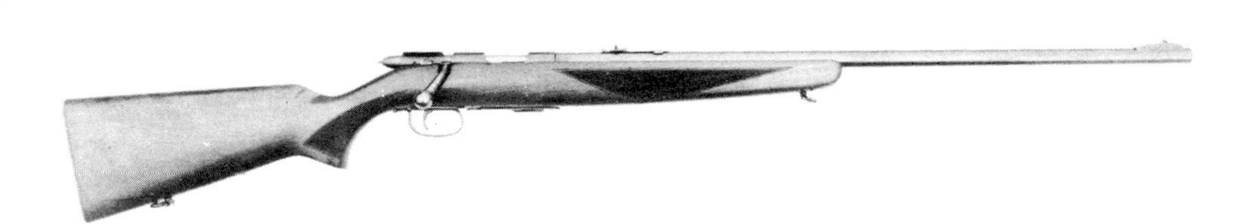

*Model 513S*. (Sporter) 22 caliber. 7 shot. Box magazine. Tapered barrel 27″. Half pistol grip walnut stock. Grip checkered. Partridge type front sight. Marble No. 3 adjustable rear sight. (Sporting version of Model 513T.) Barrel markings same as for Model 513T except for model name and number. 1941–1956

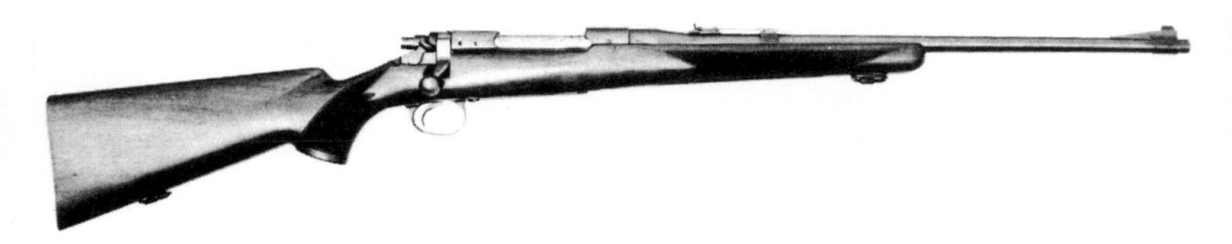

1941–1942 *Remington Model 720.* High Power Bolt Action Box Magazine. 5 shot. Calibers 257, 30-06, 270, 300 H&H Magnum. Barrel markings: *Remington Arms Co., Inc., Ilion, N.Y.* Made in U.S.A. Pat. No. 2,473,373 — 2,514,981 — others pending. Caliber designation on left rear.

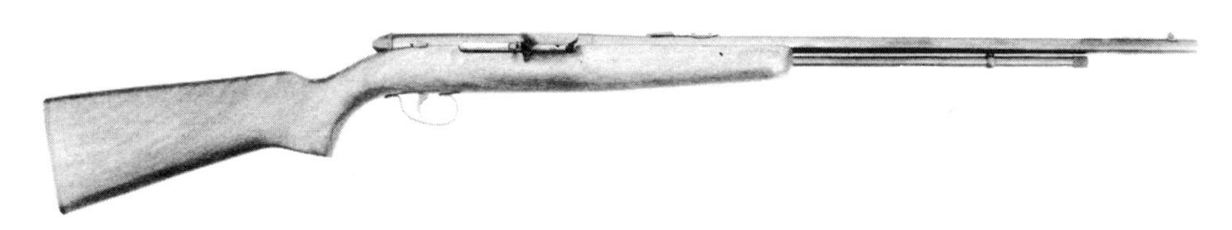

1941–1971 *Remington Model 550 Autoloader.* 22 caliber. 22, 17 or 15 shot tubular magazine. "Power piston" action. Round tapered barrel 24", crowned at muzzle. One piece, pistol grip sporting stock. Made in A, P, and 2G (Gallery) grades. First autoloading rifle to handle 22 short, long or long rifle ammunition interchangeably. Williams patent. Barrel markings: *Remington Arms Co., Inc., Ilion, N. Y. Made in U.S.A.* Williams Patents No. 2,027,892 — 2,090,656 — 2,336,146. (Model number and cartridge designations on top rear).

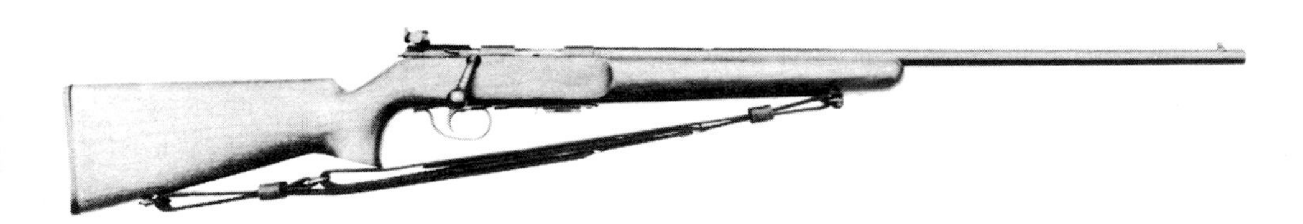

1947–1970 *Remington Model 521TL.* 7 shot. Box magazine. Bolt action repeater. Round tapered barrel, 25" crowned muzzle. Caliber 22 long rifle. Pistol grip stock. Patridge blade front sight. Lyman No. 57R rear sight. Specially designed for young target shooters. Barrel markings: *Remington Arms Co., Inc., Ilion, N.Y. Made in U.S.A.* Patent Numbers 1,908,035 — 1,913,840 — 2,356,257. Model numbers and cartridge designation on top rear of barrel.

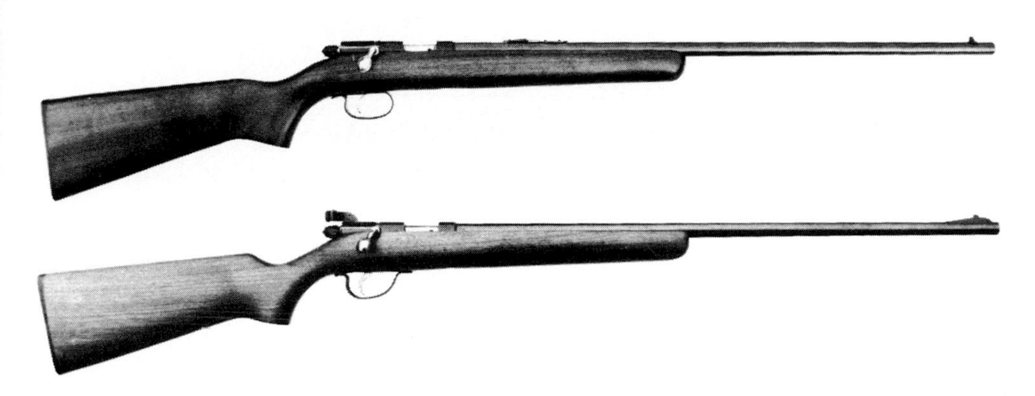

*Remington Model 514.* S.S. Bolt Action. Round tapered barrel 24¾" crowned at muzzle. Calibers 22 short, long and long rifle. One piece pistol grip stock. Light rifle specially designed for youthful shooters. A and P grade. Barrel markings: *Remington Arms Co., Inc., Ilion, N.Y. Made in U.S.A.* Patents Pending. (Model number and cartridge designation on rear left side of barrel). "P" grade illustrated also. 1948–1971

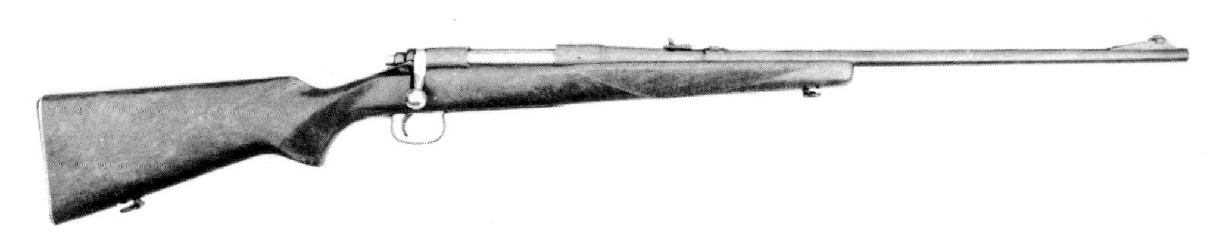

*Remington Model 721.* 5 shot. Box magazine. High power bolt action repeating rifle. Round barrel 24". Calibers 30-06, 270 Win., 300 Mag. and others. New style, pistol grip sporting stock. Adjustable trigger. A, B, D and F grades. World's strongest action in high power sporting rifle. Walker patents. Barrel markings: *Remington Arms Co., Inc., Ilion, N.Y. Made in U.S.A.* Patents 2,473,373 and 2,514,981. Others pending. (Cartridge caliber designation on left side ahead of rear sight.) (Illustrated is B Grade Special.) 1948–1962

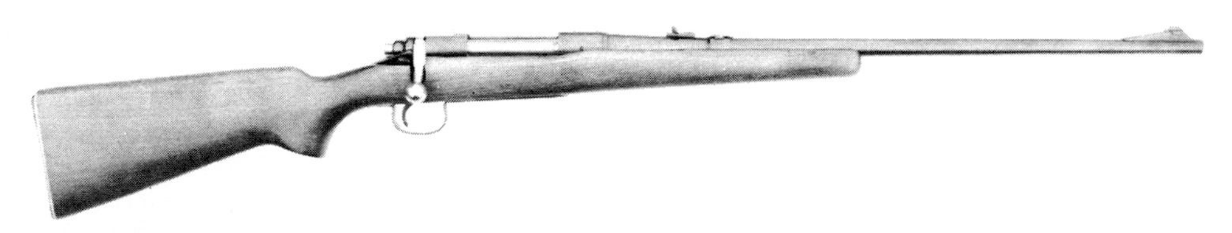

*Model 722.* Same as Model 721 except shorter action. Calibers 300 Savage, 257 Roberts, 308 Win. *Model 722* also supplied with 26" barrel and 5 shot magazine in caliber 222 Rem. and 244 Rem. 1948–1962

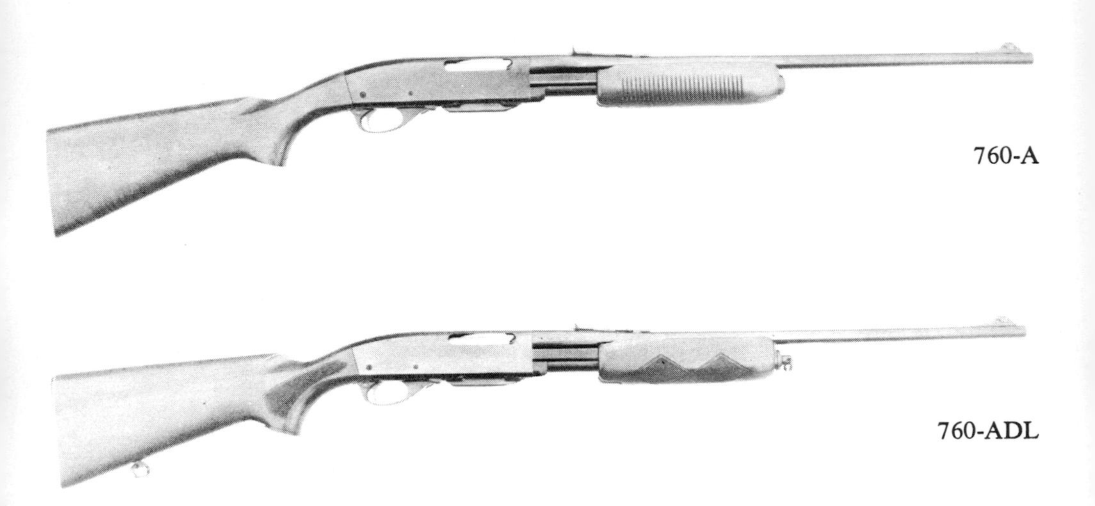

760-A

760-ADL

1952— *Model 760 Gamemaster*. 4 shot box magazine. High power slide action repeating rifle. Specially bored and rifled barrel 22″. Calibers 30-06, 35 Rem., 300 Savage. Pistol grip stock. Extension fore-end. Rotary multiple long breech bolt. Encased bolt head. This is the first slide action repeater design to handle 30-06. Caliber 270 added in 1953, Caliber 257 added in 1954. Available in Deluxe Grades. Barrel markings: *Remington Arms Co., Inc., Ilion, N.Y. Made in U.S.A*. Patent No. 2,473,373. Others pending. (Cartridge caliber designation on left side.)

1955— *Model 572 Fieldmaster*. Slide Action tubular magazine repeating rifle — chambered for 22 short, long and long rifle — 23″ round tapered barrel — half pistol grip stock — semi-beaver tail fore-end. Barrel markings: *Remington Arms Co., Inc., Ilion, N. Y., made in U.S.A. Patent pending Remington Model 572 22 S., L., L.R.*

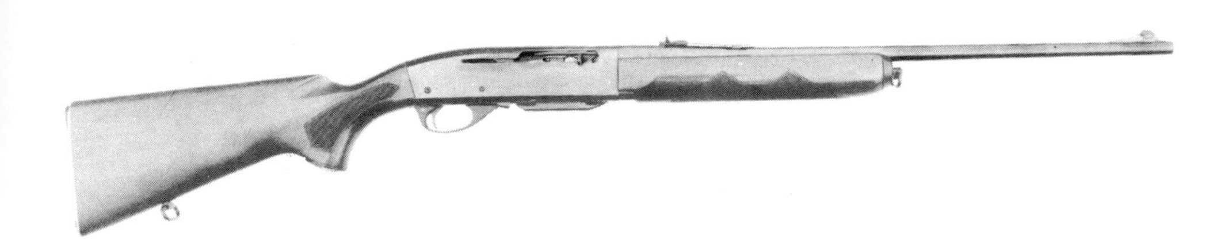

*Model 740 Woodsmaster*. Autoloading High power rifle — chambered for 30-06 Springfield cartridge. Hammerless, solid frame, side ejection. Cross bolt safety. 22-inch round barrel. Double action bars. Rotary multiple-lug breech bolt locks into barrel. Detachable magazine holds four cartridges. Furnished in standard and deluxe grades. Barrel markings: *Remington Arms Co., Inc., Ilion, N. Y. Made in U.S.A. Patent No. 2,473,373; 2,514,981. Others pending.* Cal. 308 Win. added 1956. — 1955——

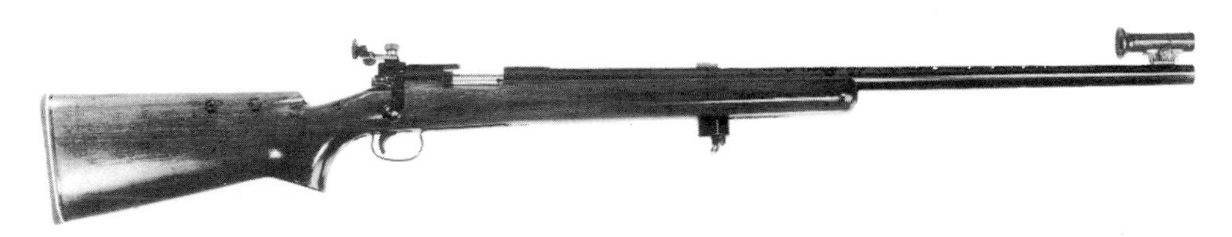

*Model 40-X Rangemaster*. S.S. Bolt Action Deluxe target rifle. Specially rifled round barrel 28″, full floating, double countersunk at muzzle. Caliber 22 long rifle high comb pistol grip stock. Sling strap. Furnished either in heavy or standard (target) weight barrel. Weight 12½ and 10½ pounds. Receiver markings: Remington Model 40-X 22 Long Rifle with Serial Numbers. — 1955——

*Nylon 66*. Automatic 22 caliber, L.R. only with tubular magazine. Stock one piece structural "Zytel" nylon. Adjustable rear sight. Top grip safety. Barrel 19½″. Barrel marking: *Remington*. — 1959——

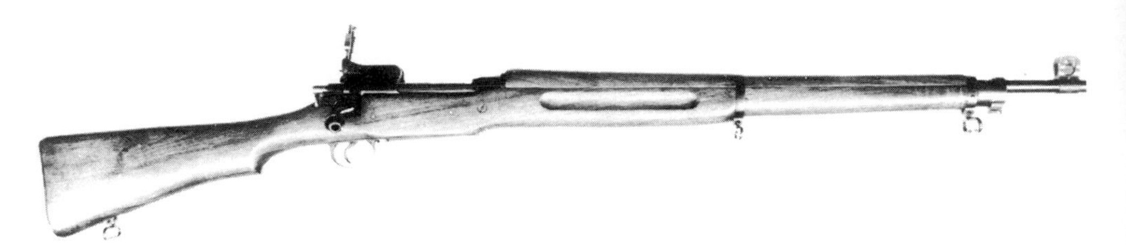

1917–1918 *U.S. Model 17*. Caliber 30 version of the Pattern 14 Enfield Bolt Action Box Magazine Repeater. Barrel length 26". Over-all length 46¼". Weight 9 lbs. 3 oz. without bayonet. Markings on front receiver ring "US Model of 1917 Remington Serial number."

1863–1866 *Harpers Ferry Musket*. Caliber 58 Muzzle Loading and with short bayonet. Described as the standard percussion rifle as used during Civil War. Barrel length 33". Over-all length 49". Weight 8½ lbs. Markings "Remington's, Ilion, NY" on lock plate.

1871–1872 *U.S. Rifle Model 1871*. Caliber 50 Rolling Block Action. Barrel 34½" Overall length 51¾". Similar rifle produced as U.S. Navy Rifle Model 1870 with 32½" barrel.

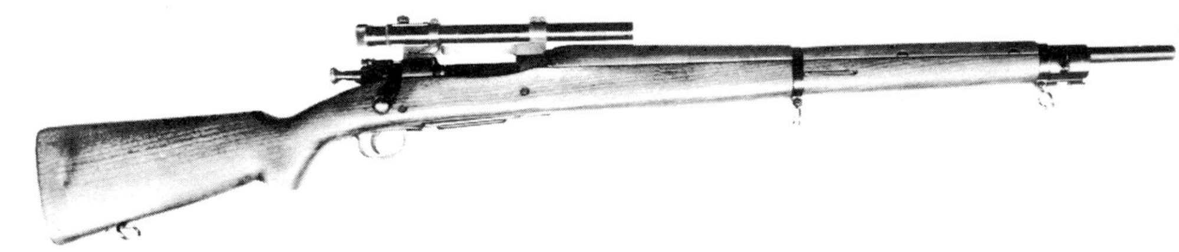

1943–1944 *Springfield Model 1903-A4 Sniper Special*. "Sniper" version of the Springfield Model 03A3 Military Bolt Action Rifle. Caliber 30-06. Fitted with optical telescopic sight mounted on top of receiver. Barrel length 24 inches. Over-all length 43 inches, approx. Weight 9½ lbs. approx. Markings on front receiver ring "U.S. Remington Model 03-A4" and serial number.

## REMINGTON SHOTGUNS

Shotguns Prior to 1840 (Unlisted)

Flintlock Single Barrel Muzzle Loading Shotguns. Cast iron, refined iron and Stubbs twisted barrels. Extra barrels. Flintlocks. (Not illustrated.) 1816–1850

Percussion Lock Single Barrel Muzzle Loading Shotguns. 1840–1888

Percussion Lock Double Barrel Muzzle Loading Shotguns.

Cast steel barrels. 6 lbs., over 6 lbs.

Iron barrels 7 lbs., 7 to 12 lbs., 12 to 18 lbs.

Stubbs twisted barrels (plain)
" " " over 6 lbs. Over 18 lbs.
" " " fine. Over 6 lbs.

Matched barrels for double guns. Cast steel.
" " " " " Plain iron.
" " " " " Stubbs twisted plain.
" " " " " " " fine.

Gun Locks, Flintlocks and Percussion locks.

Illustrated is Remington Percussion Lock double barrel Muzzleloading Sporting Gun, Mfd. 1863. Rt. Barrel Cal. 370. Left barrel 21 Gauge. Barrels 31". Weight about 8½ lbs. Nickel plated Butt Plate, Triggers and Trigger Guard. Engraved silver inlay in stock and fore-arm. Side plates marked *Remington.*

Models prior to 1856 marked *E. Remington.*

Later models marked *E. Remington & Sons, Ilion, N.Y.* or *Remingtons, Herkimer, N. Y.*

1848— (Circa) *Sporting Gun.* Double barrel. (One barrel rifled for 45 caliber. Other barrel in 32 gauge.) Percussion locks. Muzzle loading. Lock plates, trigger guard and butt plate nickel plated. Barrels 28½". Weight approx. 11 lbs. Marked: *Remington.*

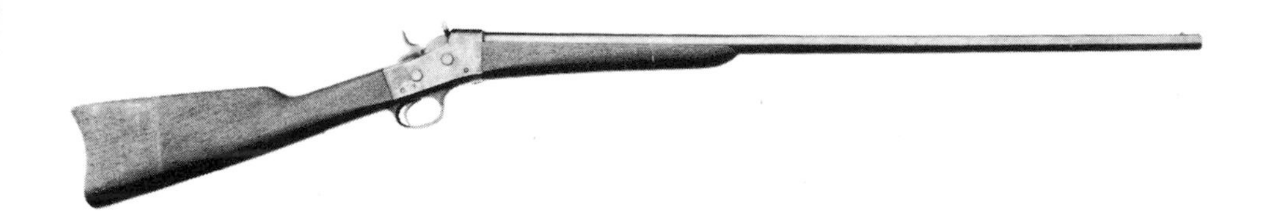

1867–1892 *Remington-Rider Shotgun No. 1.* Breech loading. Single barrel (plain) Gauge 16 and 20. (This series has Rolling Block Action.) Weight about 6½ lbs. *E. Remington & Sons, Ilion, N.Y. U.S.A.* and Patent Markings on tang.

1867–1892 *Remington Rider Shotgun No. 2.* Single barrel. (plain) Gauge 30 (Juvenile). Otherwise similar to Shotgun No. 1. (Not illustrated.)

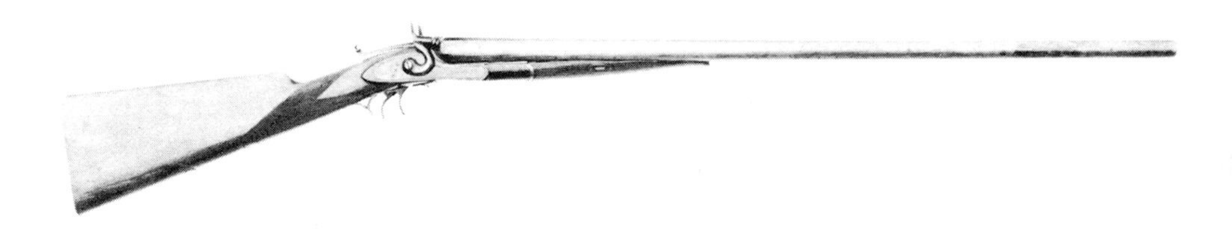

1874–1878 *Remington Whittmore, Model 1874.* Double Barrel. Break-open breech attached to frame by 2 lugs and sliding bolt. Thumb piece pushes up to open breech. Hammers, lifter action. Barrels rolled steel. (Also Damascus twist.) Gauge 10, 12 and 16. (Later models have matted rib.) First Remington Double Barrel Shotgun. Barrels marked *E. Remington & Sons, Ilion, N.Y.* Top of bolt marked *A.E. Whittmore's Patents Aug. 8, 1871, April 16, 1872.* Weight about 8 lbs.

*New Model 1882*. Double barrel. Hammers circular action. Lever moves sidewise to open breech. Barrels 28″ to 32″, plain or Damascus twist. Bar rebounding locks, low circular hammers, checkered half pistol grip, matted rib. Supplied in seven different grades. Weights: 6¾ to 7½ lbs. (16 Ga.); 7 to 9 lbs. (12 Ga.); 8½ to 10¼ lbs. (10 Ga.). Barrels marked: *E. Remington & Sons, Ilion, N.Y.* Later models marked: *Remington Arms Co., Ilion, N.Y. U.S.A.* Side plates on receivers of later models marked: *Remington Arms Co.* Metal parts of higher grades finely engraved. Serial numbers on tang of guard bow. Gauges 10, 12, 16. — 1882–1910

*New Model Heavy Shotgun*. Same as "New Model" 1882 except extension rib and rebounding locks. Made only in 10 gauge. (Not illustrated.) — 1882–1895

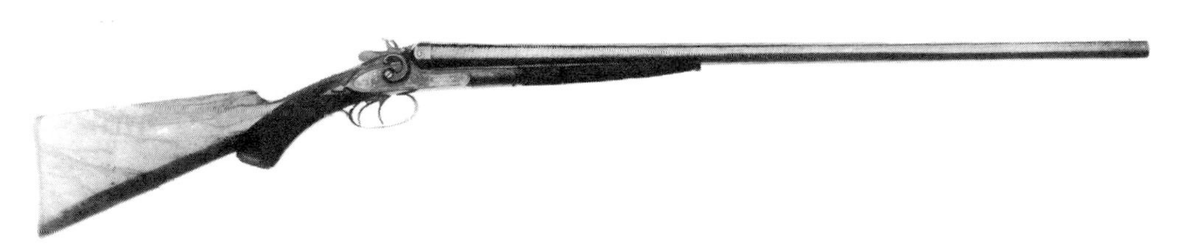

*Model 89*. Double barrel. Hammers circular action. Barrels steel or Damascus twist, 28″ to 32″. Gauges 10, 12, 16. Weight 7 to 10 lbs. Marking: *E. Remington & Sons, Ilion, N.Y.* on rib. — 1889–1908

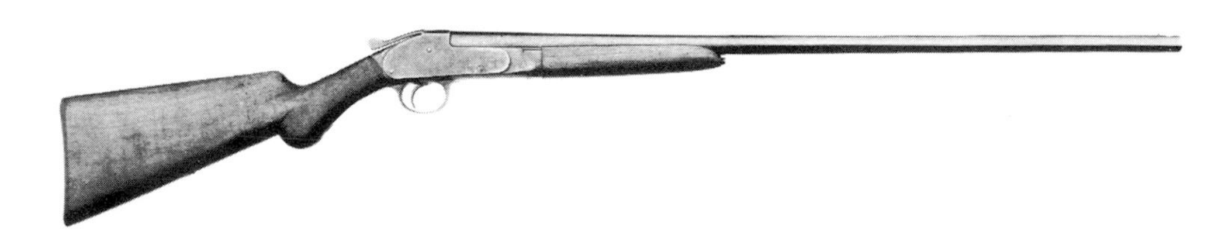

*Remington Shotgun No. 3*. Single barrel, semi-hammerless, (plain) Gauge 16, 10, 12, 20, 24 and 28. Cocks with thumb lever on left side of frame. Weights from 5¾ lbs. to 6½ lbs. Barrel lengths 30″, 32″ and 34″. Marking: *Remington Arms Co., Ilion, N.Y.* — 1893–1902

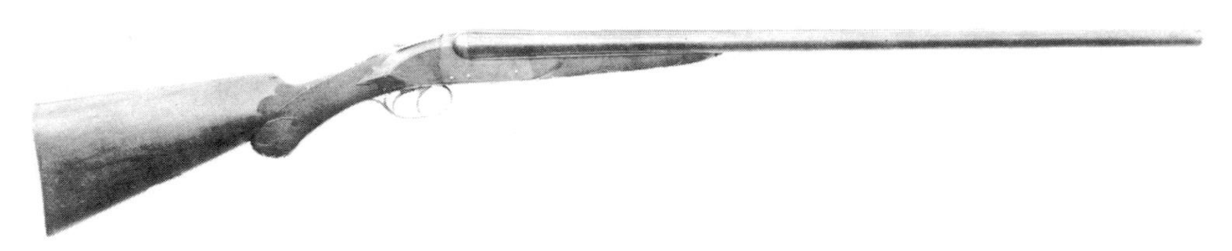

1894–1910 *Model 1894.* Remington Hammerless Double Barrel Shotgun. Automatic ejector. Automatic safety. (Also made with non-automatic ejector.) Supplied in Grades K, A, AR, B, C, D, E and Trap Grade "C.E.O." Also choice of plain or ordnance steel barrels and a variety of Damascus twist barrels, in lengths of from 28″ to 32″. Weights from 7 to 10 lbs. in Gauges 10, 12 and 16. Higher grades were ornately engraved and with finely checkered stocks and fore-arms. Fore-ends had a novel "Purdy" snap for quick take down. Early models marked: *E. Remington & Sons.* Later models marked: *Remington Arms Co., Ilion, N.Y.* Serial numbers on tang of guard bow.

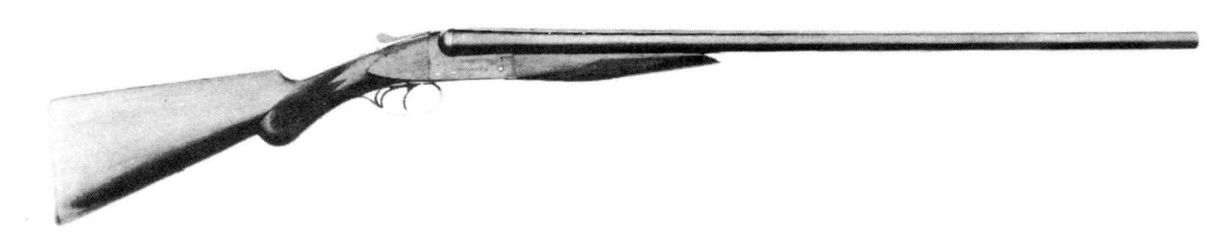

1900–1910 *Model 1900.* Remington Hammerless Double Barrel Shotgun. An improved version of Model 1894. Barrels Damascus Twist or ordnance steel. Matted rib. Gauges 10, 12, 16, 20. Fay & Humphrey patent.

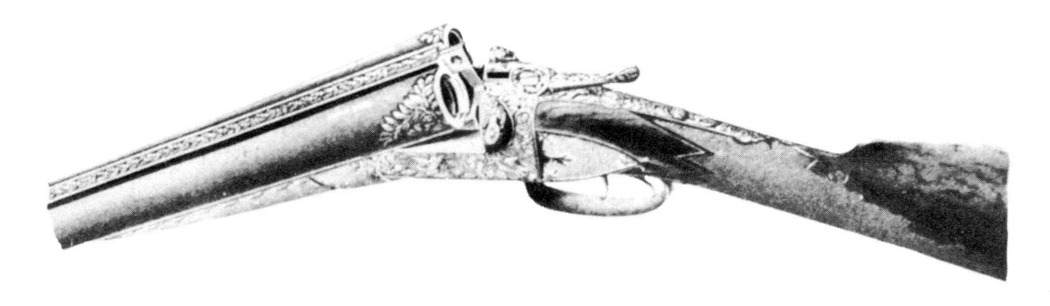

1900–1910 *Remington Special Model 1900.* Finest double barrel shotgun ever produced by Remington. Fitted with treble wedged cross bolt. Barrels ordnance, nickel or Whitworth fluid steel, 26, 28, 30 and 32 inches. Beautiful engraving. Hand-made straight grip stock of Circassian walnut, with gold inlays. Weights 6¼ lbs. to 8¾ lbs. Gauge 12. Retail price $750.00 — custom made.

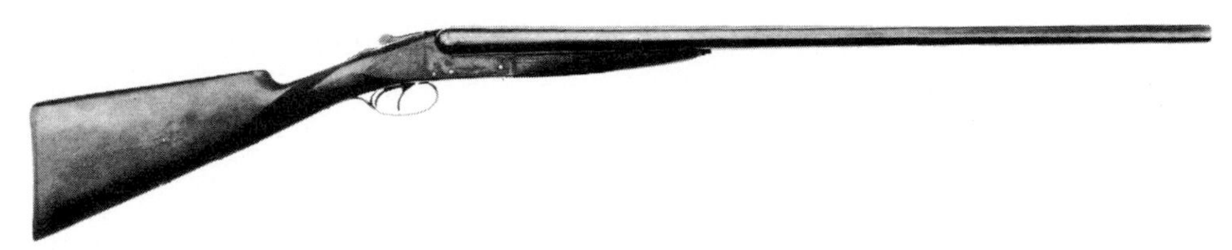

*Trap Gun.* A trap gun version of Model 1900. Straight grip. Ordnance steel barrels, 30 or 32". Gauge 12. Weight 7¾ lbs. to 7 lbs. 15 oz. Grades C, E and F. — 1902–1910

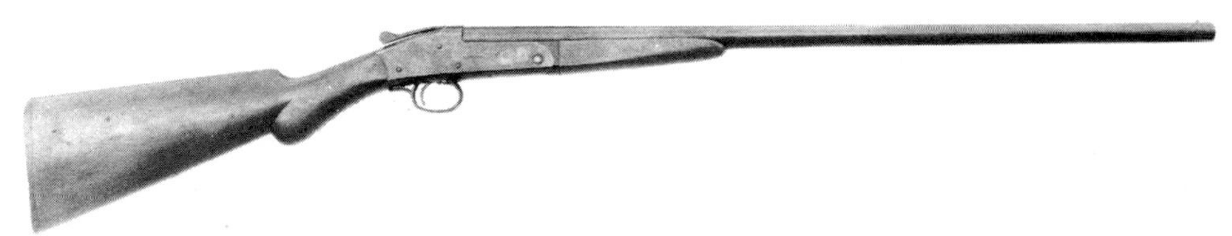

*Remington No. 9.* Model 1902. Single barrel shotgun. Improved version of No. 3 single gun. Semi-hammerless. Automatic ejector. Barrell rolled steel, 30, 32 and 34 inch lengths. Walnut stock. Gauges 10, 12, 16, 20, 24, 28. Fay patents. Weights 5¾ lbs. — 6½ lbs. Serial numbers on tang of guard bow. Barrels marked: *Remington Arms Co., Ilion, N.Y. U.S.A.* Receivers marked: Patented Oct. 30, 1894, June 16, 1902, June 28, 1904. — 1902–1910

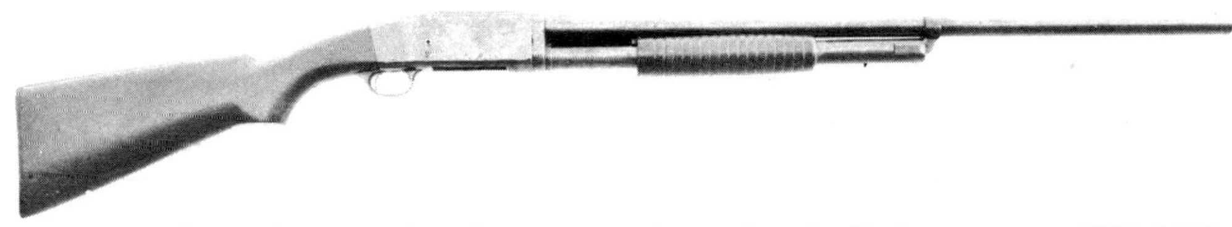

*Model 10.* Slide action repeating shotgun manufactured under Pedersen patents. Six shot. Bottom ejection. Barrels 26, 28 and 32 inches, Remington steel. (Some with matted rib.) Gauge 12, made in A, B, C, D, E, F grades. Weights about 7½ lbs. Markings: Serial numbers on bottom of receivers just ahead of ejection port. Checkered hard rubber butt plate with encircled "Remington UMC" trademark. Also "Trade Remington Mark" on action bar and "Remington UMC" trade mark on tang of trigger guard bow. Serial number on under side front of receiver. Barrels marked: *"MODEL 10" The Remington Arms Union Metallic Ctg. Co., Inc. — Remington Ilion Works, Ilion, New York, U.S.A.* Patent February 3, 1903 and May 18, 1905. — 1907–1929

Also *Model 10-C Target Version* with ventilated rib and barrel machined out of solid steel and straight grip stock. Also Model 10-S (Trap Special) with matted top surface barrel.

Also *Model 10S* (Trap Special) with straight grip. Walnut stock. Some with raised matted rib.

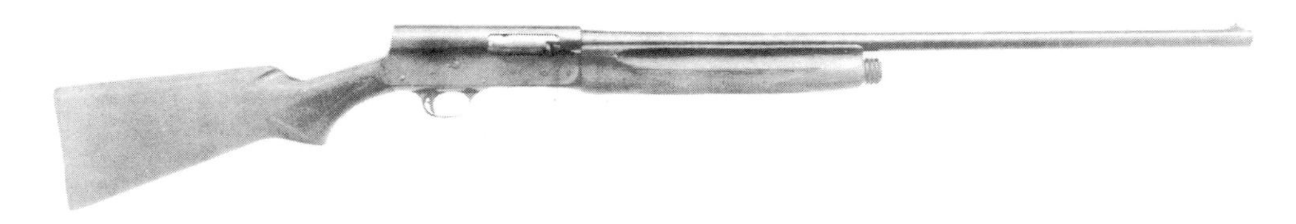

1905–1948 *Model 11*. Autoloading shotgun manufactured under Browning patents. Five shot, side ejection. Barrels Remington steel. (Some with matted rib.) Half pistol grip stock. Made in A, B, C (Trap), D, E, and F grades. Produced in 12, 16 and 20 gauges, with various barrel lengths and chokes. Weights 6¾ lbs. to 8 lbs. Receivers and/or barrels marked: *Remington Arms Co., Ilion, N.Y. U.S.A*. Browning's Patents Oct. 9, 1900, Dec. 17, 1901, Sept. 30, 1902, June 16, 1903.

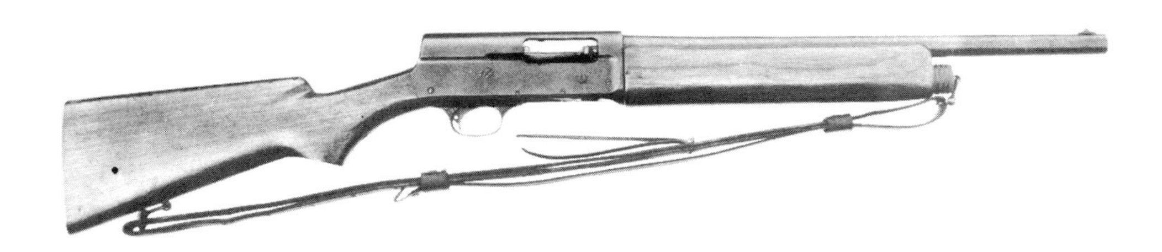

1921–1948 *Model 11 — Police Special*. Law Enforcement Officers' version with special barrel length and choke. Also fitted with sling strap and swivels. Weight approx. 8 lbs. 12 Ga. only.

1921–1948 *Model 11R*. Riot gun version of Model 11. 20 inch cylinder bored barrel, 12, 16 or 20 gauges. Otherwise same as Model 11. (Not illustrated.)

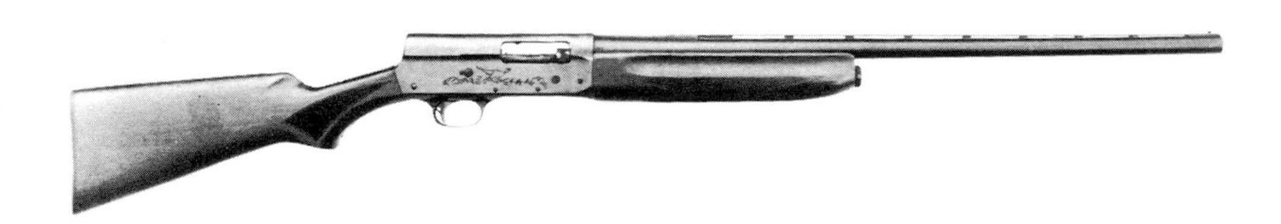

1931–1948 *Model Sportsman*. Improved 3-shot version of the Model 11, with semi-beavertail fore-end. 12, 16 and 20 gauges. Barrels 26, 28, 30 and 32 inches. Supplied in regular and high grades. Weights 6¾ lbs. to 8 lbs. Markings: Same as for the Model 11 except Breech Block marked with "The Sportsman" on ejection port side.

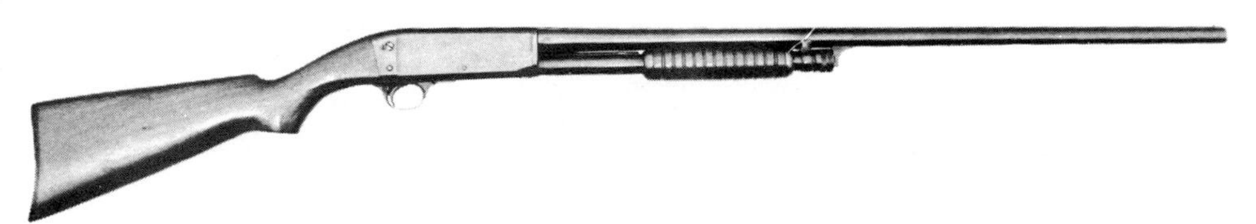

*Model 17*. Slide action repeating shotgun. Similar to Model 10 except simplified take-down. Made only in 20 gauge. Grades A, B, D, E and F. (Some with solid rib.) Browning, Pedersen and Garrison patents. Weights about 5¾ lbs. Barrels 28″ full choke (regular); also available in 26, 30, and 32 inches. 1921–1933

*Model 17 — Riot Grade*. Made with 20″ barrel. Otherwise same as standard model. (Not illustrated.) 1921–1933

*Model 17 Police*. Special police gun with pistol grip only (no stock) and 18½″ barrels. (Not illustrated.)

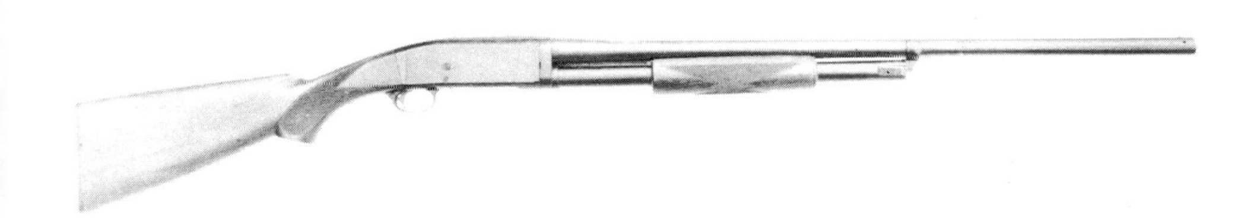

*Model 29*. Slide action repeating shotgun. Similar to Model 17. Made in 12 gauge. All grades. Loomis patent. Weight about 7¼ lbs. Receiver marked with Remington Script, model and serial numbers. Barrels marked: *Remington Arms Co., Inc., Remington Ilion Works, Ilion, N.Y. Made in U.S.A.* U.S. Patent Numbers 1,579,177 — 1,660,216. Other Patents Pending. 1929–1933

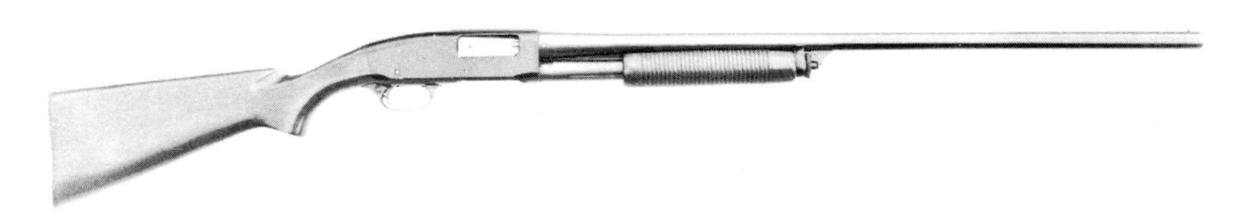

*Model 31*. Slide action repeating shotgun. New feature side ejection. Five shot. Gauges 12, 16, 20. Made in all grades; 26, 28, 30 and 32″ barrels. Barnes and Loomis patents. Weights 6½ lbs. to 7½ lbs. Barrel markings: *Remington Arms Co., Inc., Ilion, N.Y. Made in U.S.A.* Patents 1,763,665 — 1,786,213 — 1,763,714 — 1,834,410 — 2,023,929 — 2,039,814. Receivers also marked on left side with Remington Script trade mark, Model Number and serial numbers. 1931–1949

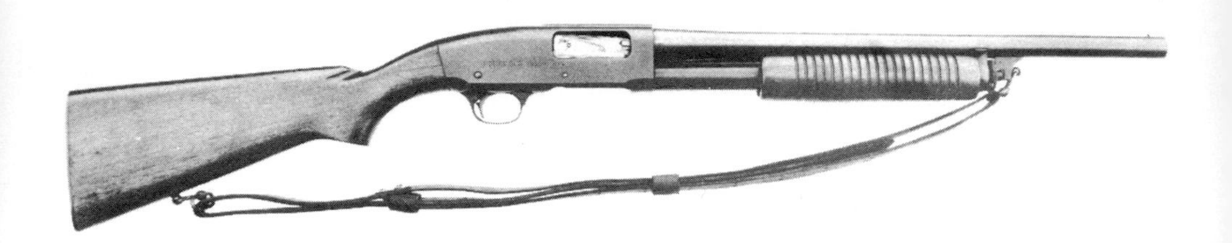

1931–1949 Also *Model 31 Police Special* Law Enforcement officers' version of Model 31, with special 18″ barrel and choke and fitted with sling strap and swivels. Weight about 7 lbs. Made in 12 Ga. only.

Also *Model 31 — Riot Grade* with 20″ cylinder bore. Otherwise same as standard grade. (Not illustrated.)

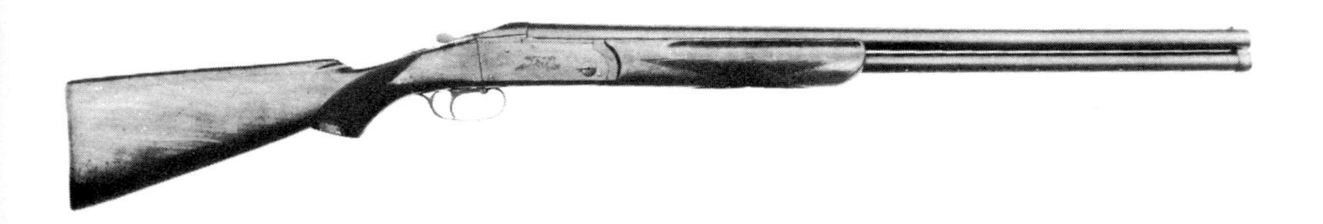

1932–1942 *Model 32*. Double barrel (over and under) shotgun. Hammerless. Gauge 12. Loomis patents. Barrels marked: *Remington Arms Co., Inc., Ilion, N.Y. Made in U.S.A*. Patent numbers 1,795,223 — 1,900,184 — 1,908,036.

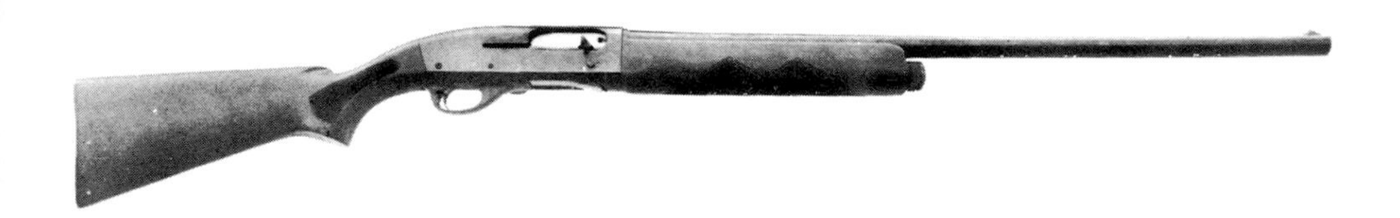

1949–1969 *Model 11-'48*. Autoloading shotgun. Five shot. Barrels, plain, matted top or ventilated rib. Half pistol grip stock. Gauges 12, 16, 20. A light, streamlined, modern version of the famous Model 11. All grades, including Police and Riot models. Crittendon patents. Weights 6½ to 7½ lbs. Barrel markings: *Remington Arms Co., Inc., Ilion, N.Y. Made in U.S.A*. Patent Nos. 2,278,589 — 2,570,772 — 2,675,638. Receivers also marked on left side with Remington Script trade mark, model number and serial number.

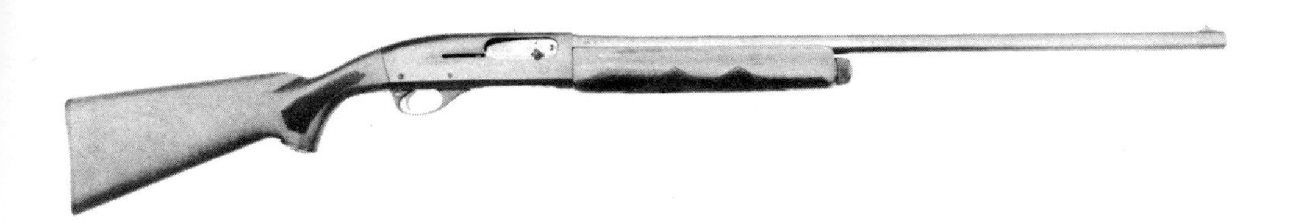

*Sportsman '48*. Same as Model 11-'48 except 3 shot capacity. All grades. Also special skeet grades with ventilated rib and ivory front-sight. Stock fitted with "Flying Duck" grip cap. 1949–1960

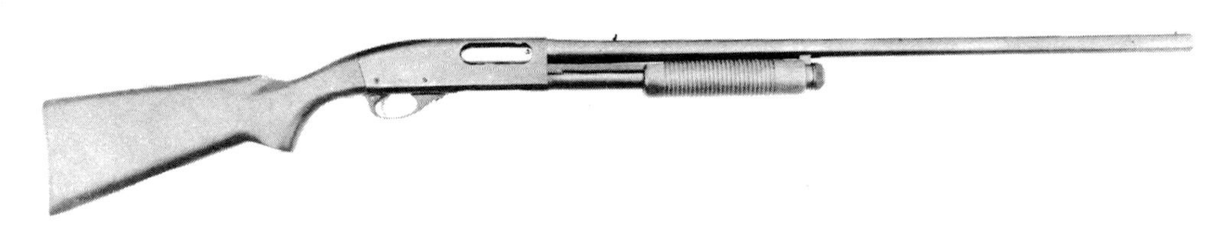

*Model 870 "Wingmaster."* Slide action repeating shotgun. Five shot, side ejection. Barrel, plain, matted top or ventilated rib. Half pistol grip stock. Gauges 12, 16, 20. Light, streamlined and made in AP, D, and F grades. Haskell and Crittendon patents. Weights 6½ lbs. to 7 lbs. 12 Ga. gun supplied with 12 oz. "Vari-Weight" magazine plug. 1950——

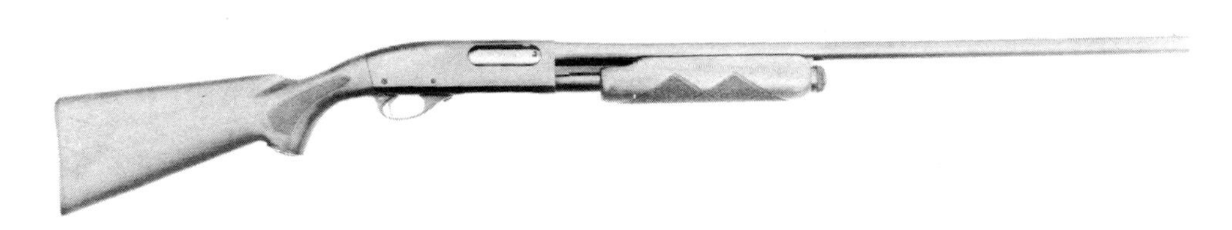

Also *Model 870 ADL* (Deluxe Grade), *Model 870 TC* (Trap Grade) with front and rear sights and ventilated rib, walnut stock, *Model 870 TB* (Trap Special) with matted top surface of barrel, steel bead front sight, walnut stock, *Model 870 SA* (Skeet Grade), *Model 870 SC* (Skeet "Target" Grade) and *Model 870 R* (Riot) — (Same as Model 870 with 20" barrel — cylinder bore — for law enforcement officers.) Barrel markings: *Remington Arms Co., Inc., Ilion, N.Y. Made in U.S.A*. Patent No. 2,039,814 — 2,645,813 — 2,675,638 — Others pending. Receivers also marked on left side with Remington Script, "Wingmaster" trademark, Model number, and serial number. 1955——

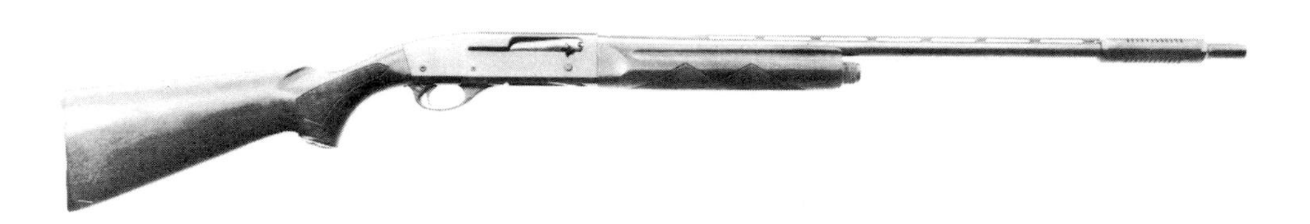

1952–1969 *Model 11-'48.* Autoloading shotgun. Four shot. All grades. First 28 gauge autoloader. Weight approx. 6¼ lbs. Similar to the 12, 16 and 20 gauges except 25" barrel length and gun capacity of four shots. (Shown is skeet model with raised ventilated rib and compensator.)

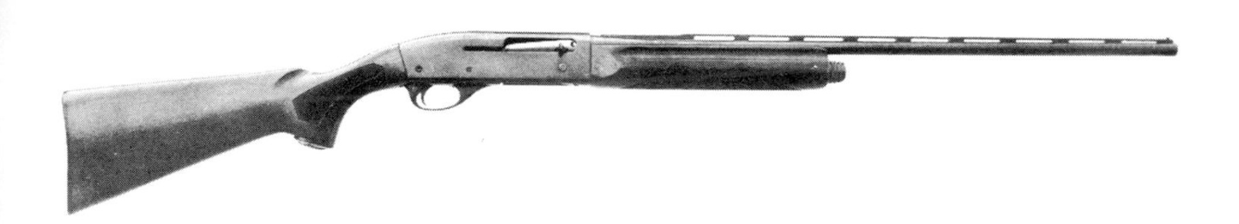

1954–1969 *Model 11-'48 — 410 Gauge Autoloading Shotgun* 4 shot. All grades. First 410 gauge autoloader. Chambered for either 2½ or 3" shells. Weight approx. 6¼ lbs. Similar to 12, 16 and 20 Gauges except 25" barrel length and gun capacity of 4 shots. All fitted with "Flying Duck" grip caps.

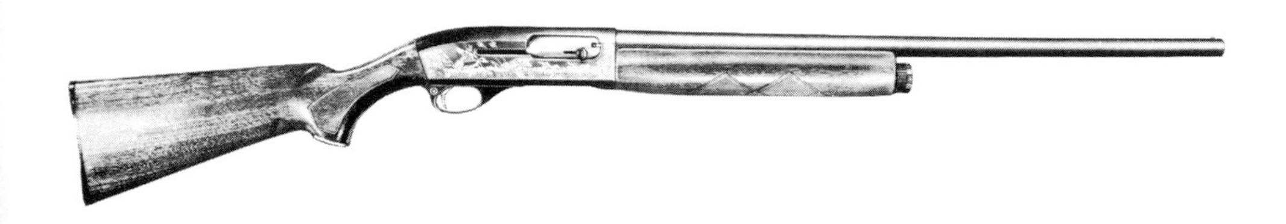

1956–1964 *Model Sportsmen 58 Autoloading Shotgun* — 3 shot capacity with "Powermatic Action" and non-recoiling barrel. 12 Gauge — Grades ADL (Deluxe), BDL (Deluxe Special), D ("Tournament"), F (Premier), SC Skeet ("Target"), SD and SF. Barrel lengths 26" to 30", weight approx. 7 lbs. Receiver decorated with game scenes and fine scroll, beavertail and checkered fore end; stock checkered and fitted with decorated metal grip cap. Barrel Markings: *Remington Ams Co., Inc., Ilion, N. Y. Made in U.S.A.*, Patent Numbers 2,039,814 — 2,645,873. Receiver also marked with Remington script trademark, model number and serial number.

## PARKER GUNS MADE BY REMINGTON

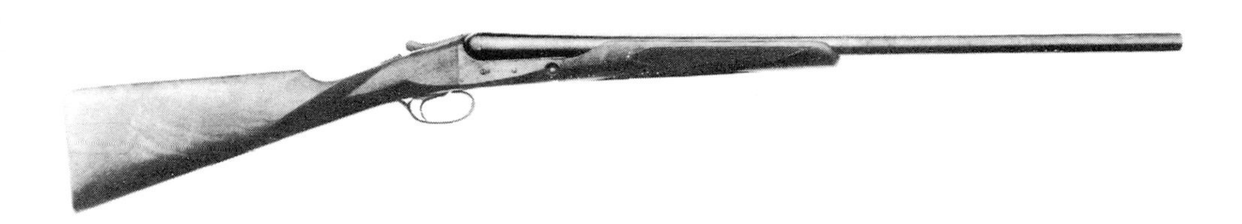

*Model 920 — Parker Double Barrel Shotgun.* Gauges 10, 12, 16, 20, 28 and 410. Supplied in Grades "VH," VHE, (Regular), also, GH, DH, CHE, BHE, AHE, AAHE, High grades and the A-1 Special Fancy grade. Also SC Trap gun and the VHE grade skeet gun. Made with full range of choke borings and a complete selection of barrel lengths from 24 inches to 34 inches. With either single or double triggers. Choke marking on barrels — front end of water table. Proof marks on rear end of water table.
Serial numbers on left side of barrel water table, also on fore end iron, guard bow, and on left side of frame. Trade mark on right flat of frame, and "Made in U.S.A., Ilion, N.Y."
"Parker" name on bottom of front frame. (Illustrated is skeet gun.) 1936–1940

*Model 930 Parker Single Barrel Trap Gun.* Made in five grades, "SC," "SB," "SA," "SAA" and "SA-1 Special." 12 Gauge only, 30, 32 or 34 inch barrels, full choke standard, with option of any other boring. All with raised vent ribs and rubber recoil pads. Weight 7¾ to 8½ lbs. Engraving, markings and other details correspond to the grade specification for the double barrel guns. 1936–1940

## REMINGTON NOVEL AND SPECIAL GUNS AND TOOLS

1923–1969 *Remington Industrial Cement Kiln Gun* 8 Ga. (Special shell) single shot breech loading. (Model 400 Illustrated)

1951–1955 *Remington — Model 450 Stud Driver* Caliber 32 R.F. Special Loads, Single Shot. Designed especially for fastening construction materials.

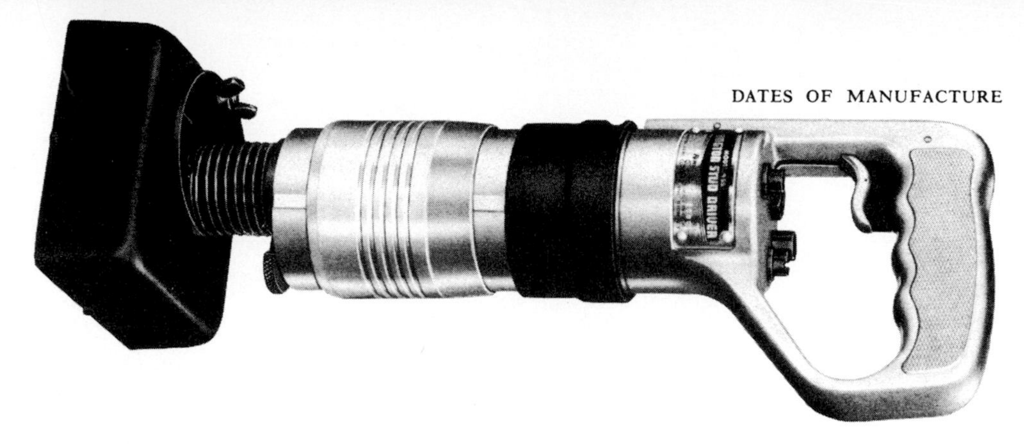

| | |
|---|---|
| *Remington — Model 455 "Double Duty" Stud Driver*. Caliber 32 RF special loads. Designed especially for fastening construction materials. ¼″ or ⅜″ dia. stud capacity, and with detachable barrel assembly for conversion to 22 Caliber RF special loads for Medium Duty. | 1955–1969 |

| | |
|---|---|
| *Remington Model 26 **Slide Action** Air Rifle*. 50-shot repeating. 20½ inch barrel and straight grip stock. Weight about 4 lbs. 5 oz. | 1928–1934 |

| | |
|---|---|
| *Remington Model 1—Cane Rifle*. Caliber 22 Rim Fire Breech loading "pull back" action, single shot. Barrel 29 inches—⅜″ round, rifled steel with molded fiber cover. Weight 1 lb. 2 oz. Dog's head cane handle with button trigger. (Some with straight handle.) A. H. Thomas Patent Feb. 9, 1858. | 1875–1888 |

| | |
|---|---|
| *Remington Model 2—Cane Rifle*. 32 Caliber Rim Fire version. Weight 1 lb. 13 oz. with plain style handle. (Some with Dog's head handle.) | 1875–1888 |

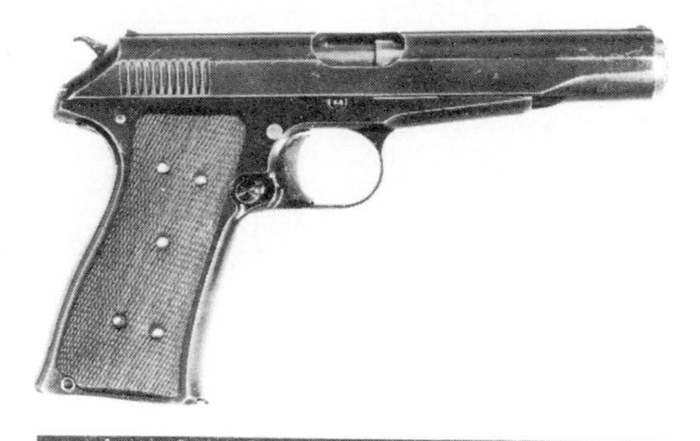

Remington Cal. 45 Automatic Pistol 1919 Government Experimental.

Early Experimental Remington Revolver

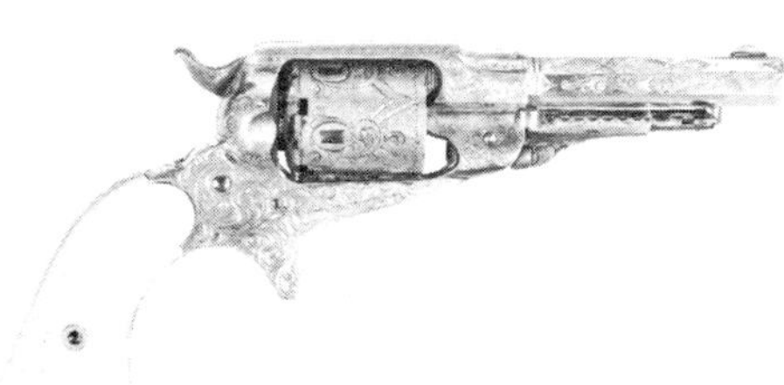

1868–1888 Remington "Pocket" Revolver conversion from percussion to cartridge model.

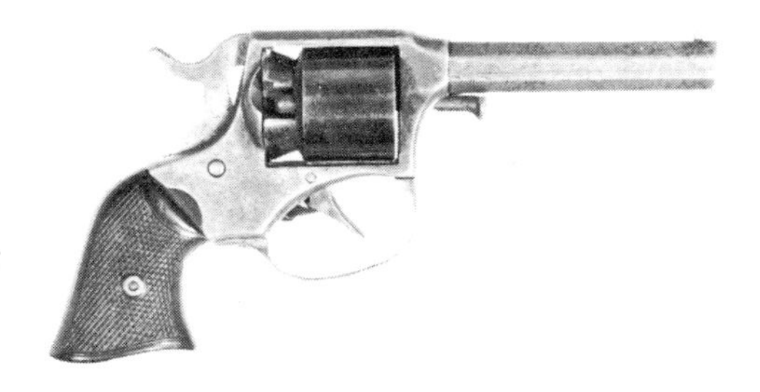

*Rider Pocket Revolver*. Caliber: 31. Barrel: 3″ octagon. Cylinder: 1¼″ long. Number of shots: 5. Rifling: 5 grooves. Trigger guard: large oval, brass. Sights: *front,* brass pin; *rear,* groove. Grips: hard rubber, checkered; pearl; ivory. Finish: blued; nickel plated frame; full nickel plated. Weight: 10 ounces. Distinctive features: "mushroom" cylinder; large trigger guard; straight trigger. Markings — top of barrel: *Manufactured by Remington's, Ilion, N.Y., Riders Pt. Aug. 17, 1858 May 3, 1859*. Serial number: underside of barrel; on frame inside trigger guard. Dates of manufacture: 1860–1888. Number manufactured: estimated at over 100,000.

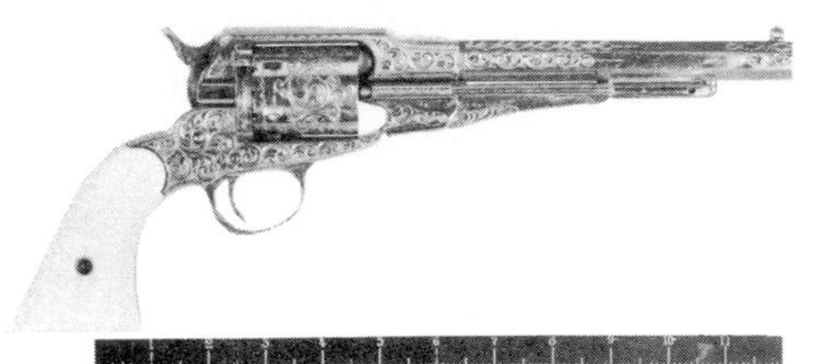

*New Model Navy Revolver* (Single Action). Caliber: 36. Barrel: 7⅜" octagon. Cylinder: 2" long. Number of shots: 6. Rifling: 5 grooves. Trigger guard: brass, oval. Sights: *front*. German silver cone or iron blade; *rear,* groove. Grips: walnut, oil finished. Finish: blued, except for case-hardened hammer. Weight: 2 pounds, 10 ounces. Markings — Top of barrel: *Patented Sept. 14, 1858. E. Remington & Sons, Ilion, N.Y., U.S.A. New Model.* Left grip: inspector's initials in script in rectangle. Serial number: underside of barrel; side of grip frame. Dates of manufacture: 1863–1888. Number manufactured: over 32,000.

*Note:* Standard New Model .36's sold the general public were produced with blued finish and varnished grips. Special engraving, finishes and grips were supplied on special order and at extra cost.

*Vest Pocket Pistol* — .22. Caliber: .22 rim fire. Number of shots: 1. Barrel: 3¼" round. Rifling: 5 grooves. Trigger: sheath. Sights: *front,* brass pin; *rear,* groove. Grips: walnut, varnished; pearl; ivory. Finish: blued; plated; engraving on order. Weight: 3⅞ ounces. Markings — Top of barrel: *Remington's, Ilion, N.Y. Patent Oct. 1, 1861.* Serial number: underside of barrel; side of grip frame. Dates of manufacture: 1865–1888. Number manufactured: estimated at over 25,000.

*Model 95 Double Deringer.* 1866-1935. Caliber .41 Rim Fire. 2 shots. Barrel length 3". Superposed. Weight 11 oz. Markings — Top of barrel: *"E. Remington and Sons, Ilion N.Y.,* Elliot's Patent Dec. 12th, 1865." Later models marked "Remington Arms Company, Ilion, N.Y." or "Remington Arms — UMC Co., Ilion, N.Y."

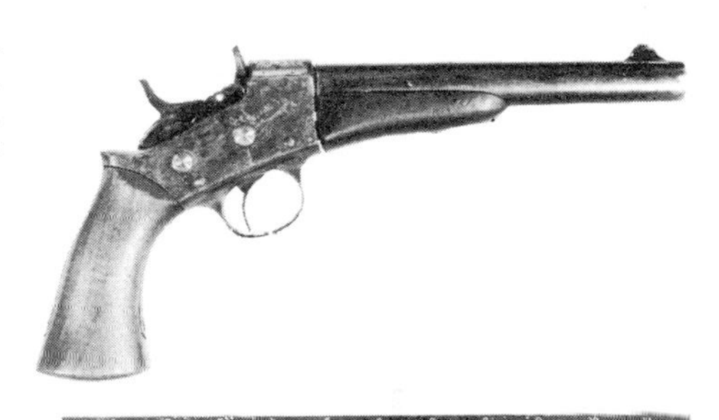

*Model 1871 Army* (Single Action). Caliber: .50 center fire. Number of shots: 1. Barrel: 8" round. Rifling: 3 grooves. Trigger guard: iron, oval. Sights: front, large iron blade; rear, V-notch in breech block. Grips: walnut, oil finished. Finish: blued barrel, trigger; case-hardened receiver, trigger guard; bright hammer, breech block. Weight: 2 pounds, 3 ounces. Markings — Left side of receiver: *Remingtons Ilion, N.Y. U.S.A. Pat. May 3d Nov. 15th, 1864 April 17th, 1866 P S.* Serial number: side of grip frame. Dates of manufacture: 1872–1888. Number manufactured: over 6,000.

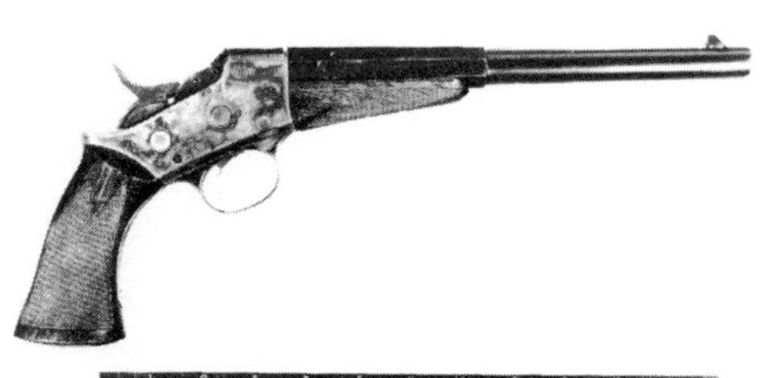

*Model 1901 Target* (Single Action). Caliber: .22 long rifle, .22 rim fire short, .25-10 rim fire, .44 S.&W. Russian. Barrel: 10″ half-octagon. Rifling: 5 grooves. Number of shots: 1. Trigger guard: iron, oval. Sights: front ivory bead; rear, adjustable wind gauge. Grips: walnut, checkered. Forearm: walnut, checkered. Weight: 2 pounds, 13 ounces in 22 caliber. Finish: blued. Markings — Top of barrel: *Remington Arms Co. Ilion, N.Y.* Left side of receiver: *Remington's Ilion, N.Y. U.S.A. Pat. May 3d Nov. 15th 1864 April 17th 1866*. Serial number: side of grip frame. Dates of manufacture: 1901–1909. Number manufactured: Approximately 700.

*Rider Magazine Pistol* (Single Action). Caliber: .32 rim fire extra short. Number of shots: 5 in magazine. Barrel: 3″ octagon. Rifling: 5 grooves. Trigger: sheath. Sights: front, brass blade. Grips: walnut, varnished; pearl; ivory. Finish: nickel plated; case-hardened; specially plated or engraved on order. Weight: 10 ounces. Markings — Top of barrel: *E. Remington & Sons, Ilion, N.Y. Riders Pat. Aug. 15, 1871*. Serial number: side of grip frame. Dates of manufacture: 1871–1888. Number manufactured: estimated at 15,000.

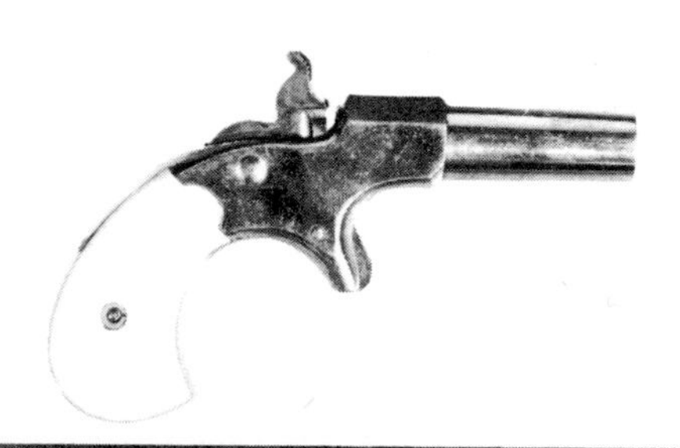

*Elliot Single Shot Deringer* (Single Action). Caliber: .41 rim fire. Barrel: 2½″ round. Rifling: 5 grooves. Trigger: sheath. Sights: front, brass pin. Grips: walnut, varnished; pearl; ivory. Finish: blued; nickel plated frame; full nickel plated. Weight: 7 ounces. Markings — Top of barrel: *Remingtons, Ilion, N.Y. Pat. Aug. 27, 1867*. Serial number: underside of barrel; underside of receiver. Dates of manufacture: 1867–1888. Number manufactured: about 10,000.

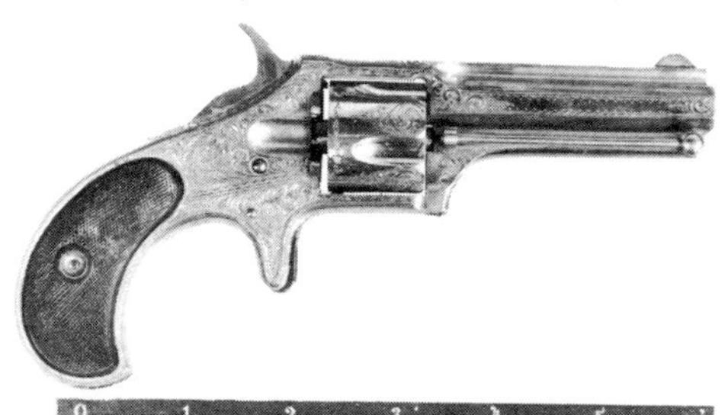

*New Line Revolver No. 1* (Single Action). Caliber: 30 rim fire short. Number of shots: 5. Barrel: 2 13/16″ octagon. Rifling: 5 grooves. Cylinder: 13/16″ long. Trigger: sheath. Sights: *front*, blade; *rear*, groove. Grips: walnut, varnished; hard rubber, checkered; pearl; ivory. Finish: blued; nickel plated; specially plated or engraved on order. Weight: 10 ounces. Distinctive feature: unique rod ejector. Markings — Top of barrel: *E. Remington & Sons, Pat. W. S. Smoot Oct. 21, 1873*. Serial number: side of grip frame. Date of manufacture: 1873–1888. Number manufactured: estimated at about 20,000.

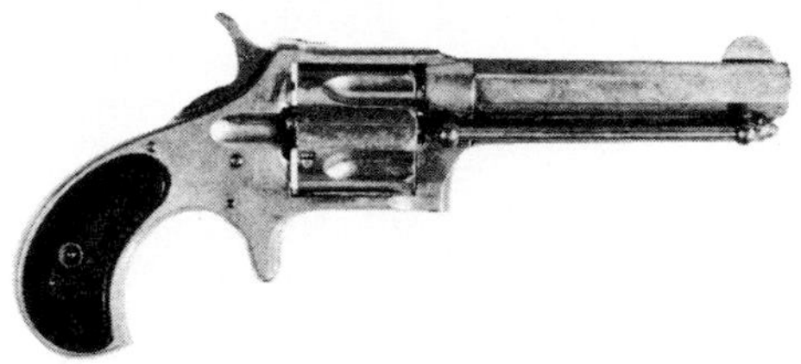

*New Line Revolver, No. 3* (Single Action). Caliber: 38 rim fire short. Number of shots: 5. Barrel: 3¾" octagon. Rifling: 5 grooves. Cylinder: 13/16" long. Trigger: sheath. Sights: *front,* blade; *rear,* groove. Grips: hard rubber, checkered; pearl; ivory. Finish: blued; nickel plated; specially plated or engraved on order. Weight: 15 ounces. Distinctive feature: unique rod ejector. Markings — Top of barrel: *E. Remington & Sons, Ilion, N. Y. Pat. W. S. Smoot Oct. 21, 1873.* Serial number: side of grip frame. Dates of manufacture: 1875–1888. Number manufactured: estimated at over 25,000 for both types.

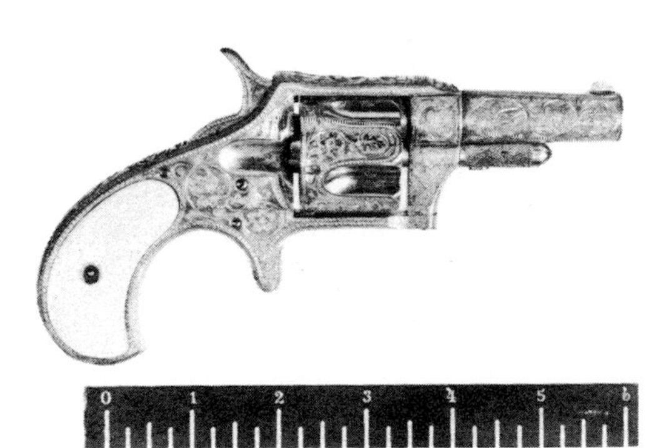

*New Line Revolver No. 4* (Single Action). Caliber: 38 center fire short; 41 rim fire short. Number of shots: 5. Barrel: 2½" round. Rifling: 5 grooves. Cylinder: 11/16" long. Trigger: sheath. Sights: *front,* blade; *rear,* groove. Grips: hard rubber, checkered; pearl; ivory. Finish: blued; nickel plated; or engraved on order. Weight: 12 ounces. Distinctive feature: no ejector. Markings — Top of barrel: *E. Remington & Sons, Ilion, N. Y.* Serial number: inside top strap; side of grip frame. Dates of manufacture: 1877–1888. Number manufactured: estimated at over 10,000.

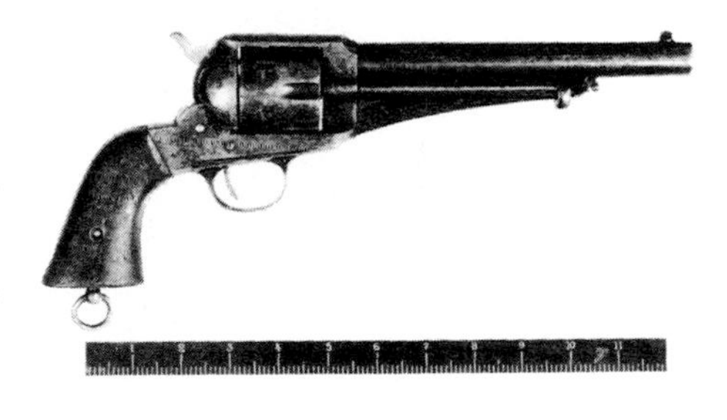

*Model 1875 Army Revolver* (Single Action). Caliber: 44 Rem. center fire 44-40; 45 Govt. Barrel: 7½" round. Rifling: 5 grooves. Cylinder: 1 17/32" long. Trigger guard: iron, oval. Sights: *front,* German silver blade; *rear,* groove. Grips: walnut, oil finished. Finish: blued, except case-hardened hammer, loading gate. Weight: 2 pounds, 12 ounces. Distinctive features: rod ejector; lanyard loop. Markings — Top of barrel: *E. Remington & Sons, Ilion, N. Y. U.S.A.* Left grip: inspector's initials. Serial number: inside top strap; side of grip frame. Dates of manufacture: 1875–1889. Number manufactured: estimated at 25,000.

*Note:* Model 1875's sold to the general public were usually nickel plated. Specially plated or engraved pieces with pearl or ivory grips could be had at extra cost.

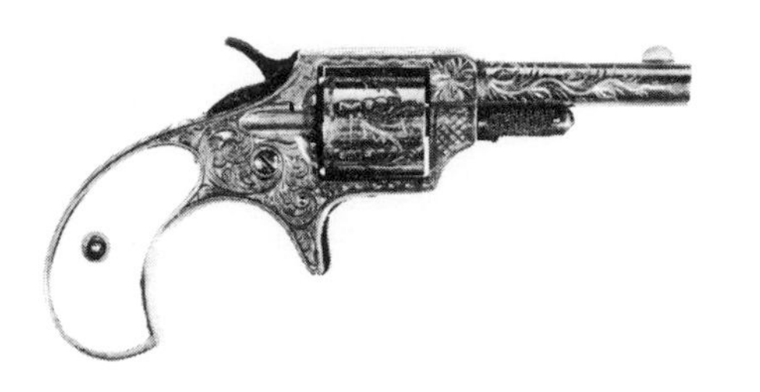

*Iroquois Revolver* (Single Action). Caliber: 22. Number of shots: 7. Barrel: 2¼" round. Rifling: 5 grooves. Cylinder: 27/32" long. Trigger: sheath. Sights: *front,* blade; *rear,* groove. Grips: hard rubber, checkered, pearl; ivory. Finish: blued, nickel plated; specially plated or engraved on order. Weight: 7½" ounces. Distinctive feature: no ejector. Markings — Top of barrel: *Iroquois*. Side of barrel: *Remington, Ilion, N. Y.* Serial number: side of grip frame. Dates of manufacture: 1878–1888. Number manufactured: estimated at 50,000.

*Model 1890 Army Revolver* (Single Action). Caliber: 44-40. Number of shots: 6. Barrel: 5½", 7½" round. Rifling: 5 grooves. Cylinder: 17/32" long. Trigger guard: iron, oval. Sights: *front,* blade; *rear,* groove. Grips: hard rubber, checkered; pearl; ivory. Finish: blued, nickel plated; specially plated or engraved on order. Weight: 2 pounds, 10 ounces (with 7½" barrel). Distinctive features: web under barrel cut away; lanyard loop. Markings — Top of barrel: *Remington Arms Co., Ilion, N. Y.* Serial number: side of grip frame. Dates of manufacture: 1891–1894. Number manufactured: approximately 2,000.

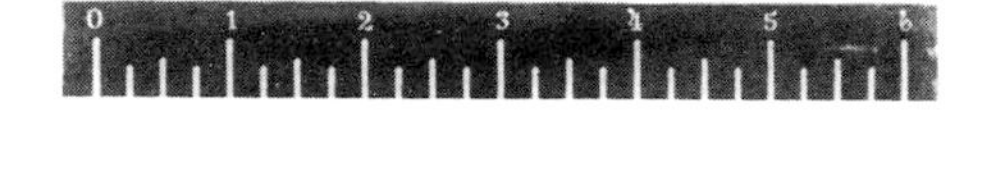

*Model 51 Automatic Pistol* (Semi-automatic). Caliber: 32 A.P. 380 rimless. Number of shots: 7 in magazine. Barrel: 3½" round (in 380). Rifling: 7 grooves. Sights: open, Patridge type. Grips: hard rubber, checkered. Finish: dull black. Weight: 1 pound, 6 ounces (in 380). Markings — On slide: *The Remington Arms-Union Metallic Cartridge Co., Inc. Remington Ilion Wks. Ilion, N.Y. U.S.A. Pedersen's Patents Pending.* Serial number: side of frame. Dates of manufacture: 1918–1934. Number manufactured: approximately 65,000.

NOT ILLUSTRATED

*Mark III Signal Pistol.* Caliber: 10 gauge. Barrel: 9" round, tip-up, steel, dull black. Trigger: sheath. Frame: brass. Grips: walnut, oil finished. Weight: 2 pounds 7 ounces. Markings — Top of barrel: *The Remington Arms-Union Metallic Cartridge Co., Inc. Mark III, Remington Bridgeport Works Bridgeport, Connecticut, U.S.A.* Dates of manufacture: 1915-1918. Number manufactured: approximately 24,500.

*Beals Pocket Revolver, First Model* (Single Action). Caliber: .31. Barrel: 3" octagon. Cylinder: 1¼" long. Number of shots: 5. Rifling: 5 or 7 grooves. Trigger guard: round, brass. Sights: *front,* German silver cone; *rear,* groove. Grips: composition, rounded, smooth. Finish: blued barrel, frame, cylinder; case hardened hammer; silver plated trigger guard. Weight: 11 ounces. Distinctive feature: Outside pawl and arm. Markings — Top of barrel: *F. Beal's Patent, June 24, '56 & May 26, '57.* Top of frame: *Remingtons, Ilion, N. Y.* Serial number: inside of trigger guard; on butt: on grip frame. Dates of manufacture: 1857–1858. Number manufactured: Estimated at 2,500.

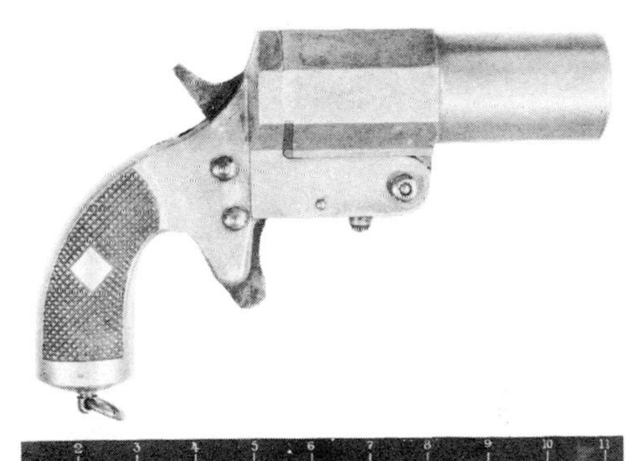

Parker 35 mm Signal Pistol Mark I — 1938

*Beals Pocket Revolver, Second Model* (Single Action). Caliber: .31. Barrel: 3" octagon. Cylinder: 1⅛" long. Number of shots: 5. Rifling: 5 grooves. Trigger: sheath. Sights: *front,* German silver cone; *rear,* groove. Grips: hard rubber, checkered. Finish: blued. Weight: 12 ounces. Distinctive feature: outside pawl and disc. Markings — Top of barrel: *Beals Patent 1856 & 57. Manufactured by Remington, Ilion, N. Y.* Serial number: underside of barrel; side of grip frame. Dates of manufacture: 1858–1860. Number manufactured: Estimated at 1,000.

*Beals Pocket Revolver, Third Model* (Single Action). Caliber: .31. Barrel: 4″ octagon. Cylinder: 1⅝″ long. Number of shots: 5. Rifling: 5 grooves. Trigger: sheath. Sights: *front,* German silver cone; *rear,* groove. Grips: hard rubber, checkered. Finish: blued. Weight: 14 ounces. Distinctive features: outside pawl and disc; lever rammer. Markings — Top of barrel: *Beals Pat. 1856, 57, 58. Manufactured by Remington, Ilion, N. Y.* Serial number: side of grip frame. Dates of manufacture: 1859–1860. Number manufactured: estimated at 1,500.

*Rider Single Shot Deringer* (Single Action). Caliber: .170. Barrel: 3″ round, brass, integral with frame. Rifling: none. Trigger: sheath. Parts: iron hammer; steel breech-pin. Sights: *front,* brass pin; *rear,* V-notch. Grips: brass, smooth, integral with frame. Finish: natural brass. Weight: 5⅜ ounces. Markings — Top of barrel: *Riders Pt. Sept. 13, 1859.* Dates of manufacture: 1860–1863. Number manufactured: estimated at less than 1,000.

*Beals Army Revolver* (Single Action). Caliber: .44. Barrel: 8″ octagon. Cylinder: 2″ long. Number of shots: 6. Rifling: 5 grooves. Trigger guard: brass oval. Sights: *front,* German silver cone; *rear,* groove. Grips: walnut, oil finished. Finish: blued, except case-hardened hammer. Weight: 2 pounds, 14 ounces. Distinctive feature: small lever rammer web. Markings — Top of barrel: *Beals Patent Sept. 14, 1858 Manufactured by Remington's Ilion, New York.* Serial number: Underside of barrel; side of grip frame. Dates of manufacture: 1860–1862. Number manufactured: estimated at 3,000.

*Model 1861 Army Revolver* (Single Action). Caliber: .44. Barrel: 8″ octagon. Cylinder: 2″ long. Number of shots: 6. Rifling: 5 grooves. Trigger guard: brass, oval. Sights: *front,* German silver cone; *rear,* groove. Grips: walnut, oil finished. Finish: blued, except for case-hardened hammer. Weight: 2 pounds, 12 ounces. Distinctive features: channel in rammer lever; noticeable space between lever and barrel. Markings — Top of barrel: *Patented Dec. 17, 1861. Manufactured by Remington's, Ilion, N. Y.* Serial number: underside of barrel; side of grip frame. Dates of manufacture: 1862. Number manufactured: over 5,000.

*Beals Navy Revolver* (Single Action). Caliber: .36. Barrel: 7½″ octagon. Cylinder: 2″ long. Number of shots: 6. Rifling: 5 grooves. Trigger guard: brass, oval. Sights: *front,* German silver cone; *rear,* groove. Grips: walnut, oil finished. Finish: blued, except case-hardened hammer. Weight: 2 pounds, 10 ounces. Distinctive feature: small lever rammer web. Markings — Top of barrel: *Beals Patent Sept. 14, 1858 Manufactured by Remington Ilion, New York.* Serial number: underside of barrel; side of grip frame. Dates of manufacture: 1860–1862. Number manufactured: over 8,000.

*Model 1861 Navy Revolver* (Single Action). Caliber: .36. Barrel: 7⅜″ octagon. Cylinder: 2″ long. Number of shots: 6. Rifling: 5 grooves. Trigger guard: brass, oval. Sights: *front,* German silver cone; *rear,* groove. Grips: walnut, oil finished. Finish: blued, except for case-hardened hammer. Weight: 2 pounds, 8 ounces. Distinctive features: channel in rammer lever; noticeable space between lever and barrel. Markings — Top of barrel: *Patented Dec. 17, 1861. Manufactured by Remington's, Ilion, N. Y.* Serial number: underside of barrel; side of grip frame. Dates of manufacture: 1862. Number manufactured: over 5,000.

*New Model Army Revolver* (Single Action). Caliber: .44. Barrel: 8" octagon. Cylinder: 2" long. Number of shots: 6. Rifling: 5 grooves. Trigger guard: brass, oval. Sights: *front,* iron blade; *rear,* groove. Grips: walnut, oil finished. Finish: blued, except for case-hardened hammer. Weight: 2 pounds, 14 ounces. Markings — Top of barrel: *Patented Sept. 14, 1858. E. Remington & Sons, Ilion, New York, U.S.A. New Model.* Left grip: inspector's initials inscript in rectangle (B.H. and O.W.A. have been noted). Serial number: underside of barrel; side of grip frame. Dates of manufacture: 1863–1875. Number manufactured: Over 140,000. *Note:* Standard New Model .44's sold to the general public came with blued finish and varnished grips; plated or engraved pieces with pearl or ivory grips could be purchased at extra cost.

*New Model Belt Revolver* (Single Action). Caliber: .36. Barrel: 6½" octagon. Cylinder: 1⅞" long. Number of shots: 6. Rifling: 5 grooves. Trigger guard: brass, oval. Sights: *front,* German silver blade; *rear,* groove. Grips: walnut, varnished; pearl; ivory. Finish: blued; nickel plated frame; full nickel plated; specially plated or engraved on order. Weight: 2 pounds, 2 ounces. Markings — Top of barrel: *Patented Sept. 14, 1858. E. Remington & Sons, Ilion, New York U.S.A. New Model.* Serial number: underside of barrel; side of grip frame. Dates of manufacture: 1863–1888. Number manufactured: over 5,000.

*New Model Belt Revolver* (Double Action). Caliber: .36. Barrel: 6½" octagon. Cylinder: 1⅞" long. Number of shots: 6. Rifling: 5 grooves. Trigger guard: brass, oval. Sights: *front,* German silver cone; *rear,* groove. Grips: walnut, varnished; pearl; ivory. Finish: blued; nickel plated frame; full nickel plated; specially plated or engraved on order. Weight: 2 pounds, 4 ounces. Markings — Top of barrel: *Manufactured by Remington's, Ilion, N. Y. Rider's Pt. Aug. 17, 1858, May 3, 1859* (or standard New Model marking). Serial number: underside of barrel; side of grip frame. Dates of manufacture: 1863–1888. Number manufactured: over 5,000. *Note:* Full fluted cylinder on special order.

*New Model Police Revolver* (Single Action). Caliber: .36. Barrel: 3½", 4½", 5½", 6½" octagon. Cylinder: 1⅝" long. Number of shots: 5. Rifling: 5 grooves. Trigger guard: brass, oval. Sights: *front,* German silver blade; *rear,* groove. Grips: walnut varnished; pearl; ivory. Finish: blued; nickel plated frame; full nickel plated; specially plated or engraved on order. Weight: 21, 22, 23, 24 ounces. Markings — Top of barrel: *Patented Sept. 14, 1858 March 17, 1863 E. Remington & Sons, Ilion, New York U.S.A. New Model.* Serial number: underside of barrel; side of grip frame. Dates of manufacture: 1863–1888. Number manufactured: over 8,000.

*New Model Pocket Revolver* (Single Action). Caliber: .31. Barrel: 3½", 4½" octagon. Cylinder: 1 7/16" long. Number of shots: 5. Rifling: 5 grooves. Trigger: sheath. Sights: *front,* German silver blade; *rear,* groove. Grips: walnut, varnished; pearl; ivory. Finish: blued; nickel plated frame; full nickel plated; specially plated or engraved on order. Weight: 14, 16 ounces. Markings — Top of barrel: *Patented Sept. 14, 1858 March 17, 1863 E. Remington & Sons, Ilion, New York U.S.A. New Model.* Serial number: underside of barrel; side of grip frame. Dates of manufacture: 1863–1888. Number manufactured: over 17,000.

*Zig-Zag Deringer* (Double Action). Caliber: .22. Number of shots: 6. Barrels: 3¾16″, fluted, with rib in each flute. Rifling: 5 grooves. Trigger: ring. Sights: *front,* brass pin each flute; *rear,* groove. Grips: hard rubber, smooth. Finish: blued. Weight: 8 ounces. Distinctive feature: grooves on rear of barrel cluster. Markings — Left side of frame: *Elliot's Patent Aug. 17, 1858 May 29, 1860.* Right side of frame: *Manufactured by Remington's, Ilion, N. Y.* Serial number: side of grip frame. Dates of manufacture: 1861–1862. Number manufactured: estimated at less than 1,000.

*Remington-Elliot Deringer* (Double Action). Caliber: .22 rim fire. Number of shots: 5. Barrel: 3″, round cluster, fluted. Rifling: 5 grooves. Trigger: ring. Sights: *front,* brass pin; *rear,* groove. Grips: hard rubber, smooth; pearl; ivory. Finish: blued; nickel plated frame; full nickel plated; specially plated or engraved on order. Weight: 8½ ounces. Markings — Left side of barrel: *Manufactured by E. Remington & Sons, Ilion, N. Y.* Right side of barrel: *Elliot's Patents May 29, 1860-Oct. 1, 1861.* Serial number: inside frame; side of grip frame. Dates of manufacture: 1863–1888. Number manufactured: estimated at over 50,000 for caliber .22 and .32 together.

*Remington-Elliot Deringer* (Double Action). Caliber: .32 rim fire. Number of shots: 4. Barrel: 3⅜″, square cluster, fluted. Rifling: 5 grooves. Trigger: ring. Sights: *front,* brass blade; *rear,* groove. Grips: hard rubber, smooth; pearl; ivory. Finish: blued; nickel plated frame; full nickel plated; especially plated or engraved on order. Weight: 13 ounces. Markings — Left side of barrel: *Manufactured by E. Remington & Son, Ilion, N. Y.* Right side of barrel: *Elliot's Patents May 29, 1860-Oct. 1, 1861.* Serial number: inside frame; side of grip frame. Dates of manufacture: 1863–1888. Number manufactured: estimated at over 50,000 for caliber .22 and .32 together.

*Vest Pocket Pistol — .41* (Single Action). Caliber: .41. Number of shots: 1. Barrel: 4″ octagon round. Rifling: 5 grooves. Trigger: sheath. Sights: *front,* brass pin; *rear,* groove. Grips: walnut, varnished; pearl; ivory. Finish: blued; nickel plated frame; full nickel plated; specially plated or engraved on order. Weight: 11 ounces. Markings — Top of barrel: *Remington's Ilion, N. Y. Pat. Oct. 1, 1861-Nov. 15, 1864.* Serial number: underside of barrel; side of grip frame. Dates of manufacture: 1865–1888. Number manufactured: estimated at over 25,000.

*Model 1865 Navy* (Single Action). Caliber: .50 rim fire. Number of shots: 1. Barrel: 8½″ round. Rifling: 3 grooves. Trigger: sheath. Sights: *front,* iron blade; *rear,* V-notch in breech block. Grips: walnut, oil finished. Finish: blued barrel, case-hardened receiver, breech block, hammer, trigger, and sheath; some barrels and receivers tinned. Weight: 2 pounds, 4 ounces. Markings — Top of barrel: anchor. Left side of receiver: *Remington Ilion, N. Y. U.S.A. Pat. May 3d Nov. 15th, 1864, April 17th, 1866.* Right side of receiver: P FCW (not on all specimens). Left grip: inspector's initials in script in medallion. Serial number: side of grip frame. Dates of manufacture: 1866–1875. Number manufactured: estimated at well over 1,000.

*Model 1867 Navy* (Single Action). Caliber: .50 center fire. Number of shots: 1. Barrel: 7″ round. Rifling: 3 grooves. Trigger: guard; iron, oval. Sights: *front,* iron blade; *rear,* V-notch in breech block. Grips: walnut, oil finished. Finish: blued barrel, case-hardened receiver, breech block, hammer, trigger, and trigger guard. Weight: 2 pounds. Markings — Top of barrel: I/W.D.W./anchor. Left side of receiver: *Remington's Ilion, N. Y. U.S.A. Pat. May 3d Nov. 15th 1864 April 17th, 1866.* Right side of receiver: P FCW. Left grip: inspector's initials in script in medallion. Serial number: underside of barrel; side of grip frame. Dates of manufacture: 1867–1875. Number manufactured: over 7,000.

*Model 1869 Target* (Single Action). Caliber: .22. Number of shots: 1. Barrel: 17″ octagon. Rifling: 5 grooves. Trigger guard: iron, oval. Sights: *front,* globe; *rear,* buckhorn. Grips: walnut, varnished. Finish: blued. Weight: not known. Markings — Not known. Dates of manufacture: 1869–1888.

*Model 1891 Target* (Single Action). Caliber: .22 rim fire, .25 rim fire, .32-20, .32 S.&W. rim fire (short or long), .32 S.&W. center fire. Barrel: 10″ half-octagon (8″ and 12″ barrel lengths have been noted). Rifling: 5 grooves. Number of shots: 1. Trigger guard: iron, oval. Sights: *front,* German silver blade; *rear,* adjustable V-notch (Rocky Mountain). Grips: walnut, oil finished. Finish: blued barrel, breech block, trigger; case-hardened receiver, trigger guard; bright hammer. Weight: 2 pounds, 13 ounces (in .22 caliber). Markings — Top of barrel: *Remington Arms Co. Ilion, N. Y.* Left side of receiver: *Remington's Ilion, N. Y. U.S.A. Pat. May 3d Nov. 15th 1864 April 17th 1866 P S.* Left grip: inspector's initials in script in medallion. Serial number: side of grip frame. Dates of manufacture: 1891–1900. Number manufactured: approximately 100.

*New Line Revolver, No. 2* (Single Action). Caliber: .32 rim fire short. Number of shots: 5. Barrel: 2¾″ octagon. Rifling: 5 grooves. Cylinder: ⅞″ long. Trigger: sheath. Sights: *front,* blade; *rear,* groove. Grips: hard rubber; checkered; pearl; ivory. Finish: blued; nickel plated; specially plated or engraved on order. Weight: 10 ounces. Distinctive feature: unique rod ejector. Markings — Top of barrel: *E. Remington & Sons, Ilion, N. Y. Pat. W. S. Smoot Oct. 21, 1873.* Serial number: side of grip frame. Dates of manufacture: 1874–1888. Number manufactured: estimated at over 20,000.

*Model XP-100.* Long Range Pistol. Caliber 221 Center Fire "Fireball". 1963— Bolt Action Single Shot. Length: Barrel 10½″; Overall 16¾″. Stock: DuPont "Zytel". Trigger: Match type, grooved. Sights: Fixed front; rear adjustable for windage and elevation. Weight: 3¾ lbs. Markings—top of barrel: *Remington Arms Co., Inc., Ilion, N.Y. Made in U.S.A.*

# Index